HC   Armstrong, Muriel.
115
.A793   The Canadian economy
1977   and its problems

DATE		

DISCARD

BUSINESS
DIVISION

D1058750

© THE BAKER & TAYLOR CO.

The Canadian Economy and Its Problems
second edition

The Canadian Economy and Its Problems

second edition

Muriel Armstrong

Department of Economics
Sir George Williams Faculty of Arts
Concordia University

PRENTICE-HALL OF CANADA, LTD. SCARBOROUGH, ONTARIO

Canadian Cataloguing in Publication Data

Armstrong, Muriel, 1925-
   The Canadian economy and its problems
   2d ed.

Includes index.
ISBN 0-13-113076-5 pa.

1. Canada—Economic conditions—1945-
2. Canada—Economic policy. I. Title.

HC115.A793 1977   330.9′71′064   C77-001136-5

Prentice-Hall, Inc., Englewood Cliffs, New Jersey
Prentice-Hall of Australia, Pty., Ltd., Sydney
Prentice-Hall of India Pvt., Ltd., New Delhi
Prentice-Hall International, Inc., London
Prentice-Hall of Japan, Inc., Tokyo
Prentice-Hall of Southeast Asia (PTE.) Ltd., Singapore

ISBN 0-13-113076-5 (Paperback)

Cover design by John Zehethofer

 2 3 4 5 W 81 80 79 78 77

Manufactured in Canada by Webcom Limited

Contents

Preface

It is apparent to all who read, watch, or listen to commentaries on contemporary Canada that many of the issues involved are economic. Economic problems are pervasive, but unfortunately, familiarity with some of the fundamentals of economics is not equally pervasive; this means that there is an inadequate foundation for understanding and discussing these problems intelligently.

This book is concerned with contemporary economic problems and their solutions; in other words, it is concerned with economic policy. However, the reader will be introduced to many of the basic tools needed to understand economic policy. Chapter 8, for example, is entirely devoted to some basic tools of microeconomic theory, such as various kinds of costs and revenues, supply and demand. Other tools such as the production possibility curve, the circular flow, the unemployment-inflation tradeoff, the concepts of comparative advantage and elasticity are introduced at the point where they are needed in order to understand a particular problem.

If one is to understand the Canadian economy and its problems, one must have more than economic theory. Many of our problems are creatures of our past and of our laws and institutions. In effect, then, the economic theory that has been omitted in this book (because it is itself subject to the law of diminishing returns) has been replaced by historical and institutional material which has a very high utility if one's objective is to understand some of Canada's problems and to find, or assess, solutions.

The "mix" of theory, history, and institutional material is not the same for every problem or for every chapter of the book. An understanding of the complex process of bank loan expansion and the creation of money requires a good deal of theory and little history. Similarly, the history of monetary policy in Canada is relatively unimportant. Chapters 5 and 6, therefore, are quite "theoretical". By contrast, in discussing the problem of regional redistribution of income (Chapter 11) economic theory is relatively unimportant, whereas our history and our institutions are very important.

The book is not primarily an introduction to economic theory, although it does introduce the student to the theory that is immediately used and useful, and requests from people who used the first edition have led me to alter my view of what *is* "used and useful", and to increase the amount of theory. The book is certainly not a history book. Instead, it is supposed to be a self-contained mixture of ingredients, mostly economics, designed to give students who are enrolled in general or terminal introductory courses, in engineering courses, or in collegial programs, or high schools an understanding of what is going on in the economy today.

Thanks are owed to my students on the Sir George Williams campus of Concordia University who pointed out changes that they would find helpful, and to Miss Linda Bonin, my secretary, who has performed many services and has been a key figure in getting the revision through its various stages. This edition has benefited greatly from the comments of a variety of users and reviewers. I am particularly grateful for the care and effort expended on it by Professor D. J. Daly of the Faculty of Administrative Studies at York University.

As in the case of the first edition, my greatest debt is to my husband, Professor D. E. Armstrong of the Faculty of Management at McGill University. His willingness to let me have an unlimited supply of that scarcest of commodities—time—is greatly appreciated.

Muriel Armstrong
Sir George Williams Faculty of Arts
Concordia University

The Canadian Economy and Its Problems
second edition

1

Making choices is what economics is all about. Resources are scarce relative to our wants, and they must be allocated among many competing uses. Decisions about how scarce resources will be allocated can be made in three ways: by tradition, by a command system and by the market.

In Canada most decisions are made in the market. Consumers by their dollar votes decide what goods and services will be produced: this is what consumer sovereignty means. Producers, responding to the profits to be made from producing goods and services consumers want, hire the necessary resources. Owners of resources are free to sell their services to producers.

Some of the solutions given by the market are not acceptable, so Canadian governments intervene and impose different ones. The Canadian economy, then, is a mixture of the market system and the command system, with the market system predominating.

The Canadian Economic System

Steak? Why not hamburger instead? A new vacuum? What's wrong with the old one? A new golf club? An absolute necessity! Derek to camp or a new coat for Dorothy? Gasoline? Dry cleaning? Paint for the living room? A get-well card for Uncle Herman, who might include us in his will? Decisions! Decisions! Decisions!

The man who brings home his weekly pay envelope with $200 in it must decide—autocratically or cooperatively with his wife and family—how that $200 should be allocated among all the goods and services that he would like to spend it on. He is faced with the central problem of economics. This economic problem has two key characteristics: first, there must be a scarce resource (money, in this case); and second, that resource must have a large number of alternative uses. A household, unable to satisfy all, or even most, of its wants out of its weekly pay envelope, must allocate that scarce resource among all its various possible uses. In making these choices, the family is administering or rationing its scarce resource. It is solving the economic problem.

Scarce Resources

Economics as a social science is not so much concerned with the problem of single individuals and how each allocates his scarce resources as it is with groups of individuals such as consumers, producers, and governments. Money may seem to be the resource that is least plentiful and most important for most individuals, but to economists it is not. Economists are much more concerned with what they call *real* resources—things that can be used to produce goods and services that will satisfy some of our many wants, or that can satisfy those wants directly. The iron ore in Labrador and the fertile farm lands and oil reserves of the Prairies are real resources, and so are the many other natural resources with which Canada is generously endowed.

But the term *resource* has a broader meaning than this: it includes not only our natural resources, but also the various raw materials used in manufacturing, such as the resins of the chemical industry and the newsprint used by *The Globe and Mail* or *The Gazette*. Resources also

3

include factories, power transmission lines, and oil rigs. The resources we have mentioned so far have been nonhuman resources; but when an economist talks about resources, or about *factors of production* (a synonym for resources), he also includes *human resources*, such as the services of labour and management.

Most but not all resources are scarce and have to be allocated among a number of competing alternative uses. *Scarcity* is the key word in any definition of economics: only scarce resources present an economic problem.

In describing the resources of our wealthy North American economies, "scarce" is not the first adjective that comes to mind; "plentiful" might be a more accurate description. But this introduces us to one of the common pitfalls in economics: economists often borrow everyday words with everyday meanings and make them into economic terms with special technical meanings. Scarce is such a "borrowed" word. It is quite true that in our affluent society resources are more plentiful than they have been for any other nation or for any other time in history; nonetheless, we describe them as scarce, because they are scarce *relative to the wants* of the people that make up our society. For example, Canadian farms produce 500 million dozen eggs a year. A lot of eggs? But if grocers distributed these eggs free (that is, if they stopped using price to ration the available supplies), we would soon find that if we arrived at the market in the afternoon there would be no eggs. Then we would agree that eggs were scarce—almost as scarce as hen's teeth.

Human wants are insatiable—not for a particular person at a particular time, but for all of us over an extended period of time. Some of these wants may not spring naturally from our needs: advertising or trying to keep up with the Joneses gives rise to a host of wants. The fact remains, however, that the total number of human wants, regardless of how they may be engendered, cannot be satisfied because there are not enough resources to produce all of the wanted goods and services. Since all wants cannot be satisfied, choices will have to be made about what *will* be produced: the economic problem of administering scarce resources must be solved.

There are a few resources that do not have to be rationed among competing uses. Air, for example, exists in such abundance in our normal habitat that we can have all we want for all the purposes we can think of. Because air is so plentiful, we regard it as a *free* resource, as opposed to a scarce one. Since air does not present a rationing problem, we regard it as a noneconomic good. But we cannot be sure that air in our normal habitat will always be a noneconomic good: if our normal habitat is a city like Toronto or Montreal, and if the commodity we are discussing is clean air as opposed to polluted air, the air may qualify as a scarce resource and thus be classified as an economic good.

Our discussion has now brought us to the point where we can define economics. Most simply, we might say that *economics is a social science whose central problem is how to allocate scarce resources among alternative uses.* As we know, allocating those scarce resources among alternative uses involves making choices concerning what will be produced. To illustrate this economic problem of allocating scarce resources, and to introduce some of the methodology (and geometry) of economics, we shall make use of a device called the *production possibility curve.*

The Production Possibility Curve

A picture can often explain what pages of written words fail to make clear. One kind of picture that is very useful to economists is the graph. A graph presents a highly simplified explanation of how the economy, or part of it, operates. It represents a *model* of the economy which has been stripped down to the bare essentials so that we can better understand a particular relationship. In most models many of the factors that might affect the relationship in the real world are assumed not to change. As long as everyone recognizes that graphs, regardless of how elaborate they may look, present a highly simplified picture, and that they make no pretence of giving a complete description of what happens in the complex, real-world economy, then these simplified pictures can be an aid to understanding.

In order to show the nature of the economizing problem by means of a production possibility curve, we must simplify. We shall start by assuming that only two commodities are produced in our economy: suits of clothes, which represent consumers' goods, and tractors, which can be regarded as representing producers' goods (investment goods or capital goods, as they are also called). Investment goods, produced now, do not satisfy our wants directly, as clothing does, but they will enable consumers' goods to be produced more efficiently and in larger quantities at a later date.

Another simplifying assumption that we shall make to start with is that the total quantity of our resources, or factors of production, is fixed and that resources are always fully employed. We can shift our factors of production from the production of suits to the production of tractors, and vice versa, but we cannot increase the total quantity of resources available. The third assumption, which will also be relaxed later, is that technology is fixed: there can be no change in methods of production.

Now let us consider the nature of the economic problem of making choices in our simple, two-product world. Assume that if all of our resources are devoted to the production of tractors, 10 000 tractors can be produced, but no suits of clothes. A situation in which we are producing nothing but investment goods is neither likely nor desirable: it is one extreme. Suppose we wish to reduce nudity and mosquito bites and produce *both* suits and tractors. Since, to begin with, all of the resources were devoted to the production of tractors, and since resources are assumed to be fixed in quantity, the only way factors of production can be made available to produce suits is to take them away from the production of tractors. Assume that the economy chooses to produce 100 000 suits of clothes, and that this requires resources that formerly were used to produce 1 000 tractors. This means that the cost to the economy of producing that first 100 000 suits is 1 000 tractors. Such a cost is referred to as the *opportunity cost*. The opportunity cost of the 100 000 suits is 1 000 tractors.

We can continue this process of "transforming" tractors into suits (the production possibility curve is also called a *transformation curve*) by transferring labour and capital from tractor production to suit production. The arithmetic table following describes the possibilities in our example.

Table 1—1
Production Possibilities

			Possible Combinations		
Suits (hundred thousand)	0	1	2	3	4
Tractors (thousand)	10	9	7	4	0

Table 1—1 shows our choices: at one extreme we can devote all of our resources to producing suits and have 400 000 suits and no tractors; at the other, we can devote all resources to producing tractors and have 10 000 tractors and no suits; or we can choose some combination in between. Notice that while the opportunity cost of the first 100 000 suits is 1 000 tractors, the cost of the second 100 000 suits is higher: it is an additional 2 000 tractors. To produce the third 100 000 suits, tractor production must drop from 7 000 to 4 000; the opportunity cost is 3 000 tractors. The cost of transforming tractors into suits steadily increases. Why should the opportunity cost of producing suits increase as more resources are shifted

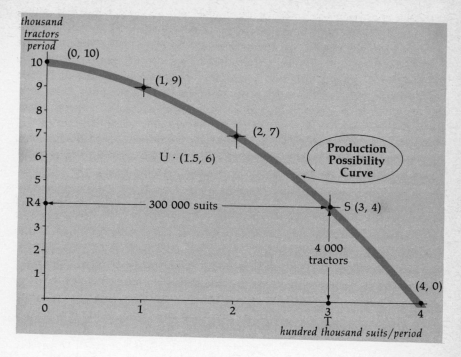

Figure 1-1

from tractor-making to suit-making? There are many reasons. Suffice it to say, however, that not all workers, managers, machinery, and raw materials are equally able or willing to move from tractor-making to suit-making. Thus, it would be logical to expect that when the call goes out for resources to shift to suit-making, it will be heeded in the first instance by those factors of production that are least at home in tractor plants and most efficient in a suit factory. The first transfers, therefore, will produce a minimum of dislocation in the tractor sector and a maximum of output in the suit industry. As transfers continue to be made, however, the tractor-making industry will begin to lose factors that are more valuable to tractor-making, and the suit industry will be employing resources which, for it, are less productive.

Now we are ready to draw a picture of the relationship that we have been discussing. In Figure 1—1 we have drawn two axes. The horizontal axis (or x-axis) is marked off from *O*, the origin, in units that represent hundreds of thousands of suits. The vertical axis (or y-axis) represents or measures tractor production and is marked in units of 1 000 tractors. Those who paid attention during their grade-school lessons in which

Cartesian coordinates were being discussed[1] will recognize that any point on this graph describes simultaneously a combination of suits and tractors. For example, point S (3, 4) represents 3 (hundred thousand) suits and 4 (thousand) tractors. Similarly, the other points on the graph, such as (0, 10) and (1, 9), merely describe pictorially the possible combinations set out arithmetically in Table 1—1. By joining the points with a smooth curve, as we have done in Figure 1—1, we have created a production possibility curve: a description of all of the possible combinations of the two commodities that can be produced if all of the resources—the services of land, of labour, of management, of raw materials, and so on—are fully employed.

If resources are not fully employed—that is, if some of the factors such as capital and labour are lying idle—then instead of being *on* the production possibility curve, the economy would be *inside* it, producing fewer tractors and suits than the maximum possible with the quantity of resources available. For example, the economy might be at point U in Figure 1—1, where the resources are not fully employed and where the output of both products is less than it could be.

The curve as we have drawn it is shaped like the inside of a circle when viewed from the origin: it is *concave* to the origin. This is what we normally expect of a production possibility curve. It reflects the increasing cost of transforming tractors into suits of clothes as we move down the curve, *i.e.*, as we increase the number of suits produced and decrease the number of tractors. The reason for this increasing cost of transformation is that all resources are not equally suited to the production of both tractors and clothing. Workers, for example, are not equally suited to working with steel or textiles. If all workers in a country had to be employed in tractor factories, we might find the personnel directors trying to stuff some very square pegs into some very round holes. The opening of a textile industry would undoubtedly be welcomed by many workers (and their bosses) as an opportunity to obtain more suitable employment.

---

[1] For those who are out of practice reading graphs, there are one or two points that need to be stressed. It is easy to see in Figure 1—1 that if we measure from the origin, which represents zero, along the horizontal axis to the figure "3", this distance represents 300 000 suits. That same distance, measured anywhere, whether above the *x*-axis (RS, for example), below it, or on it (distance OT), always represents 300 000 suits. If we draw a straight line, TS, perpendicular to the *x*-axis through the unit marked 3, then *any* point along this line will represent 300 000 suits.

Similarly, on the vertical or *y*-axis, the unit marked "4" represents 4 000 tractors. But so does any point along a straight line perpendicular to the vertical axis through that point—RS, for example. Where these two perpendiculars intersect, we have a point, S, that represents simultaneously 4 000 tractors and 300 000 suits—one of the possible combinations described in our arithmetic table of production possibilities.

As more and more resources are shifted to the production of clothing, however, suit manufacturers will begin to find that they are scraping the bottom of the manpower barrel; but their "scrapings" may very well be the top of the barrel as far as tractor plants are concerned. Similarly, other factors of land, capital, and raw materials are likely to be more efficient in one industry than in another, and these "non-homogeneous" factors will be the first to be shifted to the industry of their choice. For these reasons we can probably produce our first 100 000 suits with a relatively small sacrifice of tractors. But as we continue to transform tractors into suits, the resources being transferred grow progressively less efficient in producing suits. The cost of producing suits thus can be expected to increase.

It would be preferable, of course, to produce 10 000 tractors *and* 400 000 suits, but this is not possible because there are not enough resources to produce these quantities. Given the relative scarcity of resources, the country must make a choice: it can produce *either* 10 000 tractors *or* 400 000 suits, *or* some combination between these two extremes. What combination will it choose? How will that decision be made?

How Basic Decisions Are Made

There are three basic ways in which societies solve the economic problem of administering their scarce resources. The problem may be solved by tradition, by command, or by the market.[2]

If we were to study the economic system of a primitive society, for example, we would likely find that the decisions about what to produce and how to divide the output are made in large measure by custom: the son performs the same job as his father and the food of the society is divided among the members according to a pattern set by tradition. The caste system of India was based on custom. The decisions about what to produce, the quantity to be produced, and the way in which the output would be divided among the members of society depended on how many people were born into each caste.

Tradition still has a role to play, albeit a minor one, in allocating resources in our contemporary Canadian economy. Charitable contributions and tipping, for example, have their roots in tradition. Similarly, it is not customary for the son of an architect to become a garage mechanic. In French Canada business as an occupation has traditionally been looked down on, and as a result, a relatively small proportion of French-speaking

---

[2] For an excellent description of how the economic problems of production and distribution are solved, see Robert L. Heilbroner, *The Economic Problem*, 2nd ed. (Englewood Cliffs, N.J.: Prentice-Hall, Inc., 1970), pp. 15-22.

Canadians have sought, or been offered, education appropriate to the modern world of business or management. This tradition has had a major effect on the ethnic origin of occupants of the executive suite.

THE COMMAND ECONOMY

A command economy is one in which people are told what to produce and what to consume. Decisions are made by a central authority. In a command society economic effort can be readily directed toward whatever goals the authority may choose. The pyramids of Egypt and the Great Wall of China are examples drawn from ancient history of how economic resources in a command system were mobilized to produce remarkable public works. It is through the command system that communist countries like Russia and China have achieved such a rapid rate of industrialization.

There are important elements of command in the Canadian economy. The number of law courts and judges we have is determined by a central authority, as is the number of miles of road. The size of our armed forces —that is, the amount of defence we "consume"—is decided by a command system, not by the market. During wartime, in any economy, this kind of decision-making increases greatly.

The Canadian economy is not a command economy; it can best be described as a mixed capitalistic economy. It is capitalistic in the sense that most of the productive resources are privately owned and privately directed. It is mixed in the sense that in some important areas decisions are made by a central authority without reference to the market. For the most part, however, the problem of allocating our scarce resources among all possible uses is solved by the market.

THE MARKET

The market is a remarkable organization. It is a place where buyers and sellers meet, and yet it need not have any physical location: our bond market, for example, is operated by telephone. The market is not administered by anyone, but it is influenced by everyone. There is no central authority to run it, but it runs. No person dictates what will be produced, yet many producers make production decisions. No one issues instructions concerning who should produce what, but many "who's" produce great quantities of "what's". As a result of millions of small decisions in the marketplace some of the "who's" end up in *Who's Who*, and some remain in the "who's he?" category. Some of the "what's" flourish and become transistors and Xerox and Scotch Tape while others simply collect dust with the whatnots. Without resorting to tradition or to authority, the market determines which of the thousands of possible goods that might be produced will actually be produced. It draws resources, including millions of workers, into the production of various commodities, and it determines what share of the total output the different resources will get—all this without any central plan.

Think of the vast number of jobs to be done and products to be produced just to keep a single city like Toronto or Vancouver or Calgary operating. Everything that Calgarians need is either produced in that city or comes in by rail, truck, and air, from other provinces of Canada, from the different states of the Union, and from countries all over the world. There is no master plan. There is no commissar in Calgary—no economic Pooh-Bah. No one directs this operation, yet the restaurants are staffed with cooks and waiters; there are clerks in the stores to sell the many and varied products; television shows are produced; taxis move people from one place to another; architects are available to design buildings. Producers and resource owners operate in what they believe to be their own best interest in the market; thousands of products that Calgarians want are made available to them; and thousands of tasks are performed.

How does this remarkable market system work? The market system in Canada is not unique: all modern market systems work the same way. We have large corporations such as Bell Canada, as well as small ones; we have unincorporated businesses—partnerships, such as the local law firm—and sole proprietorships, such as the corner grocery store. These businesses produce most, but not all, of the domestically produced goods and services that Canadians consume. Canadian governments—federal, provincial, and municipal—also produce goods and services, but for the moment we shall concern ourselves with *private* rather than *public* enterprises.

Businesses organize production. They supply the initiative necessary to produce and market the goods and services that consumers want. They also find new and more efficient methods of production, so that consumers can have better and cheaper products.

Businesses employing a number of people can organize production in such a way that the resources are able to specialize in a specific operation, become skilled, and increase output per man-hour. Adam Smith, the father of modern economics, in the opening pages of his great classic, *The Wealth of Nations*, published in 1776, pointed out the economies that resulted from the division of labour in a pin factory. He suggested that a single individual, unfamiliar with the trade and the machinery used in it, might not be able to produce even a single pin in a day, and certainly could not produce more than twenty; but once the production process was broken down into distinct operations and the workers became specialized in their tasks, each could make on average almost 5 000 pins in a day.

Organizing production to take advantage of the gains from specialization and thus reducing the cost per unit of output is one of the contributions of businesses in Canada.

There may also be cost advantages to those businesses that increase the size of their operations. If output becomes large enough, a business may be able to use some highly specialized, efficient machinery that is not economical for a small output. We expect to find these *economies of scale*, as they are called, in large, modern corporations.

In addition to organizing production, businesses market, sell, and distribute their products. In markets that economists describe as purely or perfectly competitive,[3] businessmen sell at prices set by the market, though even in a market that comes as close to pure competition as does the stock exchange, the current "bid" and "asked" prices have to be bid or asked by someone. In less perfect markets, businessmen have varying degrees of power to set prices; in other words, prices, like the other terms of an offer to do business, are attached to the product. These are the so-called "administered" prices. The term "administered" might apply equally well to the packaging, advertising, credit terms, service contracts, and others, that together constitute the total offer of a businessman to a consumer or, perhaps, to another businessman. If these offers are "attractive"—that is, if they are profitable to the businessman and satisfying to the consumer—then the product will sell. If they are not, the offer will have to be altered or the product withdrawn from the market.

Businesses are also organizations that are prepared to take risks. Ideas for new products develop, either in the mind of a single individual or, more commonly in today's complex structure, in the research departments of large businesses or governments, or in universities. If an idea is ever to be translated into a product, then someone must be prepared to innovate —to assemble and organize the resources necessary to produce the new product, and to bring it to the market for people to try. Sometimes these products are highly successful, like the Polaroid camera; sometimes they are less so, as was the case with Ford's Edsel. But if new products are to reach consumers, someone or some organization must do the necessary research and take the risk involved in marketing them. Normally we expect businesses to do this.

Businesses, then, form an important part of the Canadian market system. Also important are the resources, or factors of production, whose services are used by businesses in the productive process. Workers and managers sell their working time; owners of land rent or sell the services

---

[3] One characteristic of purely competitive markets is that the number of sellers and buyers is so large that no one of them can affect price. A more detailed discussion of this kind of market appears in Ch. 8.

of land. Businesses also buy the services of factories, machinery, and raw materials—the services of what the economist calls *capital* goods. They may also "buy" the use of money capital for a given period of time.

The services of all of these resources are available in the market at a price; that is why the market system is frequently referred to as the *price system*. The price tag attached to the services of labour is usually called *wages*. The returns to managers and white-collar workers are *salaries*. If the manager also happens to be an owner of the business—one who bears risk —then he may get a reward for taking risk: *profit* is the return to owners of businesses for innovating and for taking risk. Normally profits are not fully distributed: the part that is is called dividends; what is left is either paid as taxes or retained for use in the business. The price for the use of land or other resources that are fixed in supply is usually referred to as *rent*. The price paid for the use of money or capital is *interest*.

The returns to the various resources constitute the income of the resource owners. Some resource owners have only a single resource to sell —their time; others may have several. The income from the sale of the services of these various resources, then, determines how much of the national output each resource owner is able to buy back. Thus, in the market system everyone receives money for what he sells, and in turn uses that money to buy the goods and services he wants.

Consumer Sovereignty   The process of taking the money earned from the sale of the services of various resources and using it to buy goods and services produced by businesses is really a process of voting by consumers for the products they want. This is voting, not in the political sense of putting an "X" beside the name of candidates whom voters favour, but rather *dollar* voting—taking dollars into the market and expressing support for a product or a service by buying it. The more dollars any particular person has, the more votes he has; the market does not pretend to be democratic in the sense of one individual one vote.

These dollar votes by consumers determine what will be produced by businesses. What consumers spend on goods and services provides the income of the businesses producing them. If, at the going price, the quantity of colour-television sets demanded is large, then producers, encouraged by their large sales and high profits, will want to increase the number of sets they are producing. Perhaps they can increase output with their existing plant simply by hiring more men and buying more of the necessary raw materials. Or perhaps they will have to expand the plant— to *invest* in a larger building and more machinery. Nobody orders the television producers to produce more colour sets or to increase their investment in plant and machinery. The incentive comes from the prospect of increased profits from increased sales to consumers who, expressing their own preferences by their dollar votes, have indicated clearly that they want more colour-television sets. Thus, dollar voting by consumers in the market is the major determinant of what will be produced, and of *how much* of any commodity will be produced. This is what is meant by *consumer sovereignty*—the ability of consumers through their dollar votes in the market to direct production.

Suppose now that a producer makes a mistake and produces a kind of car that consumers do not want. Who tells him to produce fewer cars of that kind? No one tells him. When he finds that consumers will not buy the car that he is producing at the price he is charging in sufficient quantities to enable him to make a profit, he will be discouraged from producing as many. He will decide to hire fewer workers and buy less steel, glass, rubber, and other materials that he needs to produce that car. As his machinery wears out, he is unlikely to replace it: he disinvests. He may close the plant down and cease production entirely. Consumers, working through the market, have dictated that that particular kind of car should be produced in smaller quantities, or should not be produced at all. By their dollar votes, consumers exercise their sovereignty in the market and determine what will, and what will not, be produced.

No one would pretend that the consumer is an absolute sovereign. It is often suggested that the advertising industry is intent on warping his judgement, and some critics of free enterprise argue that consumers are no more free than sheep being driven by dogs (advertisers) at the whim of the shepherd, who turns out to be not the good shepherd, but simply an "imperialistic American capitalist".[4] Certainly the consumer receives a great deal of advice from businessmen (who tend to speak highly of their products). They also have their freedom curtailed by governments who, by their spending, decide what will be produced by a significant proportion of society's scarce resources, and who may post keep-off-the-grass-and-other-drugs signs, without much concern for the wishes of the dollar voters.

For all of the imperfections of the marketplace, however, the consumer has the last word; for virtually all markets he has in his hands the right of effective protest. In this regard consumer sovereignty is akin to voter sovereignty. What really makes a country democratic is the existence of choice: a two-party system provides voters with the option of punishing a government that fails to meet their expectations. As a voter my real protection against the tyranny of the government is the opposition party, who will be happy to champion my cause provided, of course,

---

[4] Anyone who is going to study the market system and its alternatives must be prepared for colourful and even passionate language.

my cause has broad support from my fellow citizens. What really protects me against the tyranny of the local milkman is that he has a rival[5] who would like my business.

The Factor Market So far, we have concentrated on the market for the products that consumers buy. Factor markets, or resource markets, operate in much the same way. The increased demand for colour-television sets means that businesses producing these sets will want more men to work on the assembly line. To attract more workers they are likely to offer a higher price—a higher wage rate—so that job opportunities in the factories producing colour-television sets will be more attractive than elsewhere. When workers in less attractive jobs find this out, they will tend to shift—not ordered by anyone to change jobs, but motivated by their own interest in earning a higher income. Similarly, if television repairmen rather than bricklayers are needed, then job opportunities will improve in the television repair business: the hourly rates of television repairmen will rise relative to those of bricklayers, and workers will be encouraged to move out of bricklaying and other less attractive jobs into the television repair business. Again, resources are not forced to move; they are attracted by the prospect of greater gain.

Motivated by their own self-interest, businesmen produce the goods and services that consumers want. The basic decisions on what will be produced and in what quantity are made in the market. In precisely the same way, motivated by their own self-interest, factors of production are encouraged to offer their services to businesses that are producing the goods consumers want. The prices that resources can get for their services determine their incomes; therefore, it is in the resource market that the basic decisions about the distribution of income are made. It is no wonder that ever since Adam Smith first coined the phrase, the market has often been likened to an "invisible hand" which leads individuals who are promoting their own personal gain to promote the material welfare of society at the same time.

The Government and the Market In Canada we rely on the market to make most of the basic decisions about production and distribution. But some of the market solutions are not acceptable: our sense of justice is outraged when we discover that if we permit the market to operate freely, there may be no share of the national output for widows and orphans who are not owners of resources. Therefore we have decided that the

---

[5] Besides my husband, that is, who can pick up milk from the grocery store on the way home.

market solution in many instances needs to be altered. To that end the government steps in and either modifies the way the market operates or prevents the market from solving the basic problems. Most of us consider it right that the government should collect money in the form of taxes from some Canadians and pay it to needy widows and orphans, thus taking the solution to the problem of the distribution of income to these needy individuals out of the market and substituting the solution of a command economy. Most men, of course, make their own arrangements for the economic welfare of their wives and children: there are businesses, like trust companies, that provide a market solution to this problem.

There are other areas where we do not accept the market solution. If we relied exclusively on the price system, the Canadian economy would devote few resources to defence. We would have few law courts and judges, few fire departments or roads or sidewalks. Only the wealthy would be able to afford much education, and some who could afford education for their children might prefer not to send them to school. These are goods and services that are considered important for the health and welfare of the country as a whole; and if it were left to each individual to buy the amount he wanted in the free market, it is feared that not enough would be produced. What part of a new anti-missile missile would *you* be prepared to purchase in order to contribute to the defence of Canada?

In cases where the goods and services must be consumed communally for the benefit of all Canadians, the government steps in and imposes its total or partial solution to production and distribution problems. Most of the current economic issues in Canada today relate to this problem of substituting government regulation for the operation of the free market. But how far should government regulation go? How big a medicare plan do we want? How large should family allowances and old age pensions be? Should the government have the power to outlaw strikes? How much of our total output do we want the government to control through the command system, and how much do we want to be allocated by the free market?

We must recognize that it is not always necessary for the government to substitute authoritative decisions for decisions by the market: the government can, in some cases, operate within the market system in precisely the same way as any private business does. Air Canada, for example, is a Crown corporation (a government corporation) that reports to Parliament through the Minister of Transport, but it operates through the market in the same way as corporations in the private sector do. It is responsible for its own management, and normally it is required to conduct its business without parliamentary appropriations. CN and the Canadian Broadcasting Corporation are similar operations. Like their private counterparts, these organizations buy resources, sell services in the free market, and if they are profitable, pay income taxes. This is not to say that Crown corporations are identical to corporations in the private sector. They are not. Even the most independent of them are subject to government control and regulation in such matters as corporation budgets, bank accounts, and loans for working capital. Any surplus money must be turned over to the Receiver General of Canada. However, this kind of regulation does not alter the fact that these government corporations operate as part of the market economy: it is not the objective of Crown corporations to substitute the directives of a command system for the solutions of a free market.

2

The United States relies on the market to make most of its economic decisions. Resources are privately owned for the most part. Consumers in the United States express their preferences by spending their dollars in the market; American producers are free to determine how they will combine resources. Factors of production, which are more productive than their Canadian counterparts, are free to offer their services in the market. There is less of the command system in the United States than in Canada.

The Soviet Union, in contrast, is predominantly a command economy. Resources are owned by the state. Decisions about what to produce, how, and in what quantity are made by the government, which must formulate a vast network of economic plans. Different mixes of the command system and the market systems can be found in the economies of other countries. Yugoslavia, for example, though mainly a command economy, places greater reliance on the market than the Soviet Union. France, which is primarily a market economy, nevertheless places heavy emphasis on planning.

Some Comparisons

The Canadian economy is similar to that of the United States. However, there are major differences: Canada has a considerably smaller population with a much smaller market, and it does not have nearly as many industrial giants as the United States. Canada's labour force is not as well-educated as the American labour force, and its productivity is lower. Canadians are far more dependent on international trade than the Americans, and as a result, they are affected more by the economic conditions in other countries. It seems fair to say that the Americans as a nation have a greater distrust of concentration of power than Canadians do—whether power is concentrated in businesses, in unions, or in the government. They are strong believers in the freedom of the individual, and in the private ownership of most of the means of production.

The American Economy

The American economy, like Canada's, is predominantly a market economy: most of the basic decisions about production and distribution are made in the market. But in the United States, too, some of the market solutions are unacceptable to the American people; and so they have decided that in some cases the government should substitute solutions which have greater appeal to the sense of justice of the majority. Thus, the American government looks after needy widows, orphans, and the aged through welfare and social security payments, in the same way as the Canadian government does. However, their social security programs are not as comprehensive as Canada's: for example, they do not have nationwide family allowances.

The American economy then, like the Canadian, is a mixed, capitalistic economy. It is the price system that is the main determinant of what commodities will be produced and in what quantity, and how national income will be distributed.

Businesses in the United States, like businesses in Canada, are guided by that dynamic force, the profit motive. Of course, profits do not provide the sole motivation of businessmen: they, like everyone else, have a complex set of goals such as the desire for respectability, the urge to be powerful or to be their own bosses, and so on. Still, the desire for profits is probably the single most important force if for no other reason than without profits the business will not survive and neither will the businessman. As Tevye might have said in *Fiddler on the Roof*, if he had been incorporated, "While it's no great shame to go broke, it's no great honour either."

Profits, as we have already suggested, come from selling to consumers the goods and services they want. If consumers do not want a particular product, or do not want it at the price at which it is being offered, then the producer will find that profits are low; he may even lose money. He will therefore be encouraged to cut back on the output of that relatively unprofitable good or service and to look for other profitable ways of using his money capital. Basically, then, what he produces and how much are determined by consumers; that is, he comes under the influence of consumer sovereignty.

It is implicit in what has already been said that the American producer, like his Canadian counterpart, is free to decide how the good or service is to be produced. He can determine what resources to purchase or hire and how to organize them in order to produce the commodity in question. Since we normally assume that a businessman is interested in making a profit—the largest profit possible—it follows logically that he will want to make these decisions in such a way as to minimize cost and maximize revenue. Indeed, if his decisions are basically and consistently wrong, he will not, for long, remain "free" to make such decisions.

Decisions about investment are also the prerogative of American and Canadian businessmen. They decide whether the profits of the business should be retained and invested in more machinery and equipment so that at some future time the business will be in a position to produce more for consumers; or whether the profits should be distributed to the owners of the firm—its shareholders—and be made available for the immediate consumption of goods and services. There is no central authority to compel a businessman to replace his present plant and equipment with new and better capital. Competition from his rivals, however, may force him to modernize a plant or buy new and more efficient equipment; if he fails to invest, he may face the prospect of a decline in his profits, or even of being driven out of business. The businessman's investment decisions will always be subject to the verdict of the marketplace. Individual decisions on whether or not to invest in order to expand productive capacity affect the rate of growth of the individual firm, and collectively they affect the rate of growth of the entire economy.

The problem of distribution in the United States, like the problem of production, is solved primarily in the market. If producers want more resources to increase production of a profitable good or service, they can offer higher prices in order to attract those resources. Higher prices to resources mean high incomes to the resource owners, and hence make it possible for them to buy a larger share of the total national output. However, the solution of the distribution problem is not left entirely to the market: American governments, like Canadian governments, influence peoples' incomes through taxes and social welfare payments.

News In the American economy, as in the Canadian economy, consumers are free to purchase with their incomes the goods and services they want, with certain exceptions. Regardless of whether there exist numerous consumers who might like to purchase heroin on the free market, the governments of both countries forbid its sale.

Book 3 Like consumers, owners of resources, too, have freedom of action: they are free to sell the services of their resources—be it their own time, the services of land, or the services of money capital—for the price that is offered in the market. There is no central authority that compels them to offer their services to particular employers; and they are free to shift their resources from one use to another in response to the signals of the price system. When there are changes in consumers' demand and producers' supply, prices of goods and services change; and as the prices of goods and services change, there is likely to occur a change in the demand for the factors used to produce those goods and services, and hence a change in factor prices. If the returns to the resources used to produce the goods and services increase, owners of such resources will be free to shift them to that better-paid use; if the returns decrease, they are free to transfer the resources to alternative better-paying uses. This freedom of choice for owners of factors of production is a vital characteristic of the American as well as the Canadian economy.

Book Factors of production in the United States are more productive than those in Canada. In manufacturing, for example, the use of the same amounts of labour and capital results in a level of output that is more than 20 percent higher in the United States than in Canada.[1] Such a gap in productivity has persisted throughout this century, and there appears to be no tendency for it to close. When it comes to *returns* to the factors, right after the Second World War payments to workers, as measured by average hourly earnings, were about 50 percent higher in the United States than in Canada. This meant that although productivity in Canada was lower than in the United States, *costs* were also lower, and Canada was able to compete in international markets. That wage gap was eliminated in 1974[2]: average hourly earnings in manufacturing in Canada rose

---

[1] Economic Council of Canada, *Looking Outward: A New Trade Strategy for Canada* (Ottawa: Information Canada, 1975), pp. 29 & 74.

[2] See Judith Maxwell, *Policy Review and Outlook, 1976: Challenges to Complacency* (Montreal, C. D. Howe Research Institute, 1976), Chart 3.3, p. 80.

above those in the United States, and the effect of this was to increase the ability of the United States, relative to Canada, to compete internationally and to combat inflation.

Through the operation of the market system, the United States has become the most highly industrialized country in the world; and Americans as a nation enjoy the highest standard of living ever achieved by any nation in history. The Soviet Union, in sharp contrast, has achieved a remarkable, though not equal, level of industrialization and scientific development under a completely different system—the command economy.

The Soviet Economy

The Soviet economy must solve the same production problems as the Canadian and American economies; decisions must be made about what goods and services to produce and in what quantity, how production is to be organized, and what investment is to be made. It must also solve the problem of how income is to be distributed among resource owners.

While the Canadian and American economies are based on the system of private ownership, the Soviet economy is socialistic in form, based on state ownership. The state owns the land, the natural resources, all of the industries (with limited exceptions), the communications and transportation networks, and the banking system. About two thirds of all urban dwelling space is state-owned; for the most part rural housing is privately owned. The state owns some farms, usually large farms operated by a hired work force. Most farm land is held by these collective farms; only a very small amount is held privately by the peasants for their own use. The majority of retail outlets are government-controlled, though government-regulated cooperatives are important. There exists a small free market in the form of farmers' markets where peasants can sell freely what they grow on the small plots of ground (no larger than an acre) that individually they are allowed to own.

To understand the basic difference between our system and the command economy of the Soviet Union, we must go back to the writings of Karl Marx which provided the theoretical framework for the present Soviet system. Marx was a German-born philosopher who did most of his writing in the British Museum in London. His greatest work was *Das Kapital*, published in three volumes, the first of which appeared in 1867. In it he subjected capitalism, as he saw it in the world around him, to the most thorough and devastating analysis it had ever undergone; he concluded that capitalism contained the seeds of its own destruction, and that it must inevitably be overthrown.

Marx argued that the capitalist system would produce two distinct social classes. On the one side would be the capitalists themselves—the owners of the factories, the machines, the banks, the land, and the natural resources. On the other side would be the factory workers or the proletariat. These people owned none of the instruments of production, had nothing to sell but their own labour, and therefore had no alternative but to work for wages. Since the capitalists had a monopoly on the important means of production, they could dictate the rates that would be offered in the labour market, and, Marx argued, the wage that would be offered would be at the subsistence level—just enough to keep the workers alive and able to reproduce their kind. Marx also argued that unemployment was inherent in the capitalist system. The existence of a large pool of unemployed workers would enable the capitalists to keep workers' wages at that bare subsistence level.

One of the cornerstones of Marx's economic theory is the labour theory of value—the idea that all economic value is produced by labour, and that nothing is contributed by such other factors of production as land and natural resources. He argued that commodities produced for the market tended to have prices that were proportional to their labour content. With the machines produced by capitalist technology, a worker's output would be much more than was necessary to cover his costs of reproduction: thus there would be what Marx called "surplus value". Workers would be paid only a subsistence wage while contributing much more. The excess would be taken by the capitalists and used partly for investment and for accumulating more capital; partly for payments to land owners and resource owners in the form of rent, and to the owners of money capital in the form of interest for the use of their funds; and partly for financing the capitalists' own expenditures.

Marx underlined the inherently self-destructive nature of capitalism. He maintained that capitalists, in their search for greater profits, would overinvest. The long-term profit rate would decline. Depression would ensue, and the economy would move to even deeper depression. Through these successive crises, capital would be concentrated in fewer and fewer hands. The proletariat would grow steadily poorer. Ultimately they must rise up and overthrow the capitalists, and out of that revolution would emerge a classless society in which there would be no exploiting class and no need for a state.

It is fundamental, then, to a system that claims Marx as its founding father, that there should be no capitalist class and, therefore, no private property. This explains why the instruments of production are primarily state-owned in the U.S.S.R.

STATE PLANNING

Regardless of who owns the instruments of production, the basic decisions relating to production and distribution must still be made. In a command, or planned, economy, such decisions are not left to the market: the central government or some agent of the government must decide what to produce, how the resources are to be combined to produce the goods, where they will be produced, what the return to the resources will be, and so on. If there were a pure command system, every single decision would have to be made by the central planning authority.

The Russian economy comes as close as any to a planned or command economy, just as the American economy comes closest to being a market system. And just as the American economy, though predominantly capitalistic in form, has elements of decisions by command, so the Soviet economy, predominantly a planned economy, has a few areas in which decisions are made by the market. One might also call the Soviet system a "*mixed* command system".

Formulating the plans for the Soviet economy is a complicated process. How is any decision made about what specific industries are to have priority, or where an enterprise is to be located, or who is to work in the enterprise, or how countless other questions are to be considered?

The first task of the planning authority must be to select the general goals of the economy. The dominant goals of the Soviet Union have been to achieve a rapid rate of industrialization and economic growth, and to build up a powerful, technologically advanced military potential. These are very broad goals; more specific objectives are set out in medium-term (mainly five-year) and long-term plans. Such plans concern themselves with the size of total output and with the share of resources to be allocated to investment and military goods, to consumers' goods, and to goods that will increase what is called *social capital*, such as roads, hospitals, schools, sewage systems, and so on.

Selecting the goals and providing for their fulfilment through medium-term and long-term plans are an important part of the planning process, but such general plans do not provide directives to an individual producer about how he is to perform. This is done in the very extensive and elaborate system of short-run plans that describe in detail what is to be done in the next year, or half-year, or even in the next month.

The formulation of such elaborate plans for the entire economy requires a very extensive bureaucracy. There are many planning bodies in the U.S.S.R. At the top of the great hierarchical pyramid is the high-level state planning commission (Gosplan), below which are the planning commissions for the republics, provinces, and districts; the planning bodies that concern themselves with specialized sectors such as construction, or specialized problems such as research and development; and the planning groups that consider the problems of large areas that cut across sectors and industries. Finally there are the ministries and sub-ministries that plan for the individual industries. Up and down this immense planning pyramid must flow all of the information necessary to make the specific decisions that keep the economy operating.

When one considers the enormity and complexity of the task, it seems as if it could not possibly work. But it does. In the first place, the planning process has emerged and has been refined and modified over a period of more than half a century. It began with a relatively small number of industries, and grew until it covered virtually the entire economy. A certain amount of planning was tried out in the chaotic period after the 1917 Revolution; but the economy was so badly disrupted that in 1921 the government reverted in considerable measure to private enterprise and the market system.

In 1927 the process of achieving complete state control of the Soviet economy was put in motion again. All industry was nationalized, and private trade and manufacture were made criminal offences. The five-year plans began in 1928; this was also the period when the collectivization of agriculture was begun. Detailed central planning for the entire economy then became a necessity. Since plans for all parts of the economy have been in operation for many years now, this means that at the present time planning is mainly a matter of marginal adjustments; planners do not face the impossible task of starting from scratch each time an over-all economic plan is made. For each new period, the initial "plan" is the last period's reality, on which adjustments and, hopefully, improvements can be made.

The five-year plan, once propounded, is not irrevocably fixed. It is subject to change by the yearly, or half-yearly, or quarter-by-quarter plans that give specific directives. There is a great hierarchy of these short-run plans, and they are the ones that actually convert the more general goals and objectives of the central planners into the specific day-to-day operations necessary to achieve the goals. They are very complex; for it is at this level of planning that it must be decided which of thousands upon thousands of possible items will be produced, how much of them, the price, and enterprises in which they will be produced, and so on.

These problems cannot be solved in isolation. Obviously, for every output produced, there will be a number of inputs, including raw materials and component parts that are themselves the outputs of other enterprises. Consider, for example, a few of the problems that might arise around a single good, steel. Assume that the plan calls for a certain number of military planes and transport aircraft, tanks and automobiles, buildings using steel frames, tractors and combines, and engines and turbines. All of these demands add up to a large requirement for steel. It is apparent that the plan for steel production should be in balance with the anticipated demand for steel. This, in turn, means that there will have to be adequate amounts of iron ore and coal, of blast furnaces and steel workers, and of transportation services for the movement of the steel to places where it is needed.

Suppose that the supply and the demand are not in balance; assume, for the sake of argument, that the supply of steel is insufficient for the planned output of all of these and the myriad of other products requiring the metal. Then the plans will have to be altered to try to bring the supply into balance with the demand. Perhaps more resources can be pulled from the production of *other* commodities into the production of steel; in that case, the planned output of other commodities will have to be written down. Possibly the planned output of tractors, or cars, or turbines, or buildings will be decreased; but then the plans of these industries will have to be substantially altered. Consideration might be given to importing steel, in which case the plans of the industries exporting goods will have to be revised. More resources will have to be allocated to them so that they can produce more goods for export, and thus enable the country to earn enough foreign currency to finance the import of steel. This involves not only modifying the plans of the export industries, but also reducing the quotas of the industries from which resources have been taken. If the outputs of these industries are, in turn, the inputs of yet other industries, then the plans of the latter will have to be altered too. Thus, the process of adjustment will have to work through many different industries and regions.

In the Canadian economy, the problem of allocating a scarce resource to its various uses is handled by the market. If a resource is scarce, its price rises. The people who use it then find it profitable to cut back on the quantity of that scarce and relatively expensive resource, and to find substitutes for it. Producers, on the other hand, are encouraged to produce more of it because its price has risen. Thus, it is the market that allocates a resource to those uses that are most profitable; the price of a scarce resource acts to ration it.

In the planned economy, prices are set by the central authority, and are not permitted to fluctuate in order to ration the scarce resource. Instead, the allocation must be made according to the plan. It is no wonder that the planners encounter problems that a market economy does not. The very long lines of communication up and down the great pyramidal planning structures make action slow as compared with the movement of the market. Bottlenecks can easily develop; or unwanted inventories can build up; or the economy can go on producing a commodity that no one wants for a considerable length of time before the slow processes of a planned economy catch up. The revision of production targets and the changes in the allocation of scarce resources can, and frequently do, upset the operations of many enterprises. It is a common complaint of many Soviet managers that they have difficulty in meeting production targets when plans are changed so frequently.

THE OPERATION OF AN ENTERPRISE

In the actual operation of a plant, Russian managers, particularly at middle and lower levels, face many of the same problems as Canadian or American managers. An enterprise in any economy is very largely a miniature command system within its own operation; resources are acquired and put to work in specific jobs, are shifted from one operation to another, or are moved from plant to plant, according to the direction of the manager. There is little direct reliance on the market to shift resources within the firm. Theoretically, it might be possible for a company in Canada to use the market to shift workers with a particular skill from, say, its Toronto plant to Montreal. The company might raise the price of that particular kind of labour in Montreal and lower it in Toronto; then Toronto workers, learning of the higher wages to be earned in the Montreal plant, would be encouraged to move. In practice, it is easier to use a command system and simply transfer employees from one plant to another. This kind of technical problem is basically the same in a market economy as in a command economy.

The hired manager of a Soviet enterprise, like the hired manager of one of the plants of a large Canadian corporation, is responsible for bringing together labour and materials in order to convert them into goods and services that they sell to other enterprises, or to consumers. A most important difference between Russian managers and Western managers is their relationship to their respective environments. The Western manager faces a multitude of prices that reflect the supply of and demand for each service, commodity, or component that he buys, sells, consumes, or produces. Even when he is concerned solely with the transfer of resources within the firm, the good manager will be aware of the price at which the particular resources can be bought or sold outside the firm; he will make periodic comparisons between his own costs and external prices to determine whether he should make a component or buy it. For example, if a component of his product can be bought in the market—that is, from another firm—at, say, twelve cents, then if he is concerned with the efficiency of each facet of his operation, he should not in his costing procedure charge his assembling operation with more than twelve cents, even though the part is produced in his own plant at fourteen cents. If such a situation exists, he should question the wisdom of making rather than buying this particular component. A profit-maximizing Western manager is likely either to shake up his production manager and get his costs down, or to buy the part from someone else.

The external prices of the total assortment that the Western manager produces, together with his internal costs (most of which are the external prices of materials or services he buys) will encourage him to shift and adapt his production as often as is practical in order to increase his profits. The good Western manager has to be an adaptive opportunist.

The Russian manager, on the other hand, has a totally different environment. While he, too, faces a host of prices for everything he buys or sells, these prices reflect government planning decisions and not the supply and demand conditions in the market. A relatively low price may not indicate abundance of a commodity; it may not even indicate that the manager can buy the commodity at all at any price. More important, the rewards to the manager come from fulfilling or over-fulfilling his predetermined plan, which often includes a long list of incentive rules (a reduced electrical bill might carry a special bonus), and not from his skill in adapting to prices and bottlenecks in the system.

The price of the commodity sold in the Soviet Union is fixed. It is usually set at a level high enough to enable the enterprise to cover its production costs plus an arbitrary profit margin, much of which is taken by the government in the form of a tax. This profit margin is designed to discourage or encourage consumption of the product, and to make consumption match production. The profits that result are not used to direct production; this is done by the plan. If the firm performs better than planned, and if extra or unplanned profits result, part of this is made available as a bonus to workers and management.

Because of the bonus from the unplanned profits, managers have an incentive to produce at the least possible cost and to overfulfil their production plans. But because of the absence of consumer sovereignty, which in the market economy tends to penalize low-quality or outmoded goods, and because of a general shortage of goods of many kinds, Soviet managers have little incentive to improve style or quality. Their sole concern is to produce in order to exceed their quotas. Since they do not have to concern themselves with selling what they produce, consumers' preferences are of little concern to them.

Two examples may help to underline the differences between the American and Soviet economies. As we all know, automobile production in the Soviet Union is a fraction—a small fraction—of automobile production in North America. Why? Do the Russian people not like automobiles? Russian consumers would undoubtedly like to buy as many cars as do Americans and Canadians. The difference is that the Soviet planning agency has decided that only a small number of passenger cars will be produced, and there is no practical way for the Russian people to express their wishes effectively on this matter.

The second example concerns a Soviet plant that produces nuts, bolts, and screws. Anyone who has visited a hardware store, or taken apart a few appliances, knows that there are thousands of varieties of metal fasteners. In America the profit-maximizing manager of such an operation is sensitive to supply and demand for the simple reason that he will obtain a better price and receive a higher profit for a bolt in short supply than for one that is in excess supply. The successful North American manager shifts resources quickly from one use to another in response to the needs of his customers.

In a command economy, on the other hand, the manager is given a target, which may be expressed in tons of output. In order to meet or exceed his quota, it will be in his self-interest to produce those fasteners that have maximum weight and a minimum labour content. It would be the wildest of coincidences if such an output matched the needs of industry. To control this kind of problem, targets must be more carefully specified in terms of "assortments". But imagine trying to determine down to the last detail in Moscow the appropriate assortment for a factory in Kiev! Frequently the plan works, not because the planning is good, but because the plans are ignored. "Communist graft" is the term that is sometimes applied to the bribery—subtle or otherwise—that buyers use to persuade suppliers to provide them with the items they currently need, rather than the items that might fulfil the supplier's quota or maximize the supplier's bonus. In America it may be the salesman who has the big expense account; in Russia it seems to be the buyer. While the market system could operate quite well without high-pressure salesmen, it is doubtful that a command society would work well without its high-pressure buyers.

Another problem that arises when a specific physical quantity is the sole target is that managers may be reluctant to install new machinery and adopt new techniques that involve a slowdown in current production. Moreover, if new machinery is purchased, the planners will likely give the enterprise new and higher quotas, and high-planned profits; thus most of any benefit that accrues will go to the state, while if anything should go wrong, the manager and the workers will stand to lose.

There are indications that the Soviet emphasis on quantitative targets is decreasing and that bonuses are being increasingly used as a reward for reducing costs or increasing labour productivity, rather than merely as payment for exceeding the quota. The reforms announced in 1965 suggested that the value of *sales* was to be used as an important measuring stick of the success of an enterprise. This would put a check on the production of goods for which there was no market. The reforms were designed to increase to some extent the autonomy of the managers of Soviet enterprises and, in effect, to orient them more to profits and efficiency.

Perhaps the most striking difference between Soviet and North American enterprises is the absence of collective bargaining. Wage scales are centrally set in the U.S.S.R., and a collective struggle by a union against management for higher wages would be considered a rather serious crime against the state.

AGRICULTURE

So far we have been making comparisons in the industrial sector. Agricultural production constitutes another important part of the national output of the Soviet economy, just as it is an important part of Canada's national output.

Almost all farms in North America are privately owned. Farmers are free to produce what they want to produce. If their operations are profitable, they retain the profits; if they are only marginal, then farmers are free to change their crops or to leave the farm if they wish.

The situation is very different in the U.S.S.R. where there are three distinct kinds of institutions in the agricultural sector. First of all, there are the state farms. These are large operations, relatively few in number, which tend to specialize in certain products like wheat or cattle. They are run very much like any other state-owned enterprise: the manager and the workers are hired, and the kinds of crops and the quotas are determined by the planning agencies. The output of the state farms, which amounts to about a quarter of the total agricultural output in the Soviet economy, is turned over to the state procurement agencies.

The second form of organization is the collective farm. These farms, a product of the Stalinist era, are supposed to be run for the benefit of the peasants who work them. The collectivization process which took place in the late 1920s and early 1930s was accomplished forcibly and sometimes with violence and at a tremendous cost of human resources. Stalin needed a large source of low-priced agricultural produce to feed the great urban industrial complexes that were to spring up throughout the country. All land, cattle, and machinery were therefore taken over by the state.

Peasants on collective farms are required to sow what the central agency orders them to sow, and to harvest when told. For their labour on the farms they accumulate man-days of credit. When the crop is harvested, the state takes its large share of the output and some is set aside to take care of the replacement of capital. The balance used to be made available to the peasants, frequently in kind, on the basis of their accumulated contribution of labour. As a result, the peasants' incentive to work on these farms was always limited, for the output that remained for distribution was frequently insufficient to provide even a subsistence living for them. One of the problems is that agriculture is difficult to administer and control. The units, which are numerous, tend to be relatively small. Many of the collective farms are far from the controlling body. Moreover, targets for production are regularly upset by the vagaries of the weather. In the post-Stalinist era, great efforts were made to improve incentives on the collective farms in order to increase the dismally low productivity. An improvement occurred with the reforms of 1965 which enabled the collective farms to sell at higher prices any output in excess of the target set by the state, thereby guaranteeing a minimum monthly income to members equal to what was paid on the state farms.

The third source of agricultural output, almost a third of the total, is privately owned plots of land. This is a remarkably large output when one considers that the amount of land involved is relatively small (about 3 percent of the total sown acreage) and that individuals are not permitted to own more than an acre. On these private plots peasants can grow what they want and once the compulsory delivery quota is met, they are free to consume or sell the produce to urban workers in farmers' markets at prices that are set largely by supply and demand (like those in a market economy). These plots of land provide many of the peasants with enough to live on, and it is understandable that they should receive a great deal of the peasants' time and attention, even at the expense of the work they are expected to do on the collective farm. The productivity of this land is high because it is so intensively worked and because the peasants are able to concentrate on high-income crops for which demand is strong and for which the land is best suited.

HOUSEHOLDS

In the Soviet economy, households are linked to the productive sector in much the same way as they are in the American or Canadian economies— through their consumption of goods and services produced by that sector, and through the labour services they sell to it. In both areas—consuming and working—there is a considerable amount of freedom of choice in the Soviet economy.

With some exceptions, like the peasants who are tied to the collective farms and are not free to move of their own volition, workers in the U.S.S.R. are free to choose their jobs. Since the government does not arbitrarily allocate workers to most jobs, it becomes necessary to *attract* them to the occupations where they are needed. Thus, to enable what is regarded as an essential enterprise to get sufficient workers to fulfil the requirements of the plan, jobs will be offered at a higher wage than those in an enterprise producing a commodity regarded as less essential. There are significant wage differentials that correspond to different levels of skills and training. Observers have suggested that differences in income levels among workers in the Soviet Union are as great as differences in the United States.

Before wage differentials can provide an incentive to move from one job to another, however, workers must see that the extra money they earn is worth having: they must be able to buy things with it. Consumers in the Soviet Union are normally free to purchase in government stores the goods that the government chooses to make available; that is, consumers have freedom of choice in their purchases. This is a very different thing, of course, from consumer sovereignty, which, we said, was the most important determinant of what would be produced in our mixed capitalistic system. Consumer sovereignty means that consumers, by their dollar votes, *determine* what will be produced. In a command economy, the planners determine what goods will be available to consumers. They may make guesses about what consumers want; the decision is not left to the market. People are also free to save their money; although there are no corporate stocks and bonds, there are government bonds that may be purchased and state-owned savings banks into which money may be put.

PRICES

Prices of consumers' goods and services are set by the central authority at a level designed to equate the quantity that consumers want with the supply that the planners have decided will be made available. There are three components in these prices: the cost of production, the planned profit margin, and a very stiff turnover tax which is used to make the prices of all consumers' goods so high that the demand for them will be limited to the amount supplied. This turnover tax, which is a major source of government revenue, can be altered if there is evidence that the price is not appropriate.

Unless planners make a determined effort to find the price that equates demand with supply, there will be either shortages or unsold inventories. If the prices of coats, for example, are set too low while the prices of radios are set too high, there will be a great rush to buy coats, and coats will then be in short supply. The stage might even be set for black-market operations in coats, as those who have bought them at the relatively low price can sell at a high price to those who cannot get them. Radios, on the other hand, will be too expensive, and they will pile up on the shelves of the government stores. When goods pile up unwanted on the shelves, or when shortages occur, prices may be altered by the planners: usually the turnover tax is juggled to bring the price to a level where the quantity of the goods demanded by consumers is equal to the quantity supplied.

The attempt by the central authority to find prices that equate quantities demanded and supplied in the market for consumers' goods and for the services of labour contrasts markedly with the practice of setting the prices of produce grown on the collective farms. In the latter case, prices are deliberately set low, perhaps below cost; then in order to get the supply of agricultural produce it needs, the government is forced to set quotas that must be met.

ASSESSMENT

It is important to know something about the Soviet economy[3] for a number of reasons. First, the U.S.S.R. ranks second to the United States in military and economic power, and hence deserves some discussion. Second, the U.S.S.R. is an important example of a command economy. If we see how an economy that does not rely on the price system operates to solve most of its basic economic problems, we will be able to understand our own system better.

We must recognize that a command economy *does* work. Reputable economists in the past had suggested that the complexity of the planning process, and the distance of the planners from where the action is, would make for a completely unworkable system. But such is not the case: the system does work, though not without waste, errors, or bottlenecks. These, however, occur in the market economy as well.

For some purposes a command economy is superior to the market system. Once some relatively clear goals have been established, like the Soviet goals of a rapid rate of industrialization, a rapid rate of growth, and a rapid build-up of military forces, the command economy is potentially more efficient than the market system in achieving these goals. The central authority in a command system has the power to mobilize resources without reference to the desires of consumers. The rapid industrialization of the Soviet economy has been made possible by forcing consumers in Russia to accept a much lower standard of living than they

---

[3] For a more complete description of the Soviet economy see, for example, Robert W. Campbell, *Soviet Economic Power*, 2nd ed. (New York: Houghton Mifflin Company, 1966); Abram Bergson, *The Economics of Soviet Planning* (New Haven: Yale University Press, 1964); George R. Feiwel, *The Soviet Quest for Economic Efficiency* (New York: Frederick A. Praeger, Publishers, 1967); Gregory Grossman, *Economic Systems* (Englewood Cliffs, N.J.: Prentice-Hall, Inc., 1967); George N. Halm, *Economic Systems A Comparative Analysis*, 3rd ed. (New York: Holt, Rinehart and Winston, Inc., 1968); and Gary M. Pickersgill and Joyce E. Pickersgill, *Contemporary Economic Systems A Comparative View* (Englewood Cliffs, N.J.: Prentice-Hall, Inc., 1974).

would have been prepared to accept of their own volition, and by preventing unions or other groups from protesting effectively against the decisions of the central planners.

Industrialization and Growth: the Production Possibility Curve

Mobilizing resources to increase the rate of industrialization and the rate of growth at the expense of producing goods for consumption can be illustrated with the tool we developed in the previous chapter, the production possibility curve. In Figure 2-1, instead of putting suits and tractors on the two axes, we have used more general labels: we have labelled the horizontal axis "consumers' goods" and the vertical axis "producers' goods".

The production possibility curve, PPC, represents all possible combinations of producers' goods and consumers' goods that can be produced in a given period of time with the existing resources in the economy. A point at the top of the curve represents a combination that is heavily weighted toward producers' goods, with very few consumers' goods being produced. On the other hand, a point low down on the curve near the horizontal axis represents a combination that contains mainly consumers' goods, with little in the way of investment goods (a synonym for producers' goods).

If an economy is to become highly industrialized, it is necessary to concentrate on the production of investment goods. The government in a command economy can simply dictate that more resources will be devoted to capital goods (*another* synonym for producers' goods)—that the economy will operate at point *A*, for example, high on the production possibility curve, so that it is producing only a small quantity (Ox) of consumers' goods, but a large quantity (Oy) of producers' goods. In a market economy, where the dollar votes of consumers are the main determinant of what will be produced, the combination is more likely to end up at point *B*, with Oz of consumers' goods being produced. This means that a bigger portion of the economy's resources is being allocated to consumers' goods. If consumers' goods amounting to Oz are being produced, then the production possibility curve tells us that the output of producers' goods can amount to no more than Ow.

The next question to be asked is, what difference does this pattern of allocation of resources make to the rate of growth? We assumed in drawing the production possibility curve that, *given* its resources, the economy could be anywhere along the production possibility curve, as long as all resources were fully employed, but it could not occupy a point

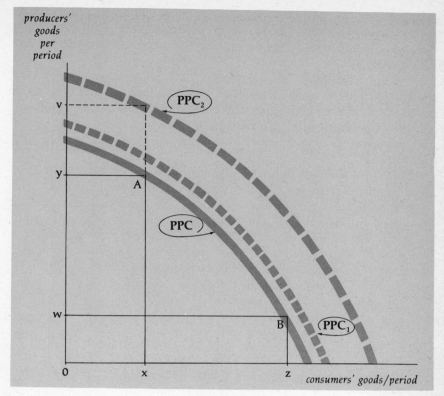

Figure 2-1

above the curve. But now consider the next phase. Having devoted more resources in period one to investment—to machines, tools, and factories in excess of the quantities needed for replacement—the economy has added to its productive resources, and these resources are available in the next period to produce either more consumers' goods or more producers' goods, or both. The decision to produce more investment goods (which, by definition, are not consumed) automatically increases the resources available for production. In the next period, therefore, we can draw a *new* production possibility curve (like PPC_1 or PPC_2) which lies outside the old one, and which shows that physical output, one of the yardsticks frequently used to measure growth, can be increased.

The greater the quantity of resources devoted to investment goods the further will the production possibility curve shift outward; in other words, the more rapidly will the potential of the economy expand. In terms of Figure 2–1, assume that the economy is operating at point A on the PPC, so that it is allocating enough resources to investment to produce Oy of producers' goods. With this concentration on capital goods, the production possibility curve in the next period might shift out to position PPC_2; and if the production of consumers' goods remains unchanged at Ox, then in that period the economy would produce an even greater quantity (Ov) of investment goods.

On the other hand, if an economy, whether market or command, chooses to allocate more of its output to consumers' goods (that is, to operate at point B instead of point A in Figure 2—1), plant and equipment will increase less rapidly, and the rate of growth will be slower. In the next period the new production possibility curve might be only PPC_1 instead of PPC_2.

This brief analysis shows in graphic form one of the controversies about whether developing countries should opt for a capitalist or a socialist solution to their growth problems. Since the developing countries are poor, there will be a natural and humanitarian desire to produce consumers' goods. Failure to emphasize the production of consumers' goods may even have to be measured in terms of the number of additional deaths by starvation. If consumer sovereignty is exercised—if peasants are given the opportunity to determine whether they will consume less now so that they can expand productive facilities in order to consume more in the future, or whether they will take more of the current output in the form of goods for immediate consumption—the economy is very likely to make a high-consumption, low-investment decision that will result in a low rate of growth. It is sometimes argued, therefore, that only such societies as those in the Communist countries, where there exists a one-party system with the power to suppress opposition, are in a position to impose growth on their people. In theory, of course, there is nothing to prevent a command economy from opting for more consumers' goods, or a market economy from developing a very high rate of capital formation and growth, as indeed Japan did in the postwar period.

Certainly in an authoritarian system it is relatively easy to give high priority to what the planners regard as the public interest, whether it is the rate of growth, a pyramid for the Pharoah, or the strength of the military forces. In the Soviet Union, the educational level and medical and health services have greatly improved because the planners have allocated large quantities of resources to them.

These are advantages of a command system; but there are disadvantages, too. The costs of these great achievements in the Soviet economy seem high to us, accustomed as we are to our political freedom, our right to criticize, and our freedom as consumers to determine what will be produced. To have to accept the secret police, who play an important role in ensuring that the goals of the Soviet economy are achieved, or the occasional purges that wipe out opposition to the incumbent regime, seem to most of us to be far too high a price to pay for this kind of efficiency in achieving the goals selected by the central authority. Moreover, the long lines of communication through the hierachical pyramid of the command economy result in inefficiencies in production, wastage of resources, and a slowness in responding to changing conditions that are more marked in the Soviet economy than in the American economy. The command economy must also find a solution to the problem of incentives, so that workers and managers will contribute their best efforts.

One of the major problems of the Soviet economy now is that the success of the command system in promoting a high rate of growth has transformed the economy from a simple, primitive one with relatively well-defined goals into a much more complex system in which the traditional kind of planning is becoming outmoded. It has been a source of concern to Soviet economists that the growth rate seems to be slowing down. Some Russian economists have been arguing for a greater degree of decentralization—that is, less planning and more reliance on the market system. As a result of the 1965 reforms, prices are now supposed to cover rent and a return on capital; they are still centrally set, however, and since they cannot respond to changes in supply and demand, they do not act to ration resources in short supply as do prices in a market economy. Managers have been given more control over their inputs and outputs, and the emphasis on targets has been changed from volume of production to volume of sales. The implication of this is that producers should pay more attention to their customers' tastes, and fewer resources should be wasted in producing unwanted, though easy-to-produce goods.

It is still a matter of controversy whether or not these reforms constitute a real move to decentralization. However, as we said at the beginning of this chapter, while we are dealing with a close approximation to a command economy, it is not a *pure* command system, any more than the Canadian or American system is a pure capitalist system. The Soviet system is a mixed command economy: decisions are made in very large measure by a central authority, but the system contains some elements of the market system.

The Yugoslavian Economy

The two most powerful economies in the world today, the American and the Soviet, lie at opposite ends of the scale. The American economy relies primarily on the market system to solve its basic economic problems, yet it has some elements of command in it; and the Soviet economy depends mainly on the command system, with some indication that the price system is becoming slightly more important. But there are many other economies that lie between these two extremes.

One interesting economy in the world today is the Yugoslavian economy. Yugoslavia became a communist country during the Second World War, closely following the authoritarian socialism of the U.S.S.R. until the country's Communist leader Tito broke with Stalin in 1948. The Yugoslavs, after this break, moved toward a rather different kind of economy: socialistic, in the sense that most of the resources are owned by the state, but far more decentralized than the Soviet economy and hence much more reliant on the market system.

Land in Yugolsavia is *not* owned by the state. Agricultural collectivization failed, and in 1953 peasants were given permission to leave the collective farms. As a result, almost 90 percent of the land is privately owned; and except for a limit of about 25 acres on the amount of land that can be held by a single family, the peasants operate as they choose. In addition, there is a certain amount of private enterprise in small-scale production and service-oriented shops: an individual is permitted to employ up to five workers in addition to the members of his own family. Apart from these exceptions, however, the means of production are primarily state-owned.

In the publicly owned sector, the Yugoslavs have come to rely more heavily than the Russians on the market system. Workers' councils manage enterprises. This means that although the workers do not own the means of production, they are responsible for the economic performance of the enterprise. They determine their own pricing policies. Instead of adhering to centrally-dictated output quotas, they plan their own output, though they are expected to adhere to the general direction of the central plan. They are interested in earning profits because they are permitted to retain them for investment purposes or for payments to workers. Wage rates are set by the workers' council; but since earnings are financed out of the net income of the enterprise, workers have an incentive to produce efficiently in order to earn their full rates and to earn bonuses. The workers elect their council, and hence are unlikely to feel alienated from the productive process. Thus, there has been some attempt in the Yugoslav economy to meet the problem of providing adequate incentives—one of the intractable problems faced by the planners in the Soviet economy.

Since the Yugoslav economy relies to a considerable extent on the market mechanism, it is faced with a number of the same problems as the Canadian economy—for example, the problem of monopolies that may charge excessive prices to consumers and make excessive profits. In Yugoslavia these high profits may mean excessively high earnings for the workers in those enterprises. The country has also suffered from strong inflationary pressures, and the government has frequently had to use price controls as a weapon against them. Price controls tend to interfere with the operation of the market system and threaten the whole idea of decentralization.

The French Economy

Further along our scale, as we move toward the mixed capitalistic system, comes the economy of a country like France. The market mechanism is permitted to solve most of the basic economic problems of production and distribution in France, but there is a large public sector by Canadian and American standards, and far more reliance is placed on comprehensive planning for the entire economy than in Canada and the United States. French plans are detailed and comprehensive: they are the most elaborate plans that exist in any of the western countries.

Planning in France is usually described as "indicative" planning. This means that the plan provides *guidelines* for future economic development, rather than standing as a coercive plan, such as that of the planning agencies in the U.S.S.R. The planning process in France is complex, involving many groups: the government, experts, and interested parties. This tends to result in a wider acceptance of the plan by the general public. Though the French government lacks the coercive weapons available to the central authorities in the Soviet Union, it does have a number of tools that can be used to help carry out the plan—tools such as tax exemptions, loan guarantees, and the power to allow rapid depreciation write-offs in order to encourage investment in specific areas. Through its own expenditure, as well as through state-financed loans, the government can directly influence more than half of the total investment in the country, and it uses its powers to help achieve the general goals of growth, modernization of the economy, stability and balance-of-payments equilibrium.

Conclusion

This rather brief description of the operations of other economies confirms our earlier statement that today there are two distinct ways in which basic economic decisions are made: the market system and the command system. These two components may be mixed in different proportions. There may be heavy reliance on the decentralized market system with a small admixture of command, as in the American and Canadian economies. At the other extreme there may be a heavy reliance on the command or planned system, with a certain limited number of decisions being made by the market. This is the case of the authoritarian socialism of the Soviet economy. In between there fall the rest of the economies of the world, of which we cited only two examples: Yugoslavia, with its adherence to a central plan, but with much more reliance on the market solution than there is in the U.S.S.R.; and France, with its heavy emphasis on indicative planning in what is primarily a market system.

3

Canada's economic goals provide a useful framework within which to discuss the country's policies and its problems. For the purposes of this study it is useful to organize our discussion around a set of six economic goals:

1. economic stability, by which we mean full employment without inflation,
2. economic growth,
3. an equitable distribution of income,
4. a viable balance of payments,
5. economic freedom,
6. the proper allocation of resources—a broad goal that permits us to talk about several problems of the Canadian economy, such as competition, the energy problem, and agriculture, which do not fit neatly in any of the other five.

These goals are not mutually exclusive. They cannot all be achieved simultaneously: policies to achieve one may defeat efforts to achieve another and compromises are necessary.

Goals, Guidelines, and Policies

We all have objectives in life—goals that determine most of our actions. Sometimes these goals are clearly stated, or explicit; sometimes they are implicit. Sometimes they are selfish; sometimes they are altruistic. Our goals may frequently conflict, and we have to find a way to resolve these conflicts. An individual at peace with himself has learned to resolve his conflicts. The same is true of a nation. If a country's economic and political systems are to operate reasonably well, there must be a general consensus about what the nation is trying to achieve. Its goals must be based on a common set of values in the country; this is what holds the community together as a cohesive unit. Once we know what the objectives are, it is possible to draw up guidelines to action or *policies* that will help the community attain its objectives. Justice, for example, is an accepted goal of most societies, and we expect these societies to look for patterns of action, or policies, that will help to establish justice.

What kind of policies will help to achieve justice? You and I would have no trouble in agreeing that justice is a desirable goal, but this still does not tell us what we should do to make sure that ours is a just society; for justice may not mean the same thing to you as it does to me. Even *economic* justice is so general a goal that it is not immediately obvious what specific actions will ensure that economic justice exists. One might argue, for example, that economic justice means equal incomes for everyone. Another might argue with equal conviction that this would be a great injustice to those who work hard, for the industrious should have a greater reward in an economically just society than those who are lazy and unwilling to do their share.

Economic justice is probably regarded as an acceptable goal in the U.S.S.R., but it has a different meaning for the Russians than it has for us. We have already said that the Russians argue that the only factor of production that makes a contribution to the productive process is labour; this is the essence of the "labour theory of value". Other factors such as land, capital, and entrepreneurship (the organizational skill of the innovator or promoter and his willingness to take risk) do not deserve any share when the national income pie is being distributed. The Communist dogma says that in our capitalist system, since the price of the product is greater than the return to labour—allowing as it does for a return to land, capital, and the skill of the entrepreneur—the workers are being exploited; this, they argue, is unjust. Economic justice in the Soviet economy, therefore, involves state ownership of the instruments of production.

To many Canadians, on the other hand, the Soviet system may seem unjust, for it is argued that without the skill of the innovator to organize labour, land, capital, and raw materials, less would be produced. Money capital is necessary to build plants and machinery. In order to persuade people to forgo spending on current consumption voluntarily, and thus make money available for the productive process, we consider it fair that there should be a return in the form of interest. Thrift, like hard work, should be rewarded. Most of us regard private ownership of the greater part of the means of production as a freer, more productive, and more equitable system than public ownership. It is apparent that goals are closely associated with value systems: different value systems will lead to different objectives.

Establishing the Goals

Establishing goals is a complex process even for a single individual. The first objective of an individual is to fulfil his physical needs in order to survive; but "survival" may have different meanings for different people. For some it may have the literal meaning of living at the margin of subsistence; for others "survival" may mean nothing less than a comfortable home in suburbia with two cars and a swimming pool. Beyond survival come the "higher" goals, some of which are attainable with money and some of which cannot be bought. The pursuit of happiness or achieving "the good life" are possible goals, but they are too general to give any guidelines to behaviour. The pursuit of happiness for one may involve spending all possible spare time in the garden: planting, weeding, and watering. Gardening for another may be anathema: a state of well being for him may be achieved by reading good books and attending concerts, or visiting museums and art galleries. For someone else it may mean spending every night "on the town". The good life for one may involve serving others; for another it may mean focusing attention exclusively on himself.

A company is made up of a group of workers who have a common objective—for example, making cars. If there are different objectives in the same company—with half of the workers wanting to make power mowers and the other half wanting to make cars—then it is unlikely to be a viable company. To get along in the same organization, groups must have similar objectives. Indeed, it is the existence of common goals that molds heterogeneous individuals into a single group. If there are not at least some common goals—whether in a marriage, in a company, or in a nation—then the group will not be a viable entity.

It is important then for a country to reach a consensus about its principal goals; this is the essence of nationhood. Given the diversity of individual objectives, one can see that it may be difficult to arrive at common goals for the entire economy. Citizens may have goals that differ from those of the government making the policy decisions. When this happens in a democracy, we expect one government to be voted out of office and replaced by another whose objectives conform more closely with those of the people. It is not so easy, of course, in an authoritarian government where the central authority imposes its own goals. The Soviet Union, for example, has decided that it wants a rapid rate of industrialization and growth and strong military power at the expense of consumers' goods; and there is no easy way for Russian citizens to register their approval or disapproval.

Within any country, moreover, competing groups may have different goals. We saw this in the United States with the problem of the war in Vietnam; the absence of a consensus caused a deep split in the country. It is one of the problems that Canada must face up to: if French Canada and English Canada have common goals, then there can be a workable partnership. If their objectives are diametrically opposed, then there may be reason to dissolve the partnership.

The Goals of the Canadian Economy

It is difficult to find a classification of goals that provides a completely satisfactory framework within which to discuss the problems of the Canadian economy, but since the rest of the book is organized around these goals, it is important to find a classification that is workable. We can group various objectives together and reduce the number to two or three broad goals—or even to a single one—but then we end up dealing with goals so broad that they cannot provide guidelines to action, and so general that they might apply equally well to the Soviet economy as to the Canadian economy. On the other hand, if we define the goals narrowly, they may become distinctly Canadian in flavour, but we may find ourselves dealing not so much with the goals themselves as with *means* to broader ends. When we discuss goals for the country, we face the further problem that while our main concern is with the *economic* goals of the Canadian economy, they are closely interwoven with the social goals and we cannot completely separate economics and ethics.

Kenneth E. Boulding, in his book *Principles of Economic Policy*[1], suggests that there are four objectives of policy: economic progress or growth,

---

[1] K. E. Boulding, *Principles of Economic Policy* (Englewood Cliffs, N.J.: Prentice-Hall, Inc., 1958).

economic stability, economic justice (an equitable distribution of income), and economic freedom. In Canada the most comprehensive discussion of goals is to be found in the various publications of the Economic Council of Canada, a group made up of a chairman, two directors, and up to twenty-five members drawn from various sectors of the economy including industry, labour, agriculture, and finance and commerce. The function of this body is to advise the government on economic matters. To fulfill its mandate the Economic Council originally built its work around five basic economic goals: full employment, a high rate of economic growth, reasonable stability of prices, a viable balance of payments, and an equitable distribution of rising incomes.[2] These five goals provide a useful framework within which the Canadian economy and its problems can be studied, but the list is not comprehensive enough for our purposes. For example, it omits Boulding's objective of economic freedom. Economic freedom may be interpreted to include the freedom to pay the cost of being Canadian, or the freedom to pay the cost involved in retaining the French culture—problems of major concern in contemporary Canada.

Moreover, there is a large body of economic policy relating to issues which are important to any discussion of the Canadian economy and its problems but which do not fit neatly into the above framework. For example, various aspects of policies relating to the regulation of business —whether through taxation, legislation to protect consumers' rights, or regulations designed to maintain a reasonable degree of competition and prevent unfair business practices—might be dealt with under one of several of the above goals. They might be included in a discussion of growth (because progress is enhanced by competition); economic freedom (because competition reinforces consumer sovereignty, and by encouraging greater output increases the range of choice of jobs); achieving a viable balance of payments (because competition, to the extent that it increases efficiency, enables Canadian goods to compete in the international market), and so on. The same is true of policies dealing with current problems in the natural resources sector including energy and agriculture. Both of them have had a sharp destabilizing effect on the economy; both have a major influence on the distribution of income; both have implications for achieving a viable balance of payments. Rather than break such problems up and consider them under a variety of goals, it would be more convenient to find a somewhat wider framework for their discussion. Policies relating to competition and monopoly are frequently discussed as part of a broader goal of *achieving a proper allocation of resources;* policies relating to energy and agriculture could readily fit under the same heading. But the inclusion of such a broad goal creates its own problems:

---

[2] Economic Council of Canada, *First Annual Review* (Ottawa: Queen's Printer, 1964), p. 1.

earlier we defined economics as "a social science whose central problem is how to allocate scarce resources among alternative uses", and this means that the proper allocation of resources is a goal that could be as broad as economics itself. It could encompass virtually every objective we could name. Allocating resources *properly* means achieving the optimum level of welfare for the community as a whole. This is at the same level of generality as "achieving the good life", and it is at the same high level of desirability as motherhood, virtue, and green leafy vegetables. It could include all of Boulding's four goals. This is too broad a meaning to be useful to us, and it would not suit our purposes to discuss all contemporary problems as part of a single goal.

The Economic Council is in the process of developing a new and broader framework of socioeconomic goals within which it may be possible to develop policies for a wide range of emerging needs and concerns in Canada. It has begun the difficult task of developing a set of *social indicators* to help measure the achievement of the country in areas that the Council considers to be primarily social but with strong economic implications, such as national identity, health, education, the environment (both natural and man made)—the latter to encompass such current issues as the physical environment of the city including, for example, housing and transportation.[3]

The rest of this book is organized around a set of six economic goals. They provide a broader framework than the five performance goals of the Economic Council that are listed above, but are somewhat more specific than the new socioeconomic goals promise to be. They are not mutually exclusive; nor can they all be attained simultaneously. They include: (1) economic stability (full employment without inflation), (2) growth (economic progress), (3) an equitable distribution of income (economic justice), (4) a viable balance of payments, (5) economic freedom, and, notwithstanding the broad interpretation that might be attached to the goal, (6) the proper allocation of resources, which will provide us with a convenient peg on which to hang the discussion of such issues as consumerism, maintaining a reasonable degree of competition, and problems in the resources sector like energy and agriculture.

These could be the goals of any democratic economy; they would also be acceptable to the Soviet economy. Some of them need to be defined more precisely, particularly economic freedom, for it is the interpretation of the meaning of this goal that distinguishes most clearly the market system from the command system. While it is true that these could be the goals of any economically advanced country, there is a great difference in

---

[3] Economic Council of Canada, *Eleventh Annual Review: Economic Targets and Social Indicators* (Ottawa: Information Canada, 1974), Chs. 1 & 4.

emphasis in different economies. The freedom to be Canadian, for example, has been a dominant objective throughout Canadian history, and it is an objective that has major economic implications.

It is important at this point to have some understanding of the meaning of these goals. For that reason the remainder of this chapter will be devoted to a brief discussion of each of them in turn. They will be treated in greater detail in later chapters.

ECONOMIC STABILITY

One of the problems of the Canadian economy, as well as of the economies of other developed countries, is that progress is not *steady*. The economy moves forward in a wave-like motion; output fluctuates from a high level in boom times to too low a level in times of recession. When output reaches a high level and presses on capacity, and when all resources are fully employed, the economy is likely to be plagued with rapidly rising prices. On the other hand, when output is too low, many factors of production are unemployed, and the output that these resources might otherwise produce is irrevocably lost. Everyone agrees that it would be desirable to prevent, or at least mitigate, economic fluctuations.

Stability of the economy is a desirable goal. It is not enough to say that we want stability, however; for we do not want the economy to be stable at the level it was back in 1933, when almost 20 percent of the labour force was unemployed. We want stability at a level where the factors of production are fully employed. On the other hand, we want to avoid inflation: we do not want prices to increase at a rate of one percent per month, as they did just after World War II; nor do we want the double-digit inflation that reappeared in 1974 and 1975. Stability at full employment without inflation is the goal we hope to reach.

Stability is difficult to achieve because there is an inherent conflict in the goal. There are two variables involved—prices and employment—and the conflict arises because efforts to stabilize one may cause the destabilization of the other. Should we attempt, then, to have stable prices at the expense of having an increased number of our resources unemployed? Or, should we try for full employment and let prices rise? Or, is there a compromise position, and if so, how do we decide on the appropriate trade-off between rising prices and unemployment? The choice becomes even more complex when *both* inflation and unemployment are at an unacceptably high level as they were in the mid-1970s.

Rising prices cause a redistribution of income and wealth because inflation decreases the purchasing power of money. The *real* value of a dollar is determined by what goods and services it will buy. If prices double, a dollar will buy only half as much as before. In this case, we say that the purchasing power of money has declined. When prices go up, people on fixed salaries, or those living on old age pensions, find that their incomes and their savings command fewer goods and services. On the other hand, businessmen who find that the prices of what they are selling are increasing may make windfall profits during an inflationary period. People who owe money gain from inflation, because the dollars that they pay back are not as valuable as the dollars they borrowed. If prices are stable, such problems of income redistribution are avoided; thus we must conclude that, other things being equal, stable prices are a desirable objective.

Full employment is another desirable goal. If the economy does not operate at capacity, then the output that might be produced if all resources are used is irrevocably lost. If a man remains unemployed for a year, there is no way in the future of getting back the services he could have rendered while he was out of work.

So far, we have carefully sidestepped the difficult question of precisely what we mean by full employment. First, we should distinguish between the full employment of human resources and the full employment of non-human resources. Human resources get the largest share of national income. As we shall see in Chapter 9, wages and salaries account for more than 70 percent of net national income, and this understates the return to labour as a productive resource. Under-utilization of any factor of production is an economic waste. Our humanitarian instincts, however, lead us to emphasize the importance of the full employment of labour. An idle machine does not suffer; an unemployed man may.

Second, when considering the full employment of labour, we must recognize that at any particular time there will be people who are changing jobs and who, therefore, are out of work. This "frictional unemployment" is inevitable if the labour force is to be mobile: it is a necessary part of the operation of the market system that workers should move to jobs that are offering higher prices for their services. Obviously then, full employment does not mean 100 percent of the work force employed for this is neither attainable nor desirable. But what percentage of the labour force can be without work and still allow us to describe our economy as being fully employed? Two percent? Five percent? Somewhere in between? And is this figure to be an average level for the year? Unemployment in Canada is seasonal in nature: it typically reaches a peak in February or March each year and reaches a low in August or September. Thus, when we say that full employment exists when 97 percent of the labour force is employed, are we referring to the periods when unemployment is at its low or at its high, or are we talking about an average for the entire year? The objective of achieving stability at full employment without inflation is difficult to attain; and failure to achieve it caused some people in the mid-1970s to ask whether traditional economics and traditional economic policies would work at all. Economic stability is a problem to which we shall return in Chapter 6 after we have acquired some of the tools necessary to understand the problem better.

GROWTH

The decade of the 1960s was a period of remarkable growth. By any measure one cares to use—rising total real output, rising real output per person, rising productivity of the factors of production (increasing output per person employed, or per unit of physical capital employed, or per acre of land employed), or rising consumption per person—the Canadian economy grew rapidly. Canadians became accustomed not merely to maintaining their standard of living, but to improving it every year, and to this firmly entrenched expectation has been attributed some of the blame for the vicious wage-price spiral of 1974 and 1975[4] as various parts of the labour force tried to fulfill their expectations of improving their material welfare in years when real output was either rising little, or for short periods was actually declining.

There has been more and more debate over whether or not improvements in *material* welfare mean improvements in the *general* welfare of society: critics are expressing concern over the effects of growth on the environment and the implications of the rapid rate of consumption of resources, particularly nonrenewable resources. The question is being asked more frequently: does *more* necessarily mean better? More attention is being focused on the costs of economic growth and the need to weigh them against the benefits. However, there is little evidence to suggest that Canadians are prepared to forgo growth as one of the important goals of the economy, for it is apparent that with growth it is easier to achieve some of the broad socioeconomic goals like improving health and education, reducing pollution, improving the quality of life in cities, eliminating poverty, and enabling job creation to keep up with a growing labour force. The debate on the benefits and costs of growth has reinforced the idea that the goal is to achieve, not the maximum rate of growth, but the *optimum* rate.

AN EQUITABLE DISTRIBUTION OF INCOME

From our description of the way the market system works, we know that resources, or factors, have prices that are determined in the factor market. The owners of these resources sell their services in the market, and what

---

[4] See, for example, Judith Maxwell, "The Vicious Circle of Inflation" in *Policy Review and Outlook, 1975: Restructuring The Incentive System* (Montreal, C. D. Howe Research Institute, 1974), pp. 9-10.

they earn from all of the resources that they own constitutes their income. Some individuals have only their labour services to sell, and they get a return in the form of a wage or salary. Others have, in addition, land, money capital, or organizational skill; and they may earn rent, interest, or profit in addition to or instead of a wage or salary. If we operated with a pure market system, the sum of these returns would determine the share of income of the owners of the various resources. But we do not regard the market solution to the problem of the distribution of income as entirely just. For example, what about the penniless mother who was left with young children to support when the breadwinner of the family died? In the pure market system, if she could not leave her children and go to work, she would not have any income. This violates our sense of justice, and so we have welfare plans that ensure that she and her children will get some financial aid even if she does not work. The same is true of the orphans, the handicapped, and the aged.

It has been the general consensus that the market solution leaves too large a gap between rich and poor. Therefore, Parliament has passed tax laws that require those who earn incomes above a given amount to pay taxes. To reduce the spread in incomes, those who move into higher and higher income brackets must pay as taxes a larger and larger percentage of the extra income they earn: this is what is meant by a progressive tax system.

But how far do we push our attempts to alter the solution given by the market and to even out the distribution of income in the name of justice? Does justice require *equality* of incomes, as some argue? Not many people regard equal incomes for all as just, for—as we have noted—this implies that those who work diligently earn the same amount as those who loaf. There must be some kind of incentive to encourage people to contribute their best efforts. If economic growth and progress are to be encouraged, producers must be rewarded for the risks they take in developing a new machine or in marketing a new product. For a few, recognition as the inventor of a new process may be a sufficient reward, but for most there must be a greater incentive than merely the self-satisfaction that comes from a job well done. The Russians have discovered that there must be some tangible reward to encourage initiative, and we have already noted that the spread of incomes appears to be as wide in the U.S.S.R. as it is in the United States. Thus, even if one believed that ideally incomes should be equal, such a principle would conflict so strongly with the goal of growth and progress that some kind of compromise would have to be reached.

The objective of achieving an equitable distribution of income, then, really boils down to achieving a less *unequal* distribution of income than the market system would give, and establishing a level of income that ensures a basic minimum standard of living for all. It is generally agreed that poverty in our affluent Canadian society is a pressing problem. But what *is* poverty? What is the minimum income in Canada necessary to permit someone to buy a basket of goods and services that enables him to live at the minimum decency level? It is difficult to suggest exactly how much this minimum should be because as the average standard of living increases, our concept of what constitutes a basic minimum also increases. We shall return to the question of the distribution of income in Chapter 9.

It is not only the inequitable distribution among individuals and groups that creates a problem of economic justice in Canada: there also exist wide and persistent differences in the incomes of different regions. If we divide total Canadian personal income for 1974 by total population we get an average income for each man, woman, and child of $4 966. Such an average, however, conceals the fact that the personal income per person of $5 559 in Ontario, the province with the highest average, was 70 percent higher than the average of $3 274 that existed in Prince Edward Island, the province with the lowest income per person.[5] Numerous policies have been implemented to reduce these income disparities—policies like equalization and stabilization payments, which are part of the federal-provincial fiscal arrangements, and the various development policies of the Department of Regional Economic Expansion, which we shall look at in more detail in Chapter 11. But the wide disparities still persist, creating serious strains on the Canadian nation.

A VIABLE BALANCE OF PAYMENTS

The balance of payments is a summary of all payments to foreigners and receipts from them. These receipts and payments arise mainly because countries trade: they export and import goods and services. In addition, individuals and governments give and receive gifts. Borrowing, lending, and investing, whether for short periods or long, take place across international boundaries and give rise to foreign payments and receipts. Receipts and payments for goods and services can get out of balance, and when that happens borrowing or lending or investing will be necessary to bring the accounts back into line. If an imbalance persists, then a country's reserves of foreign exchange or its foreign exchange rates may be affected in such a way as to have an adverse impact on the domestic economy, and in that case the objective of a viable balance of payments is not being achieved.

---

[5] Based on information from Statistics Canada.

The objective of achieving a viable balance of payments is of major importance to Canada because international trade is so important. Trade has played a crucial role in the development of this country, and it has had a major impact on the level of national income and the rate of growth. According to the Economic Council of Canada, exports account for more than half of the output of Canadian industries that produce goods (as opposed to services), and the value of imports by 1973 amounted to more than half the value of the output of the goods-producing industries in Canada.[6]

Trade in goods and services, foreign aid, and flows of capital across the border (foreign investment)—transactions that show up in the balance of payments—also have a major impact on efforts to achieve other goals like full employment and price stability, the optimum rate of growth and economic freedom. One has only to think of the effect on domestic prices of the drastic price increases in oil imposed by the governments of the cartel of oil-producing countries (OPEC) to realize this. Canada's great dependence on international transactions means that the changing framework of world trade has serious implications for the entire economy. Canada is no longer dealing with some twenty individual industrialized countries as was the case a couple of decades ago; instead the country is dealing mainly with three economic giants: the United States, the European Common Market, and Japan. This raises questions about the efficiency of Canada's industries and the future ability of such a small economic unit with its limited domestic market to compete in a world of giants. In view of the crucial importance to the Canadian economy of such matters, it is not surprising that achieving viability in the balance of payments should have been adopted as one of the basic economic goals. We shall return to a discussion of the goal in Chapter 12 and shall consider foreign investment in Chapter 13.

ECONOMIC FREEDOM

Economic freedom is a complex goal: it has a number of component parts, some of which we discussed in connection with the comparison between the market economy and the command economy. An important part of it is freedom of choice, and one of the great advantages of the market system is that it ensures the greatest degree of freedom of choice. Freedom of choice applies in a number of areas. For a worker, there is freedom to choose his job, to quit his present one if conditions are not

---

[6] Economic Council of Canada, *Looking Outward: A New Trade Strategy* (Ottawa: Information Canada, 1975), p. 18.

suitable, or to move to one that pays more. As long as the labour market is operating properly, workers can benefit from these choices. However, if the economy fails to achieve full employment, the freedom to quit one's job may be an empty one, for there may not be another job to go to. For this freedom to exist in a meaningful way, the market for labour must work efficiently; this means that there must be alternative job opportunities (full employment), and information about these opportunities must be readily available.

For consumers in the market economy, freedom of choice means not merely the freedom to buy any of the goods that are brought into the market—this is a freedom open to consumers in the Soviet economy—but it also means that consumers are free to determine what goods and services will be produced. In other words, freedom of choice for consumers in the market system implies consumers' sovereignty. This freedom does not exist in a command system. Even in our own economy, consumers do not have *complete* freedom to determine what will be produced; there are certain limits. For example, consumers do not determine the amount of defence that will be produced. The government makes this decision, as well as decisions that involve the quantities of all other collectively consumed goods and services. A certain amount of education is compulsory; people have no freedom of choice about whether or not they will send their children to school to consume an elementary education. Consumers do not have the option of purchasing heroin (not legally, at least) since its free sale is forbidden by law. Within such limits, however, consumers have the right not only to select the goods they want, but to determine what will be available to them. The rise of consumerism, which will be discussed in Chapter 14, can be interpreted as a move on the part of consumers, with the aid of the government, to assert their freedom and preserve what they consider to be their rights.

In the market economy there is also the freedom to decide whether to consume or to save and, if we save, the freedom to do what we want with our savings. If an individual wants to take a high flier on a speculative oil stock, he is free to do so. If he wants to give up his factory job in favour of being his own boss on a chicken farm, he can spend his savings on a small piece of land somewhere and set up a business. Related to what we have just said is the fact that we have the freedom to be owners of the factors of production, and this is the freedom that does not belong exclusively to the rich: subsistence farms, for example, can be purchased cheaply, and it does not take too much capital to start a corner grocery store.

A final freedom that we should include for Canadians is the freedom to pay the cost of being Canadian. The freedom to maintain national identity has economic implications, because it involves such actions as putting tariffs on foreign goods to encourage the growth of Canadian industry, paying higher defence costs, perhaps controlling the quantity of foreign capital coming in or even sending it home. Such actions are very likely to be detrimental to the interests of Canadian consumers. Tariffs make imported goods more expensive to buy; higher defence costs mean higher taxes; foreign capital and know-how have given a major impetus to Canada's growth rate and have meant a more rapidly rising standard of living than Canadians could have achieved on their own. One of the contentious issues of our time is the question of how high a price Canadians are willing to pay to maintain their national identity.

Precisely the same considerations are relevant to the discussions of the separation of Quebec from the rest of Canada. The costs would be high to the people of Quebec as well as to the rest of the country.

Economic freedom deserves an important place in our list of objectives for Canada. As was the case with the other goals, attempts to achieve it have given rise to a number of current problems.

THE PROPER ALLOCATION OF RESOURCES

Because there are several important contemporary problems that do not fit neatly into a discussion of any one of the goals described so far, it is convenient, as mentioned earlier, to add a sixth goal that can provide a peg on which to hang the discussion of such problems of the Canadian economy: the proper allocation of resources. One of the most important problems to be dealt with under this broad heading is maintaining competition through the regulation of business, whether by means of devices like regulatory boards or the Combines Investigation Act or by consumer protection legislation.[7]

For the free market economy to work satisfactorily, there must be competition. Profits are supposed to be the signal indicating that consumers like a product and want more of it. That is, they want more of the economy's scarce labour, raw materials, and entrepreneurial skill allocated to the production of that good or service. If producers earn high profits, they are encouraged to expand their plants and to buy more machinery so that they can increase output. Other businessmen, seeing the profits to be made, will try to get into that business. Thus, the wishes of consumers are likely to be fulfilled.

But this process of fulfilling consumers' wishes can be short-circuited

---

[7] See Chs. 14 & 15.

if, for one reason or another, old firms do not expand and new firms are not established. This can happen when there exists a high degree of monopoly in the industry. Monopoly, in the rather loose sense that we have used it here, means simply that there are barriers that make entry into the industry difficult.[8] Such barriers may be caused by control over strategic raw materials, or special patents, or recipes, by the very large amount of capital necessary to get into the industry, or by some other obstacle. In such a case, the signal of high profits may be present, but if new firms cannot get in and the old firms will not expand, then the operation of the free market is frustrated. The monopolist may raise his price, thereby discouraging sales, and a misallocation of resources will occur in the sense that not enough factors are being directed toward the product consumers want. Thus, economists who see consumer sovereignty as an important objective and who want to see the market system operate efficiently support competition and condemn monopoly.

Competition is also supported on the grounds that it promotes economic growth. When one company introduces a new and better technique in a competitive industry, other companies must follow suit quickly if they are to continue to be able to compete. Thus, competition encourages firms to innovate and to increase productivity.

Unfortunately, competition is another of those ambiguous words in economics which have a number of meanings and which, therefore, make communication difficult. To say that our objective is to have a reasonable degree of competition is to make a statement that anyone could agree with, but what does "a reasonable degree of competition" mean? As we shall see, economists have a model of competition (they refer to it as *perfect* or *pure competition*) that assumes an industry which one can get in and out of easily and which contains a large number of small firms producing a homogeneous product. Farms producing No. 1 Northern Wheat in Canada might be an example, if we ignore the operation of the Canadian Wheat Board. This kind of competition is sometimes called "atomistic" competition. Clearly, the objective in Canada cannot be to establish atomistic competition. This would not be reasonable: how could we produce cars at anything less than a prohibitive price unless we used large plants like the Ford plant at Oakville? It is in large corporations that the cost advantages of assembly-line techniques are achieved, and this, in turn, is what permits us to have one of the highest standards of living in the world.

But how large should these corporations be? Have we already allowed them to grow too big, and should we break them up? Many argue that

---

[8] Later on we shall use the word "monopoly" in the strict economic sense of an industry in which there is a single seller.

bigness in whatever area means an undesirable concentration of power. If we permit giant corporations to develop, along with giant unions, will we come to a stage where competition is virtually eliminated—where the economy is dominated by huge organizations that either do battle or negotiate with each other?

On the other hand, it may be that the full potential of our advanced technology necessitates large corporations. These firms, with their large profits, can afford to do research—to find new and better techniques and to produce new products. Because other smaller firms cannot easily get into the industry, these corporations know that while they have to take the risk of failure, they will also be able to keep any profits as a reward for success. Therefore, large corporations may encourage economic progress, not impede it. Perhaps what we mean by "a reasonable degree of competition" is enough competition to ensure a satisfactory performance of the firms in any given industry. A precise definition of "a reasonable degree of competition" is just not possible. Judgement will be required, and perhaps the most that we can say is that reasonable suggests that we use our "reason" in a pragmatic way to ensure that the price, growth, and innovative performance of each industry are "satisfactory". Our policies must ensure that prices are neither too high nor too low, that reasonable growth occurs in the industry, and that companies constantly improve their products and their productive processes.

The allocation of *natural* resources is another important contemporary issue. A shortage at prevailing prices of domestic supplies of energy has been foreseen for many years, but government intervention in the market has resulted in the allocation of fewer resources than are necessary to find and develop alternative sources of energy. Fossil fuels, our major source of energy, are an exhaustible resource. This creates serious allocation problems: should new oil and gas reserves be developed for export to improve the trade position, or should they be conserved for future use by the next generation, or indeed, should they be developed at all in view of their potential to harm the environment? The entire issue of energy sources will be a contentious problem during the late 1970s and the 1980s.

Agriculture is another sector of the economy where policies affect the achievement of several goals. Incomes in agriculture have traditionally been much lower than in other sectors of the economy, and this has been an important cause of the very large shift of labour resources out of agriculture, particularly since World War II. Numerous actions have been taken by various governments in Canada (such as establishing marketing boards and tariffs and non-tariff barriers) to lessen the insecurity that goes with atomistic competition and to improve the distribution of income. Agricultural products are an important component of international trade: exports of agricultural products in 1975, for example, accounted for close to 13 percent of Canada's total exports. Resource allocation in this sector is a long-standing and ongoing problem that merits attention. Problems related to both energy and agriculture will be considered in Chapter 16.

Conflict among Goals

Conflict is inherent in economics. It is not the sole prerogative of economics, of course: conflict and conflict resolution in our social lives are basic to the study of sociology and psychology. Political scientists concern themselves with conflicts in the area of politics.

In economics it is impossible to think of a decision that does not involve some conflict, be it a conflict within an individual, between individuals, within a group, or between groups. Take, for example, the very simple economic operation of buying a loaf of bread—there is nothing controversial about that, surely! But there is an element of conflict: the fifty cents spent on the loaf of bread is not available for the purchase of cinnamon buns, or a milkshake. Every time an individual uses his money for one purpose, he does not have it for any other. The whole process of allocating scarce resources is a process of resolving conflicts: steel used for cars, for example, is not available for the production of tractors. Such economic conflicts must be resolved. Market societies resolve them largely through competition. The producers of loaves of bread compete for the consumer's dollar with the producers of cinnamon buns and the producers of milkshakes. Car producers and tractor producers also compete for consumers' dollars, and the competitive process ultimately determines how much steel will be allocated to each industry.

Competition is not the only way that conflicts are resolved in our economy. Social, moral, and political pressure may be exerted in order to settle conflicting issues. Lobbying by pressure groups and strikes are examples of such pressures. Some problems are resolved by laws. The minimum school-leaving age, for example, requires that Canadians "consume" at least a basic amount of education.

From what has already been said, it is apparent that there are numerous conflicts among the economic goals of the country. Decisions must be made about which of the chosen objectives will be pursued, and in what order of priority; for policies to achieve one may defeat efforts to achieve another. For example, policies designed to make the distribution of income more equitable, involving as they do progressive tax rates, may slow down the growth rate as well as circumscribe the economic freedom of a large group in the economy. Policies to improve the balance-of-payments position by exploiting new sources of energy may adversely affect the government. The

most acute economic problem of the second half of the 1970s—unacceptably high inflation rates combined with unacceptably high unemployment—
involves so many issues of conflict with other goals, and conflict over the
priority of stability as a goal, that discussion of it has been left until the
final chapter, which deals in more detail with the question of the conflicts
among goals.

4

The best-known indicators of how the economy is doing include the unemployment rate, Consumer Price Index, money supply, and national income. Gross National Product and Gross National Expenditure measure the value at current prices of all final goods and services produced in a country in a given period. GNE comprises expenditures for consumption, investment, government, and exports minus imports. There are pitfalls in comparing national income over time: prices, population, and quality of goods and services may change; the composition of GNE may change; and the value of some goods and services are excluded.

Simplified models can help us understand how the level of income is determined; for example, we can think of national income as a circular flow of real goods and services in one direction and money in the other. Investment and government spending are injections that increase the size of that flow. Savings and taxes are leakages that diminish it.

The National Scoreboard

The goals of the Canadian economy that provide us with a framework for our discussion of the economy and its problems include stability, growth, an equitable distribution of income, a viable balance of payments, economic freedom, and the proper allocation of resources. They have been defined rather narrowly. Now new questions need to be raised. "How is the economy doing?" "Is Canada achieving these goals or not?" "How can we tell?"

Mr. Jones next door is usually prepared to tell you in no uncertain terms how the economy is doing. "Business is bad." "Everybody is out of work." "Prices are rising." "The country is on the verge of bankruptcy; why doesn't the government *do* something?" What is the basis for neighbour Jones' assessment of the economy? Perhaps he has looked at the relevant indicators, and perhaps his pessimism is well-founded; or it may be that he has lost his job, or worse still, perhaps his wife has lost hers! If Mrs. Jones was laid off because of incompetence, however, this hardly calls for a national war on unemployment. But if many people are out of jobs and seeking work, then fast government action may be imperative. Obviously Mr. Jones' private scoreboard (Mrs. Jones) is not reliable enough to provide the basis for government policy.

How *do* we find out whether unemployment is serious enough to require government policies to counteract it? Clearly we need a national scoreboard that gives unemployment figures. Is the economy growing? We cannot tell unless we can say where the economy was, say, last year or five years ago. Is the economy booming? Or is it in a recession? The only sure way of knowing is by certain reliable indicators.

How comprehensive does our national scoreboard have to be? Every important policy decision, if it is to be made rationally, is likely to require a large amount of statistical information. Suppose, for example, that the industry producing flat glass is putting pressure on the government to impose a tariff on Japanese imports, which, they argue, are harming their Canadian sales. Should the government accede to their request? There is no basis for a rational decision unless the government has sales and output figures for the flat glass industry, as well as figures on imports from Japan, figures on our balance-of-payments position with Japan, and information on transportation costs. And this is just one small problem.

Economic Indicators

Can we get all indicators of performance that we need? One problem is that progress toward some goals like economic freedom is very difficult to measure. The time is unlikely ever to come when we shall have *all* the statistics we require for making decisions, but a great deal is known about the Canadian economy. Information is available from many sources, the most comprehensive being Statistics Canada, the official government agency that collects data. Statistics Canada is the largest and most important source of information on all aspects of the economy, but it is by no means the only one. Many other government departments and agencies publish statistical information—the Department of Labour and the Department of National Revenue, for example. The Bank of Canada provides financial statistics. Bodies like the Economic Council of Canada and various Royal Commissions also publish information about the Canadian economy. In 1972 the Economic Council began to publish a set of fifteen *performance indicators*—medium-term targets that are assessed annually in the light of new statistical information and changing objectives. World agencies like the Organisation for Economic Co-operation and Development (OECD) and the United Nations and its affiliated agencies provide a wealth of material which permit comparisons of performance between Canada and other countries. In a comprehensive study of the health of the economy, many indicators would have to be consulted. We shall make do with four or five.

UNEMPLOYMENT RATES

If we want to study progress over time, the indicators must go back for some years; how far back depends on the specific problem we have in mind. In other words, we want *time series*. Figures on unemployment are one useful time series. Are we achieving our objective of full employment? Did we *really* have massive unemployment in the 1930s, or was it all an insidious plot on the part of a few malcontents who had lost their jobs through incompetence and were trying to draw attention to themselves? A time series of annual unemployment rates going back to the early 1930s gives us some indication, and we can get a visual picture if we plot the data on a graph.

The chart shows us that unemployment reached a high in 1933, when close to 20 percent of our total labour force were without jobs and seeking work. This is a conservative estimate because it takes no account of the many so-called "hidden unemployed"—the boys who stayed on the farm even though there was little work for them, or those who worked in their fathers' stores just to keep off the streets and out of the ranks of the

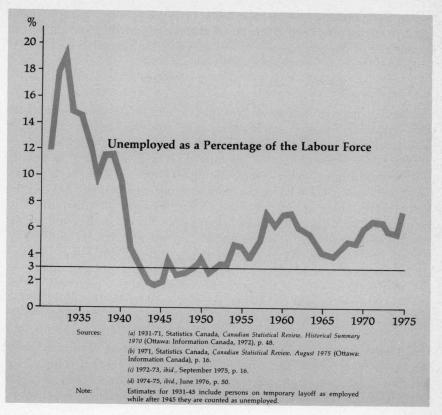

Figure 4-1

unemployed. The data from the chart also enable us to determine whether or not we are achieving our objective of full employment, if we can agree on what we mean by full employment. Figure 4-1 shows us how infrequently the level of 3 percent (the maximum rate if the economy is to be described as having full employment, according to the *First Annual Review* of the Economic Council of Canada) has been achieved.

The unemployment rate is one of the most quoted indicators of the general state of the economy. One of its advantages is its simplicity, but its disadvantage is the loss of detail. For example, it conceals great differences in performance within the economy, such as the different rates of unemployment in different regions and industries, and different rates in different age and sex categories. Being an aggregated indicator it does not tell us, for example, that the component of teenagers in the labour force has increased rapidly in recent years, and yet this is important information to have because the teenage category is one where unemployment rates are consistently high. Thus, it needs to be used with some caution as an indicator of the general state of well-being of the entire labour force.

PRICE INDEXES

The various indexes that show how prices behave are also useful measures of the way the economy is performing. Statistics Canada calculates a number of price indexes. There are indexes of wholesale prices, which include prices of the output of manufacturers and of those who deal in primary products, as well as wholesale prices proper. The general wholesale price index itself is a composite of a number of indexes. Besides the general index, there are indexes for specific purposes like the indexes of the prices of building materials and farm prices. Such data have numerous uses. Some contracts, for example, contain a price-adjustment clause which is based on one or another of these indexes.

In addition to the wholesale price index, there is a group of indexes of security prices, which give the prices of common stocks, preferred stocks, and bonds. Best known of all the price indexes is the Consumer Price Index.

The Consumer Price Index   The release of the latest consumer index number is always news, and when it reaches an unprecedented high, as it so often does, it is front-page news. The popularity of this index is understandable because it is the best measure we have of the effect of rising prices on the lives of a large number of people. It must be used with caution, however, for it is concerned with only one sector of the economy—the consumers' sector—and it traces what happens to the prices of goods bought by just one particular group in that sector—a representative cross-section of the Canadian *urban* population in the lower middle-income group.[1]

But if you happen to live in a rural area, or a small city or town, or if you happen to be a good surgeon, say, or a good engineer, with a high level of income, then this index may not give an accurate description of what is happening to the prices of the things that you are buying. It does not take into account improvements in quality. It also makes the erroneous assumption that people continue to buy the specific items in the basket no matter what happens to their price; in other words it makes no

---

[1] The consumer price index is based on some 300 goods and services bought by Canadian families. The families covered by the index live in cities with populations of 30 000 or more and range in size from two adults to two adults and four children. Their incomes range from $4 000 to $12 000.

allowance for substituting baked beans for beef when the price of beef rises.

In September 1976, the consumer price index stood at 150.7.[2] This means that the prices of goods in the basket were almost 51 percent higher than they were in 1971, the year that is used by Statistics Canada as a base year for its comparisons. This one figure gives us some useful information: prices have risen rapidly since 1971. However, if we wanted to know about the pattern of these increases since, say, the Second World War—to know whether prices had gone up at a steady rate, or whether there had been periods of rapid increase followed by periods of stability, or even decline— we would have to consult a time series of the consumer price index.

Such a time series would reveal that price increases in the postwar period occurred, for the most part, in four periods. The first one came just after the Second World War: prices between January 1947 and October 1948 rose at a rate of about one percent per month. The Korean War brought on another bout of rapidly rising prices: the rate of increase between February 1950 and January 1952 was close to three quarters of one percent per month. The next period of rising prices occurred between May 1956 and April 1958, when the increase was at a rate of something less than one third of one percent per month—4 percent per year. This rise in prices was caused by the investment boom of 1956, when business-men began to buy factories and equipment in such large quantities that the economy could not produce the investment goods rapidly enough, and prices began to rise.

Prices started moving up again around 1962, reaching annual rates of increase of more than 4 percent in 1968 and 1969. The Federal Govern-ment established the Prices and Incomes Commission in mid-1969 prima-rily as an investigative and research body. The Commission made an active but unsuccessful attempt to control inflation by persuading busi-nessmen and union leaders to establish a voluntary program of price and wage restraints. In 1972 the Commission was disbanded. Through 1974 and most of 1975 the rate of inflation averaged about nine tenths of one percent a month—not far from the rate after the Second World War when price controls were removed. Food was one of the main culprits, urging the government in 1973 to establish the Food Prices Review Board to look into the problem. Finally, in October 1975, when there seemed to be no evidence that the rate of inflation was slowing down, the Federal Government moved to impose wage and price controls, which were described as voluntary, but with teeth. The Food Prices Review Board was

---

[2] Statistics Canada, *Canadian Statistical Review, October 1976* (Ottawa: Information Canada, 1976), p. 76.

superseded by the Anti-Inflation Board. We shall return to a more detailed discussion of inflation in the final chapter.

OTHER INDICATORS

The index of industrial production and real domestic product are two other useful indicators of the behaviour of the economy. The index of industrial production measures the volume of goods produced in Canada in industries such as manufacturing and mining. Real domestic product is more comprehensive since it covers both goods and services. Both are good indicators of economic fluctuations, although the index of industrial production experiences wider cyclical swings.

Many other statistical series are a valuable help in determining the state of health of the economy. There are financial series that tell us about the money supply, the rate of interest, consumer credit, and loans. There are also measures of purchases of various kinds—purchases of automobiles and retail goods, for example—as well as statistics on steel operating rates and freight car loadings.

For our purposes, perhaps the most important indicators are the national income and expenditure accounts. These are comprehensive indicators that combine both the physical output of goods and services in the economy and price changes.

The National Accounts: Income and Expenditure

The total value at market prices of our national output in 1975 amounted to $161 billion. This sum has two technical names: Gross National Product (GNP) and Gross National Expenditure (GNE). If you read the financial press, you probably are not aware that there *are* two names: most reports use only the term GNP when referring to the total value at market prices of our national output. Why should the same sum have two names? Do we need both? For technical reasons it is more convenient to have two because two distinct methods of calculation are involved, and it is helpful, for our purposes, if we keep the two separate.

We can arrive at the value of national output, first of all, by using the *expenditure approach*: we can add up the price tags on all of the final goods and services on which various sectors spend money and arrive in this way at Gross National Expenditure. But every time a consumer, a producer, a government, or a foreigner buys a Canadian-produced good or service, this expenditure provides some other Canadian with an income. Because this is so, we can arrive at the same total for the value of our national output (with a few adjustments) by adding up the incomes paid to all of the various resources that produced the goods and services. This is the *income approach*, and when we use it, we designate the aggregate that we arrive at as Gross National Product.

DEFINITION

Since we are talking about an aggregate figure that can be calculated in two different ways, it should not be surprising to find that GNP and GNE have the same definition. Both are defined as *the total value at market prices of all final goods and services produced in the country in a given period of time.*

This is an important definition, and it is necessary to understand all of its terms. What are *final* goods and services? They are goods and services that are not going to be sold again in the period we are talking about. If we add up the value of *all* goods and services produced in the period, intermediate as well as final, we shall end up by counting some of them twice, or three times, or even more.

An example might help. Assume that in one year a tiny agricultural economy produces wheat worth $8 million, that all of the wheat is ground into flour valued at $11 million, and that, within the same year, all of the flour is used to bake bread, bearing price tags that add up to $20 million. What is the total value of the output of that tiny economy? Is it $8 million plus $11 million plus $20 million? No, because the value of the flour already includes wheat worth $8 million; since the wheat was produced only once during the period, we cannot count it a second time. As for the final product, bread, its total value of $20 million includes the $11 million the bakers paid the flour millers, which, in its turn, included the $8 million the flour millers paid the farmers. If we add $8 million plus $11 million plus $20 million (the value of the intermediate and final goods), we double-count the flour and count the same crop of wheat three times. To avoid this kind of over-counting, then, we take the price of only the final products—bread in this case; this means that the national income of our tiny economy adds up to $20 million.

Our definition requires us to include *all* final goods and services. That means that we must include the cars produced by automobile workers, the services of the local dry cleaner, the bread sold by the baker, this book, and the myriad of other goods and services produced in Canada. These final goods and services comprise our *real* national product. The only common denominator we have for adding together cars, units of dry cleaning, and loaves of bread is their money value; therefore we take the *market price* of each final good and service and multiply it by the quantity produced in the period. This enables us to arrive at the total value, in money terms, of our national output.

Since we are dealing with current market prices, GNE and GNP are expressed in what are called *current* dollars. As a result, even if the quantity of output does not change, if prices rise our aggregate value figure will increase. If we want to consider changes that eliminate the effects of price increases, we must calculate in what are called *constant* dollars: instead of using current market prices, we use the prices prevailing in some chosen year.[3] This kind of calculation enables us to compare the value of output now with that of the chosen base year and thereby avoid the complication of price changes.

THE COMPONENTS OF GROSS NATIONAL EXPENDITURE

In theory, Gross National Expenditure is easy to calculate: all that Statistics Canada has to do is send out a vast army of people to add up the price tags on all of the final goods and services sold in the economy. In practice, this is impossible: Statistics Canada has neither the manpower nor the money available for this massive data collection service. Nor is it necessary, because a reasonably accurate figure can be estimated by using a carefully selected sample.

In the expenditure approach, the value at market prices of all final goods and services is broken down into four main categories. First of all, there are personal expenditures on consumers' goods and services (C) such as smoked meat sandwiches, raincoats, cars, personal services such as those we buy from the barber, the dentist, the National Ballet, and so on.

Investment (I) is the second category. It includes two items—inventories and gross fixed capital formation. The latter sounds complicated, but is not. It is simply a technical term that covers expenditures on machinery and equipment, and construction, both residential and non-residential; it also includes the building of items like new factories, mines, pipelines, railways, dams, houses, and apartments, as well as the machinery and equipment necessary for the productive process. Inventory changes comprise the other item in investment. If stocks of goods pile up on businessmen's shelves, then the value of this increase in inventories will show as a positive item in the investment component of the expenditure accounts. If, on the other hand, stocks are run down in the period, then the value of this physical change in inventories will be negative.

The third category is government expenditures on goods and services (G). These include current government expenditures at the federal, pro-

---

[3] Since the base year at present is 1971, we often use the expression "1971 dollars". For example, we might say: GNP in 1975 was $111 billion in (constant) 1971 dollars. Translated, this means that if we had calculated the value of all goods and services produced in 1975 at 1971 prices, GNP would have been $111 billion. To convert the value at current market prices to 1971 dollar prices, we use what is called the *Implicit Price Index, Gross National Product* as a deflator.

vincial, and municipal level, such as salaries of judges and civil servants. For our purposes it is useful to group governments' expenditures on investments such as schools, hospitals and highways with their current expenditures on goods and services. This means that all government expenditures, current as well as expenditures on gross fixed capital formation, are lumped together into G, while investment (I) is reserved for investment by the private sector.

The final item in GNE, except for an allowance for statistical errors, is exports (X) minus imports (M)—*net exports* we might call it. Some of the goods and services produced in Canada are sold to other countries: the wheat, newsprint and turbines bought by other countries are part of Canada's national output, and we must include them when we tally the value of Canadian production. On the other hand, the oranges and bananas imported from Florida are part of the output of *American* producers; even though Canadians spend money on them, they form part of the national income of the United States. Since GNE is an aggregate of expenditures on Canadian-produced goods and services, we must deduct the value of imports from the national accounts.

We can summarize all of the components of GNE in a rather simple little equation:

$$GNE = C + I + G + (X - M)$$

PROBLEMS IN USING THE NATIONAL ACCOUNTS

The national accounts have many uses. They provide an indication of how fast the economy is growing. They help to locate trouble spots, and thus can be used to guide the government in making decisions about whether its policy should be directed to the entire economy, or to restraining or activating particular sectors. These accounts also provide the basis for economic forecasting, another essential activity in formulating appropriate policies.

The uses to which the national accounts are put involve making comparisons with other periods of time. These intertemporal comparisons have pitfalls that we should be aware of if we are not to fall into traps either when we use them or when we read reports based on them. We shall consider briefly four such problems.

Price Changes First of all there is the problem of price changes. Suppose we want to know how much output increased in the five years between 1970 and 1975. If we look up GNE[4] for 1970, we find that it amounted to

---

[4] The information in this section is drawn from Statistics Canada, *National Income and Expenditure Accounts, First Quarter 1975* (Ottawa: Information Canada, August 1975), Tables 1 and 20, and *ibid., Second Quarter 1976* (Ottawa: Information Canada, October 1976).

almost $86 billion. In 1975 it was close to $161 billion—more than 85 percent higher. Does that mean that the standard of living improved that much in five years? Unfortunately, no. As the definition of GNE indicates, those are values at *current* prices: $86 billion is the value of the goods and services produced in 1970 at 1970 prices; $161 billion is the value at 1975 prices of final goods and services produced in 1975. But this gives us no indication of what part of that increase of $75 billion was caused by an increased volume of output, and what part was accounted for by the fact that prices had risen. To make a comparison of real output, we need to value the output of both years in terms of the *same* prices—in constant dollars, in other words. The 1975 output was worth about $111 billion in 1971 dollars: that would have been the value of output in 1975 if prices had not risen since 1971. The 1970 output was worth more than $88 billion in constant (1971) dollars. This means that in *real* terms GNE increased by just over 25 percent instead of over 85 percent—the difference when we calculate in current dollars.

Because of price increases, we can almost always count on an increase every year in national income, and politicians can say, "Look how well we are doing: GNP has risen 4 percent this year!" If that rise was accounted for by a price increase of 4 percent, however, we are no better off. And if the price increase happened to be 6 percent, then even though national income was higher, the economy would be worse off. That explains why GNE and GNP have occasionally been dubbed "GNT—the Great National Tranquilizer". While we may look as if we are forging ahead, in fact we are crawling at a snail's pace, or standing still, or, even worse, sliding back. Price changes, then, cause a problem in measuring national output over time, but this is a problem that can readily be solved by working in constant dollars instead of current ones, that is, by using the Implicit GNE Price Index to eliminate the effect of price increases.

Population Changes   An increase in real GNE means that the economy is growing, but it does not necessarily mean that our standard of living is rising. If population increases more rapidly than real output, the standard of living of the average Canadian will fall. This is what happened after the 1956 boom, and it took about six years to get back to the level of real income per person reached in 1956. From 1962 to 1974 real income per person rose annually: this explains why there grew up such a strong expectation on the part of Canadians that their real position would improve every year.

This problem, like the problem of changing prices, has an easy solution. If we want a good yardstick of economic welfare—one that permits us to say whether Canadians are better off on average—we must take population changes into account.

Composition of the Basket   One difficulty that cannot so easily be overcome is the fact that the goods and services that comprise national output may vary from year to year, and this change in composition may have a significant effect on our welfare. During the Second World War, for example, national output increased rapidly, but that was largely the result of the output of war materiel: the higher output did not mean any increase in our living standards.

Technology causes changes, too: three decades ago no television sets appeared in our national accounts. There are fewer wages of domestic servants in the national accounts today than there were a generation ago, but there has been a great increase in the number of labour-saving devices. Are we better off or worse off as a result?

There is also the problem of quality changes. Men's shirts, for example, may have increased in price, but now buttons stay on longer, button holes are less likely to ravel, collars are more likely to stay fused, and the need for ironing has been reduced if not eliminated. If these quality changes fully compensate the shirt buyer so that he prefers today's shirt, at today's price, to the 1950 shirt at the 1950 price, is it correct to say that the price of the shirt has risen?

Excluded Goods and Services   The final problem that we are going to mention is the fact that some goods and services are not traded in the market, and, as a result, they are not counted in our national output. The vegetables that are grown in our own gardens, the furniture we make, and the rooms we build add to our welfare, and the amounts produced vary from year to year; but these changes do not show up in the national accounts. A classic example of a service that does not show up in GNP is the service of a housewife. However, if a housewife decides to take a paying job and to use the money to hire a housekeeper to perform the jobs she used to do, then the housekeeping services will enter into the national accounts, whereas when the housewife performed them herself, they did not. National income, in such a case, shows an increase, but part of that increase is spurious.

THE CIRCULAR FLOW MODEL

The national accounts are a valuable tool of analysis. One of their important uses is that they provide the foundation for building simplified economic models that help us to understand the factors that determine the level of national income. The only model that we shall consider is the circular flow model.

It is important to recognize that national income is a *flow*. One might compare it to the operation of a swimming pool. There is a circular flow in a swimming pool as the water moves from the pool through the skimmers to the filter, and from the filter back into the pool. There are leakages from the pool: evaporation removes some of the water, as do the "cannon balls" and "belly flops" of the swimmers. These leakages must be compensated for if the water in the pool is to remain at the proper level.

National income also is a circular flow. Money flows from households to producers of goods and services (the producers may be either businesses or governments) in payment for goods and services purchased. Producers, for their part, use the money earned by selling what they produce to buy the services of the resources they need for production. This means that two things are flowing in circles: money is flowing in one direction, and goods and services in the other.

The circular flow can be shown on a simple diagram such as Figure 4-2. For the moment, we shall ignore the foreign trade sector and assume a "closed" economy. Assume that we have two sectors, the producers' sector on the left and the household sector on the right. Consider the lower flows first: according to our diagram, goods and services (such as hamburgers, taxi rides, and doctors' services) flow to households in exchange for dollar payments. These household expenditures on goods and services provide producers with income. From the upper part of the diagram, we can see that producers, for their part, receive a flow of services in the form of labour, land, capital, and entrepreneurial skill from the households who own them. In return, they pay money in the form of wages and salaries, rent, interest, and profit. These payments give households the incomes necessary to buy the goods and services that producers want to sell.

The outer circle is thus a money flow: dollars flow from producers to households and back to producers again. If we were to fit a gauge in at point *e* to measure the flow of dollars, we would be measuring the payments flow by the *expenditure* approach. Similarly, if we put a flow gauge in at point *i* and measured income there, we would be using the *income* approach to calculate national income.

The inner circle represents *real* inputs and outputs. The flow of services rendered by the factors of production is represented on the upper part of the counter-clockwise flow. The lower part represents the physical goods and services on which money is spent.

As we are well aware from our study of the expenditure approach to the national accounts, the actual flows of money and of goods and services are much more complex than this, but even this very simple model helps us to understand more about how the economy works. It emphasizes the important fact that when we talk about national income we are

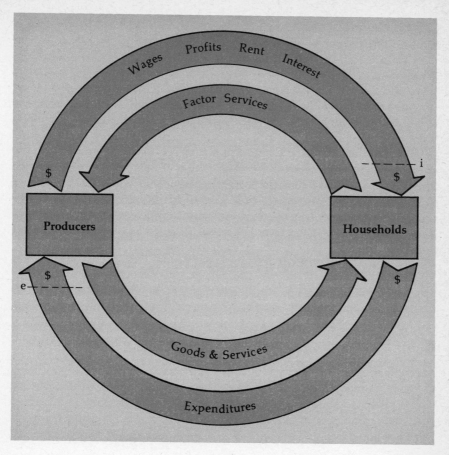

Figure 4-2

talking about flows—a flow of money in one direction in payment for a flow of real goods and services in the other. The model emphasizes the difference between real output (real income) and money income—the real income being the flow of goods and services, and the money being the dollar payments for them.

The model also helps us to understand the relationship between the expenditure approach and the income approach in calculating the total value of our national output. One group's expenditures are the incomes of another group; because of this, we can use either expenditures or incomes to arrive at an aggregate figure for the value of our national output. The payments by businesses and governments to purchase the services of the factors of production provide those factors with an income out of which they can purchase the goods and services, which, in turn, provide producers with their income. If one group increases its expenditures, the income of another group goes up.

The circular flow model can be made much more complex. Before the development of the computer, some economists were building complicated hydraulic machines involving 25 or 30 variables in order to get a clearer understanding of how changes in these variables affected the level of income. One's artistic ability is the only effective limit to the degree of complexity that can be introduced. The expenditures flow, for example, might be broken down into consumers' goods and producers' goods; we could separate out the government sector to see how money and goods and services flow to and from the government. We might introduce the whole financial sector comprising banks, trust companies, and all of the other financial institutions. If, by that time, the diagram were not completely unmanageable, we could make it so by incorporating a set of flows to handle exports and imports.

The Level of Income   The simple circular flow model is an aid to understanding national income, but there remain some important questions that need to be discussed. Why is GNE what it is? What makes it rise? Or, why is it not rising? We can adapt the circular flow model to help us to understand the modern theory of how the level of income is determined. This theory is based in large measure on the famous book, *The General Theory of Employment Interest and Money*, written by John Maynard Keynes who contributed a new vocabulary and a new way of thinking about aggregate economic activity, or *macroeconomics*, as it is usually called. Keynes' work has had a tremendous impact on economic policy as well as theory; it has particular relevance for the goal of achieving economic stability. He emphasized the role of fluctuations in the various components of aggregate expenditure (illustrated in the lower half of Figure 4-2). He regarded the fluctuations in investment in the private sector as a major source of instability which would need to be countered by deliberate changes in government policies if economic stability was to be achieved.

To begin with, we shall simplify our model still further by eliminating the real flow and dealing only with the flow of dollars. We shall adhere to our assumption of a closed (no-trade) economy, and we shall go further, for the moment at least, and assume the government out of existence.

Our simplifications leave us with a money flow from producers (businesses) to households (consumers) in payment for the factor services that households sell. Assume, for the sake of argument, that these payments amount to $60 billion. Households can dispose of that $60 billion as they choose: they are free either to spend it all, or to spend some and save some. (Since we assumed the government temporarily out of existence, we have also assumed taxes out of existence.) If they spend it all, then payments amounting to $60 billion will flow back to producers, who once again will have the $60 billion to pay for factor services. If we were to put in a gauge to measure the flow of income, it would register a steady $60 billion. In terms of our swimming pool analogy, we have ruled out any leakages from the flow system; the level in the pool remains unchanged.

Saving: A Leakage Canadian consumers on balance do not spend all of their income on goods and services. There are some who spend more than they earn; some who spend all of their income; and some who spend less —in other words, some who save. The amount people spend on consumers' goods and services depends primarily on the level of their present income, although such factors as their expected income, the ease with which they can get consumer credit, and their estimates of how much they must save to finance their old age, or to finance themselves or their children in university, can have an important influence on their consuming and saving habits.

Assume in our numerical example that people save $6 billion out of the $60 billion they receive as income, and that they spend the rest on goods and services. These dollars of saving are an outflow from the system; and, like evaporation and other water losses from the swimming pool, they result in a lowering of the level. Instead of getting back $60 billion from consumers, producers get only $54 billion, and this leaves them with a smaller sum available to pay factors for their services. The saving leakage causes a decrease in the national income flow. If households in the next period decide to save another $6 billion out of the $54 billion, then only $48 billion dollars will remain in the system to be passed on as incomes to the factors, and the gauge will record another large drop in the income flow.

Investment If there is an injection to offset the leakage, then the level will not decline. In the swimming pool we can turn on the hose. In the case of the income flow, there are several injections that can offset, or more than offset, the leakages. Investment is one such injection. Businesses buy investment goods and services and use them to build and equip factories, or to build power transmission lines, and so on. Such investment may be necessary because machinery now in use has worn out, or because the businessman anticipates that if he buys new capital, it will yield him a greater profit.

Whenever they contemplate making an investment, businessmen will forecast (implicitly or explicitly) the rate of return they expect on that investment. In economic jargon, the anticipated or expected rate of return on the last dollar invested is called the *marginal efficiency of investment*. The marginal efficiency of investment is affected by a number of factors. One is the businessman's forecast of the demand for his product. If population is increasing, or if he sees a new market opening up for his product either at home or abroad, or if incomes are rising so that consumers can afford more of his product, then he might logically expect the demand for his product to increase. This, in turn, means that he would anticipate a higher rate of return on any planned investment in new plant and equipment than would be the case if the demand for his product were expected to remain static.

Technology and innovation can cause an improvement in a producer's expectations about his rate of return. Advances in technology may permit him to produce a better product, or to produce the same product more cheaply. In either event, the marginal efficiency of investment will be higher.

The final factor that we shall mention that may influence the marginal efficiency of investment is the general outlook for the economy. This is a complex factor that is, itself, a function of many things. A great deal of uncertainty is involved in a major investment: will the economy forge ahead, or is a recession in the offing? Will tax rates continue at their present level, or does the government have increases in mind? Will an innovation make a new machine obsolete in a year or two? Will the Parti Quebecois lead Quebec out of Canada, thus splitting the country into two markets? Since the rate of return that we are discussing depends on expectations about the future, the general outlook, which is important in shaping that state of mind we call "business confidence", is bound to play a major role in influencing producers' decisions about whether or not to invest.

The expected rate of return on his proposed investment is one of two major components in the businessman's decision to invest. The second arises from the fact that he needs money to finance any investment; and whether the money is available to him from earnings that have been retained in his firm, or whether he has to borrow it from the bank, there is a cost involved. Interest, the cost of using money, is the second major component in the investment decision. When a businessman goes to his banker to borrow money, his banker tells him how much he will have to pay for its use. He can then compare that cost with the expected rate of return on his proposed investment and decide whether or not to go ahead with his plan. If the rate of interest is 10 percent and his marginal efficiency of investment is only 5 percent, then as long as he is interested in making a profit, he will not make the investment. On the other hand, if the marginal efficiency of investment is 50 percent and the rate of interest is 10 percent, he is likely to invest. Somewhere there exists a relationship between the anticipated rate of return and the rate of interest that marks his boundary: if he is interested in maximizing profit he will not carry his investment beyond the point where the interest rate is equal to the expected rate of return on the last dollar invested. Most businessmen want the expected rate of return to exceed the rate of interest by some margin in order to allow for risk.

Suppose the firm itself has enough money to finance the proposed investment. Since the businessman will not have to pay the banker any interest, surely he can afford investments that he otherwise could not? Many businessmen, in fact, look at internal financing this way, but such an approach will not lead them to maximize profits. Regardless of the source of the money capital, the businessman should consider the rate of interest: if he does not invest in his own business, he can undoubtedly lend his money to someone else and earn a rate of return equal to the interest rate quoted him by his banker. The interest forgone on the money that he invests is as much a cost to him as the interest he has to pay to his bank.

Businessmen, then, invest because they expect to make a profit, and their investments are an injection into the payments flow that counterbalances the leakage of saving. In the example that we have been using, we assumed that when the income flow was $60 billion, consumers decided to save $6 billion, so that only $54 billion flowed back to producers. But now, assume that coincidentally businessmen decide to invest $6 billion. The saving leakage would be fully offset by the investment injection, and the income level would continue at $60 billion; it would be in *equilibrium*, in other words, continuing at the same level period after period.

A simple diagram that shows only the money flows may make this clearer. In Figure 4-3, consumers are assumed to pay producers $54 billion for goods and services (C), and to save $6 billion (S) out of the $60 billion they have received. Producers, then, inject $6 billion in the form of payments to other producers for investment goods (I), so that total expenditures, (C+I), add up to $60 billion, and the sum of $60 billion, once again, is available to pay for the services of the various factors of production.

Suppose that businesses decided to invest $10 billion instead of $6 billion. In that case the injection into the expenditure flow of $10 billion exceeds the leakage in the form of saving, (I is greater than S), and national income, which equals C+I, will rise to $64 billion instead of remaining at its former level of $60 billion. An increase in any expenditure results in an increase in the income flow, while an increase in any leakage decreases that flow.

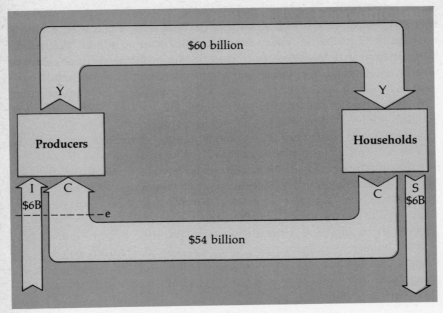

Figure 4-3

The Return of Savings to the Income Stream One must not get the idea from our diagram that the saving flow,[5] which we have called a leakage, is forever lost to the system. This is not true. Savings can be directed into a number of channels. In the first place, they may flow directly into investment. Businesses commonly retain some of their earnings (which belong to the shareholders) and, in effect, force their shareholders to save. These savings are often plowed directly back into new plant and equipment. Moreover, one of the investment components of GNE, as we have seen, is residential construction, and personal savings may flow into this form of investment. If savings flow directly into investment and get back into the income stream in the time period that we are talking about, there is no leakage at all.

People frequently save by putting money into banks or trust companies, or by buying life insurance. Businessmen, for their part, may borrow these collected savings from the financial institutions in order to finance their investments, and in this way the money flows back into the payments stream. How long it remains out of the expenditure flow depends

---

[5] A distinction is sometimes made between the act of *saving* and the resulting accumulation of money, which is called saving*s*. Saving, like GNE or consumption, is a flow or a rate; one might say, "I am saving at the rate of fifty dollars a month." In that case, savings (the stock) would amount to $600 at the end of a year.

on how willing various savings institutions are to lend, and how willing the businessmen are to borrow in order to invest.

The saving flow may also be channeled into the purchase of existing wealth—things like houses that have already been built, used cars, or stocks and bonds. If in the period in question you forgo consumption and use part of your income to purchase ten shares of, say, Home Oil stock, then, since you are not spending it on final goods and services produced in this period, and since only spending of this kind is relevant to the income flow, this form of saving constitutes a leakage from the payments stream.

Finally, money can be hidden in a mattress—hoarded, in other words. Saving in this form is a leakage from the payments system. At some time or another, however, if an heir or a thief comes into possession of that idle cash, it is likely to be "dis-hoarded", i.e., put back into the expenditure stream in payment for goods and services.

The Government Sector   Our model is still too simple to be very useful because we have assumed the government out of existence. This is too idealistic an assumption for some, too callous an assumption for others, but a wholly unrealistic assumption in any event. Setting up a separate sector for government raises the immediate question of whether the principles that apply to the public sector are so different from those that apply to the private sector that such a separation is warranted. Many people would say no. The late Charles Wilson, when he moved from the presidency of General Motors into the Eisenhower Cabinet, made a statement to a U.S. Congressional Committee in January 1953 that will long be quoted by economists: "I thought what was good for the country was good for General Motors and vice versa." Such a statement is made on the assumption (a false one) that the government is just another big business. Certainly there are similarities between government and business, and many things—efficiency, for example—that are good for General Motors *are* good for the government. However, the differences are vital, particularly when the government we are considering is the federal government, which controls the money supply.

THE PUBLIC SECTOR AND THE PRIVATE SECTOR

Perhaps the most important difference between the public sector and the private sector is that the federal government can do a great deal as a matter of deliberate policy to help achieve the goal of stability through its control of the money supply and through its budgetary surpluses and deficits. It would be folly, and indeed it would be impossible, for firms or individuals to run surpluses or deficits for any length of time with the express purpose of stabilizing employees' incomes.

Another difference lies in the motivation for spending. If the market system is working properly, the dominant motive behind business expenditure is profits, whereas the government's motive is to promote the general welfare. Normally, no direct revenue is expected to result from government spending, although there are exceptions. Most of these exceptions occur in Crown corporations.

A third important difference is that governments can compel people to provide them with revenues, and this element of coercion is not available to individuals and businesses. Government policy in this country is usually arrived at more democratically than business policy, but once tax measures, for example, are determined, they are coercive. We cannot avoid the sales tax unless we refuse to buy taxed goods, and not buying taxed goods raises awkward problems for anyone concerned about his standard of living. The only way to avoid paying income tax (legally, that is) is to refuse to earn more than about $1 700 a year. One might argue that coercion is not totally lacking in the business world: if there is only one firm producing an essential good, there may be an element of coercion in the fact that we must buy the product and thus provide revenues for that monopolist.

GOVERNMENT EXPENDITURES

The three levels of government—federal, provincial, and municipal—spend on current goods and services and on investment goods about one quarter of the Gross National Expenditure—a sizable and growing share of national output. This does not include some large sums of money that governments collect and hand over to other people to spend—transfer payments such as family allowances, for example, and Canada Pension Plan payments. By the time all expenditures by all levels of government were included (apart from intergovernmental transfers) the proportion in 1974 rose to 39.1 percent,[6] and it rose again in 1975. We have already mentioned several reasons why the government is such a big spender: we look to the government to provide goods and services that the market, left to itself, would not provide or would provide in insufficient quantities. These are the collectively consumed goods like defence, education, the services of Statistics Canada, and the services of policemen and judges. Expenditures on such collectively consumed goods are intended to promote the welfare of all of us; but since the benefits cannot be accurately attributed to individuals or businesses, such goods must be purchased by the government.

---

[6] Government of Canada, *Attack on Inflation A program of National Action*, Policy Statement tabled in the House of Commons by the Honourable Donald S. Macdonald, Minister of Finance, 14 October 1975, p. 5.

The government also spends in order to achieve the goal of stability: if the private sector is not spending enough on consumption and investment to keep the factors fully employed, then we expect the government to step in and spend in order to help achieve that important goal. We are also aware that the market solution to the problem of income distribution is not entirely acceptable to us, and we expect the government to improve that distribution by its welfare programs—Old Age Security, income supplements for the elderly, unemployment insurance, medicare, and so on. Sometimes the government finds itself in business by default: if the market had been left to decide, the CN would not be in existence now; however, there was a widespread feeling that we needed that railroad, so the government had no alternative but to step in and take over. The government may also get into business because it is more efficient than private enterprise. Sidewalks might be built as a private venture, and toll collectors could be given the job of making the users pay, but it is more efficient for municipal governments to build the sidewalks and levy property taxes to pay for them.

The Payments Flow There must be revenues to finance these expenditures, and government revenues, for the most part, derive from taxes. Over 80 percent of the total revenue of governments comes from taxes.[7] The remainder comes from such sources as returns from natural resources, profits of Crown corporations, income from government investments, and monies collected by the Post Office. In our simplified circular flow model, we shall ignore the non-tax revenues.

When businesses and consumers pay income taxes, sales taxes, and property taxes, the money they turn over to the government is not available for spending on consumption and investment. Taxes, in other words, constitute another leakage from the payments flow. If we wished, we could adapt our flow diagrams and put in arrows showing taxation leakages from both producers and households.

The government, for its part, does not collect taxes merely for the purpose of hanging on to them: it spends its revenues on all kinds of goods and services. These dollars of expenditure, then, are an injection into the income stream, in the same way as are dollars spent by the private sector on investment, or on the purchase of consumers' goods and services. Thus, government expenditures (G) would have to be shown as an inflow arrow into the payments stream along with consumption and investment.

Assume that the payments flow is in equilibrium at $60 billion, with the saving leakage equal to $6 billion, and the investment injection of $6

---

[7] Calculated from Canadian Tax Foundation, *The National Finances 1975-76* (Toronto, 1976), Table 2-13, p. 22.

billion just exactly offsetting it. We shall hold these two variables, S and I, constant for the time being and consider what happens to the level of payments when government expenditures and revenue vary. If the government balances its budget, then its revenues equal its expenditures, and this means, in terms of our simplified analysis, that the leakage in the form of taxes is just balanced by the injection in the form of government expenditures on goods and services. If we assume, for example, that the leakage in taxes amounts to $12 billion out of the payments flow of $60 billion and that government spending (the injection) amounts to $12 billion, then the level of income (which equals C + I + G) will remain unchanged at $60 billion. The government, in other words, is affecting the composition of the national income pie, but not its size.

The government does not have to balance its budget: it can deliberately vary its flows of revenues and expenditures. Suppose that expenditures exceed revenues (G is greater than T)—that is, that the government is running a deficit. This means that the injection into the system is greater than the leakage from it. The income flow will increase. If we use a hose and put into the swimming pool more water than is being removed by evaporation and by people splashing about in it, the level of the water rises. The same can be said of the payments flow: if the government spends more than it collects in revenues, the income level will rise.

What is so different about this? Businesses and individuals, too, can decide to spend more or less than their revenues. The difference lies in the fact that there is no way for businessmen or consumers to make *collective* decisions to spend more or less, according to the need to maintain stability in the economy.

If the government unbalances its budget to achieve a surplus—not a very common occurrence in the postwar Canadian economy—its revenues will exceed its expenditures, and the leakage from the system will be greater than the injection. As a result the payments flow will be decreased.

It is a general, if somewhat simplified, rule that the income or expenditure flow will remain in equilibrium (remain at any given level) if the leakages from the system are counterbalanced by the injections. So far we have considered two leakages: the act of saving and payments to the government in the form of taxes. There have been two offsetting injections: investment and government expenditures. If the combined injections exceed the combined leakages, income will rise. (If G + I exceed S + T, income will rise.) On the other hand, if the injections of government spending and investment are less than the leakages caused by saving and taxing, the level of income will fall. Finally, as we said initially, if the leakages and the injections are equal, the national income will neither rise nor fall but will continue at its current equilibrium level.

Exports and Imports We ended the initial discussion of the components of GNE with the summary equation, GNE = C + I + G + (X − M). We have now built all of the components into our flow model except exports and imports. For the sake of completeness, we should discuss them briefly, and while we shall make no attempt to incorporate them into our diagram, it would be quite possible to do so. When consumers buy products produced in other countries, or when producers buy machinery or parts not made in Canada, then the dollars they spend do not flow back to Canadian producers; instead they flow to foreign firms. Thus, as far as our circular flow is concerned, these dollars are a leakage from the domestic payments flow. On the other hand, when Americans buy Otter aircraft or when Russians purchase Canadian wheat, their payments are an injection into the system. And, as is the case with other components of GNE, if the injection (exports) is greater than the leakage (imports), the payments flow will be increased. If the injection is less than the leakage (if exports are less than imports), then the total expenditure stream will be decreased. Finally, if they are equal, the income level will not change.

In discussing the components of the expenditure side of the National Accounts we have been talking about aggregate demand in the economy. When we consider stabilization policy in greater detail (in Chapter 6), we shall discuss the ways in which the government can influence the level of aggregate demand through monetary and fiscal policy. Before we begin this discussion, however, there is one more area that must be explored, the money supply and the banking system.

Time series on changes in the money supply constitute an important indicator on our national scoreboard. Like the national accounts, the money supply is more than just as an indicator. It is a tool of monetary policy. The way money is created by the banking system and the way the central bank (the Bank of Canada) controls the supply are an important part of macroeconomic theory to which we shall turn before continuing with our discussion of the problems of achieving the goals of the Canadian economy.

5

Money is anything that is generally accepted in payment for goods and services or in settlement of accounts. It makes the cumbersome process of barter unnecessary. For our purposes the money supply is defined as currency outside chartered banks plus chartered-bank deposits.

Chartered banks are not required to hold reserves equal to their customers' deposits but to keep fractional reserves instead. The size of these reserves determines how much money the banking system can create.

The Bank of Canada, the central bank, employs various techniques to control the money supply. It can affect banks' reserves by buying or selling bonds in the open market, altering the legal reserve ratio, or switching the deposits of the federal government in to or out of the chartered banks. Another technique is to alter the Bank Rate, its lending rate. Finally, it may use moral suasion to control the money supply.

The Money Supply

Money—the root of all evil or the key to happiness? A veil that enshrouds (and confuses) economic activity or the oil that greases the skids of industry? We use money every day, so presumably we should know what it is. Surely, for once, we do not need a definition. Those nice, crisp, green, purple, or better still, brown or orange bills issued by the Bank of Canada are money. So are the coins we carry around to put in the coffee machine. But what about your current account at the bank, or your personal chequing account? What about the figures in the passbook for your savings account—are they included in the money supply? What about a Canada Savings Bond? Your banker will be happy to take it as repayment for a loan: is it money or is it not?

Perhaps we need a definition after all. Money is sometimes defined very broadly as *anything that is generally acceptable within a given society in payment of accounts or for goods and services.* It is this general acceptability as a means of payment that distinguishes what is money from what is not.

Money is an alternative to barter. Barter, for its part, is an awkward and complicated process whereby two commodities are exchanged, neither of which has general acceptability. Money makes this trading process much simpler by serving as a *medium of exchange.* It is the means by which a garage mechanic, for example, can exchange his time and skill in tuning engines for the groceries, clothing, furniture, and the hundreds of other items that he and his family want, without resorting to the cumbersome method of barter.

Assume that in a barter economy the garage mechanic wants meat for dinner. He can undoubtedly find a number of people who would be prepared to sell meat, but that is not enough: he needs to find a butcher with the kind of meat he wants, who also has a car whose engine needs tuning. Having found such a butcher, he has to come to some agreement about the ratio in which engine-tuning exchanges for kilograms of meat. And meat is only *one* of the many items he needs.

Multiply the complexity of this one transaction by the number of transactions he would have to undertake to get all the things he needs, and it becomes evident why barter is a cumbersome method of carrying out exchange and why it would cause a fast-moving and complex economy to slow down to a snail's pace.[1] Money as a medium of exchange greatly expedites the exchange process. Instead of spending time looking for appropriate individuals with whom to trade and instead of establishing mutually acceptable exchange rates for thousands of different commodities, people can specialize in their respective tasks, earn money, and use that money to buy the goods and services they want. Money permits the specialization necessary to develop an advanced economy.

In addition to serving as a medium of exchange, money is a useful unit for keeping accounts. Moreover, because it is durable it can be held as a store of value until the holder wants to use it—something that cannot be done with the time of the garage mechanic. It is also used to arrange payments that are deferred until some future time. Money, in other words, is the basis of credit transactions, and these are very important in a developed economy.

Money in Canada

A wide variety of items has served as money in Canada. Arrowheads were an early one. Wampum—small tubes made from sea shells—was used by the Indians, and even for a time by the white colonists; it lost its usefulness when it was rendered valueless by the import of large quantities of cheap substitutes from Europe. Furs, particularly beaver pelts, were a common form of money at one time.

Until the middle of the seventeenth century, what coins there were in Canada came from such diverse countries as France, England, Portugal, Spain, and Mexico. Coins were scarce, and because of the scarcity, there developed a unique form of money: in 1685 the French colonial authorities issued the famous "playing-card money". They cut playing cards in quarters, affixed the wax seal of the treasurer and the signature of the governor and intendant, and put them into circulation. Later, halves of cards and whole cards were used for higher denominations. Playing-card money was used for about three quarters of a century.

After the fall of Quebec in 1759, the British brought their crowns, shillings, and pence into New France and sterling became the official accounting unit. There was so little sterling currency, however, that trade was carried on mainly in American, Spanish, and Portuguese currency. With the circulation of coins of many countries of the world, exchange became very difficult.

---

[1] One explanation, perhaps, for the unfavourable attitude of academic economists towards barter might be the rather frightening prospect of trying to find butchers who would be prepared to exchange meat for lectures on the national income accounts!

During the War of 1812, Sir Isaac Brock issued paper money in the form of army bills—not in sterling, the official unit, but in Spanish dollar denominations. Shortly after the Bank of Montreal was chartered in 1817 it began to issue notes, and the first issue was, again, in Spanish dollar denominations, not sterling. In the nineteenth century, Canadian banks also began to issue coins. These supplemented the great variety already in circulation, which included many kinds of brass and copper tokens issued by merchants in various areas. One unique coin was the "made-beaver" of the Hudson's Bay Company, which was equivalent in value to the skin of an adult male beaver.

Because of close commerical connections with the United States, in 1857 the Province of Canada decided to use dollars rather than pounds, shillings, and pence, as the monetary unit. Shortly before Confederation the government started issuing notes; and when the dollar became the monetary unit of the entire Dominion, Parliament (through the Dominion Notes Act of 1870) prohibited the banks from issuing notes except in multiples of five dollars. This gave the government a monopoly on notes of one- and two-dollar denominations.

After the central bank (the Bank of Canada) went into operation in 1935, it gradually took over full responsibility for issuing currency. The notes of the chartered banks were gradually retired; the last of them went out of circulation in 1950.

THE MONEY SUPPLY IN CANADA

As we have said, money is anything that is generally accepted as a means of payment, and our brief historical sketch indicates that different items achieved general acceptability at different times in Canada. Our money supply today includes the currency declared as legal tender by the government. Legal tender money includes all the coins—the pennies, nickels, dimes, quarters, half-dollars, and dollars—that are produced by the Canadian Mint. These coins, valued at more than $730 million in August 1976, are normally of the token type. This means that the face value of the coins is greater than the value of the metal in them, so that it does not pay to melt them down. In 1968, however, with the sharp increase in the price of silver, there developed a fairly brisk, if illegal, trade in Canadian silver coins of vintage 1966 and earlier, and American coins dated 1963 and earlier; these were bought in bulk and melted down for their silver content. This gave rise to an acute coin shortage in Canada; as a result, the metal content of some coins was changed.

The bank notes issued by the Bank of Canada comprise an important part of our money supply. In August 1976 they amounted to about $6.2 billion. Canadian currency has no gold backing: it is what is called "fiat" money. The only backing it has is people's confidence in the federal government. The money is as good as the government that backs it and that has the power and self-discipline to control its supply. The note itself is lawful money and must be accepted by all Canadian creditors in payment of goods and services or for a debt. Strange as it may seem, not all coins and notes are included when we calculte the money supply in Canada: only currency *outside the banks* is included. Currency lying idle in bank vaults is not counted.

Currency outside the banks forms an important but relatively small part of a total money supply that amounted to about $78 billion in August 1976. Ninety percent of what is usually considered to be our money supply consists of neither coins nor bills: it is made up of entries on the books of the chartered banks, which are called chartered bank deposits. People sometimes object to calling bank deposits money, saying that bookkeeping items should not be included under that heading. But the definition of money does not state that money is only legal-tender money, or that it consists solely of currency. According to the definition, money is anything that is generally accepted as a means of payment, and orders to pay (cheques) drawn against deposits with chequing privileges do have general acceptability as a means of payment. It is true that *you* may have to show your driver's licence in order to get a personal cheque accepted, but this is not required of governments or large companies. In terms of value, most of the business transacted in this country is paid for out of bank deposits.

An anomaly in the Canadian system is that deposits in savings banks like the Montreal City and District Savings Bank are not included in the money supply even though these institutions closely resemble the savings departments of the chartered banks. The same is true of deposits in trust companies. Because these institutions are not regulated by the Bank Act, they are not considered chartered banks; instead they are *near banks*, and deposits in them are not part of the money supply.

As an exercise we might draw up a list of items according to their degree of liquidity or "money-ness". The first item on the list would be coins and bank notes—but not all notes, since those of large denominations are not universally acceptable. Items like travellers' cheques, certified cheques, and government cheques like family allowance cheques, would rank high on the list. Lower down the list would be bank accounts of various kinds: chequing accounts of governments, businesses, and individuals; savings accounts in chartered banks; and accounts in savings banks, trust companies, and credit unions. Near the bottom of the list would be items like government bonds: Canada Savings Bonds, short-term bonds like treasury bills, long-term bonds, provincial and municipal bonds, and corporation bonds and stocks.

Now, having made up the list, where do we draw the line of demarcation between what is and what is not to be counted as money? In Canada, most economists draw the line after savings deposits in chartered banks; the American definition of the money supply excludes savings accounts. For some purposes in Canada, federal government deposits are excluded from the definition, though provincial and municipal government deposits are included; the money supply in this case is defined as currency outside the banks and chartered bank deposits *held by the public*. This suggests that what is called "money" rests on a rather arbitrary decision. Perhaps the most common definition of the Canadian money supply includes *currency outside the banks and all chartered bank deposits*.

THE PROBLEM OF INSTABILITY

Whether or not one agrees that money is the root of all evil, it is certainly true that it lies at the root of one of the major problems of our advanced industrial society—the problem of instability. In a barter economy, people who come to the market to sell also come to buy: the man who brings his surplus of corn is prepared to exchange it for someone else's surplus of hunting weapons, or yarn for cloth. There is nothing to interrupt the exchange of good for good. Money makes possible specialization, growth, and progress; it also makes possible saving, and with saving comes instability, for when people save, the exchange of good for good typical of a barter economy can be, and usually is, interrupted.

Consider an impossible but illustrative example. Suppose everyone decided that spending had been going on at far too high a rate and that, to compensate, everyone was going to save *all* of his income. That means that there would be no customers in the barber shop; nobody but the clerks would be at Eaton's and Simpsons; and nobody but the ushers, ticket seller, and projector operators would be in the movie theatres. If such a situation continued for any length of time, the department stores would have to stop calling in the clerks; the movie houses would have to dismiss the ushers, the ticket seller, and the projector operators; in a very short time savers would find themselves with no income. Their decision to save all income would have resulted in their having none left to save. Such an extreme situation is impossible, but occasionally we do have spending strikes. Businessmen are more volatile in their expenditure patterns than consumers, and they quite frequently go on spending strikes and decide to cut back on outlays on plant and equipment. This is a major source of instability in the economy.

The recognition of how important it is to have a carefully managed money supply was very slow in coming to Canada: the country struggled through almost seventy years of Confederation without a central bank and went through the depression of the 1930s without any attempt to control the supply of money. However, people knew that something was wrong: Canada was a land of plenty, yet poverty was everywhere. Out of the awareness that something was amiss in the system grew Social Credit, an economic theory based on the conviction that there was a chronic insufficiency of spending power. While there seemed to be plenty of goods about, people did not have enough money to buy them. This observation led to the Social Credit idea of social dividends—payments by the government that would put money into people's hands so that they could buy the food that was rotting on the farms and the goods that were standing idle on merchants' shelves. Today most economists who are followers of Lord Keynes would agree that the Social Credit position was right for that time. This is not to say that good Keynesians would adhere to the *doctrine* of Social Credit. They would not, for the doctrine is based on the false premise that there is *always* a shortage of purchasing power, and that the money supply *always* needs to be increased. We recognize that this is not true. Gifts of cash all around would hardly have been appropriate in the severe inflation of 1975, for example.

In an advanced economy, people are highly interdependent. The very existence of many of us depends on money and its proper management. If money were removed from the system and we reverted to barter, many would starve. Given the importance of the money supply, it would be advisable for us to know how it *can* be managed, and how it *ought* to be managed, even though the process is rather complex.

The Chartered Banks

In Canada there are many financial institutions—banks, trust companies, insurance companies, consumer finance companies, investment dealers, and stock brokers—as well as government financial institutions such as the Central Mortgage and Housing Corporation. Each plays an important role in the economy, but most essential for a study of the money supply and its management are the chartered banks and the central bank, the Bank of Canada.

The importance of the chartered banks should already be apparent, for we have noted that they hold deposits that comprise about 90 percent of the money supply. Moreover, their importance is even greater than this for not only do they hold these deposits, but within certain limits they also have the power to *create* deposits and *destroy* them. In short, they have the power to create and destroy money.

Eleven privately owned banks[2] chartered by Parliament and operating under the Bank Act comprise the commercial banking system in Canada. The newest, the Canadian Commercial and Industrial Bank, was chartered in July 1975. This bank is also the smallest; its operations are to be focused on short-term loans to business, and for this, like the Mercantile Bank of Canada, it will need branches only in the main cities.[3] IAC Ltd., Canada's largest sales finance company, is seeking a bank charter.[4] Two other banks—the Banque Canadienne Nationale and the Banque Provinciale du Canada—operate mainly in the Province of Quebec. The remaining banks have a network of more than 6 000 branches throughout Canada and a number of branches in foreign countries.

The Canadian commercial banking system resembles the British system; it differs markedly from that of the United States where there are some 14 000 different banks. This large number of individual, or unit, banks is the result of American legislation that prevents banks from operating in more than one state of the Union. Since many states forbid branch banking within their borders, this has favoured the development of a large number of relatively small independent banks. There are exceptions: in California, the Bank of America, the largest bank in the world in terms of assets, has numerous branches all over the state.

Chartered banks in Canada are corporations established for the purpose of making a profit. Their funds come in part from their shareholders and in part from depositors who bring money in for safekeeping and, in some cases, to earn a return on it. The fact that these banks operate under the provisions of the Bank Act is what differentiates them from all other financial insitutions.

FRACTIONAL RESERVES

When we go to the bank to deposit money, we know that we can get it back any time we want; the bank is legally obligated to return the amount of the deposit in whole or in part, to the depositor personally or, except in the case of some special kinds of savings accounts, to anyone else whom the depositor may designate on his cheque. The money we put into the bank, which is an asset to us, is a *liability* of the bank: it is part of what they owe.

---

[2] The Bank of British Columbia, The Bank of Montreal, The Bank of Nova Scotia, Banque Canadienne Nationale, Banque Provinciale du Canada, The Canadian Commercial and Industrial Bank, The Canadian Imperial Bank of Commerce, The Mercantile Bank of Canada, The Royal Bank of Canada, The Toronto-Dominion Bank, and The Unity Bank of Canada.

[3] *The Gazette*, Montreal, 12 June 1975.

[4] *Financial Times of Canada*, Toronto, 29 September 1975, p. 3.

Since banks are legally bound to pay out money whenever depositors want it, this raises a question: do they keep on hand all the money deposited with them, just in case all customers should simultaneously ask for their money back? The answer is no. They keep only a small fraction of it as a reserve and lend the rest to businessmen and consumers who want to borrow money.

The recognition that it was not necessary to keep 100 percent reserves was made by the medieval goldsmiths, our first bankers. Goldsmiths had to build strongboxes to keep their gold secure, and it soon became a practice among wealthy people to leave their gold with them for safekeeping. While all gold depositors had the right to ask for their gold back at any time, goldsmiths soon found out that they never did so simultaneously: while some people were withdrawing gold, others were depositing it, so that a large amount of the gold in the vaults was just lying idle. The goldsmiths discovered that under normal circumstances it was safe to keep on hand only part of the gold deposited with them; they found, in other words, that they could operate with *fractional* rather than 100 percent reserves. Then they began to lend out some of their excess reserves to credit-worthy clients, and modern banking methods got their start.

This is precisely what the chartered banks do today. They hold a portion of what is deposited with them either in the form of currency, which they keep in all of their various branches in order to meet customers' demands, or in the form of deposits in the central bank, the Bank of Canada. These holdings constitute their legal reserves. The rest they put to work to earn money, either by lending it to customers or by using it to buy government bonds. It is because banks hold only fractional reserves that they can expand the money supply by creating the deposits that comprise the largest part of the money supply.

A growing supply of money is as important to a growing economy as an expanding supply of steel. Banks and willing borrowers together have the power to expand the money supply by creating deposits. Furthermore, banks and willing (or unwilling) repayers of bank debt can destroy deposits and thus contract the money supply. Sometimes they go too far. We associate contractions and excessive expansions in the money supply with economic fluctuations, which are a sign of the failure of the economy to meet its objective of achieving stability.

THE CREATION OF MONEY

How do banks create and destroy money? Consider again the goldsmiths who started the process. When the wealthy deposited gold for safekeeping, goldsmiths issued receipts for it, and it was not long before these

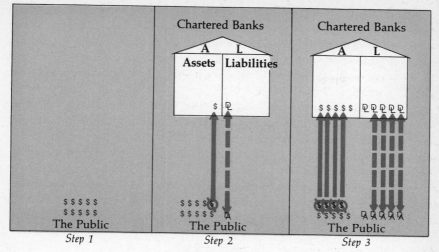

Figure 5-1

receipts began to be accepted in payment for goods and services and in settlement of debts. They were more convenient than heavy bars of gold. When the goldsmiths discovered that they needed to hold only fractional reserves, they began to lend some of the gold deposited with them, and it circulated alongside the receipts. Thus, items with general acceptability in settling accounts included both the receipts issued by the goldsmiths and the gold lent to credit-worthy clients. Money had been created. The money supply had been increased.

This sounds like sleight of hand, and so, to many people, does the money-creating process of our chartered banks today. A simplified example with some diagrams may help.[5] Assume, to begin with, that the currency in the hands of the public amounts to ten units. We shall designate every unit of currency with a dollar sign, and each unit can represent $10, $1 000, or $1 million (the size of the unit does not alter the argument in any way). The money supply includes currency outside the banks and chartered bank deposits; and if we assume for the moment that there are no chartered banks, then the total money supply is ten units, as shown in Step 1 of Figure 5-1.

In Step 2, a chartered banking system has been established. Banks are convenient places to store money, so we shall assume that some individual takes a unit of currency and deposits it in a bank. The solid arrow indicates the move. One unit of currency, formerly an asset in the hands

---

[5] The process is not very diffcult, but the examples that follow will sound like incomprehensible sleight of hand unless you are prepared not merely to *read* them, but to work through them step by step.

of the public (now circled and stroked out) has become an asset of the bank and, being an asset, has been put on the asset side (left side) of the books of the chartered banking system. As for the customer, when he places the currency in the bank, he gets in exchange a deposit. As far as he is concerned, that deposit is an asset. This is shown as a D (for deposit) with an A (for asset) through it. (D_A). That same figure, though an asset to the customer, is a liability to the bank, and it shows up on the bank's books in the right hand, or liability, column as a D (for deposit) with an L (for liabilities) through it (D_L). To indicate that we are talking about the same thing—a figure in the bank's books—we have joined the two with a broken line.

Has anything happened to the size of the money supply? Before any deposit of currency was made in the banks, the money supply stood at ten units. The present situation is that there are nine units of currency outside the chartered banks plus one unit of deposits, making a total money supply of ten units—precisely what we had before. Remember that currency inside the chartered banks is not included in the money supply.

Assume now that the public finds that it needs only five units of currency for its cash payments, and that it can perform all other transactions with cheques drawn on its deposits. By value, most transactions are carried out by cheque. If cheques were always cashed—that is, converted into currency—there would be no point in including bank deposits in the money supply, for in the end, payment would always be accomplished by a transfer of currency, and it would not matter whether the buyer of the merchandise went to the bank and withdrew the currency to make the purchase or whether he wrote a cheque which the seller promptly cashed. However, this is not what usually happens. Assume that we both bank at the same bank, and I make a payment to you by cheque, which you deposit in your account. The bank merely makes two bookkeeping entries; it writes down (debits) the balance in my account and writes up (credits) your balance, and a payment has been made without the use of currency at all. Even if we bank in different banks, the transactions can be carried out without the use of currency, for all cheques go through a clearing process.[6] Thousands of transactions occur daily, and chances are that a bank's customers will make about as many payments to customers of other banks as they receive. In the clearing process, the value of most

---

[6] The clearing process, carried out by the chartered banks, facilitates interbank payments made necessary when any bank receives cheques drawn on other banks, either local or out of town, that are to be credited to the accounts of its customers. The process used to take place in many bank clearing houses, but it has been streamlined by the introduction of centralized data processing. The ultimate settlement of accounts takes place through the chartered banks' deposits with the Bank of Canada.

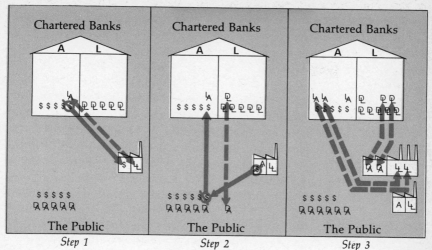

Step 1   Step 2   Step 3

Figure 5-2

cheques simply cancels out, and only relatively small residual sums have to be transferred from one bank to another at the end of a day.

In Step 3 of Figure 5-1 the total money supply remains unchanged at ten units, but the public, satisfied to hold only five units of currency, has deposited four more units. The corresponding deposits are a liability (D_L), from the point of view of the banks, and an asset (D_A) from the point of view of the depositors. The assets of the chartered banks (five units of currency) are equal to their liabilities (five units of deposits). The money supply, which comprises currency outside the banks and chartered bank deposits, is made up of five units of currency and five units of deposits; all that has happened in this step is that the public has changed the form in which it is holding its money.

Banks, like the goldsmiths of the middle ages, recognize that they do not need to hold 100 percent reserves. While some people come in to withdraw currency, others come in to deposit it; therefore on balance the quantity of currency held by the public remains relatively stable. This means that instead of holding as reserves all the dollars deposited by the public, the banks can safely keep fractional reserves, use the excess to make loans, and in that way, earn a higher profit for their shareholders. Assume now that a businessman comes along wanting to borrow a unit of money to finance a bigger inventory of raw materials for his small factory. The bank considers him to be a credit-worthy client, so it makes the loan and in this case, gives him currency; the solid arrow in Step 1 of Figure 5-2 shows the move of the dollar from the banking system to the factory owner. In exchange for this unit of currency, the businessman gives the bank manager his note (his IOU), showing that he has incurred a debt; in the diagram, this is shown as a loan liability (L, for loan, with an L for liability through it—L_L. The businessman's liability is an *asset* to the bank; it is shown as a loan asset (L with an A, for asset, through it—L_A). The bank has exchanged one form of asset, a unit of currency on which it earns no return, for another, a loan on which it charges interest. Its books still balance. Assets equal liabilities; both stand at five units.

The interesting item is the money supply. Currency outside the banks now amounts to six units, the five previously in the hands of the public, plus one that the factory owner borrowed. These, together with the five units of deposits, make a total money supply of eleven units. A unit of money has been created. Notice that the banks are no longer holding currency equal to their deposit liabilities: the ratio of currency to deposits is 4:5—80 percent instead of 100 percent reserves. Because of the willingness of the banks to hold fractional reserves, their willingness to lend money, and the willingness of businessmen to borrow, money has been created.

The factory manager originally borrowed the money to purchase some raw materials, so presumably he will promptly pay it to his suppliers. The assumption was made earlier that the economic system could operate with five units of currency; the public now has six, which means that one will be deposited. The two solid arrows in Step 2 of Figure 5-2 show that the company has received an asset (A) and has paid the unit of currency to the supplier, who in turn deposits it in the bank and obtains a deposit asset (D_A) in exchange. These two transactions (the purchase of the raw materials and the deposit of the unit of currency) do not result in the creation of money; they merely change the form in which the public is holding its money. Cash outside the chartered banks amounts to five units, and chartered bank deposits amount to six, leaving the total money supply unchanged at eleven. The banks are now holding cash equal to five sixths or 83.33 percent of their deposit liabilities.

Normally, when a businessman borrows money, his banker does not give him currency. As soon as the bank manager agrees to lend money, he increases the balance in the businessman's account, and the latter can make his payments by drawing cheques on this account. Assume now that a large-scale entrepreneur wants to borrow money for an innovation which he thinks will enable him to cut his costs of production; but he needs a good deal of money—say, two units—to get that innovation operative. The banker agrees that his idea is a good one, and is prepared to finance it; so in exchange for the businessman's note, he writes up the latter's balance by two units. In effect he has converted the businessman's credit-worthiness or debt into money: in economic jargon, he has "mone-

Chartered Banks				Chartered Banks			
Assets		**Liabilities**		**Assets**		**Liabilities**	
Currency	$5	Deposits	$5	Currency	$5	Deposits	$8
				Loans	3		
	—		—		—		—
	5		5		8		8
a				b			

Figure 5-3

tized private debt". Step 3 of Figure 5-2 shows that deposits in the banking system have increased by two units; that amount shows on the businessman's books as a deposit asset (D_A), and on the bank's books as a deposit liability (D_L), the broken lines in Step 3 indicating as usual, that both symbols stand for the same thing. By this transaction the bank once again has created money: chartered bank deposits amount to eight units and currency outside the banks remains unchanged at five. The total money supply has increased from eleven to thirteen units. The assets of the chartered banks (three units of loans plus five units of currency) still equal their liabilities (eight units of deposits). However, the reserves are no longer equal to 83.33 percent of the deposit liabilities. The five units of currency are now supporting eight units of deposit liabilities; the reserve ratio has been reduced to 62.5 percent.

Having worked through our examples step by step, we can now summarize what has happened in the chartered banks by drawing up simple balance sheets in the form of "T" accounts and tracing the changes through them. As in the diagrams, assets are on the left and liabilities on the right. Figure 5-3 shows what the balance sheet would look like if we started from the position in Figure 5-1 and went through the transactions illustrated in Steps 1 to 3 of Figure 5-2. Assets must equal liabilities. From Figure 5-3b we can tell that there has been an increase in the money supply because deposits in the chartered banks have increased from five to eight units, and the public is continuing to hold its five units of currency outside the banks. By making loans of three units ($3 million, perhaps?) the banks have *created* a corresponding amount of money. The ratio of deposit liabilities to currency in the banks (their cash reserves) is 8:5; in other words, reserves, as noted earlier, are 62.5 percent of deposit liabilities.

Chartered Banks

Assets		Liabilities	
Currency	$5	Deposits	$10
Loans	5		
	—		—
	10		10

a

Chartered Banks

Assets		Liabilities	
Currency	$5	Deposits	$15
Loans	10		
	—		—
	15		15

b

Figure 5-4

The Limits to Expansion Can this process of expanding the money supply go on indefinitely? If credit-worthy businessmen want more loans, the banks can safely let the ratio of reserves to deposit liabilities drop below 62.5 percent. If the banks lend two more units, and if the loans are made by creating deposits, then cash will be five units, loan assets will amount to another five, and these assets will be balanced by deposit liabilities of ten units, as shown in Figure 5-4a. The money supply will have increased to fifteen (ten deposit units plus five units of currency outside the banks) and the reserve ratio will be down to 50 percent (five units of cash supporting ten units of deposit liabilities). The ratio of dollar reserves to deposits decreases steadily with each loan: to begin with, there were 100 percent reserves; the ratio is now down to 50 percent. With every decrease in the reserve ratio, the supply of money increases.

How far can the reserve ratio go down: to 25 percent? 10 percent? one percent? zero? Banks have the legal obligation to pay their depositors cash on demand. Normally they can expect that for everyone in the lineup at the teller's wicket wanting to withdraw money, there will be a customer behind him wanting to make a deposit. But it does not necessarily work that way, and banks must be prepared for the possibility that at times the currency withdrawn will exceed the currency deposited. This means that banks need *some* cash reserves on hand, probably more than one percent.

As long as there is a stable banking system and people trust the banks, and as long as their withdrawals occur in an orderly manner, there is unlikely to be much need for reserves. Sometimes, however, there is a run on banks: for some reason people lose confidence, and they rush to take their money out. Not too many years ago, there was a run on one of the smaller banks in Montreal triggered by a rumour that resulted from a misunderstanding of a press report. At this point it should be stressed that a run on a bank does not mean that the bank is bankrupt. Far from it. As shown in our diagrams, every deposit liability of a bank is matched by an asset, but those assets are not held entirely, or even predominantly, as cash. If the customers who were late in the queue during a run were prepared to take some of the bonds the bank held, or some of the notes or IOUs of businessmen to whom the banks had lent money, there would be no problem. In the midst of a run, however, this does not happen; all that people want is currency. Banks, then, need large amounts of *cash* to assure people that if they want their money in the form of currency, they can have it. In the case of the Montreal run, the banking community, including the central bank, poured in large quantities of currency, and the situation did not get out of hand. As soon as depositors discovered that they could get cash from the bank, they no longer wanted it.

Canada has a very sound banking system, and a small reserve ratio would probably be adequate. However, the banks are not free to set their own reserve ratio: it is set by law. The Bank Act states that on demand deposits (like current accounts and personal chequing accounts) the legal reserve ratio must be 12 percent, while on so-called "notice" deposits (savings and term), the required ratio is 4 percent. The average required cash reserve ratio varies considerably with the relative size of current and savings deposits, but it fluctuates around 6 percent. In addition, the Bank of Canada (the central bank) has the power under the Bank Act to vary the amount that the chartered banks should hold as secondary reserves. Secondary reserves are short-term assets like treasury bills (three-month Canada bonds) and day-to-day loans (callable loans to certain investment dealers to finance their portfolios of treasury bills). These assets, though not as liquid as cash, still have a high degree of liquidity, and their advantage is that, unlike currency and deposits in the Bank of Canada, they earn some return for the banks.

When the banks reach the point where they are fully "loaned up", that is, where (ignoring the secondary reserves) for every $100 in demand deposits they are holding $12 as reserves either in the form of cash or as a deposit with the central bank, and for every $100 in notice deposits they are holding reserves of $4, then the expansion of the money supply through monetizing private debt has gone as far as it can go.

An Example An average cash reserve ratio of around 6 percent makes the arithmetic too complicated for our simple diagrams. Assume instead that banks must hold currency equal to 33.33 percent of their deposit liabilities. This means that every unit of currency in the chartered banks will support up to three units of deposit liabilities but no more; otherwise the ratio of reserves to deposit liabilities will drop below the legally allowable limit in our hypothetical system. We shall not change our assumption that the public is content to hold five units of currency outside the banks, and that the banks have five units. We started with a reserve ratio of 100 percent, but because of the banks' willingness to lend, the businessmen's willingness to borrow, and the system's recognition that a reserve ratio of 100 percent was not necessary, we ended up in Step 3 of Figure 5-2 with reserves equal to 62.5 percent of the money supply. Under our new assumption, banks can continue to lend until the ratio declines to 33.33 percent. As credit-worthy businessmen come to borrow money, then, the banks can continue to increase their loans and their deposit liabilities until the latter are three times the number of units of currency in the banks.

The expansion of loans and deposits that brought the reserve ratio from 62.5 percent to 50 percent, and then to 33.33 percent (which, we have assumed, is the legal ratio set by the monetary authorities) is shown in Figure 5-4. Figure 5-4b shows that when the banking system has made all the loans it legally can, there will be ten units of loan assets and five of currency, making a total of fifteen units of assets. On the liability side banks have created ten units of deposits by making loans to businessmen, and there are the original deposit liabilities incurred when customers brought in the five units of currency. The money supply has increased from the ten units it was at the beginning of our first example to twenty units—fifteen units of deposits in the chartered banks and five units of currency held outside the banks.

Suppose that still more money is needed in the system: an expanding economy needs an expanding supply of money, and since private debt has been monetized to its legal limit, how is the money supply to grow? Before we can answer this question, we shall have to find out about the origin of those dollars that we started out with. Step 2 of Figure 5-5 provides a basis for analysis. Step 2 incorporates Step 1, which showed a banking system that had lent all the money the law allowed it to lend, and the public, who were holding five units of currency; and we have added the Bank of Canada (the central bank) and the government.

How could the ten units of currency that we started with in Figure 5-1 have been introduced into the system? In theory, the government might have printed them and put them into circulation by paying for some items it needed. However, governments that print money are regarded as irresponsible by most voters: too many countries have suffered when their governments resorted to the printing press. The government therefore goes about it in a little more subtle manner. It has a central bank that prints the currency. In fact, the Bank of Canada does not do the actual printing either: it is done for the Bank of Canada by the Canadian Bank Note Company and the Royal Canadian Mint, but we shall ignore this slight complication.

Strange as it may seem, that currency which comprises an important part of the assets of the public, the banks, and the government is a *liability* of the Bank of Canada. Those units of currency are, in effect, the

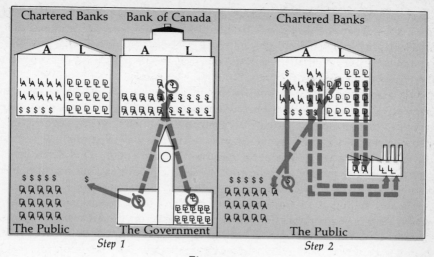

Figure 5-5

IOUs of the central bank, just as the note the businessman signed for the bank manager when he borrowed money was *his* IOU; it was a liability for him and at the same time it was an asset for the bank. As long as the "notes" of the Bank of Canada—the bills of various denominations— remain inside the bank, they are nothing but rather attractive pieces of paper of different colours. They are not assets of the central bank. If this idea seems strange, it might help to consider the following situation: suppose you sat down and wrote yourself twenty IOUs each with a face value of $50. Would you be wealthier by $1 000? No, those IOUs in your own hands are valueless bits of paper. In someone else's hands—your banker's, for example—your notes for $1 000 are a liability to you and an asset to the holder. Similarly, for the Bank of Canada those notes on highgrade paper stating "This note is legal tender" are nothing but "stationery", which is what they are often called as long as they remain in the vaults of the Bank of Canada. When they go into circulation, they become assets to those who hold them (as your note becomes an asset to your banker) and a liability to the issuer, the Bank of Canada (as your note in your banker's hands is a liability to you).

The next step is to find out how these notes get into circulation. The central bank does not just give them away; there must be value received in exchange. This is where the government comes in: the government does not actually print money; what it does instead is print bonds, which are simply interest-bearing IOUs. In Step 2 of Figure 5-5, we have shown as liabilities of the government ten units of bonds (B for bonds with an L for liabilities through it—B_L). These have been sold to the Bank of Canada (and show on the Bank's books as bond assets, B_A) in exchange for ten units of currency, which the government has then exchanged for goods and services of various kinds purchased from the public. This explains how the ten units of currency that we started with in Figure 5-1 got into the hands of the public in the first place.

We are now ready to return to the question that we asked at the beginning of the section: how are we to get new money into a system that is fully "loaned up"? This can be done by "monetizing the government debt" in the very same way as the money supply was expanded earlier by the monetization of private debt. Assume that the government finds itself in need of more money in order to finance its operations, and that it plans to borrow. It does so by printing another unit of bonds (a government IOU) and selling it to the Bank of Canada. These bonds bear interest, which currency does not. (Sometimes, to make fun of our system, Communists point out that the government, by issuing bonds rather than printing currency, is merely substituting interest-bearing debt for non-interest-bearing debt.) In this operation, the government's bond liabilities increase by one unit, and the central bank's bond assets increase by one unit. In exchange, the bank gets out one unit of "stationery" from its vaults and turns it over to the government, an action that results in a one-unit increase in its dollar liabilities. Its assets and liabilities are now equal at eleven units.

In Step 1 of Figure 5-6 we have moved one stage further to show that the government has turned that currency over to the public to pay for goods and services for which it initially borrowed the money. As to the money supply, when that unit of currency came out of the central bank's vaults into circulation, the money supply was increased. Step 1 shows that there are six units of currency outside the chartered banks and fifteen units of chartered bank deposits, making a total money supply of twenty-one units instead of the twenty we had in Figure 5-5.

If we retain the assumption that the public can get along very nicely with just five units of currency, then one of the six now being held outside the banks will be deposited. Step 2 of Figure 5-6 shows a cash deposit of one unit. This reduces the currency outside the chartered banks to five units and increases the number of units inside to six. When the currency is put into the bank, the customer's deposits are increased by that one unit; this means that from the bank's point of view deposit liabilities have increased, and from the public's point of view, deposit *assets* have been increased by one unit. The money supply has not changed because of the deposit: a unit of currency has simply been transferred into a bank deposit so that the deposits in the chartered banks amount to sixteen units and the currency outside the banks to five, giving the same total of twenty-one units.

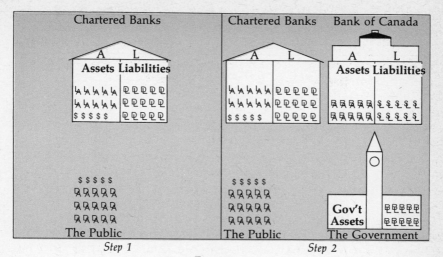

| Chartered Banks | Chartered Banks | Bank of Canada |

Figure 5-6

The stage is now set for a further expansion of the money supply, because the chartered banks are holding six units of cash reserves against sixteen units of deposit liabilities. The ratio of reserves to deposit liabilities is 6:16, or 37.5 percent; 33.33 percent is all that is required. Suppose, now, that some credit-worthy entrepreneurs come along who need working capital. The banks can accommodate them by making loans of up to two units. In Step 2 of Figure 5-6 they make these loans by increasing the businessmen's deposits; the banks' loan assets rise from ten to twelve units, and their deposit liabilities rise to eighteen, as do the matching deposit assets of the public. The reserve ratio is six units of reserves to eighteen units of deposit liabilities, or 33.33 percent, as required. The banks' books balance; loan assets are twelve units and cash reserves are six units, making a total of eighteen, to balance deposit liabilities of eighteen. As for the money supply, currency outside the banks amounts to five units, and chartered bank deposits amount to eighteen, which means that the money supply has risen to twenty-three units. The injection of one unit of new money into the system, issued by the central bank to finance government borrowing, has resulted in a three-unit increase: the money supply rose from twenty to twenty-three units.

Once again we can use balance sheets to summarize the changes that have been made in the money supply. In Figure 5-4b (as in Step 1 of Figure 5-5) deposit liabilities of the chartered banks amounted to fifteen units, against which the banks were holding currency reserves of five units, thus meeting the required reserve ratio. After one more unit of currency is introduced by the government, perhaps through increased payments to civil servants, and after the extra funds have flowed back

Chartered Banks

Assets		Liabilities	
Currency	$ 6	Deposits	$16
Loans	10		
	—		—
	16		16

a

Chartered Banks

Assets		Liabilities	
Currency	$ 6	Deposits	$18
Loans	12		
	—		—
	18		18

b

Figure 5-7

into the chartered banks, the system's balance sheet will look like that in Figure 5-7a: cash reserves have risen by one unit, to six; deposits have increased by one unit, to sixteen, leaving the banking system with extra cash reserves, which put it in a position to increase its loans. In Figure 5-7b the banking system, once again, is fully "loaned up": it has lent two more units, raising its loan assets to twelve units and deposits to eighteen, and its ratio of reserves to deposits is again at the maximum permitted, 1:3. As for the money supply, since cash outside the banks remains at five units, the increase in deposits from fifteen to eighteen has meant an increase in the money supply from twenty to twenty-three units.

The major conclusions to be drawn from the step-by-step analysis we have done is that, provided that banks are willing to lend and business-men are willing to borrow (conditions that are not always met in the economy), the fact that banks keep fractional reserves enables them to expand the money supply. The amount of that expansion depends on the amount of reserves they are required to keep, and on whether the reserves they actually hold are, in fact, greater than their required reserves. We saw that when the banks were fully "loaned up"—that is, when the ratio of reserves to deposit liabilities was just equal to what the law required —then the banks could not expand any more. They could do nothing until there occurred an injection of new reserves into the system.

In our example, we assumed a reserve ratio of one third. This meant that every unit of reserves was capable of supporting three units of deposit liabilities, and these deposit liabilities were created by lending money to businessmen who wanted to borrow—"monetizing private debt", as we called the process. Suppose the reserve ratio had been 10 percent, or one tenth, then each of those five units of currency inside the chartered banks would have supported deposit liabilities of ten units; loans could have been made until deposit liabilities reached fifty units, and these, together with five units of currency outside the banks, would have given a money supply of fifty-five units—a much greater expansion than in our example. The smaller the reserve ratio, the larger the possible expansion of the money supply. There is a rule that tells us how to calculate the maximum possible expansion. It states that as long as banks have excess reserves, they can create *new* money by an amount equal to the reciprocal of the reserve ratio multiplied by the amount of excess reserves.[7]

It should be apparent by now that anything that affects the size of the reserves of the chartered banks can influence the size of the money supply. The Bank of Canada (the central bank) virtually controls the reserves of the chartered banks within certain limits set by Parliament and hence has the power to alter the money supply. Altering the money supply in order to achieve the economy's objectives with respect to unemployment, prices, and growth is what is meant by monetary policy. The Bank of Canada, in other words, controls national monetary policy under normal conditions. Obviously it is an important institution.

The Bank of Canada

The Bank of Canada has only one shareholder, the federal government. The Bank was established in 1934 as a privately owned corporation with shares held by the public, but it was nationalized in 1938 when the government bought all outstanding shares held by the public. The central bank, offspring of a typically Canadian procedure—a Royal Commission—was created by Parliament as an autonomous corporation with a governor (currently Gerald K. Bouey), its own board of directors, and an executive committee. Though the members of the board of directors are all appointed by the government, and though the capital stock is owned entirely by the government, the Bank is designed to be relatively free from political interference. The Bank must have independence of action in formulating and carrying out monetary policy, because monetary policy, when it aims at controlling inflation, is likely to be politically unpopular. Notwithstanding this independence and freedom of action, the Bank's

---

[7] In Step 2 of Figure 5-6, when the unit of money was deposited, the banking system, with a reserve ratio of one third, needed one third of it for legal reserves and was left with excess reserves of two thirds of a unit. The reciprocal of one third, the reserve ratio, is three. The further expansion of the money supply was the reciprocal of the reserve ratio times the excess reserves (three times two thirds) or two units. Had the reserve ratio been one tenth, then one tenth of the money deposited would have been required as reserves, nine tenths would have been excess reserves, and the expansion would have been the reciprocal of one tenth (ten) times nine tenths which, of course, equals nine units.

monetary policy must, in a democratic society, conform with the views of the government. In the case of a disagreement, the government has the power to issue directives, which the Bank must follow.

RESPONSIBILITIES

The preamble to the *Bank of Canada Act* places great responsibilities on the central bank. It is required "to regulate credit and currency in the best interests of the economic life of the nation, to control and protect the external value of the national monetary unit, and to mitigate by its influence fluctuations in the general level of production, trade, prices and employment, so far as may be possible within the scope of monetary action, and generally to promote the economic and financial welfare of the Dominion."[8] These are major responsibilities. It is up to the central bank to see that the chartered banks are increasing (or decreasing) the money supply at a rate appropriate to the economic conditions of the country. It must try to prevent the money supply from increasing so rapidly that serious inflation and balance-of-payments problems result; but it still must permit enough of an expansion to support a growing economy. If there is a contraction, the Bank must do what it can to prevent a contracting money supply from pushing the country into a recession. Regulating credit and currency is a difficult and delicate task that requires the skillful use of a number of tools of control.

The Bank of Canada is a bankers' bank: it is not an institution in which we, as members of the public, can deposit our money. The banks we deal with keep deposits there, and these deposits in the central bank are part of their legal reserves. The central bank helps the clearing process, for any inter-bank debts that remain after cheques have been cleared through the clearing house may be settled by cheques drawn on the accounts of the chartered banks in the Bank of Canada. The central bank also lends money to the chartered banks—if the banks want to borrow—in practically the same way as chartered banks lend to consumers and businessmen. The rate (called the *Bank Rate*) at which the Bank of Canada lends to the chartered banks is of particular importance in monetary policy. The central bank also stands ready to provide money in case a run should occur in any bank: in other words, it is prepared to act as a lender of last resort.

The central bank acts as banker and advisor to the federal government. The government keeps deposits in the Bank of Canada. It keeps them in the other banks, too, but the central bank serves as more than merely a holder of deposits: it acts as fiscal agent for the government,

---

[8] R.S.C. 1952, c. 13, as amended by R.S.C. 1952, c. 315, 1953-54, c. 33.

which means that it administers the government's debt. It issues bonds for the government, calls them in when they have matured, and looks after interest payments. The Bank of Canada, in other words, manages the *national debt*. This system differs from that of the United States, in that the Federal Reserve, the American central banking system, does not have this function.

In order to help fulfill its responsibility of protecting the external value of the dollar, the central bank deals in foreign exchange, gold, and foreign securities. It used to hold gold on its own account before the Second World War, when our money was backed by gold and when it was the duty of the Bank of Canada to act as custodian of our basic monetary reserves. The requirement that the Bank hold gold reserves equal to 25 percent of its combined note and deposit liabilities disappeared early in the war, when it became apparent that the Canadian money supply would have to be greatly increased—by much more than four times the gold supply— and that the gold would be needed for other purposes. Canadian money has had no gold backing since then. The central bank now deals in gold, not on its own account, but as agent for the Exchange Fund Account, the fund used to help stabilize the value of the Canadian dollar.

TECHNIQUES OF CENTRAL BANK CONTROL

As one might expect from our discussion of the chartered banks and the creation of money, the most important technique of control available to the Bank of Canada to regulate the money supply is altering the reserves of the chartered banks. There are two others that we should mention: one is altering the Bank Rate, the rate at which it will lend to the chartered banks; and the other is *moral suasion*, the process of using central bank influence or persuasion to get the chartered banks to follow certain patterns of action.

Altering Chartered Banks' Reserves Altering the chartered banks' reserves is the central bank's most important control technique. The Bank of Canada can influence these reserves in a number of ways, the most important of which is by open market operations. The others that we shall consider are switching government accounts and altering the reserve ratio.

OPEN MARKET OPERATIONS

The central bank's open market operations consist of buying and selling bonds in the bond market, the objective being to increase or decrease chartered banks' reserves and hence to affect the size of the money supply. The effect of the central bank's sales and purchases can be shown

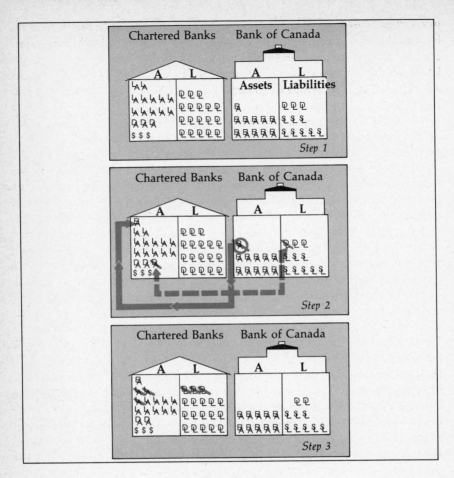

Figure 5-8

in another step-by-step diagram similar to the ones we used to show changes in the money supply. To begin with, we shall remove another simplifying assumption: the assumption that the chartered banks keep all of their reserves in their own vaults. Now we shall assume, as is in fact the case, that they keep part of their required reserves in the form of deposits in the Bank of Canada. In the final step of Figure 5-6, chartered banks were holding cash reserves amounting to six units. In Step 1 of Figure 5-8, we have assumed that the banks have decided to retain three units of currency, and to deposit three units in the Bank of Canada which, for its part, opens deposit accounts for the banks. These deposits are assets for the chartered banks and comprise part of their legal reserves. The central bank can simply put those three units of currency back in the "stationary" department (leaving only eight outstanding); its *dollar* liabilities will now be decreased by three units, and its *deposit* liabilities will be increased by a corresponding three units. All that the Bank of Canada has done is switch one form of liability for another, while the chartered banks have switched one form of asset for another. Since six units of reserves are supporting eighteen units of deposit liabilities in the chartered banks and since we have assumed a required reserve ratio of 33.33 percent, there is no room for further expansion. In Step 1, the only change that has been made is to bring the system a step closer to reality by including deposits in the central bank among the assets of the chartered banks.

Assume now that the Bank of Canada decides to undertake some open market operations like selling a unit of bonds. Assume further that the buyers of those bonds are the chartered banks. So far, the assets of the chartered banks have included only loans to businessmen, currency, and deposits with the central bank. This has been another oversimplification: banks lend not only to businessmen, but also to consumers and to people who need mortgages. While loans of various kinds comprise by far the most important asset of the banks, banks do invest, to a considerable extent, in government bonds. Step 2 shows the chartered banks as buyers of the unit of bonds sold in the open market by the Bank of Canada. They can pay for the bonds either by transferring a unit of currency to the Bank of Canada or by having their deposits with the central bank decreased by that amount. Assume that they choose the latter method: in Step 2 the bond (an asset) is transferred to the chartered banks, as shown by the solid arrow. To pay for it, chartered banks' deposits are debited: as indicated by the broken line, there is a decrease in the deposit liabilities of the Bank of Canada (a unit is stroked out) and a decrease in the deposit assets of the chartered banks (one unit stroked out). In the Bank of Canada the remaining ten units of bond assets are balanced by eight units of currency liabilities and two units of deposit liabilities. The books of the chartered banks also balance: they are holding as assets three units of currency, two units of deposits with the Bank of Canada, twelve units of loans, and one unit of bonds, making a total of eighteen units of assets, to balance the eighteen units of deposit liabilities.

However, the banks face a new problem. Their reserves can take the form of currency or of deposits with the Bank of Canada; bonds are not part of their cash reserves. By switching the form of assets from deposits with the Bank of Canada to bonds, the banking system's reserves were reduced from six to five units; those five units are supporting deposit liabilities of eighteen, making a reserve ratio of about 28 percent. We have assumed the legal reserve ratio to be 33.33 percent. The chartered banks must somehow reduce their deposit liabilities to fifteen units in order to bring the ratio of reserves to deposit liabilities up to 33.33 percent. One way to do this is to reduce loans.

Banks may reduce their loans by "calling" them: that is, they may say to businessmen who have loans, "You owe us money; you must come in and settle your debt." These businessmen, in turn, may collect funds from the people who owe *them* money and then write cheques on their accounts in favour of the bank, thereby reducing simultaneously the loans and the deposit liabilities of the banks. But since bank loans are constantly maturing and being paid off or renegotiated, it is much more likely that banks will merely refuse to make new loans as old ones mature, or will fail to renew those that fall due. However it is accomplished, both loans and deposit liabilities will be reduced. With our reserve ratio of 33.33 percent, the loss of one unit of reserves must be counterbalanced by a reduction of three units of deposit liabilities, as shown in Step 3. The bank's loan assets have been reduced by three units (stroked out); and deposit liabilities were reduced by three units (stroked out) at the same time. The system, then, is left with assets of one unit of bonds, nine of loans, two of deposits with the Bank of Canada, and three of currency—fifteen units of assets in all. This is balanced by deposit liabilities of fifteen units. The reserve ratio is again 33.33 percent: legal reserves of five units (three units of currency and two of deposits with the central bank) amount to a third of the fifteen units of deposit liabilities of the chartered banks. As for the money supply, it has been *reduced* by three units. Currency outside the banks has not been affected by the open market operations of the Bank of Canada: it still stands at five units, just as in Step 2 of Figure 5-6. However, chartered bank deposits are now only fifteen units, bringing back the total money supply down to twenty from the previous total of twenty-three.

These transactions can be summarized in balance sheets. Figure 5-9 shows balance sheets for both the chartered banks and the Bank of Canada that encompass all of the same assumptions as Step 1 of Figure 5-8. The chartered banks' reserves (currency plus deposits in the Bank of Canada) are at the required ratio of 33.33 percent of their deposit liabilities. The central bank's liabilities (the chartered banks' deposits plus currency in the chartered banks and currency in general circulation) are matched by its holding of bonds.

In Figure 5-10 the assumption is made that the central bank has sold a bond, which the chartered banks have paid for by using their deposits in the central bank. Since these deposits constitute part of their reserves whereas bonds do not, the chartered banks, finding themselves with only five units of reserves—fewer than the number required to support eighteen units of deposits—have responded by reducing their loans from twelve to nine units, and hence their deposits by three units, bringing them down to fifteen. This drop in deposits, which constitute part of the money supply, means that as a result of the sale of bonds by the Bank of Canada, the money supply has decreased by three units.

Chartered Banks

Assets		Liabilities	
Currency	$ 3	Deposits	$18
Deposits in Bank of Canada	3		
Loans	12		
	—		—
	18		18

Bank of Canada

Assets		Liabilities	
Bonds	$11	Currency	$8
		Deposits	3
	—		—
	11		11

Figure 5-9

Chartered Banks

Assets		Liabilities	
Currency	$ 3	Deposits	$15
Deposits in Bank of Canada	2		
Loans	9		
Bonds	1		
	—		—
	15		15

Bank of Canada

Assets		Liabilities	
Bonds	$10	Currency	$8
		Deposits	2
	—		—
	10		10

Figure 5-10

Our diagrams indicate that the central bank can decrease the size of the money supply (as long as the chartered banks have no excess reserves) by selling them bonds in the open market. We can reverse the process and have the central bank *buy* bonds in the open market. If the bonds belong to the chartered banks, then the Bank of Canada may pay for those bonds with currency or by increasing the deposits of the chartered banks. In either event the result will be to increase the reserves of the banking system and pave the way for an increase in the money supply.

We have assumed that the bonds bought and sold by the central bank belonged to the chartered banks; this has made our diagrams considerably simpler. However, the result would have been no different if the bonds had been sold to, or bought from, members of the public. As long as the public wants to hold five units of currency, we can assume that any bond it buys will be paid for by cheque, which constitutes a claim of the central bank against the chartered bank that must cash that cheque. Even if the bond is paid for in cash, we can assume that when the public is short of cash, it will make a (net) withdrawal from the chartered banks. The result, in either event, is a reduction in the reserves of the chartered banks.

The Bank of Canada makes considerable use of open market operations to influence the reserves of the chartered banks. To increase their cash reserves, it buys bonds on the open market, and this paves the way for an increase in the money supply through bank loan expansion. To decrease the banks' reserves, it sells bonds on the open market. This has the effect of "absorbing" the excess reserves of the chartered banks, thus limiting the potential expansion of the money supply, or if the banks do not have excess reserves (as was the case in our example) of actually causing a decrease in the money supply.

To help manage cash reserves, the central bank supplements its use of open-market sales and purchases of bonds with sales and purchases of foreign exchange, through temporary swap transactions with the Exchange Fund Account. Such transactions have precisely the same effect on cash reserves as buying and selling bonds in the open market.

SWITCHING GOVERNMENT ACCOUNTS

When the Government of Canada collects its revenues, it will probably put them into a bank account the way an individual or business does. Since it has access to the Bank of Canada, the government has the option of making deposits in the Bank of Canada, or in the chartered banks, or both. In practice, it keeps deposits in both the central bank and the chartered banks.

The Bank of Canada, with the cooperation of the Minister of Finance, can control these government deposits: it can switch them from one bank to another, or switch them from the chartered banks to itself, or vice versa. Consider the effect of the switch of some government deposits from the Bank of Canada to the chartered banks. It can be done by a set of very simple bookkeeping entries—the same kind of entries made when you and I banked in the same bank and I paid my debt to you by cheque: my account was debited by the amount of my cheque, and your balance was increased. In this case, since the Government of Canada and the chartered banks both bank with the Bank of Canada, the transfer of federal funds out of the chartered banks can be accomplished merely by increasing the figure representing government deposits with the Bank of Canada and decreasing chartered bank deposits in the Bank. On the books of the chartered banks, deposit liabilities are diminished by the withdrawal of government funds, as are their deposits with the Bank of Canada, and the switch has been completed. This simple transaction has important implications, because to decrease chartered banks' deposits in the central bank is to decrease their legal reserves; and anything that decreases the legal reserves either paves the way for a decrease in the money supply or absorbs excess reserves and thus checks the size of the expansion that might otherwise occur.

If the central bank wishes to *increase* the reserves of the chartered bank, it can do so by the reverse operation of switching government accounts *to* the chartered banks. It transfers funds by simply decreasing the figure on its books for government deposits and increasing the deposits of the chartered banks. The chartered banks then find themselves with increased deposit liabilities and, more important, increased deposits in the central bank, or increased legal reserves.

Switching government accounts thus provides the central bank with a very fast method of altering the reserves of the chartered banking system; this is a tool the Bank of Canada uses almost daily. The Government of Canada deposits, then, are different from those of the public and are regarded by the banking community as more of a control tool than a genuine part of the money supply. Thus, when bankers calculate the money supply, for some purposes at least, they tend to exclude Government of Canada deposits.

CHANGING THE RESERVE RATIO

In our example, we discovered that the size of the reserve ratio was important in determining the size of the possible expansion or contraction of the money supply. The larger the reserve ratio, the smaller the possible expansion (or contraction). Obviously, if the central bank can control the size of the legal reserve ratio, it can, by changing it, affect the size of the required reserves and hence the size of the potential expansion or contraction of the money supply.

Under the terms of the 1954 *Bank Act*, the central bank had the power to vary the minimum legal reserve ratio between 8 percent and 12 percent, but this was a power it never used. The 1967 *Bank Act* fixed the legal reserve ratio at 4 percent for notice deposits (savings deposits) and 12 percent for demand deposits; that is, it removed the Bank of Canada's power of altering the legal reserve ratio. However, the Bank was given the power to set a ratio for *secondary* reserves (excess cash reserves—day-to-day loans to money market dealers, and treasury bills—short-term bonds issued by the federal government) of up to 12 percent. Between 1956 and

1967, by agreement with the Bank of Canada rather than by law, the chartered banks carried secondary reserves equal to 7 percent of their deposit liabilities. The 1967 *Bank Act* legalized these secondary reserves and gave the central bank control over their size. During the next eight years the ratio was altered occasionally: it ranged between a high of 9 percent, set in May 1970, and a low of 5.5 percent, set in February 1975.

Altering the Bank Rate   Altering the Bank Rate is a traditional control tool of central banks everywhere. In some countries the Bank Rate is called the discount, or rediscount, rate. The United Kingdom has a very highly developed money market[9] with a hierarchy of interrelated interest rates, and when an interest rate as important as the Bank Rate moves, many other rates move with it. The repercussions of these changes may be felt throughout the economy. A high interest rate, for example, discourages the commercial banks (in Canada, the chartered banks) from borrowing from the central bank. The central bank also uses alterations in this rate to indicate the monetary policy it intends to pursue. In Canada, the Bank Rate is the minimum rate at which the Bank of Canada makes loans (advances) to the chartered banks.

Although the Canadian money market has advanced greatly in recent years, it is not as well developed as those in London and New York. While there exists a sizable quantity of short-term securities of various kinds, these securities, once purchased, usually stay put instead of being actively traded. Moreover, the chartered banks borrow infrequently from the central bank. In Canada, therefore, the Bank Rate's most useful function has been to act as a signal of intent about the monetary policy that the central bank proposes to pursue. If the Bank wishes to indicate a "tight" money policy, then it raises the Bank Rate. Thus, there were five increases in 1973 that took the Bank Rate from 5.25 to 7.25 percent, and three more increases in 1974 took it to an unprecedented 9.25 percent. The purpose was to restrain strong demands for credit and to slow down the rate of growth.[10] On the other hand, if an "easy" money policy is in order, it can indicate this by lowering the rate. Not every change in Bank Rate can be considered a signal: the rate must be kept in proper relationship to rates like the treasury bill rate and the rate at which banks lend to money market dealers—the day-to-day loan rate.[11] The Bank Rate traditionally lies above them. This means that when chartered banks run short

---

[9] The term "money market" is generally used to describe the market in which short-term securities are bought and sold. The broader term "capital market" is usually used to describe the arrangements for buying and selling long-term securities.

[10] Bank of Canada, *Annual Report of the Governor to the Minister of Finance and Statement of Accounts for the Year 1974* (Ottawa: 1975), p. 31.

of money, they will rely on the money market and call in their day-to-day loans rather than borrow from the central bank. However, the Bank Rate should not be so far above the day-to-day loan rate that even in times of stringency the chartered banks will be reluctant to borrow. Such a situation might cause the banks to take actions that would disrupt the securities market. Therefore, there must be changes in the Bank Rate that are simply technical adjustments, rather than announcements of intentions with respect to monetary policy.

Moral Suasion The third technique of control of central banks is moral suasion. As the name implies, this is simply an attempt by the central bank to persuade the chartered banks to follow a policy that is considered beneficial to the economy. Moral suasion may be used to affect specific regions or sectors or groups in the economy. For example, banks might be encouraged to make more credit available to less developed regions of the country. Because there are few banks in Canada, it is easy for the Governor to talk to all bank presidents and urge them to take certain actions. Moral suasion is a less useful tool in the United States where there are many thousands of banks; but even there, pronouncements by the Governor of the Federal Reserve System may have an influence on the commercial banking system. Moral suasion is a powerful control technique of the Bank of England.

In Canada, probably the best known example of moral suasion was the implementation of the secondary reserve ratio of 7 percent accepted reluctantly by the chartered banks in 1956 on the advice of James Coyne, then Governor of the Bank of Canada. More recently, moral suasion has been used to persuade the chartered banks to limit the rates paid on large short-term deposits.

This chapter has focused on money: how it is created and destroyed and the tools available to the Bank of Canada to control the supply. In the next chapter we shall use this information to explain how the money supply can be used to help achieve the objective of full employment without inflation. We shall consider the demand for money, the way the price of using money (the interest rate) is affected by changes in the supply, and how the interest rate affects the level of demand in the private sector. Finally, we shall turn our attention from the money supply to the use of government revenues and expenditures as tools to help achieve stability in the economy.

---

[11] Day-to-day loans, as noted earlier, are callable loans made by the chartered banks to certain investment dealers to finance their portfolios of treasury bills. If the banks ask for their repayment before noon, these loans must be repaid in the same day; they are very liquid assets, in other words. The rate of interest charged (the day-to-day loan rate) is relatively low because of the high degree of liquidity of these loans.

6

The federal government uses monetary policy (changing the money supply, and hence the interest rate) and fiscal policy (altering its revenues and expenditures) to help achieve economic stability. The problems of using monetary policy include forecasting accurately, time lags before the effects are felt, and economic disparities between different regions of Canada, as well as the effects of a high rate of interest on the costs of servicing the public debt and on the capital inflow.

Over time governments have built automatic stabilizers into their expenditures and revenues; progressive income taxes and payments to the unemployed are examples. Parliament also makes discretionary changes in revenues and expenditures to help stabilize the economy. Unfortunately there is a trade-off between policies to achieve full employment and policies to control inflation.

When expenditures exceed revenues, governments borrow money and the public debt increases. Public debt has increased rapidly in the last thirty years, though not as rapidly as national income.

Stabilization Policies

When the economic goals were introduced in Chapter 3 it was pointed out that the economy does not progress at a steady rate: when we plot output over time on a graph it shows a wave-like pattern. The swings in output are accompanied by undesirable fluctuations in prices and unemployment, and it is an accepted goal of the Canadian economy that we should try to get rid of these cycles and aim for economic stability—for full employment without inflation. Unfortunately it is difficult to quantify this goal. The Economic Council of Canada has indicated that its definition of a high level of employment in the *First Annual Review* as a situation with a maximum rate of unemployment of 3 percent, though desirable, was rather ambitious. Figure 4-1 showed how infrequently the rate of 3 percent had been reached. When the Economic Council began the practice of publishing medium-term performance indicators, it set the unemployment target somewhat higher at 4.5 percent, a target maintained for 1976 and 1977.[1]

The Economic Council's first definition of inflation as anything more than 2 percent as measured by the Implicit (GNE) Price Deflator also proved to be ambitious. As the double-digit inflation of the 1970s made clear, price increases in the countries with which Canada trades can have a major effect on prices in Canada. Thus, the new performance indicator used by the Economic Council is a relative price indicator. There is no specified target for inflation; instead the Council suggests that the rates of price change in Canada should keep in step with price changes in the major OECD countries. The objective for the differential between Canadian and foreign prices was given a zero value, plus or minus 0.5 percent.[2]

It is customary to classify policies aimed at producing more stability in the economy into two categories, monetary policy and fiscal policy. Monetary policy involves using the money supply to help achieve full employment without inflation. When it uses fiscal policy the Federal Government employs its own revenues and expenditures as its policy tools. Alterations in revenues and expenditure to help achieve stability are likely to affect the size of the public debt.

---

[1] Economic Council of Canada, *Eleventh Annual Review: Economic Targets and Social Indicators* (Ottawa: Information Canada, 1974), p. 23.

[2] See Economic Council of Canada, *Twelfth Annual Review: Options for Growth* (Ottawa: Information Canada, 1975), p. 82.

Monetary Policy

The rationale for our venture into macroeconomic theory in Chapter 5 was to find out how the money supply could be controlled and hence, how it could be used as a tool of government policy. Since the central bank has the power to alter the money supply, it follows that monetary policy must be administered by the Bank of Canada.

TIGHT MONEY

Assume that we are experiencing inflation: prices are rising rapidly. Assume further that factors of production are fully employed and that the economy is encountering bottlenecks so that real output is unlikely to be increasing much. National income, however, will be rising rapidly, reflecting those rising prices. Since inflation is unlikely to occur without an increase in the money supply, it follows that to keep inflation in check, the appropriate monetary policy is one of tight money. This means that the central bank should operate in such a way as to decrease or constrain the reserves of the chartered banks. The most effective method of doing this is to sell bonds in the open market. This action might be reinforced by switching government accounts out of the chartered banks into the central bank, or possibly by raising the secondary reserve ratio. If the banks have no excess reserves, then such a policy can bring about a decline in the money supply, as Figure 5-8 showed. If the banks *have* excess reserves, the effect of the central bank's tight money policy will be to absorb some of these reserves and prevent the expansion from being as large as it otherwise might be. The central bank might make clear its intent to pursue a tight money policy by raising the Bank Rate, and it might possibly use its powers of persuasion to encourage banks to limit their expansion of credit.

As a deliberate matter of policy, money has been made scarce. This means that when loans are being requested, bankers may either refuse to make them at all or, if they do make them, may charge a higher price for the use of money—that is, they may raise the interest rate. This will affect consumers, for some go directly to banks for loans, and when money is tight, there will be many who cannot get money at all. Those who get it will have to pay a higher rate of interest for it, which may encourage them to borrow less than they otherwise would. Other consumers rely on installment finance companies to finance car purchases, or on retail stores to finance their purchases of durable goods such as television sets and refrigerators. However, most retailers and finance companies are able to extend more credit to consumers only if they can increase their own borrowing from the banks. When the central bank makes money scarce, consumers may be compelled to cut down on their purchases.

Consumption is not the only variable that may be affected. A tight money supply also affects investment in housing. Housebuilders rely heavily on borrowed funds and when monetary policy makes funds scarce in the economy, less is available from financial institutions for mortgages. Moreover, when interest rates rise, monthly mortgage payments rise too, and this means that prospective homeowners are either discouraged from buying houses or else they buy smaller ones. Studies of the housing market in the 1950s and 1960s have suggested that the market is quite sensitive to changes in the interest rate on mortgages.[3]

In an inflationary boom, businesses need more money to meet larger payrolls, buy more raw materials, and finance larger inventories. They also need funds to expand their plants and purchase equipment. Some of the extra money may come from rising sales and profits, but businesses will most likely have to turn to the banks for help. However, when money is in short supply, bank managers may have to say no to many would-be borrowers and refuse to extend the loans of others; and those who *can* borrow funds will likely pay higher rates of interest. The marginal efficiency of investment theory that was described in Chapter 4 suggests that when the spread between the interest rate and the anticipated rate of return is reduced because of the increased cost of money, some investment may be discouraged. Any reduction in investment (and consumption) will cause a decrease in the payments flow and reduce the demand for goods and services; this, in turn, will reduce the upward pressure on prices.

We discussed above the possible consequences of a tight money policy and the resultant high rates of interest. However, a good question to ask is how sensitive investment will actually be to increases in the interest rate. There are other considerations that may be even more important to the businessman than interest costs, such as the fact that much investment is regarded as essential for survival or at least for the maintenance of a share of the market. In such a case, investment is likely to be rather insensitive to changes in the rate of interest. If investment is financed from internal sources, businessmen tend to ignore the opportunity cost of using their own funds. Moreover, in calculating a rate of return, businessmen are subject to such wide margins of error that the cost associated with an increase in the interest rate may well fall within the margin of error usually allowed on a project.

---

[3] Economic Council of Canada, *Toward More Stable Growth in Construction* (Ottawa: Information Canada, 1974), p. 149.

In the conditions that existed in the mid-1970s, the problems of using a tight money policy were even greater. Prices were spiralling upward, but at the same time unemployment was unacceptably high. There was widespread concern that if the money supply was tightened enough to control the inflation, consumption and investment would be discouraged, and the result would be a further increase in unemployment.

EASY MONEY

During a recession when the rate of unemployment is high, the appropriate monetary policy to follow is to increase the money supply in order to encourage an increase in consumption and investment so that some of the unemployed may be put back to work, and the level of national income may rise. The central bank, to signal its intent to pursue an easy money policy, could lower the Bank Rate. It should also make sure that the chartered banking system has adequate reserves, through such devices as buying bonds in the open market, switching government accounts out of the central bank to the chartered banks, and perhaps, lowering the secondary reserve ratio. When money is plentiful, banks will charge less for its use; the reduced interest rate will increase the availability of credit and, hopefully, consumers will be encouraged to buy more, and businessmen will be encouraged to invest more.

In a serious recession, however, an easy money policy may do little to bring about an increase in investment. Banks may be quite prepared to lend at low rates of interest, but businessmen may not want to borrow. One of the important factors influencing the businessman's anticipated rate of return is the economic outlook. In a recession, when prospects are anything but bright, the expected rate of return on an investment may itself decline, offsetting any encouragement that may come from the drop in the interest rate. Moreover, in a recession there is likely to be unemployment, not only of labour but also of capital; and if there is already excess capacity, the businessman's expected rate of return on new investment is likely to be zero. Thus, some economists argue that decreases in the rate of interest are likely to be a relatively unimportant factor in helping check a recession.

There are other economists who argue that interest costs are an important factor in influencing at least certain kinds of investment. For example, reductions in the rate of interest make a difference in the size of the monthly or yearly mortgage payments an individual will have to make and may have an important influence on the size of house he can afford to build. Then, too, if the cost of using money is low enough, such projects as the Chignecto Canal in the Maritimes or the Richelieu Canal in

Quebec may become economically feasible.

Even those who feel that a low rate of interest may not be too effective in stimulating investment and consumption still advocate an easy money policy in time of recession to ensure that banks have plenty of reserves to lend to those who are willing to borrow at low rates. That is, the central bank should do what it can to *encourage* an increase in consumption and investment even though it cannot *force* the community to borrow and spend.

PROBLEMS IN USING MONETARY POLICY

Forecasting The effectiveness of monetary policy is only one of a number of problems the monetary authorities face in using the tool. Another problem is forecasting. Accumulating statistics takes time, and as a result, statistics for many time series are not very recent. While we may know where the economy was four or five months ago, we do not know precisely where it is now. Moreover, when statistics for the large number of indicators necessary to make a good forecast are assembled, one inevitably finds that they are not all pointing in the same direction: some are moving up, others are moving down, and some are not moving at all. It is difficult enough to tell where the economy is at any given time; it is even more difficult to tell where it is going even though forecasting techniques are improving steadily and the computer is making possible many refinements. Since the timing of corrective measures in both monetary and fiscal policy is crucial, our inability to see ahead with certainty creates serious problems for achieving the goals of full employment, stable prices, a viable balance of payments position, and an appropriate rate of growth.

Time Lags There may be a lag between the time a problem occurs and the time it is recognized, and between the time it is recognized and the time monetary policy is actually implemented. This lapse in time comprises what is sometimes called the *inside lag*. There is also the *outside lag*—the time that elapses between the implementation of the policy and its effect on businessmen and consumers. Assume, for example, that the Bank of Canada sells bonds in the open market. If the chartered banks resist this attempt to decrease their reserves by letting some of the maturing securities "run off", and if businesses and individuals respond to the situation by cutting down on the amount of money they normally hold in the form of currency and depositing it instead (so that the banks have more reserves), then it may be some time before the effects of monetary policy are felt. On the other hand, if the central bank's actions have an adverse effect on public opinion, and if optimism turns to pessimism overnight, the effect may be very sudden. No one knows how long the lags will be. If they are very long, then the full effect of a tight money policy may be felt at a time when money should be made easily available again.

Because of the variability and unpredictability of these time lags, some economists (perhaps the best known being Professor Milton Friedman) have argued that the economy would be better served if the discretionary element in monetary policy was eliminated. Instead, the money supply should be increased at a specified rate—somewhere between 3 and 5 percent annually—about equal to the rate of growth in real output.

Disparities in the Economy　An important economic problem in Canada is that not all regions are equally well off. For example, while central Canada may be experiencing economic prosperity, the Atlantic Provinces may be suffering from a high rate of unemployment. Monetary policy is a blunt instrument that makes its influence felt over the entire economy rather than in a particular region. Thus, if restraint is needed in Ontario or B.C. but not in the Atlantic Provinces, it is only natural to expect the latter to fight the tight money policies that are likely to aggravate their economic problems.

There are disparities of another kind in the economy: disparities between the abilities of investors to get funds. Not all companies depend on banks. Some are profitable enough to finance expansions out of undistributed profits, and a tight money policy will not prevent them from using their funds for investment. Others may be able to borrow funds from financial institutions such as insurance companies and trust companies. Some borrowers can go to outside sources—the New York market, for example. American subsidiaries may be able to get funds from their parent companies. Even among those who depend on banks for funds, the effects of tight money may not be uniform. Small borrowers often complain that when money is tight, they are discriminated against, while the larger customers who do a lot of business with the banks get preferred treatment.

Interest Payments on the Public Debt　When money is in tight supply and the cost of using it rises, the interest charges on the national debt increase. The federal government is a large borrower: not only does it borrow to finance new projects, but also to refinance issues that are maturing. When interest rates increase, then interest payments on newly floated government bonds must also increase because these bonds must be attractive enough to compete for customers in the open market. This is a problem that the Bank of Canada, the government's fiscal agent, must bear in mind when it formulates and implements monetary policy.

The Capital Inflow   A tight money policy means a high rate of interest. If the Canadian rate is higher than the American rate, then Canadian securities will look attractive to American buyers, and there may occur a large enough inflow of funds from the United States to influence Canada's balance of payments.

This issue gained prominence when James Coyne was governor of the Bank of Canada. At the end of the 1950s and the beginning of the 1960s, Canada had a very large trade deficit: imports were much in excess of exports. Mr. Coyne made statements about Canadians living beyond their means and the necessity of tightening their belts. However, one of the major causes of the unfavourable balance was Mr. Coyne's policy to keep money tight: the interest rate was considerably higher than that of the United States, and as a result, large amounts of American money capital flowed in to take advantage of the relatively attractive return on Canadian securities. At the same time, Canadian businessmen as well as provincial and municipal governments who wanted to borrow funds looked for the lowest interest rate available; as a result many issues were floated in New York. This reinforced the inflow of money capital into Canada. Canadians who sell securities on American markets do not want American dollars: they need Canadian dollars to spend in Canada; thus American dollars have to be sold in the foreign exchange market to purchase Canadian dollars. The great demand for the Canadian dollar in this period drove its price up until by late 1957 it had reached a premium of almost 6 percent: it cost more than $1.05 in American funds as compared with the 92.5 cents it was pegged at from 1962 to 1970.

When there is a premium on the Canadian dollar, export industries suffer. Foreigners buying Canadian goods pay not only the domestic price but also the premium for the Canadian currency. Consequently, the prices of Canadian goods in the world market rise and sales decline. Some commodities like newsprint are sold in the world market at world prices. When the Canadian dollar was at a premium, the newsprint companies that converted their earnings into the Canadian funds they needed to pay their Canadian workers and suppliers found that every American dollar gave them only about 95 cents in Canadian money. Their profits fell accordingly, and a lower rate of profit discouraged exports. At the same time, a premium on the Canadian dollar meant that the prices of imported goods became more attractive as compared with the prices of competing goods produced in Canada. As a result, consumers were encouraged to increase their purchases of foreign-produced goods.[4] In effect, the tight money policy in Canada at that time taxed exporters and subsidized consumers of imported goods. Thus, it was not surprising that with imports far exceeding exports, the problem grew to crisis proportions, and emergency measures had to be taken in June 1962.

A question that became an important part of the great debate during that time was whether Canada could afford to have a monetary policy independent of that of the United States. The experience of that period seems to suggest that Canadian monetary policy cannot safely get too far out of line with that of the United States. If Canada attempts to follow a monetary policy tighter than that of the United States so that interest rates rise high enough to attract American money capital, then this capital inflow may cause balance-of-payments problems for Canada.

Applied long and firmly enough, monetary policy can be used to restrain a boom. But it is such a blunt weapon that even if properly timed, it must be used with great care lest it go too far and precipitate a recession, increase unemployment, and cut down on the rate of growth. In a recession, if we are looking for a method of getting unemployed factors of production back to work, we are unlikely to rely solely on monetary policy. Help may be needed from fiscal policy involving government expenditures and revenues. Monetary and fiscal policies should complement each other: either one alone may not be sufficient.

Fiscal Policy

Fiscal policy, which involves government expenditures and taxes, hits voters in a place where they are likely to be most sensitive—their pocketbooks. Major controversies rage around this area of vital public interest in Parliament, in the press, and on the street. The fundamental ideas of fiscal policy are not difficult to comprehend. If the level of spending (effective demand) by the private sector is too low to permit the economy to achieve its potential output, then the government should step in and either do some spending itself (act directly to increase the payments stream) or else take measures to encourage private spending. If the government is deliberately spending in order to stimulate the economy, then it seems logical to suggest that it should not offset the effect of that spending by financing

---

[4] Assume, for example, that a domestic and an imported vacuum cleaner both sell for $100. If the Canadian dollar goes to a premium, the price of the domestically produced machine will not change, but the imported product can now be purchased for less—for about $95 in the case of the premium we discussed above. Such reduction in price will encourage some buyers to switch to the foreign product.

it with new or increased taxes: the government should *borrow* rather than tax—that is, it should incur a deficit and increase the public debt.

Rather than adopt the policy of affecting the payments stream by its own spending, the government may follow a less direct approach to the problem of increasing aggregate demand. It may lower the level of taxes (without reducing government expenditures) so that the after-tax revenues of consumers and businesses will be increased. With more revenue, it is almost inevitable that consumers and businesses will spend more and, directly or indirectly, bring about an increase in employment and output.

On the other hand, if the economy is in a situation in which its resources are fully employed and if the level of private spending is so high that inflation is a threat, then as far as possible the government should limit its own spending. In times of excessive demand, its objective should be to have its revenues *exceed* its expenditures. This may involve not only limiting its own expenditures, but also increasing taxes in order to attempt to bring about a decrease in consumption and investment by the private sector, and thus relieve the pressure of demand on the scarce resources.

The view that a government should deliberately unbalance its budget in order to help the economy achieve its goals with respect to employment, prices, and growth is in stark contrast to the view of classical economists that the government should not interfere with the operation of the economy. According to the arguments of the classical economists, the economy, left to itself, would return to a position of full employment. Before the 1930s, almost no one questioned the wisdom of balancing the federal budget every year. Sometimes a government did not manage to achieve a balanced budget, but if it failed, it was always very apologetic about it. However, in the midst of the depression of the 1930s, it became impossible for governments to balance budgets, hard as they tried, and an increasing number of economists, led by John Maynard Keynes, began to argue that it was a good thing that they could not. The budget does not have to be in balance on a weekly or monthly basis, so why should the government try to balance it every March 31? Why not balance it over two years? or five? Better still, why not balance it roughly over the length of the cycle? Or why not aim for a balanced budget at a level of income where the economy would be operating at its *potential* output, with no unemployment and no production gap?

The Canadian government officially accepted the validity of this approach more than thirty years ago when it published the White Paper on Employment and Income. It recognized that to achieve the objective of a high and stable level of employment and income, the government would have to be prepared to run deficits or surpluses as the economic situation required. This view seems to have gained some acceptance in this country although successive governments have consistently felt obliged to explain their surpluses or their deficits.

THE BUDGET

Expenditures by provincial and municipal governments are important in the economy; but when the problem centres around the deliberate balancing or unbalancing of a budget for the sake of stabilizing the economy, then our attention must be concentrated on the budget of the government that controls the money supply—the federal government.

To many people, the budget means budget night when the Minister of Finance informs an attentive House of Commons, assembled for a post-dinner session, of the changes in taxes that are to be implemented in the coming year. However, it comprises much more than just the budget speech, though this is one of the most important budgetary documents. Like any budget, it has two sides, expenditures and revenues; and it consists of a number of documents.

Expenditure Estimates   The main estimates of expenditure are drawn up by the various government departments many months before they are passed by the House of Commons. These estimates reach Parliament after a long journey through the individual departments and through the Treasury Board—a powerful committee of Cabinet ministers that acts as a watchdog on expenditures and plays a key role in determining Canada's financial policy. After clearance by the Treasury Board and, finally, by the Cabinet, the estimates are presented to the House of Commons (sitting as the Committee of Supply) by the appropriate department minister. Because the main estimates are drawn up far in advance of the time the money will actually be needed and spent, some errors and omissions are inevitable; therefore there are provisions for *supplementary* estimates and even *further supplementary* estimates. The House of Commons considers all estimates, and ultimately all of the individual votes are combined into an Appropriation Bill which, when passed through Commons and the Senate, becomes law. Expenditure estimates take up a considerable amount of Parliament's time—so much, in fact, that some of the reforms proposed for the House of Commons include having the estimates thoroughly studied by a small working committee rather than in detail by a Committee of the Whole House.

The budgetary expenditures of the federal government were estimated at $35 billion in the fiscal year that ended in March 1976, more than triple the expenditure of a decade before. The largest amounts of money in the government budget were spent on health and welfare (almost 29 percent of total budgetary expenditure; and this figure included Old Age Security Pensions but not payments under the Canada Pension Plan), public debt charges (11 percent), and defence (under 9 percent). Other government departments accounted for a much smaller percentage of expenditures: public works, for example, accounted for only a little over 2 percent.[5]

Revenue Estimates Revenue estimates and proposals for changes in the various revenue bills appear only in the budget speech delivered by the Minister of Finance. The revenue provisions have traditionally been announced on budget night by the Minister of Finance, after all stock markets—those most sensitive of financial institutions—have closed, and when most business has ended for the day, so that no one can rush out to try to circumvent or take advantage of the new tax provisions.

Quite apart from the information it gives about tax changes, the budget speech is a valuable document because of its review of the economic conditions of the country and of the government's operations of the previous year and because of its forecasts of revenues. The Budget White Paper that accompanies the speech is an important source of economic information and statistical data on the Canadian economy.

The major sources of federal government revenue are personal income tax and corporation income tax. These two account for about 60 percent of the government's total budgetary revenue. The sales tax accounts for over 10 percent. The balance comes from excise taxes, customs and excise duties, oil export charges, and non-tax sources.[6]

The Various Budgets Federal government budgeting is a big, complex operation, and its complexity is compounded by the fact that revenues and expenditures are calculated on several different bases. We have been discussing *budgetary revenues and expenditures*. These budgetary accounts cover the largest part of the government's operations, but there are some important non-budgetary items such as Old Age Security, the Canada Pension Plan and unemployment insurance which are accounted for separately and which traditionally have not been consolidated to provide an overview of total government activities. Since 1964, the Minister of Finance has also presented his budget on a *national accounts* basis, the form favoured by economists because it provides a better means for studying

---

[5] Canadian Tax Foundation, *The National Finance 1975-76* (Toronto, 1976), pp. 26-30, and 1976-77.

[6] *Ibid.*

the impact of the budget on the entire economy. As its name suggests, this approach takes into account those revenues and expenditures that would appear in the national accounts. A government purchase of existing capital or land, for example, is omitted, whereas Old Age Security taxes and payments, employee and employer contributions to the Unemployment Insurance Fund, and Unemployment Insurance Fund benefits are included.

One can also look at the government's *cash* budget, which is different again. It takes account of *all* inflows and outflows of federal funds, including borrowing on the revenue side and loans to government agencies such as the Central Mortgage and Housing Corporation on the expenditure side. These items do not appear in either of the other two sets of accounts.

STABILIZERS

Taxes and expenditures provide the federal government with its tools of fiscal policy. These tools can be of two general kinds. First of all, there are stabilizers that automatically go into operation without any action on the part of the government; they have been built into the economy by previous actions of Parliament and they automatically go to work to provide corrective influences. Such stabilizers automatically contribute to surpluses in periods of prosperity and to deficits in periods of slack. As one might expect, they are called *automatic* or *built-in* stabilizers. In addition, there are the stabilizers that go into operation only after Parliament has enacted a law putting them to work; these are called *discretionary* stabilizers.

Stabilizers in the Private Sector   Our prime concern is government stabilizers, but there are stabilizing forces in the private sector, too. The fact that consumers are reluctant to alter their buying habits acts as a stabilizer: when their incomes drop, consumers tend to do their best to maintain their standard of living. On the other hand, if incomes rise sharply, consumers do not react immediately; they change their buying patterns relatively slowly. This has a stabilizing influence on national income.

Contracts that extend over a number of years also act as stabilizers: the two-year lease on the apartment you rent, or the mortgage payments that are fixed for five years stabilize the payments of some groups and hence the incomes of other groups for that period of time. Corporation dividend policies tend to act as stabilizers, too, for even when profits fluctuate, companies try to keep dividend payments to shareholders fairly stable and allow the retained earnings of the company to fluctuate.

Built-in Government Stabilizers One important built-in stabilizer in the government's revenues is the progressive personal income tax structure, which requires an individual to pay to the government successively higher portions of additional increments of his income. The higher incomes rise, the greater the percentage (not merely the greater the absolute amount) that goes to the government. The lower incomes fall, the smaller the government's relative share; in other words, the government gets a smaller percentage of a smaller income.

Taxes on luxuries like jewelry are built-in stabilizers: when incomes fall, the purchase of luxuries declines, and the government's revenues from this source also decline. In prosperous times when people are buying more luxuries, government revenues increase accordingly. Another automatic stabilizer on the revenue side is payments into the Unemployment Insurance Fund: they decrease with a decline in employment and increase when employment is high.

On the expenditure side, too, there are outlays that vary *inversely* with changes in national income. That is, when national income increases, these expenditures automatically decrease; conversely, in times when national income is falling, there are expenditures that increase without any deliberate action on the part of the government. Disbursements from the Unemployment Insurance Fund are one of the best examples: when employment is falling, more people become eligible for unemployment insurance, and there occurs an immediate increase in government outlays. Welfare payments that are tied to need can also be automatic stabilizers: in a recession when many are out of work, more people qualify for such assistance. Relief payments and some of the government's payments to the blind and to widows under the Canada Assistance Plan fall into this category. Another kind of payment that works as an automatic stabilizer is price supports, which are paid to farmers on some of their products. When national income falls, prices of farm products are likely to fall; if they fall below the support price, there will be increased government payments to the agricultural sector, and these will help to stabilize the income of farmers.

Advantages and Disadvantages of Automatic Stabilizers There are advantages to stabilizers that have been built into the economy, for one of the biggest problems facing those responsible for fiscal policy is when to do what. Deliberate decisions to enact fiscal policy involve deciding how the economy's actual output compares with its potential and where the economy is going. Inevitably there will be time lags between recognizing the need for policy and implementing that policy, and between the time of its implementation and the time its effects are felt. Timing is as much of a problem for discretionary fiscal policies as it is for monetary policy. Automatic stabilizers, however, have the great advantage in that they eliminate the necessity for forecasting. They respond immediately to changing conditions in the economy without any of the intervening time lags. Moreover, with built-in stabilizers, it is much less apparent to businessmen that the government is indulging in what many of them regard as meddling with the economy. Thus, they do not have the adverse effect on the business climate that deliberate actions may have.

Since they seem to be such good devices, it is logical to ask why we do not build in all kinds of automatic stabilizers and just forget about the discretionary ones. The problem is that all of the expenditures that can practicably be made into automatic stabilizers may not be enough to get the economy out of a serious recession. Furthermore, unique situations may arise for which these expenditures are inadequate or inappropriate. In such cases we also need discretionary stabilizers.

Discretionary Stabilizers Discretionary stabilizers involve deliberate policy decisions on the part of the government in the light of actual and expected economic conditions. On the revenue side, the government can alter tax *rates* in such a way as to help stabilize the economy. If there is excessive demand and if inflation is threatening, tax rates should be increased so that less money is left in the hands of individuals and businessmen for consumption and investment. The government may alter tax *exemptions*: instead of allowing the first $1 700 as a tax-free exemption, the government might cut the exemption down to $700 or $800. This would mean that individuals would then be paying more taxes and, therefore, would have less money available for consumption. On the other hand, if the government wanted to encourage consumption, it might raise the basic exemption to, say, $2 500.

Another action that the government can take to encourage expenditure by the private sector is to vary the rate at which it will permit businesses to "write off" their investment in plant and equipment. High allowable rates of depreciation mean a higher rate of return on a new investment and thus encourage investment in general.

The discretionary stabilizers that we have mentioned so far act indirectly on the payments stream. By decreasing its own revenues, the government leaves more money in the hands of individuals and businesses in the hope that consumption and investment will increase and hence, that output and employment will increase because of the extra spending by the private sector. Government expenditures, on the other hand, provide a direct method of increasing the national income flow. If the government increases its spending on public works, that extra expenditure represents an addition to the payments stream. Extra government spending, if it is to have the desired effect, must be a *net* increase: it must not cause an offsetting drop in private investment or in consumption. This means that the government should not finance the investment out of new taxes, for that money, left in the hands of individuals and businessmen, might have been used for consumption or for investment. Nor will the addition to the income stream be net if the government invests in something that the private sector would otherwise have invested in, or if its spending creates a climate that is unfavourable to investment so that businessmen cut back on *their* investment.

Other government outlays that can be used as a discretionary stabilizer are the so called transfer payments such as Old Age Security, family allowances, and various other welfare payments. In times of high unemployment and low demand in the economy, the government can increase individual incomes by increasing these transfer payments. The problem, however, is that such actions are likely to be a one-way street: increases, once given, cannot easily be taken away. It would be politically inexpedient to cut back on such payments in times of prosperity; imagine the public outcry if, even at a time when inflation was a serious problem, the government proposed to *cut* the payment to the elderly by $10 a month! This suggests that if transfer payments are to be altered as a deliberate policy measure, then the ones chosen for this purpose should be those that vary inversely with national income—those that already act as automatic stabilizers, such as unemployment insurance and welfare payments based on need.

In 1966 the Canadian government, under strong pressure to increase pensions, chose not to increase them across the board but to offer a Guaranteed Income Supplement which ensured a minimum monthly income of $105, subject to upward adjustments in step with the cost of living, to those who received Old Age Security payments. The program went into effect in 1967. By 1976 the guaranteed monthly income had more than doubled, and more than half of those who got the basic pension were eligible for the income supplement. To a degree at least, such payments will tend to vary inversely with national income and hence act as a stabilizer, since in times of recession there will be an increased number who will be eligible for a supplement.

PROBLEMS OF USING FISCAL POLICY

There are problems associated with the use of fiscal policy, just as there are problems associated with the use of monetary policy. Some of the problems, in fact, are the same.

We have already mentioned lags and timing as a problem. The time lags in implementing fiscal policy may be even longer than those involved in monetary policy. The budgetary process itself is a slow one, much slower than the process of changing the interest rate or deciding to operate in the open market. Once the decision has been made to implement a policy, it takes more time to get a causeway or an irrigation dam under construction than it does to buy bonds in the open market.

The lags in spending on public works can be very long. Plans must be drawn and blueprints made. Often land must be acquired. Tenders must be let and contractors must be given time to study the specifications and submit bids (unless, of course, patronage is used). Only after contracts are awarded can men be hired and by that time the economy may be facing the problem of inflation rather than unemployment.[7] The time lag might be reduced if the government has a shelf of projects with the plans and blueprints already made and the project ready to go. But even then, it would not be easy to bring about a rapid increase in the expenditures flow because there is still the outside lag—the time it takes to let tenders, award contracts, hire the men, get the construction started, and raise the employment on the site to a level high enough to be of significance. The larger the project, the longer the lag tends to be.

Another major complication in using fiscal policy is the fact that government expenditures and revenues are influenced by many considerations, stabilization being only one of them. If by happy coincidence these other considerations—political and social demands, for example—also encourage spending and cutting taxes at a time when this is the appropriate stabilization policy, then all is well. But if there is a conflict between the interests of stabilization policy and other reasons for spending, then the success of fiscal policy will depend on the government's willingness to give stabilization policy priority. From the point of view of a nation's economic health, it would be better if all elections, especially at the provincial and municipal levels, could be held during periods of recession.

A further limitation on using government expenditures to achieve stability is the fact that there is a limited part of total federal spending that can be deliberately varied for stabilization purposes. The total expenditure by the public works department, for example, is not much more than 2 percent of the federal government's budgetary accounts, and much of this cannot be varied. The government cannot very well alter defence expenditures or civil service salaries in response to fluctuations in

---

[7] The administration of one Canadian city was apparently so concerned about these lags that it had the successful contractor move his equipment onto the site the day *before* the tenders were opened.

the economy; and while investing in post offices and opening up new federal parks may be helpful, these projects are unlikely to involve expenditures large enough to pull the economy out of a recession. The Royal Commission on Banking and Finance estimated that out of a total budgetary expenditure of $6 billion in 1960-61, only $415 million could be varied from year to year.[8] This expenditure, which was on capital projects, amounted to only 5 percent of the total public and private spending on capital formation; the picture is unlikely to be very different today.

The fact that Canada is a federation rather than a unitary state creates problems for fiscal policy. Most public works like schools and hospitals, roads, sewage systems, and urban renewal projects are under the control of either provincial or municipal governments. Together, the junior governments spend more than four times as much as the federal government on construction, machinery, and equipment.[9] In the past, their expenditures have tended to reinforce fluctuations in the economy. The junior governments have money to spend in prosperous times, and often they spend it on capital projects at a time when inflationary pressures suggest that it would be helpful if government expenditures were cut. When a level of unemployment is high and the economy is in a recession, provincial and municipal revenues tend to drop, and this leads governments to cut back on expenditures which, in turn, makes the recession worse.

If expenditures are to provide a useful tool of policy, then cooperation is needed among all three levels of government. The government tried in the postwar period, without success, to find some way of encouraging provincial and municipal governments to reinforce the federal government's deliberate use of spending to help achieve stability. During the Reconstruction Conference of 1946, for example, the federal government proposed planning and timing grants as means of controlling public works. The idea was that provincial governments would plan in advance a shelf of public works projects and the federal government would help defray the costs through "planning grants". These projects could be undertaken at any time, but the amount the federal government was prepared to pay would depend on the economic conditions of the day: if there was inflation, the government might not contribute anything. If, on the other hand, there was a recession, the "timing grants" would cover a substantial part of the cost in order to encourage implementation of the projects. The provinces never accepted the proposals; Alberta and Quebec

---

[8] *Report of the Royal Commission on Banking and Finance* (Ottawa: Queen's Printer, 1965) p. 518

[9] See Statistics Canada, *Private and Public Investment in Canada Outlook 1976* (Ottawa: Information Canada, 1976), Table 34.

walked out of the conference. The Economic Council of Canada recently proposed an investment levy and an incentive program on private construction (excluding housing) to counter booms and slumps in that industry.[10]

There exist possibilities of encouraging provinces and municipalities to spend in order to help achieve the economic goal of stability. The annual federal-provincial meetings of finance ministers and treasurers provide a forum for discussion of the economic situation in Canada and of the appropriate kinds of budgeting at all levels, given those economic conditions. There are also federal grants to provinces and municipalities, and projects that are carried out on a shared-cost basis. These can be planned in such a way as to encourage stability of outlays on construction by the junior governments.

Federalism may also cause complications in the use of tax *revenues* as stabilizers. The rapid rate of expansion of demands on municipal and provincial treasuries has put them in the position where they are constantly trying to find additional sources of revenue. Education, welfare services, roads, and urban renewal are provincial and municipal responsibilities under the terms of the British North America Act; and the rapidly mounting need for funds to finance them is the source of much of the conflict between the provinces and the central government. Thus, there is always the danger that when the central government tries to use a tax cut to encourage expenditure by businesses and consumers, the provincial governments, always short of funds, may simply step in to raise their own tax rates, thus frustrating the stabilization policy of the federal government.

Nevertheless, this area of government revenues offers the greatest possibility for improvement in the use of the stabilization tools. If the government can find methods of shortening the budgetary procedure so that prompt action can be taken to impose, say, a temporary surtax on personal or corporate incomes (like the 10 percent temporary surtax imposed on corporations for the year commencing May 1, 1974) when inflation is a problem, or to increase certain excise taxes, or to grant a fast change on rates of depreciation allowed to businesses in order to encourage or discourage investment, then the effectiveness of fiscal policy can be greatly enhanced. Perhaps such policies might be imposed for only a month or two. The problems of speed and flexibility may not be so difficult to solve when tax *cuts* are in order; it may be politically much more difficult to solve them when resources are fully employed, when

---

[10] Economic Council of Canada, *Toward More Stable Growth in Construction* (Ottawa: Information Canada, 1974), p. S-25.

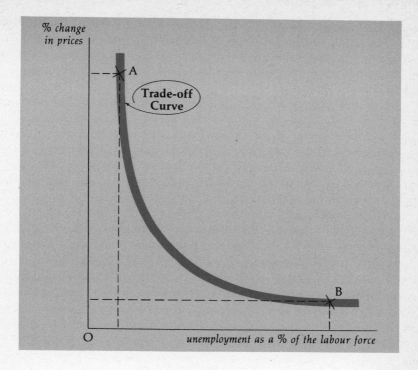

Figure 6-1

inflation is a threat, and tax increases and decreased write-off periods are the appropriate policy.

The Trade-off

Our discussion of monetary and fiscal policies so far may have left the impression that the goals of full employment and stable prices are capable of simultaneous realization. This impression needs to be corrected, for there is a conflict between these objectives. The problem is that there is a trade-off between the two: policies to achieve stable prices can cause an increase in the rate of unemployment, and conversely, policies to increase employment can produce higher prices. Economists sometimes illustrate the problem by means of a graph called a "trade-off curve" or a "trade-off range" that shows the relationship between the percentage change in prices and the unemployment rate. The downward-sloping curve in Figure 6-1 suggests that lower levels of unemployment can be "purchased" only at the price of higher levels of inflation. The cost of more price stability is higher unemployment. Thus, the problem of choosing the optimum policy is the problem of accepting a trade-off between two objectives. The shape of the curve further suggests that as one moves toward either of the extremes, the trade-off between price changes and unemployment rates can be made only at a high cost to the economy. Monetary and fiscal policies, it is to be hoped, can keep the economy away from both extremes of the curve—the one extreme (illustrated by point A) where unemployment is low and where any further decrease in its level can be brought about only at the expense of rapidly rising prices, and the other extreme (point B) where further decreases in the rate at which prices are rising can be brought about only at the expense of a rapid increase in the rate of unemployment.

In the middle range, however, if actual output is below potential and if unemployment rates are high, then expansionary monetary and fiscal policies should help to reduce unemployment and cause an increase in prices that is small compared with the increase that would occur at the upper end of the curve. Conversely, if actual output is not much different from potential and if resources are fully employed, then fiscal and monetary policies designed to restrain the economy should be able to exert a downward pressure on prices and costs without causing too great an increase in unemployment.

More complex problems arise when what is needed is to *shift* the entire trade-off curve down to the left because the economy finds itself in the position where there exist simultaneously a high rate of inflation and an unacceptably high level of unemployment. Measures to cope with such a situation must go beyond traditional monetary and fiscal policies and involve policies related to the achievement of other goals such as growth and a viable balance of payments. The price and wage controls imposed in October 1975 for the first time since the Second World War constituted a policy whose objective was to shift the entire trade-off curve to the left, so that for any given level of unemployment there would be a smaller rate of inflation. We shall return to this problem in the final chapter after we have considered all of the various goals of the Canadian economy.

The Public Debt

We have seen that when actual output is close to potential, when resources are fully employed, and when prices are rising, appropriate fiscal policy requires that the government have a surplus: its revenues should exceed its expenditures. The flow of payments to the government, mainly in the form of taxes, should exceed the flow of government expenditures so that there is, on balance, a leakage from the payments stream (to use the language of Chapter 4) and national income tends to contract. On the other hand, if resources are unemployed and output is below potential, then the government should resort to deficit financing: it should unbalance its budget in such a way as to make its expenditures exceed its revenues. When this happens, the government must find some way to raise money in order to fill the gap between expenditures and revenues. Deficit financing by either the government or indeed, by one's own household gives rise to the interesting question: how can this money be raised?

We have suggested that the federal government always has the option of paying for its expenditures by issuing newly printed currency. The advantage of this is that there are no interest payments to be made on currency. If the government uses the other approach and finances its deficits by borrowing, then it must offer its securities in the market in competition with the securities of corporations and other governments. The bonds of the Government of Canada are regarded as the safest in the market, and therefore, they can be offered at a relatively low rate of interest; but the government still must *pay* people for the use of the money it borrows from them. We said that in the budgetary estimates of the federal government, public debt charges—mainly interest payments— amounted to about 11 percent of total budgetary expenditures for 1975-76. If the federal government printed the money, interest payments would be eliminated, and by far the largest part of the debt charges would be avoided.

The great disadvantage of printing money is the adverse public reaction that would result: it might frighten businessmen and citizens, and the effect on the business climate and public opinion could be drastic. Moreover, if pushed to excess or used at a time when rising prices are a problem, it can cause inflation. The government, therefore, normally borrows the funds with which to finance its deficits. When it borrows to finance the excess of expenditures over revenues, the public debt increases.

It should be noted that the interest on the government debt provides income to the holders of that debt. The Bank of Canada is a very large holder of these securities. If interest payments on the national debt were not available, the government would not save the entire 11 percent of its expenditures; for example, the expenses of the Bank of Canada would still have to be met. Moreover, many retired people who have invested in bonds (or who participate in retirement plans that hold large quantities of government bonds) would find their income reduced, and unless suitable alternative investments could be found, there would likely be many cases in which the government would have to step in to make up for lost investment income

Government deficits caused by efforts to combat unemployment are one major contributor to the national debt. The other major factor is war: no war has ever been financed on a pay-as-you-go basis, and the greatest increases in the public debt have occurred in wartime. Rightly or wrongly, it has always been decided that the sacrifice required to finance a war by taxation alone would be too great: the adverse effect on public morale of the extremely high taxes just could not be afforded by any nation.

THE SIZE OF THE DEBT

Many myths surround the public debt. It is frequently said that at the rate it is growing the debt is putting a staggering burden on us and is likely to drive the country into bankruptcy. Some are convinced that *any* government deficit, and hence any increase in the debt, automatically means inflation. To refute such erroneous ideas we need to have some statistics.

The net debt of the federal government (gross debt minus the Government's assets that offset that debt) is increasing. This is illustrated by the bar graph in Figure 6-2 which shows the debt for a few selected years since 1940. The left-hand bar of each set represents net debt measured in billions of dollars. If we ignore the sudden jump during the war years (the year 1946 in our diagram), the chart shows the debt's almost steady upward trend. The jump between 1940 and 1946 also enables us to see the vast increase caused by the war: it rose by more than $10 billion, from $3.3 billion in March 1940 to $13.4 billion in March 1946. Surpluses during the years of prosperity after the war resulted in a reduction of the debt to $11.3 billion by 1956. Deficits in most years from 1950 to the mid-1970s raised the debt to record levels.

Another way of looking at the debt picture is to divide the total by the number of people in Canada to find the net debt per person. In 1975 it stood at nearly $850 for every man, woman, and child in Canada,[11] not far from three times as high as it was before World War II. Does that mean that the burden on Canadians is three times as great?

The ability of a country to bear a debt depends, first of all, on the size of its income. The same thing applies to an individual. A $25 000 debt for an individual whose income is $2 500 imposes an unbearable burden. That same $25 000 debt imposes a relatively small burden on an individual whose annual income is $100 000. In the case of a country, the larger its national income, the greater the public debt it can carry. The public debt in Canada today is more than seven times as large as it was in the mid-1920s. Are we therefore in a worse position than we were then? The

---

[11] Canadian Tax Foundation, *op. cit.*, Table 9-1, p. 117.

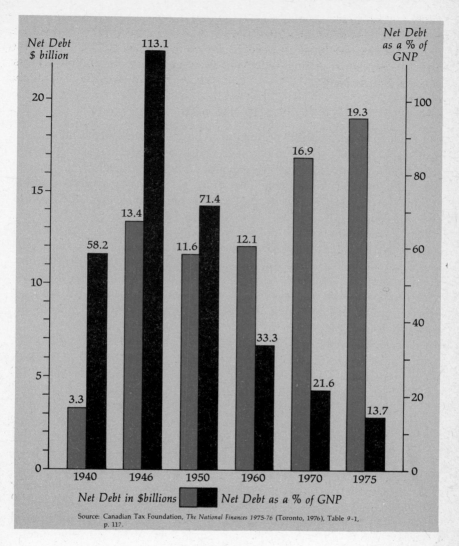

Net Debt
\$ billion

Net Debt
as a % of
GNP

113.1

19.3

16.9

71.4

58.2

13.4

11.6

12.1

33.3

21.6

13.7

3.3

1940   1946   1950   1960   1970   1975

Net Debt in \$billions   Net Debt as a % of GNP

Source: Canadian Tax Foundation, *The National Finances 1975-76* (Toronto, 1976), Table 9-1,
p. 117.

Figure 6-2

answer is no because the level of our income is more than twenty-five
times as high today.

In Figure 6-2 the right-hand bar of each set shows what has been
happening to debt as a percentage of GNP. If we ignore the effect of the
war, which sent the debt skyrocketing to a record 113 percent of GNP, we
can see that debt as a proportion of our national income has been declining steadily. In 1940, the year when total debt was a mere \$3.3 billion,
that debt amounted to 58 percent of GNP. By 1975, when total debt

achieved a new record high of $19.3 billion, it had decreased to 14 percent of GNP. Thus, a rising debt does not necessarily mean insolvency or fiscal irresponsibility: as long as debt is declining *relative to GNP* then our financial position is getting better, not worse, because our ability to carry the debt is increasing.

CORPORATE DEBT VERSUS PUBLIC DEBT

We seem to worry about two kinds of debt: consumers' debt and government debt. Nobody seems to be much concerned about the size of corporate debt. Concern is frequently expressed about the level of consumers' debt, although we know from our study of the national accounts that consumers, on balance, save money: in 1975 personal savings amounted to over $11 billion.[12] Corporate debt is much larger than the debt of the federal government, yet we do not worry about corporations. It does not seem to matter what the borrowed money is actually spent for—building a new plant, designing a new package, or increasing advertising; we assume that corporations are borrowing money in order to generate an increased stream of payments. We assume, in other words, that there is producing power behind the debt that will earn sufficient dollars to enable the company to repay it.

The public debt worries many people, and by implication, these people must regard it as *not* having any earning assets behind it. Yet part of the expenditure that gives rise to the public debt has been made for what we call "social capital" (harbour facilities, airports, roads, post offices, and educational institutions, particularly at the post-secondary level) as well as certain services such as air and rail transport (to the extent that deficits of Air Canada and CN have been covered by the government). It is not accurate to regard social capital as failing to bring forth a stream of payments. Consider the expenditures on higher education, a field in which the federal government has spent a considerable amount of money. Such spending must be regarded as an investment in human capital, and it is a most productive investment. The earning power of an individual is increased by education. Given our progressive income tax structure, the government takes a sizable bite of higher incomes; this means that by investing in education, it is generating for itself a larger stream of payments in the future.

The same thing can be said of other social capital such as harbour facilities, airports, roads, causeways, and dams. Deficits incurred to provide such things are as productive of income and as essential as the cash

---

[12] Statistics Canada, *National Income and Expenditure Accounts, First Quarter 1976* (Ottawa: Information Canada, 1976), Table 5, p. 11.

deficits that corporations incur in order to provide us with their production facilities. National output is a function of both social and private capital formation. The well-known American economist J. K. Galbraith argues in *The Affluent Society*[13] that there is an imbalance in the economy: it is understocked with social capital relative to private capital. National income, he suggests, would increase more rapidly if there were larger expenditures on social capital.

THE CREDITORS

An important question that must be considered in discussing the burden of the debt is, who are the creditors? Canadians or foreigners? In other words, is the debt held internally or externally? Interest payments on the bonds of the federal government amount to more than $2 billion annually. Suppose foreigners owned those bonds: interest payments on them would give foreigners command over $2 billion worth of Canadian goods and services, which would not then be available to Canadian consumers, and would therefore lower the domestic standard of living accordingly.[14] However, less than one percent of total unmatured debt was payable outside Canada at the end of fiscal year 1975.[15]

Because almost all our debts are internally held, there can be no question of bankruptcy, the prophets of doom to the contrary. It is rather like the debts within a family: if Mother runs out of grocery money before the end of the week and borrows from Father, or if Junior finds that the Engineers' Ball is going to cost him more money than he has and he borrows from his sister, then regardless of the size of the debts incurred within that one family as a result of borrowing from each other, the family as a unit will not go bankrupt. The same holds true for Canada. Since the debt is internally held, the payment of interest and the repayment of principal involve transfers from one group of Canadians to another: the money is taken from taxpayers and paid to the bondholders, who are often the same people.

PROBLEMS CAUSED BY THE PUBLIC DEBT

In our attempt to do away with some myths about the public debt, we must not go too far and assume that there are *no* problems associated with

---

[13] J. K. Galbraith, *The Affluent Society* (Boston: Houghton Mifflin Company, 1958). See especially Chs. 18 and 19.

[14] When the foreign debt was incurred, of course, Canadians presumably received goods and services that increased the country's ability to service the debt.

[15] Canadian Tax Foundation, *op. cit.*, p. 118.

it. On the contrary, a large debt does cause problems: the greater the debt, for example, the more money the government will have to raise in order to pay the interest on it. Normally more government revenue means higher taxes, and higher taxes, it is argued, may alter people's behaviour. If the government takes a large part of each additional dollar earned, the incentive to work decreases relative to the incentive to enjoy extra leisure time, and this may discourage people from working as hard as they otherwise might.

If the government resorts to borrowing rather than taxing to pay the debt charges, and if this happens in time of full employment, inflationary pressure on the economy may increase. If inflation occurs, it reduces the value of the dollar so that such an action by the government may be regarded as a method of repudiating part of the debt: creditors will get back dollars with a smaller value (commanding fewer goods and services) than the dollars they lent.

A large debt also creates problems for monetary policy. If there is a tight money policy and interest rates are allowed to rise, interest costs to the federal government will rise accordingly. As bonds mature and the government issues new ones to get funds to repay the principal due on the maturing ones, the new issues will have to carry a higher rate of interest. The larger the debt, the greater the problem; thus, by increasing the debt in order to combat unemployment and underproduction, the government may be creating problems for fighting a future inflation.

The whole question of how to manage the public debt creates a number of problems for the Canadian economy. Should the government try to minimize its costs by issuing bonds only when interest rates are low; or alternatively, should it use its issues and reissues of bonds in a counter-cyclical manner in order to alter interest rates in the short-term or long-term bond markets? The government can affect the interest rate by the timing of its issues, and this makes it possible to reinforce the prevailing monetary policy. There are those who argue that, given the massive size of our public debt, any "manipulation" can upset the sensitive bond market in Canada and, therefore, that no attempt should be made either to minimize costs or to reinforce monetary policy. Instead, they suggest that government bond issues should appear at regular intervals in the market so that the effect of debt management is largely neutral rather than disruptive.

Just because there are problems involved in applying the tools of both monetary and fiscal policies and because there are limits to their usefulness, one must not conclude that these policies are not worth using. There is no one panacea for the ills of instability in the economy, and a broad program that includes a number of different measures is more likely to help the economy to achieve its goals. Moreover, we have had a relatively short time in which to learn to use these tools and to gain public acceptance of their use: the tools were not even tried until after the Second World War. With practice our skill in using these tools should increase.

7

Growth, which is an increase in real GNP per person, entails benefits and costs. Benefits include the possibility of raising living standards (especially the living standards of the poor), and increasing the number of jobs available. As for costs, investment, which fosters growth, occurs at the cost of current consumption when full employment exists. Environmentalists oppose it. Growth also involves change, which is painful for some industries and workers.

An increase in the quantity of resources or in their productivity can cause growth. The expansion of the Canadian labour force, brought about by the postwar baby boom, immigration, and increased participation by women, has promoted growth. Unemployment reduces the growth rate.

Because increased productivity (more output from a given quantity of resources) is the most desirable source of growth, Canada's poor productivity performance, particularly in manufacturing, is a current problem. More economies of scale, research and development, and lower tariffs could raise productivity.

Growth

In the 1950s and 1960s growth was fashionable in economics. Economists devoted a great deal of time and energy to its study and produced a large volume of literature on its benefits and costs, the factors that influence it, the various ways of measuring it, and so on. The emergence of growth as an important goal was attributable in part to a recognition that came during the Second World War and the ensuing years of the cold war that in an era of costly weapons, increasing economic strength was essential to military power and defence. Interest in growth was stirred by the competition between the two great powers, the United States and the Soviet Union, for the support of the uncommitted nations of the world. The success of the Communist system in achieving an impressive rate of growth won a great deal of favourable attention among the underdeveloped nations and drew the attention of democratic systems, with their reliance on the market, to their own growth performance. There was also concern over the growth rates of underdeveloped countries for humanitarian reasons that had nothing to do with the cold war, as well as an interest in understanding why real incomes per person in countries like Germany and Japan were increasing more rapidly than in the United States and Canada.

Growth is still accepted as one of the important goals of the economy; however, more attention is being paid to the costs of growth, particularly the adverse effects it may have on the environment. There is increasingly an agreement that the objective should be to achieve an *appropriate* or *optimum* growth rate rather than to strive for a high or maximum rate regardless of the costs.

The Meaning of Growth

Growth can be defined in a number of ways, and thus it is difficult to find an acceptable measure of it. Growth differs from stability (which we discussed in the previous chapter) because it is a long-term rather than a short-term goal. Moreover, when we discuss stability, we tend to emphasize demand: when demand is excessive, the chief problem of the economy is likely to be inflation; and when demand is deficient, unemployment results. An economy may be unstable, whether or not it is growing; if it is growing, however, the alternate periods of prosperity and recession

143

will take place around a rising trend. Policies to influence the rate of growth are aimed primarily at the supply side rather than the demand side of the economy. Their objective is to bring about an increase in productive capacity, which in turn enables the economy to increase output. The increase in productive capacity is, in fact, one way that growth can be measured.

Sometimes growth is taken to mean an increase in productivity—in output per person employed, or output per unit of capital or unit of land in use. The easiest definition of growth is as an increase in real output per person; hence, a country's growth is commonly cited in terms of the rate of increase in real GNP per person. The disadvantage of this method of measuring growth is that it fails to take into account improvements in the quality of products: a 1970 car is not the same product as a 1925 car, even though both are simply called "cars". It also fails to take into consideration the fact that leisure time per person is steadily increasing. Both of these factors have a strong influence on our general welfare.

The Benefits of Growth

Growth is widely accepted as a desirable goal. It removes the threat of stagnation, which was a great concern to economists after the Great Depression of the 1930s. At that time, economists began to express fears that the economy would become stagnant, that there would be a chronic deficiency in private investment and chronic unemployment of the factors of production. In the stagnation thesis propounded by the eminent American economist Alvin Hansen, it was argued that the great expansions of the past rested on investment generated by three factors: the rapid growth of population, the opening of vast new territories, and innovations. In the 1930s it looked as if only one of these three pillars of prosperity remained —innovations. The rate of increase of the population had slowed down greatly so that there appeared to be no hope of a growing domestic market to encourage large amounts of investment; and there seemed to be no new territories to open. There was no reason to expect that innovations would cease, but neither was there any reason to believe that they would speed up sufficiently to offset the effects on investment of the decline in population growth and the absence of new frontiers. This spectre of economic stagnation at chronically high levels of unemployment provided another incentive to economists to look for policies that would encourage growth and thus avoid the irreplaceable loss of output and the hardship wrought on the economy by continuing unemployment.

An increase in population means an increase in the size of the domestic market, and this provides an incentive for growth. As the population grows, the labour force also expands, and more jobs need to be created to keep people out of the ranks of the unemployed. Moreover, we have come to expect output per person—productivity—to increase; this means that total output (and the demand for it) must expand rapidly enough to keep not only a larger labour force, but also a more productive one, fully employed. One of the benefits of a growing economy is that the number of job opportunities increases rapidly.

An important economic and social problem is the amount of poverty that exists in Canada in spite of its wealth. The pursuit of a just society means that efforts must be made to reduce poverty, and this task is made easier if the economy is growing. Poverty is difficult to define. If we take it to mean some absolute *real* level—a minimum number of calories, enough clothing to keep warm, and subsistence-level housing—then as the economy grows, fewer people fall below this minimum absolute standard, and the amount of poverty is reduced. However, if we define poverty in more subjective terms, such as failure to achieve a decent minimum standard of living, we are likely to find truth in the biblical forecast that the poor will always be with us. As the level of income and standards of living increase, our concept of what constitutes a decent minimum also increases. It is a good question, of course, whether this increasingly affluent poverty will be easier to accept, or will be less disruptive socially than the old-fashioned subsistence poverty.

Clearly, there are benefits to growth, which explains why it is regarded as a desirable objective of policy, and why it became so prominent a goal after the Second World War. However, growth has costs as well as benefits, and before society makes a decision about how fast the economy should grow, the two should be weighed against each other.

The Costs of Growth

Some of the costs of growth can be illustrated on a diagram that we have used before, the production possibility curve. We have already said that investment is fundamental to growth, whether it is investment in new capital equipment or investment in *human* capital—through education, for example. If we measure investment goods along the vertical axis and consumers' goods along the horizontal axis, then the production possibility curve tells us the various maximum combinations of investment goods and consumption goods that can be produced by the economy if all of the factors of production are fully employed. If the economy is at point B in Figure 7-1, then most of its resources are being devoted to the production of consumers' goods: the output of consumers' goods is measured by the distance OC_1. On the other hand, if it is at point A, then many more of its resources are being used to produce investment goods; in this case the output of consumers' goods is measured by the distance OC_2, which represents a much smaller output than before, while the output of capital goods is equal to OI_2 which is much greater than OI_1.

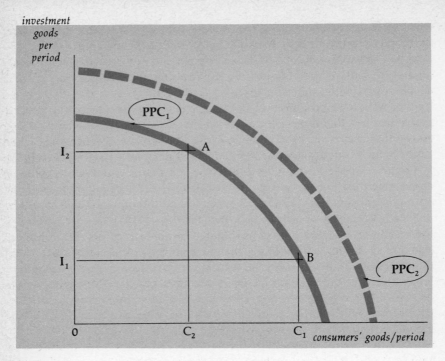

Figure 7-1

The diagram makes it clear that when an economy is at full employment, increasing growth involves sacrificing present consumption for investment. If no extra resources are available for more investment, then resources must be shifted from industries producing consumers' goods to industries producing investment goods. This means that consumers must be prepared to accept lower levels of consumption in the present period in favour of a later benefit: high standards of living compete with growth (high *current* standards of living compete with high *future* standards of living) as objectives in a fully employed economy, and consumers have to be prepared to pay the costs of growth. Growth and current consumption may not be competing objectives if resources are idle (if the economy is *inside* rather than *on* the production possibility curve), for then the actual production of consumption and investment goods is less than the potential. In that case, an effective stabilization policy that puts all factors back to work is likely to increase both current and future levels of living standards.

Present and future living standards can grow simultaneously if we can increase the supply of the factors of production or improve their skills. The production possibility curve that we have drawn assumes a given amount of resources. If we can increase their number or improve their quality, then more can be produced of either investment goods or consumption goods, or both: the entire curve will shift outward—to PPC_2, for example. Such an outward shift in the production possibility curve could be accomplished if the labour force increased through immigration; if people who previously had not been working were brought into the labour force; or if the labour force, though fixed in size, increased its productivity so that the same number of workers could produce more. An outward shift of the curve might also be accomplished if there occurred an increase in the quantity of capital, and this could be brought about if more resources were devoted to investment goods. An economy operating at position A will have a greater outward shift in the production possibility curve in the next period than an economy operating at point B, because more resources are being devoted to the production of investment goods. During the period in question, however, this increase in the output of investment goods would take place at the expense of consumers, who would have to be persuaded or forced to consume less and save more.

Another cost of growth that must be taken into account is the cost of change. Growth involves change, and sometimes it appears to have undesirable results. Canadian railroads increased their efficiency by shifting from coal to oil; but Canadian coal miners, particularly in the Maritimes, suffered because the decline in demand meant that it ceased to be economical to work some mines and many miners lost their jobs. Factories may increase their productivity by automating their assembly lines, but some factory workers may lose their jobs as a result. Although jobs are being created to produce automated equipment, for reasons of required skills or location these jobs may not be immediately suitable to the workers whose jobs were eliminated. Innovations may cause an enterprise to go bankrupt because it cannot, or will not, install new machinery that its thriving rival is using, and the entrepreneur and his entire work force may all find themselves out of work. Sometimes change can make ghost towns out of prosperous communities. Change is a painful process; it creates the problem of retraining people for new jobs, of moving them to places where jobs are available, and of finding alternative sources of income. These are major costs of growth, and they must be taken into account.

Today we often hear about the adverse effects of growth on the environment and on the quality of life. The British economist E. J. Mishan,[1] for example, has loudly lamented the traffic congestion, urban

---

[1] E. J. Mishan, *The Costs of Economic Growth* (Harmondsworth, England: Penguin Books Ltd., 1969), Ch. 1. For strong and reasoned counter arguments to statements made by Dr. Mishan, see Wilfred Beckerman, *In Defence of Economic Growth* (London: Jonathan Cape, 1974). The section where he puts some of the anti-growth arguments in historical perspective (pp. 65 ff.) is particularly relevant in this context.

sprawl, highway blight, absorption of land, and the pollution of air, land, and water, which he sees as costs of growth.

Factors Contributing to Economic Growth

It has been estimated that from the time of Confederation to 1963 real income in Canada grew at an average rate of 3.3 percent a year.[2] Progress during that time was by no means steady; there were periods when real national income increased rapidly and others when the rate of growth fell well below the 3.3 percent average. In the 25-year period that ended in 1975, the annual real rate of growth averaged just about 5 percent.[3] Canada's growth rate between 1960 and 1973 was higher than that of the United States and the average of the six countries in the European Economic Community, where the rate was less than 5 percent, and much higher than that of the United Kingdom, where it amounted to less than 3 percent. However, Japan's rate of growth in the same period was 10 percent.[4]

A considerable amount of attention has been devoted to the two basic factors that contribute to economic growth. First of all there is the increase in productive capacity: in terms of our previous diagram, the production possibility curve has shifted outward owing to an increase in the *quantity* of physical and human resources. The second source of economic growth is the increased *productivity* of resources—that is, greater output per unit of labour or per unit of capital or land used. We know that factors like education, research and development, and the efficiency with which resources are organized affect productivity, but it seems to be impossible to establish precise, quantitative relationships among these variables.

THE QUANTITY OF RESOURCES

When we discuss the productive capacity of the economy, we shall consider the quantity of two kinds of resources—human and nonhuman or physical resources. Physical resources include capital (the stock of productive resources that has been built up as a result of investment in plant and equipment), as well as natural resources. The quantity of human resources is the *labour force*.

---

[2] Economic Council of Canada, *First Annual Review: Economic Goals for Canada to 1970* (Ottawa: Queen's Printer, 1964), p. 13.

[3] Statistics Canada, *National Income and Expenditure Accounts, Fourth Quarter and Preliminary Annual 1975* (Ottawa: Information Canada, April 1976), p. xv.

[4] Economic Council of Canada, *Tenth Annual Review: Shaping the Expansion* (Ottawa: Information Canada, 1973), p. 90.

The Labour Force A rapid increase in the labour force has been one of the major factors encouraging growth throughout much of Canada's history. The total supply of labour (the civilian labour force) is made up of that part of the total population 15 years and older that is willing and able to work for a wage or salary. To calculate the number of people in the labour force, we start with the total civilian population 15 and over (about 16.5 million in 1975) and subtract the number not in the market. The latter includes those who keep house or go to school, those who are unable to work because of age or other reasons, or those who have retired or are idle by choice. The annual average figures for those not in the labour market totalled about 6.4 million in 1975, which left a civilian labour force of 10.1 million. If we calculate the labour force as a percentage of the population 15 years and over, then the result is the *participation rate*, which in 1975 totalled 61.1 percent.[5]

The labour force in Canada has been growing at a rate greatly exceeding that of other industrialized countries, and this is expected to continue until the 1980s. According to one forecast, the growth in the Canadian labour force from 1970 to 1980 will be about 30 percent, as compared with a growth rate in the United States of about 17 percent, and of just over 3 percent in Germany.[6]

The rapid increase in the supply of labour derives from three sources. First, the labour force has been augmented by the higher domestic birth rate and the declining death rate of the postwar period. The products of the postwar baby boom are now working their way through the labour force, and the impact of the dramatic decline in birth rate that took place after the mid-1960s will not be felt until the 1980s. At that time there will likely occur a sharp decline in the rate of growth in the labour force: the Economic Council has forecast that between 1982 and 1985 only about 170 000 Canadian-born workers will enter the labour force annually as compared with about 290 000 in 1974.[7]

Second, the female participation rate (the female labour force expressed as a percentage of the female population of age 14 and over) has risen dramatically since the war. Between 1946 and 1975 it rose from 24.7 percent to 40.9 percent, largely as a result of the growing proportion of married women entering the labour force. The greater number of women in the labour force is closely related to a rapid increase in employ-

---

[5] Statistics Canada, *Canadian Statistical Review, October 1976* (Ottawa: Information Canada, 1976), p. 48.

[6] W. D. Wood, *The Current Industrial Relations Scene in Canada 1974* (Kingston: Industrial Relations Centre, Queen's University, 1974), p. 5-MP-8.

[7] Economic Council of Canada, *Looking Outward: A New Trade Strategy for Canada* (Ottawa: Information Canada, 1975), p. 63.

ment in the service industries as compared with the goods-producing industries. The expansion of the female labour force has been large enough to offset the decline that has taken place in the male participation rate as young men delay entry into the labour market in order to get more education, and as older men retire earlier. The percentage of males 14 years and older in the labour force declined between 1946 and 1975 from an average of 85.1 percent to 77.2 percent. The total participation rate, however, has not changed significantly.[8]

The third source of increase in the labour supply is immigration. In certain periods (the first half of the 1950s, for example) net immigration was *the* major source of increase in the quantity of labour. It is a volatile and unpredictable component which can be influenced by immigration policies, especially if the intent is to limit it. From 1975 to 1985 the Economic Council expects immigration to account for a little more than one fifth of the total increase in the labour force.[9]

An increase in the quantity of labour paves the way for growth in total real output. Moreover, since the labour force as a percentage of total population is growing and is expected to continue to grow, we can anticipate not only that *total* output will rise, but also that total output *per person* will rise. This is important to Canada, for total output per person is a better measure of the material welfare of Canadians. In the postwar period increases in real output per person in Canada have lagged far behind those of many major OECD countries.

THE UNEMPLOYED

It is not merely the size of the labour force that affects the rate of growth because, as we are well aware, not all of those in the labour force have jobs, and therefore not all are adding to total output. When the labour force surveys are taken, some people report that they are without jobs and seeking work; others are not working because they have been temporarily laid off. These people comprise the unemployed.

Unemployment has a number of causes. First of all there is the *minimum*, or *frictional*, unemployment which means that some members of the labour force are between jobs. This situation exists regardless of the state of the economy not because people are lazy, or unwilling to work, or technically incompetent, but because the labour force is mobile: people quit jobs for some reason and move to different ones. When the labour

---

[8] The data in this paragraph are drawn from Statistics Canada, *Canadian Statistical Review, July 1976* (Ottawa: Information Canada, 1976), p. 50; and *Canadian Statistical Review, Historical Survey 1970* (Ottawa: Information Canada, 1973), p. 48. They do not incorporate changes in the revised Labour Force Survey.

[9] Economic Council of Canada, *Looking Outward*, p. 63.

force survey is conducted each month, it is inevitable that a certain percentage of the work force will be out of jobs and seeking work. Mobility is important to the operation of the market system, and frictional employment is something that we must expect even in times of high employment. For this reason it is unrealistic to define full employment as meaning 100 percent of the labour force with jobs.

Unemployment may also be caused by the *seasonal* nature of certain jobs. It can be the result, for example, of some annual events like the shutdown for retooling of automobile plants or the manufacture of seasonal commodities such as Christmas tree ornaments. In the spring, the black flies chase the loggers out of the bush. More important, seasonal unemployment may be related to climate: our cold weather brings to a halt many economic activities such as coastal fishing, farming, and inland shipping. Because workers are laid off in the winter months, unemployment in February or March is always higher than it is in August or September. The seriousness of seasonality has declined in the last decade as industries like construction have developed techniques that enable them to keep their workers on the job through the winter months, but the problem has by no means been eliminated.[10]

Statistics Canada publishes its data on unemployment at *seasonally adjusted rates* so that we can see what the level of unemployment would be if there were no seasonal fluctuations. This enables us to look at *cyclical* unemployment—unemployment that occurs in response to a deterioration in economic conditions rather than the season. It is against cyclical unemployment that the government traditionally uses its stabilization tools; such tools are not effective in controlling seasonal unemployment; easier credit conditions are of no help to the man who is being chased out of the woods by the black flies.

The last kind of unemployment we shall consider may be described as *structural*. In this case, there are job vacancies, but the people who are out of work and looking for jobs cannot be employed because they do not have the necessary qualifications. To cite an example, the computer department of a company may be in dire need of programmers but all that the personnel department has on file is a long list of high-school dropouts who want a job. Structural unemployment also occurs when natural resources in an area run out (when a mine is exhausted, for example) or when tastes of consumers change so that a product is no longer wanted.

While it is relatively simple to sort out the different kinds of unemployment in theory, in practice it is virtually impossible. Structural as well as seasonal unemployment would exist regardless of the economic condi-

---

[10] See Economic Council of Canada, *Toward More Stable Growth in Construction* (Ottawa: Information Canada, 1974), p. S-10.

tions in the economy, but the fact is that a great deal of seasonal unemployment disappeared during the boom period of World War II. Employment in the coal mines in Alberta, for example, had always been highly seasonal, but during the war it became a year-round operation because people, fearing that they would face a shortage later on, bought coal whenever it was available.

Physical Resources   We have mentioned on several occasions the importance of investment to growth. All investment over and above that necessary for replacing depreciated buildings, machinery, and equipment (in other words, all *net* investment) adds to our supply of physical capital and causes an outward shift of the production possibility curve. We have also talked about the two general kinds of capital: industrial capital (such as factories, machinery, pipelines, and so on), which results from investment by business; and social capital such as schools and hospitals. Canada ranks among the most advanced industrial countries in the world in terms of the amount of capital in existence.

Natural resources also constitute an important part of physical resources. There are great disparities in the natural endowments of different countries. A generous endowment, however, does not guarantee a rapid rate of growth. Although Indonesia, for example, is rich in natural resources, its development has been slow, and it still remains a poor country. On the other hand, lack of natural resources does not preclude growth, as in the case of countries like Israel, Japan, and Switzerland which are relatively poorly endowed but highly developed. Nevertheless, natural resources are factors that increase the potential for growth.

Canada is well-endowed with natural resources in the form of minerals, forests, fresh water, oil, and agricultural land. Agricultural land provided one of the cornerstones for much of the country's early growth. This is unlikely to be the case in the future: the importance of agriculture in the economy is declining, and there is not likely to be any impetus to growth from bringing new land under cultivation.

One of the problems of natural resources is that their supply is relatively fixed. It is not completely fixed, however, for we have found new uses for some resources (like uranium for power generation); and technology has resulted in our being able to use others which hitherto have been useless (like low grades of iron ore). We have also been able to improve some of our resources: land through fertilization and forests through reforestation. By and large, however, we must regard the supply as given, and the problem for growth is to find the appropriate rate of exploitation and conservation of the country's natural resources—an issue that has caused serious problems (as in the case of energy resources).

THE PRODUCTIVITY OF RESOURCES

An increase in the quantity of resources makes growth possible. But whether the quantity changes or not, growth can occur if the *quality* of the resources improves, if the resources are combined in a more efficient way, or if human resources become more highly motivated so that a given quantity of them produces a greater output than before. This is what economists mean by increasing productivity: increasing the output per unit of input. Many measures of productivity are possible; they will differ according to the definition of output and input.

However it is measured, low productivity in Canada is a matter of serious concern. The Economic Council of Canada has suggested that in the mid-1970s output per person was more than 20 percent lower than in the United States, and according to some projections, the rate of increase in productivity in the 1970s will be less than that of most other industrialized countries.[11] The relatively high growth rate has been due mainly to the remarkable increase in the *quantity* of labour and capital rather than to an increase in the efficiency with which these factors have been used, or to improvements in their quality or motivation.[12] In contrast, the growth in other countries has resulted mostly from an improvement in productivity. This means that real incomes in Canada are not as high as they should be for a given level of employment, and it raises the question of what will happen to real national income when the effects of the sharp drop in the birth rate are felt, and the large increase in the quantity of labour is removed as a spur to growth.

However, productivity has an importance that goes beyond growth: it is directly related to the cost of output and to the price of products and hence, to the goal of achieving stability. The lag in productivity in the Canadian manufacturing industry is also a matter for concern in the objective of maintaining a viable balance of payments because price performance is important in enabling Canada to compete internationally.

The Productivity of Human Resources Motivation is an important factor affecting human productivity. Obviously, any group that has taken the vow of poverty has no incentive to increase productivity. The less materialistic are our goals, the less productive are we likely to be, and this is

---

[11] Economic Council of Canada, *Looking Outward*, pp. 28, 29, & 74.

[12] This is not true of agriculture where the labour force employed dropped (from almost 25 percent just after the Second World War to under 5 percent in 1974), and total agricultural output rose.

true whether we are talking about workers or managers. Social values and attitudes, then, are an important consideration in productivity. The effect on productivity of attitudes toward material possessions can be seen if we take an extreme case and compare the output of a man raised in a western industrial society with a primitive man who attaches little importance to material things once his minimum requirements have been met. Unlike modern man, the primitive man is content once he has adequate shelter, has enough food to eat, and has found material to fashion some crude clothing for himself. Even within a country we can find variations among different cultural groups that can affect productivity. Different emphasis may be placed on the family and the need for the head of the household to be with them. If there is a strong emphasis on family ties, a worker may not consider accepting a job that takes him away from home; this affects the kind of work he can do, restricts his mobility, and is likely to result in decreased productivity. Research done for the Royal Commission on Bilingualism and Biculturalism indicates that this difference in attitudes exists between the French and English Canadians, resulting in a lower productivity of the former group.

Education increases productivity by enhancing the quality of human resources. It improves workers' skills and knowledge and teaches them how to do their jobs better. It conditions people to accept change and facilitates discoveries and the dissemination of new ideas. Expenditures on education constitute an investment in human capital, and the return on this investment takes the form of higher income for the factors of production. Studies made of earning differentials associated with differences in formal schooling suggest that education accounts for 60 to 70 percent of these differentials.[13] The rate of return on investment in a university education a few years ago was regarded as relatively high—from 11 to 13 percent. Recent report suggest that the rate has fallen considerably: the return in 1974 reportedly dropped to 7 or 8 percent in the United States.[14]

Scale and Specialization   There are ways of improving Canada's rather dismal productivity performance. One is to increase scale and specialization in manufacturing. When a manufacturing plant increases the scale of its operations and produces more of a certain product, the cost per unit declines over a considerable range of output. This is what is meant by "economies of large-scale production" or, more simply, "economies of scale". Obviously, the size of the market has an important effect on

[13] Economic Council of Canada, *Eighth Annual Review: Design for Decision-Making* (Ottawa: Information Canada, 1971), p. 207.

[14] Quoted from *Change*, a journal of higher education, in the lead editorial in *The Gazette*, Montreal, 18 August 1975.

economies of scale. If the market is limited, then the businessman will either build a smaller plant and thus not benefit from the advantages of large-scale production; or if he builds a large plant, he may have to use it to produce a number of products or a number of varieties of the same product. In either case, the size of the production "run" for any one product is likely to be short, and time will be lost in shutting down the plant for changeovers. Moreover, studies have shown that changeovers may reduce workers' efficiency and slow down the rate at which the assembly line moves. These factors tend to decrease productivity.

On the average, plants in Canada are smaller than those in other major industrial countries.[15] In addition, while the range of products produced in Canada is about the same as in the United States, the number of plants producing them is considerably smaller,[16] which means that the length of the production run must be very much shorter. If Canadian markets were larger, productivity would increase: firms could expand their scale of production and reduce the number of production runs. Since the Canadian population is small, the country needs either to rationalize its industry or to look for external markets. Trade is a matter that we shall consider in more detail later, but we cannot ignore it in any discussion of growth. It is argued by a number of economists, as well as by the Economic Council, that Canada does not have access to large external markets because of high tariffs, and that the tariff wall has protected a number of inefficient industries which would either learn to compete or be eliminated by the forces of international competition if tariffs were removed.

Research and Development Advances in technology have contributed to growth by the invention of new and better machines (improving the *quality* of capital), by increasing the skills of the labour force, and by developing new and more efficient ways of organizing the factors of production. In recognition of the important role of research and development, Canada, since the mid-1960s, has taken a number of steps to establish a *science policy* for the country. It set up the Science Council of Canada, an independent Crown corporation whose task is to assess the country's scientific and technical resources and, through its published reports, to make recommendations. It also set up a Special Senate Committee on Science Policy which produced a two-volume report on the subject. In 1971 a separate department, the Ministry of State for Science and Technology, was established.

There exists in Canada the belief that if the market were left to itself,

---

[15] Economic Council of Canada, *Looking Outward*, p. 33.

[16] Economic Council of Canada, *Fourth Annual Review* (Ottawa: Queen's Printer, 1967), p. 154.

considerably less research and development than is desirable would be undertaken. This has prodded the government to step in and encourage indigenous research through three important granting agencies: the National Research Council, the Medical Research Council, and the Canada Council. The government also carries out in-house research through organizations like the Atomic Energy of Canada and the Departments of Industry and of Defence Production. Many research programs are funded by the Department of Agriculture in research institutes, on experimental farms, and in universities.

To encourage more research and innovation by companies as opposed to governments and universities, the federal government has developed assistance programs like the Program for the Advancement of Industrial Technology (PAIT) and the General Incentives for Research and Development (GIRD). It has also made research and development expenditures deductible expenses under the Income Tax Act.

Expenditures on research make an important contribution to productivity and growth. Canada has lagged behind many of the industrialized countries in these areas, and some have argued that the lag is primarily due to the limited research carried on by the subsidiaries of foreign companies. However, through these same subsidiaries, Canada has ready access to the vast technological research efforts of the United States. Such know-how can often simply be picked up and applied in Canada. What is of prime importance for productivity is not so much indigenous research, but rather *innovation*—putting to work the results of research and development. In this regard, the willingness of management to take the initiative and the risk of putting new techniques to work is crucial. Innovation depends on such factors as the adaptability of management to change and the degree of dedication to what is supposed to be a manager's prime objective—maximizing profits. The degree of competition in the market also influences the speed with which inventions are put to work. If a rival firm innovates and thereby gains a competitive advantage, other firms in the industry, spurred on by competition, will be encouraged or forced to innovate. A note of pessimism is to be found in the suggestion that Canadian manufacturing firms are slower to adopt new processes than are manufacturers in the United States and Europe.[17]

A low level of productivity in Canada has relevance for a number of current Canadian problems. The domestic price level is an example. Wage increases will not exert an upward pressure on prices if they are matched by increases in productivity. In manufacturing, if the great potential for increases in productivity is realized, wages can increase steadily without

---

[17] See, for example, D. J. Daly and S. Globerman, *Tariff and Science Policies*, Ontario Economic Council Research Study (Toronto: University of Toronto Press, 1976).

affecting the prices of manufactured goods. This potential is usually lacking in the *service* industries, where productivity increases are difficult to achieve. The waiter in the restaurant, the barber and the hairdresser, the stenographer and the teacher all want a share of rising national income, but the possibility of financing that share by their increased productivity seems rather remote.

Productivity is also important if Canadian products are to compete in the international market. The foreign price of Canadian goods has two components: the domestic price and the price paid for Canadian dollars (the exchange rate). If higher productivity results in lower domestic prices, then the competitive position of Canadian goods will be improved. Unfortunately, as a result of the very rapid increase in average hourly earnings in Canadian manufacturing since the Second World War, the wage differential that has traditionally existed between Canada and the United States disappeared in 1974. Because there has not been an offsetting increase in the level of output per man-hour in manufacturing, the competitive position of Canadian manufacturers has been eroded. This has adverse implications for domestic prices and employment, as well as for international trade in manufactured products.

Canada's productivity lags behind that of the United States and this disparity is the main reason for the lag in real incomes. It is particularly relevant when one considers the demand of various workers' groups in Canada for wage parity (equality of wages) with their American counterparts. In the Canadian economy, parity in real terms will not be possible until there is also parity in productivity. Wage equality may be feasible in some industries in this country where productivity is as high as in the same industries in the United States, but the problem is that when one group achieves an equal wage rate, others are apt to demand the same treatment regardless of their relative level of productivity. Granting parity across the board without simultaneously closing the gap in productivity is likely to result in inflation, and since the value of higher wages would then be wiped out by rising prices, no change in the *real* economic position of Canadians *vis-à-vis* Americans would result.

At present, we do not know precisely what weight to attach to the various factors that influence the growth rate. Those who want to promote free trade argue that if we just eliminate tariffs, economies of scale will emerge, productivity will rise to the same level as that of the United States, and the income gap will virtually disappear. Others argue that most weight should be attached to education if the gap is to be reduced. Psychologists tend to emphasize the motivation aspect, the respective functions of workers and managers, and the conflict in their roles. Scientists promote technological improvements. All are related to productivity, but there is no consensus regarding the relative importance of each or the importance of interconnections between them.

8

We need some microeconomic tools to understand the theory of setting price. In our first model, we use these tools to set the price of cinema tickets. To maximize profits, the theatre owner must operate at the price and quantity where marginal cost (the additional cost of one extra viewer) equals marginal revenue (the additional revenue from the sale of the extra ticket).

A purely competitive market is one where there are many buyers and sellers, a homogeneous product, and no barriers to entry or exit. Price is determined by market demand and supply. Since price is given, the entrepreneur should try to produce the output at which price (which, in pure competition, equals marginal revenue) equals marginal cost. Profit per unit is the difference between average revenue (price) and average cost.

Pure competition lies at one end of a spectrum of markets. Monopoly lies at the other. Most firms fall between, into oligopoly or monopolistic competition.

Some Microeconomic Tools: A Digression

To help us understand the problems related to the goals of stability and growth we have made use of a few macroeconomic tools such as GNP (and its components) and the money supply. We now come to the point where if we want to discuss other goals such as a viable balance of payments and economic freedom, or if we want to consider some of the problems related to the proper allocation of resources, we must digress and develop some *microeconomic* tools. Many tools of microeconomic analysis are elegant, sophisticated, and for the devotee of the science, a pleasure to work with. The difficulty is that many of them are more elegant and more sophisticated than we need if what we are after is an understanding of the major problems in the Canadian economy. While it is not necessary for our purposes to delve deeply into microeconomic theory, we do need *some* tools with which to build simple economic models that will help explain how the economy operates. Such models omit many of the complexities of the real world and do not give a complete and accurate picture of the economy. However, as long as the assumptions are clear and the model is carefully used, what we lose in terms of reality we gain in comprehension of how a complex economy operates. To understand the effects of government intervention in the market by means of taxes and regulations, we need tools to explain how prices are set in a market economy, as well as tools that will help us comprehend problems like foreign exchange, the role of agricultural price supports, and the energy crisis. We also need some idea of the different kinds of market structures that exist.

Our first task will be to learn how price is set for a single product. We shall begin with a simplified model of a movie theatre. Armed with an understanding of an equilibrium market price for a single product, we shall then be in a position to use our tools to predict what will happen when changes occur in the underlying market forces.

Setting the Price

Consider the case of Mr. Black who, with the aid of a small legacy and a large bank loan, has just purchased a small movie theatre in a prosperous suburb. Since running the theatre is to be a business venture and not a hobby, we can safely assume that Mr. Black's objective in buying it is to make a profit, that is, to have the total revenue from ticket sales exceed the total costs to be paid for the salaries of the manager, the projectionist, the ticket sellers and ticket takers, the ushers and the cleaning staff, the interest on his bank loan, the interest forgone on the legacy which could have been invested in Canada Savings Bonds (which, in 1976 could have earned a return of 9.25 percent), not to mention the costs of his license, insurance, repairs and maintenance, and the rental costs of the films.

COSTS

For the sake of simplicity we shall assume that when Mr. Black took over the movie theatre the contracts for the entire schedule of films had been signed and the rental on them fixed for the next year, and that the staff all had contracts running for a year. These contracts give rise to costs that he cannot avoid: they must all be paid during that year whether one customer or 50 000 come to see the films scheduled to be shown. Like his insurance and interest, they are *fixed costs*—costs that do not vary with the quantity of tickets sold. Such an assumption does not violate conditions in the real world too drastically, and it makes our analysis much easier, for it leaves no costs that *will* vary with the number of customers. Whether only one customer arrives or whether all 400 seats are filled two or three times a day, no additional costs will be incurred: in other words, the *variable costs*—those costs that *do* vary with the number of tickets sold—are zero, given our assumptions. This does not mean that there can be no variable costs; if one of the scheduled films proves to be very popular and there are long queues, Mr. Black may have to hire a security guard to keep the crowd lined up close to the building so as not to block traffic, or he may have to hire an extra usher at peak periods to help customers find seats once the lights are turned down. Perhaps the cleaning staff may have to stay overtime to get all the gum off the seats and the popcorn containers off the floor. However, these are complications that we shall simply ignore.

Given our assumptions, we can say that as each extra customer comes in, from the first to the 400th, who takes the last seat, the *addition to total cost from selling one more ticket is zero*: the extra, or incremental, cost of seating one more customer is zero. This is just another way of saying that until he reaches the capacity of his theatre, Mr. Black's *marginal cost* is zero.

REVENUES

Mr. Black, then, is all set to do business: he has a movie theatre, a staff hired for the next year, other payment commitments that are fixed, a film advertised on his marquee, and a potential audience for his films; as yet, however, he has not posted a price in his box office window. What should he charge? Since this is a business venture, we assume that Mr. Black's objective is to make as much profit as possible, so the appropriate question to ask is, what price should he charge to maximize profits? Total profit is the difference between total revenue and total cost (total profit = $TR - TC$), so his objective will be to maximize that difference. However, if Mr. Black has made a bad investment, his total cost may exceed his total revenue no matter what he does, in which case his optimum price will be the one that *minimizes* his losses.

Even though Mr. Black is not familiar with the movie theatre business, common sense will tell him something about the price-quantity relationship: he will realize that if he charges $15 for a ticket, his prospective audience will number very few. Even if he charges a third of that price he will probably not attract too big an audience. On the other hand, if he charges 25 cents he will probably lure from the street a large number of tired shoppers, or dead beats, a gang of juveniles, and even passers-by who simply want to seek shelter from the rain or use his washrooms: he will probably attract far more customers than either his movie theatre or his washrooms can accommodate. Common sense, in other words, will tell him that his sales are dependent on the price he charges and that they are *inversely* related to that price; that is, the higher the price, the fewer tickets he will sell; the lower the price, the more tickets he will sell.

If we were to draw a picture of that relationship, we would put the price ratio on the vertical or y-axis, and the quantity of tickets sold in a week on the horizontal, or x-axis. The price-quantity relationship would slope down and to the right, as shown in Figure 8-1. Since the price of a ticket is revenue for Mr. Black—his *average revenue*—the price-quantity relationship, which shows the number of tickets he can sell at various prices, is called his *average revenue curve*.

Mr. Black's sales, of course, depend on (are a function of) other factors besides price, such as the kind of film he is showing (the quality of his product) and the condition of his theatre—whether it is old, dirty, and musty, with broken-down seats, or whether it is comfortable, clean, and air-conditioned. Sales are also a function of the weather and of the number of people who know what film is showing. The quantity of tickets sold also depends on what movies are being shown on television or what concerts, live theatre, or sports events are on elsewhere in the community. For the moment, we shall assume that all these other variables do not change, and we shall simply say that sales are a function of price. Our immediate problem is to find out more about that price-quantity relationship.

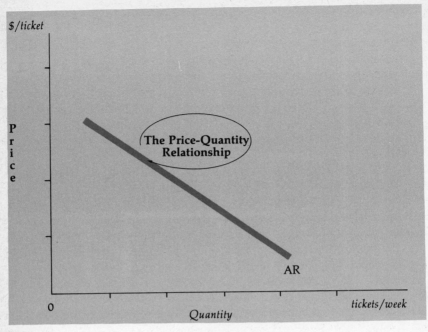

$/ticket

P
r
i
c
e

The Price-Quantity Relationship

AR

0

Quantity

tickets/week

Figure 8-1

Since Mr. Black bought an ongoing enterprise, presumably it was operating the previous week, which means that he should know one point on that price-quantity relationship: the price charged last week and the number of tickets sold. Assume that the price was $3.00 and that 4 000 tickets were sold. How could he establish any other points on that price-quantity schedule? He could make a guess: "If I wanted to sell another 1 000 tickets a week, I'd probably have to drop the price to $2.00." Or, "If I charged $6.50 a ticket I could probably get a few customers, but *nobody* would come at a price of $7.00." Alternatively, he might seek information about a similar theatre in a suburb of about the same size with about the same family income, which actually charged a price of $2.00, or perhaps a different price was charged not long ago in the theatre he has just purchased. One way or another, let us assume that he comes up with some estimates of the number of tickets that could be sold in a week at various prices like those in Table 8-1.

With such a set of prices or average revenues and the quantity of tickets sold at each price, Mr. Black can calculate his total revenue, which is equal to average revenue times the quantity of tickets sold ($TR = P(AR) \times Q$). At a price of $1.00, his total revenue equals $1.00 × 6 000, or $6 000; at $2.00 his total revenue is $10 000, and so on for the rest of the

Table 8-1

Price $/ticket	Quantity tickets/week	Total Revenue $/week
$7.00	0	0
6.00	1 000	$ 6 000
5.00	2 000	10 000
4.00	3 000	12 000
3.00	4 000	12 000
2.00	5 000	10 000
1.00	6 000	6 000

table. It is apparent from the table that Mr. Black must earn his maximum revenue at a price somewhere between $3.00 and $4.00.

THE OPTIMUM PRICE

We have talked about the kinds of costs Mr. Black would incur, but to calculate his profit we need a dollar value for his costs. Assume that his costs amount to $11 000 a week for everything including salaries, film rental, insurance, and so on. We have assumed that these costs are all fixed, which means that he will incur them no matter what quantity of tickets he sells. Knowing his costs and his estimated revenue, we can now calculate his profit. From the total revenue figures in Table 8-1 we can see that at most prices Mr. Black would not cover his costs at all and would therefore incur a loss. At a price of between $2.00 and $3.00 his total revenue would just equal his total cost. However, at higher prices on our schedule (up to a price about midway between $4.00 and $5.00), his total revenue would exceed his total cost, and he would make a profit. What then will be the *best* price—the one at which he can maximize profit? Table 8-1 suggests that the optimum price lies somewhere between $3.00 and $4.00. We can be more precise if we plot the total revenue data and Mr. Black's total fixed costs on a graph.

In Figure 8-2 the total revenue calculated in Table 8-1 has been plotted on a graph which shows *total dollars* a week on the vertical axis (instead of price, which is a ratio—dollars *per ticket*) and tickets per week on the horizontal axis; the points have been joined by a smooth curve labelled *TR*. Figure 8-2 shows that Mr. Black's revenue comes to a maximum of $12 250 when he sells 3 500 tickets. His costs are fixed at $11 000 a week, and this is shown on the diagram by a horizontal straight line at the level of $11 000, labelled *TFC*. Total revenue exceeds total cost by the maximum amount (which means his profit is at a maximum) when ticket

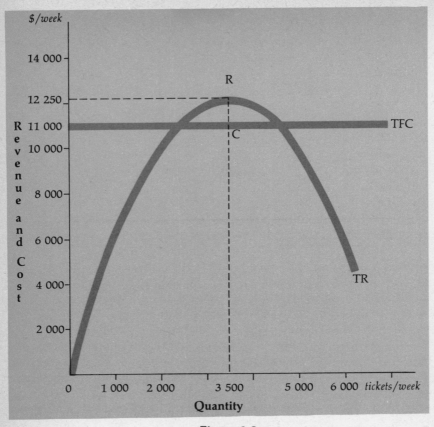

Figure 8-2

sales are 3 500. His profit $(TR - TC)$ is shown on the diagram as CR, the distance between TR ($12 250) and TC ($11 000). The price he should charge for his tickets can be calculated by dividing total revenue by the quantity of tickets sold [price $(AR) = TR/Q = \$12\ 250/3\ 500$]. The optimum price then is $3.50 a ticket.

Marginal Revenue   There are several ways of finding the optimum price, some of them much more sophisticated than the route we have just taken. One of the most useful is to use *marginal* cost and *marginal* revenue rather than total cost and total revenue. Marginal cost, as we already know, is the addition to total cost involved in accommodating one more customer. Marginal revenue is an analogous concept (once again "marginal" implies something additional or incremental). Marginal revenue, then, is the additional revenue from selling one more unit of a product—one more theatre ticket in this example.

Table 8-2

Price $/ticket	Quantity tickets/week	Total Revenue $/week
$4.00	3 000	$12 000
3.90	3 100	12 090
3.80	3 200	12 160
3.70	3 300	12 210
3.60	3 400	12 240
3.50	3 500	12 250
3.40	3 600	12 240
3.30	3 700	12 210
3.20	3 800	12 160
3.10	3 900	12 090
3.00	4 000	12 000

How can these concepts guide us to the profit-maximizing price and quantity? If the additional revenue from accommodating an extra customer is greater than the additional cost, then clearly Mr. Black will increase his profit providing he adjusts his price and quantity and attracts the extra customer. If, however, by lowering the price of his product enough to sell an additional unit of it Mr. Black ends up with an addition to revenue that is *less* than the addition to cost, then such an action will reduce profit, and he should not lower his price. This gives us a rule for establishing the profit-maximizing output: sell every unit for which the marginal revenue (MR) exceeds the marginal cost; sell no units for which the marginal cost exceeds the marginal revenue. This implies, of course, that the profit-maximizing entrepreneur should aim as close as possible for the output at which marginal cost equals marginal revenue. "Operate where $MC = MR$" is a concise way of stating the profit-maximizing rule even though in the real world it may not be possible to get precisely to that output or even to know exactly what that output is.

The next problem is to *calculate* marginal revenue. In Table 8-1, changes in price and quantity were really too large to be used for calculating marginal revenue. We know that the profit-maximizing price must lie somewhere between $3.00 and $4.00, but there is not enough detail in the table to calculate the precise price and output; we solved the problem before by drawing a diagram. Table 8-2 gives some details about what happens to the quantity of ticket sales as prices vary between $4.00 and $3.00.

The built-in assumption in the table must be made explicit: the entrepreneur, in making estimates about ticket sales at various prices, is assuming that if he charges $4.00 *for all tickets*, he will sell 3 000 and earn a revenue of $12 000. If he wants to sell 100 more, he must drop the price of *all 3 100 tickets* to $3.90—not just the price of the extra 100 he wants to sell. While there are a few complex markets in the economy where uniform pricing is not the normal procedure and customers can bargain over price or get secret rebates, this is not the case with Mr. Black's movie theatre: he posts his price in the box office window and everyone (including senior citizens and children) pays that price. He does not sell 100 tickets and then post a price 10 cents lower, sell another 100 tickets, post a lower price, and so on.

According to Table 8-2 Mr. Black has calculated that if he charges $3.70 each for all tickets, he can sell 3 300 and earn a revenue of $12 210 in a week. He estimates that if he drops the price to $3.60 for all tickets he can increase sales by 100 and earn $12 240—an addition of $30 to his total revenue. We have defined marginal revenue as the addition to total revenue from selling *one* more unit, but in our example the addition of $30 to total revenue resulted from the sale of an additional *100* tickets. It is apparent that to calculate the addition to total revenue from a *single* ticket we must divide the change in total revenue by the change in the number of tickets sold. If we use the Greek upper-case letter "delta" (which looks like a triangle) to mean "the change in", then we can describe the calculation in shorthand form: the change in total revenue can be written as ΔTR, and the change in quantity as ΔQ. Marginal revenue, then, is $TR / \Delta Q$, or $30/100$, which amounts to 30 cents a ticket.

Is $3.60 the right price for him to charge? The profit-maximizing rule said that the entrepreneur should sell all units whose marginal revenue exceeded marginal cost; when the price is $3.60, marginal revenue is 30 cents a ticket, and according to our earlier assumption, marginal cost is zero. Can we get marginal revenue closer to equality with marginal cost? If the ticket price is dropped from $3.60 to $3.50, then according to Table 8-2 sales will rise from 3 400 to 3 500 tickets a week, and total revenue will rise from $12 240 to $12 250, a change of $10; marginal revenue ($\Delta TR / \Delta Q = $10/100$) is 10 cents a ticket; marginal cost is still zero. Mr. Black will increase his total profit if he sells 3 500 tickets at $3.50 instead of 3 400 tickets at $3.60 a ticket.

Should he drop his price still further and sell 100 tickets more? At a price of $3.40 Table 8-2 indicates that his total revenue is $12 240: it has *dropped* by $10 with the sale of the extra 100 tickets. This means that the marginal revenue is negative: it is *minus* 10 cents a ticket. A marginal cost of zero is greater than a marginal revenue of minus 10 cents; a price of $3.40 is too low, and profits will fall if Mr. Black sells 3 600 tickets. His profit-maximizing price, then, is $3.50 with sales of 3 500 tickets.[1]

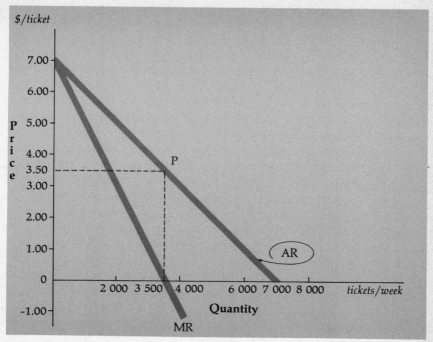

Figure 8-3

A Graphical Solution We can plot the information about average revenue and marginal revenue on a diagram and find visually or graphically the output at which $MR = MC$. In such a diagram the quantity of tickets sold each week is again measured along the horizontal axis and, as in the case of Figure 8-1, price ($/ticket) is measured on the vertical axis. The average revenue schedule, which shows Mr. Black's estimate of the number of tickets he can sell in a week at various prices up to $7.00 (the information in Table 8-2), slopes down and to the right illustrating the inverse relationship between quantity sold and price, as shown in Figure 8-3.

---

[1] If we wish to have a more mathematically precise measure of marginal revenue we can resort to differential calculus and find the marginal revenue at a *point* on our price-quantity relationship rather than over an arc or segment of our function. Even with arithmetic we can test the validity of our choice of $3.50 as the profit-maximizing price. Since the price-quantity function we are using is: $P = .001Q + 7$, it follows that if Mr. Black wanted to sell 3 501 tickets he would have to drop the price (if it were possible) to $3 499, and his total revenue would drop by a tenth of a cent. Although such a price might not disturb a mathematician, it cannot enter into an entrepreneur's thinking. For that reason we shall stick to our cruder measure of marginal revenue.

If we calculate all the marginal revenues that correspond to the increasing ticket sales, we can plot a marginal revenue curve. Since our average revenue curve is a straight line, the marginal revenue curve will also be a straight line[2], which has the the very convenient property, when it comes to drawing it, that it bisects the horizontal distance between the average revenue curve and the vertical axis. For example, when we extend the average revenue curve to the horizontal axis, we can see that it intersects it at sales of 7 000 tickets; the marginal revenue curve, then, will cut the horizontal axis at 3 500 tickets.

With a diagram, it is easy to determine the profit-maximizing quantity of ticket sales. Mr. Black should try to come as close as possible to the quantity at which $MC = MR$. Since we have assumed that marginal cost is zero, the horizontal axis serves as our marginal cost curve, which means that he should operate where the marginal revenue curve crosses the horizontal axis. This occurs, as we already know, at a quantity of 3 500 tickets. Up to this quantity, as can be seen from Figure 8-3, marginal revenue exceeds marginal cost. Beyond it marginal revenue becomes negative and hence is less than marginal cost. The price that Mr. Black should charge if he wants to sell 3 500 tickets can be read from the average revenue curve at the quantity of 3 500 tickets: as indicated by the broken line drawn from the x-axis to point P on the average revenue curve, it is $3.50. To be realistic, we must recognize that once Mr. Black sets that price, his ticket sales will rarely, if ever, turn out to be exactly 3 500 a week: they may be more one week and fewer in another, depending on the weather, the popularity of the film being shown, the competing entertainment in town, and so on. But over time, if Mr. Black was right in his original estimates, they will average to about 3 500 a week. Needless to say, since variables like incomes, tastes, and competing forms of entertainment are subject to change it would be advisable for him to reexamine his "guesstimate" of the relationship between price and sales fairly regularly.

Changing the Offer

Undoubtedly Mr. Black is aware that the total entertainment package he is offering can be varied in a number of ways that will affect the quantity of tickets sold. Instead of keeping a meticulously clean theatre, he can reduce the size of his cleaning staff, cut his costs, and leave the gum on

---

[2] As you may already have noticed, in describing mathematical functions, as in describing women, it is considered acceptable and even desirable on occasion to use the word "curve" when the line in question may be perfectly straight.

the seats; he would expect this to result in a reduction in ticket sales as customers who respond negatively to dirty theatres decide not to patronize his theatre again. He might substitute friendly, attractively underdressed usherettes for ushers. He might stop relying exclusively on his marquee and the pictures in his showcases to let potential customers know what is playing; instead he might advertise, perhaps in the neighborhood newspaper where ads are relatively cheap, or by spot advertising on radio or television, or by putting ads in the large-circulation dailies. Perhaps he can run a sales promotion of some sort: he might give away a set of dishes or a pair of airline tickets to the lucky ticket-holder, or give away a container of popcorn to the first hundred patrons. Devices of this kind will change his offer in such a way as to increase his ticket sales and revenues; they will also increase his costs.

Having settled his first problem of setting the price, Mr. Black begins to wonder whether it might be a good idea to advertise. Before he actually spends any money, he should do a little arm-chair theorizing on how advertising might affect his ticket sales. Without any advertising, and at a price of $3.50 a ticket, Mr. Black has about 3 500 customers a week. He should recognize that in addition to those who actually go to the theatre there exists a pool of potential customers, some needing very little persuasion and others needing a great deal before they actually buy tickets. Some might be planning to go to a movie that week anyway and just need to know what film is being shown at what time; at the other extreme will be those who can be persuaded to go only if the manager himself pays a personal visit and gives a pep talk on the merits of a particular film. His potential customers can, in theory, be lined up in order of their increasing reluctance to buy a ticket. From this, Mr. Black might conclude that if he spends just a little money on advertising he will attract quite a few customers; to increase ticket sales still more, he will have to increase his selling costs, perhaps by a substantial amount. The quantity of tickets sold, in other words, will vary with his advertising costs, and as we already know, costs that vary with sales are called *variable* costs. To increase his sales, he must increase his expenditures on advertising, so the relationship between costs and quantity of sales is a *direct* one. Mr. Black might pursue his armchair theorizing further and come to some conclusion about the *rate* at which he will have to increase his selling costs. Since he anticipates increasing consumer resistance as more and more customers come to his theatre, he might logically expect to spend more and more *per customer* as ticket sales increase.

Mr. Black decides that is now time to test his theories, so he buys a two-column block ad in the entertainment section of the Friday edition of a large-circulation evening daily at a cost of $200. After running the ad for a few weeks, he finds that his sales have gone up to about 3 700 tickets from the previous level of 3 500: he is selling about 200 tickets more, still at a price of $3.50 a ticket, and he has incurred an additional cost of $200—an additional cost of about a dollar a ticket, in other words. Clearly, he has improved his profit position: he is earning an additional revenue of $3.50 on each of his 200 tickets, for an additional advertising outlay of $1.00 per ticket.

Given his success, he decides to run a weekend ad for some time in the morning paper at an additional cost, again, of $200. This boosts his sales to about 3 800 a week—an increase of another 100 customers for the outlay of the extra $200, or an additional cost per ticket of about $2.00. We know that the additional revenue from selling each ticket is $3.50. With an additional advertising cost that works out to about $2.00 a ticket, his extra revenue still exceeds his extra cost, and that means that the ads in both the morning and the evening papers are worth continuing.

The next best possibility seems to Mr. Black to be to try an ad in the evening newspaper on Saturday, as well as on Friday, again at a cost of $200. After trying this for a few weeks, he finds that his ticket sales have increased, though only by about 50 tickets a week, to about 3 850. The *additional* selling cost divided by the *additional* sales ($SC/\Delta Q$) gives us an extra cost per ticket of $4.00 ($200/50). Should he keep running the Saturday ad or not? Every ticket he sells adds $3.50 to his revenue; the extra advertising on Saturday costs $4.00 a ticket. Clearly, if he is interested in maximizing his profits, Mr. Black should *not* continue to run the ad on Saturday.

We can summarize what we have said in a table, and even though the advertising has been done in large lumps, we can still draw a picture to help clarify the ideas. The first column in Table 8-3 shows the *additional* selling cost that Mr. Black incurs with each extra ad. We can also calculate his *total* advertising bill. If he takes out only the first ad, his total outlay will be $200; if he takes out the second, his total cost will be $400— the cost of the first ad plus the additional cost of the second; if he takes

Table 8-3

$\triangle SC$ $/week	Quantity sold tickets/week	$\triangle$ Quantity tickets/week	$\triangle SC/Q$ $/ticket
0	3500		
		200	$1.00
$200	3700		
		100	$2.00
$200	3800		
		50	$4.00
$200	3850		

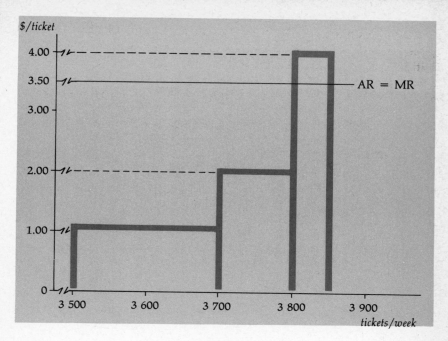

Figure 8-4

out three, then his total advertising cost will be $200 plus $200 plus $200, or $600. In other words, to get to his total selling cost, we must sum each of the incremental additions to cost.

His total ticket sales behave in the way shown in the second column, and we can see that the change in the number of customers (ΔQ) as a result of taking his first ad is $200. When he inserts the second ad, the change in the quantity of tickets sold is the difference between total sales with two ads (3 800) and the total sales with only one ad (3 700), or 100 extra tickets, as shown in the third column. The change in selling cost (ΔSC) divided by the change in the quantity sold (ΔQ) is worked out in the final column, giving us a crude measure of his marginal selling cost.

Because of the "lumpiness" of the expenditures on the ads, the diagram, as illustrated in Figure 8-4, turns out to be a type of bar chart; we cannot really call the "bars" the marginal cost, but they are useful in helping Mr. Black reach the proper decision. The quantity of tickets sold per week is plotted along the horizontal axis, but because we are not concerned now with the first 3 500 tickets which were part of our earlier pricing problem, the horizontal axis shows a break, which means that the section representing the range of 0 to 3 500 tickets has been omitted. The vertical axis measures dollars per ticket and can be used for both revenue and cost.

We have assumed that Mr. Black has already fixed his price (his average revenue) at $3.50 a ticket and has decided to vary a different part of his offer in order to influence his ticket sales. Since the price will not change with successive sales of tickets, his average revenue curve must be a horizontal straight line at the level of $3.50; it shows that no matter how many tickets he sells he will continue to charge $3.50. But such an average revenue curve means more than that: since every ticket he sells at a price of $3.50 yields him an *additional* revenue (a marginal revenue) equal to the price of $3.50, his price (AR) in this case is identical to his marginal revenue; this is always true when the price is fixed and the average revenue curve is a horizontal straight line.

The height of the bars illustrates the data in the final column of Table 8-3 ($\Delta SC / \Delta Q$); their width shows the quantity of tickets sold. By advertising in Friday afternoon's paper, for example, Mr. Black's ticket sales increased from 3 500 to 3 700; he sold an extra 200 tickets at a selling cost of $1.00 a ticket. Notice that the *area* of that bar (200 tickets $\times$ $1.00) amounts to $200—the addition to his costs for the first ad. Clearly the bar showing the extra cost per ticket for a block of 200 tickets lies below his marginal revenue, indicating that it pays to advertise. The same is true of the second bar which indicates that he can sell another 100 tickets if he puts another ad in Friday morning's paper at a cost of $200; it also lies below his marginal revenue curve. If we want to find out what his total advertising expense has been so far, then we must add the area of the first bar to the area of the second: it adds up to $400.

It is easy to see from the diagram that a third ad will not be profitable. The height of the bar is greater than the marginal revenue, indicating that the extra cost of selling each of the 50 seats exceeds the extra revenue. Mr. Black should not spend a total of $600 on three ads; instead, he should stop at two and spend only $400.

We need not restrict our analysis to such big items as large two-column ads at $200 apiece. It is quite conceivable that Mr. Black can use other kinds of ads—like small ones at a quarter of the cost, or short radio spots—and in that way get much smaller increments of selling costs and of ticket sales. If we were to plot such information on a diagram, our bars would begin to look more like bars, and the smaller they got, the more like a curve they would begin to look. We can do precisely the same kind of analysis: if we want to find out how long Mr. Black should continue to advertise, we can see where a bar crosses his marginal revenue curve, and we know that he should not spend money on any ad or spot commercial that puts the bar at a level higher than $3.50—his marginal revenue and also, in this case, the price of his ticket. If we want to calculate his total outlay on advertising up to that point, we should sum the area of all those bars.

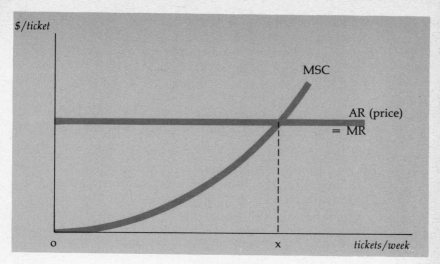

Figure 8-5

If we go one step further in our theoretical analysis and assume that we do not have to think of advertising in discrete steps but can think of infinitely divisible incremental costs and ticket sales, then we can draw a smooth curve like the one in Figure 8-5, which is a marginal selling cost (*MSC*) curve. In this example in which we have assumed that all of Mr. Black's other costs are fixed so that his other marginal costs are zero, this curve actually represents *all* of his marginal costs. The rule for maximizing profits is the same: he should not spend extra dollars on advertising if the marginal cost of selling the extra ticket is greater than the marginal revenue from it. Figure 8-5 suggests that the entrepreneur should continue to spend on advertising until he is selling Ox tickets—the quantity at which $MR = MSC$. We can arrive at his total advertising bill in precisely the same way as when we were discussing the three large ads: sum the extra dollars spent to increase sales by the first ticket, the expenditure for the second, and the third, and so on right up to the Ox^{th} ticket. The total cost of advertising, in other words, is the area under the MSC curve.[3]

In finding out what price Mr. Black should charge if he wanted to maximize his profits, we encountered a number of cost concepts—fixed and variable, average and marginal costs. We also looked at his revenues, both average and marginal. We discovered the very useful rule for an entrepreneur who wants to maximize profits: operate at the output and price at which marginal cost equals marginal revenue; and we found that

---

[3] Those who know calculus will recognize that the area under the curve can be calculated by integration.

the rule still applied when Mr. Black decided to try to increase his sales by spending some money on advertising. The next step is to progress from the example of a single seller to a market comprising many sellers.

The Purely Competitive Market

In the example we have just worked through we were dealing with a market in which Mr. Black did not have too many competitors. There may have been one or two other movie theatres in the suburb as well as those in the downtown area. It is likely, however, that his theatre was the only one showing that particular film. It is apparent that he is offering a *differentiated* as opposed to a *homogeneous* product. In such a market the entrepreneur must solve the problem of setting his own price, and thus of determining the quantity to be sold. The entrepreneur is a *price maker* as opposed to a price taker, and his price is referred to as an *administered* price.

Most prices in Canada are administered. This means that most entrepreneurs face the problem of deciding what price to set, and once the price is set they undertake (as far as is physically possible) to supply all customers with whatever quantity they want to buy at that price. There are a few markets in which entrepreneurs do not set the price: the price is set for them by the market because their output is too small to affect it. In this case, entrepreneurs are *price takers* rather than price makers: the best they can do is adjust their quantity to the price determined by the forces of the market. This manner of setting price is assumed in the economic theory of pure (and perfect) competition.

A number of conditions must be met in order to have a perfectly competitive market. First, there must be a very large number of buyers and sellers: there must be so many producers, for example, that none by himself is large enough to affect price, whether he withdraws his total output from the market or whether he produces the maximum possible. Second, the product must be homogeneous: all units must be identical in the eyes of the buyers. Finally, the market must be easy to get into and out of, with no barriers to entry and exit. These three characteristics are common to both pure and perfect competition. Perfect competition has additional requirements that must be met: the market must be made up of experts with full knowledge of all transactions at all prices, and the factors of production must have complete mobility to enable them to get into and out of the market instantaneously. In summary, the three key characteristics of a purely competitive market include 1) a very large number of buyers and sellers, 2) a product that is homogeneous, and 3) free entry into and exit from the market. If, in addition, there exist perfect knowledge about the market and full mobility of the factors, then the market is described as perfectly competitive.

It is apparent that very few markets can come close to meeting these requirements: the market for blue chip stocks—provided we can keep out the professionals and others who trade in large blocks of stock—is an example. The theory of pure or perfect competition provides a reasonable explanation of how some of the commodity markets—like the sugar market in London where the price of raw sugar for the entire world is set, or the cotton exchange in Manchester, or the livestock market in Chicago—work.

Some of the characteristics of pure competition exist in agriculture. First, there are thousands of wheat farmers, or dairy farmers, or cattle ranchers, none of whom alone is able to influence the price. For this reason, agriculture is sometimes referred to as an "atomistically" competitive industry. Second, agricultural products can be graded—Number 1 Northern Wheat, Grade A-1 large eggs, Grade A butter—and when that is done, although the units are not identical, they come close enough to it to be called a homogeneous product. Third, it is relatively easy to get into or out of farming.

For simplicity we shall not consider the characteristics of perfect knowledge and perfect mobility; instead we shall discuss agriculture as a *purely* competitive (rather than a perfectly competitive) market. Even this classification can be challenged today because of the existence of government bodies like the Canadian Wheat Board, the Canadian Dairy Commission, and the Agricultural Stabilization Board, which intervene in the market to affect price. If we wish to describe the market for agriculture as purely competitive, then we shall have to assume that these government agencies that administer prices do not exist. For the sake of argument, let us discuss the market for butter as if in fact it were a purely competitive market in which there was no subsidy and no Canadian Dairy Commission. This will enable us to develop some of the tools of analysis essential to an understanding of some of our contemporary problems. Our immediate task is to draw a demand curve and a supply curve so that we will know how the market price is set through the free movement of supply and demand.

DEMAND

The demand curve in economic analysis shows the relationship between the *price* of a product and the *quantity* that consumers are willing to take off the market, at a certain price and at a particular time. Demand may be defined as *a schedule of the quantities of a good or service that consumers are willing to buy at various prices, in a given period of time, ceteris paribus* (other things remaining unchanged). The *ceteris paribus* constraint is very important because there are many factors besides price that can influence the quantity of a particular commodity consumers are willing to buy. Some examples include consumers' incomes and tastes, the climate (one would not expect to sell too many refrigerators to the Inuit, for instance) the quality of the product, the amount of advertising, the prices of related goods—goods that compete, as margarine competes with butter, and goods that are "go-togethers" or "complements" like bread and butter. In our definition of demand we assume that all factors remain constant, and we construct a schedule of the different quantities that will be purchased by consumers as the price, and *only* the price, is varied.

What kind of relationship exists between price and quantity? A little introspection, together with past experience in purchasing goods and services, should suggest that normally, if the price of a given commodity is relatively high, less of it will be purchased than if the price is low. In other words, there exists an *inverse* relationship between price and quantity demanded.

Diminishing Marginal Utility This inverse relationship, which illustrates the reluctance of consumers to buy additional units except at a lower price, is often explained by the diminishing amount of satisfaction consumers get from consuming additional units of a good or service at any one time. For example, on a cold snowy night after you have finally shovelled all the snow off your sidewalk, the first cup of coffee gives you a great deal of satisfaction. You may enjoy the second cup, too, but the *extra* satisfaction yielded by that second cup is likely to be less than the satisfaction—or utility—that you derived from the first. Similarly, the third cup, while still enjoyable perhaps, is likely to give you less satisfaction than the second, and the fourth may threaten to keep you awake all night. Your response to the fifth cup is likely to be, "I wouldn't drink it if you paid me!" This is precisely what the economist has in mind when he talks about "the law of diminishing marginal utility". *Utility* is a synonym for satisfaction. Marginal, as usual, means extra or incremental. Thus, the law of diminishing marginal utility simply states that the extra satisfaction derived from each additional unit of a commodity in any given time period is less than the satisfaction derived from the previous unit of the product.

If we tried to extract the minimum amount of money that a cold snow shoveller would be willing to pay for his first cup of coffee, chances are that we could get a high price because that first cup yields him so much satisfaction. The second cup is likely to yield less satisfaction than the first, and the snow shoveller probably would not buy it unless we charged a lower price; the extra satisfaction added by the fourth or fifth cup consumed in one sitting is probably very small, if there is any at all. In such a case, the price that the consumer would be willing to pay for the fourth or fifth cup would be small. If the point of satiation had been reached or passed, we would probably have to pay the snow shoveller to drink that extra cup of coffee, if we could persuade him to take it at all. The law of diminishing marginal utility thus provides a good explanation of the inverse relationship between price and quantity: the greater the quantity of the good one has consumed in a given time period, the smaller the price one would be prepared to pay to get the next unit, because it yields less satisfaction.

Individual Demand The inverse relationship between price and quantity may be discussed for an individual or household, or for an entire market; it may be described by an arithmetic table, by a graph, or by an algebraic function. Assume that we are considering the demand for butter in a week by the Smiths, a good-sized family of two parents and six children. Table 8-4 describes the possible reaction of Mrs. Smith to various prices that might exist at a particular time. If butter is expensive, for example $3.00 a kilogram, Mrs. Smith would limit consumption to table use only and buy just 1.0 kg a week. If the price were lower, say $2.40, she would buy 1.5 kg for her family. At a very low price of 60 cents a kilogram, she might buy as much as 3.0 kg a week and use butter lavishly in cooking and in baking such treats as shortbread cookies.

This price-quantity relationship for the individual family can be shown diagrammatically. As usual, the price—dollars per kilogram—is measured along the vertical axis. The commodity we are talking about, kilograms of butter per unit of time, is put on the horizontal axis. At a price of $3.00 a kilogram, we have assumed that Mrs. Smith would buy 1.0 kg of butter. From the vertical (price) axis, we can determine the distance that measures $3.00. If we draw a horizontal line at that distance,

Table 8-4
THE SMITHS' DEMAND FOR BUTTER

Price $/kg	Quantity kg/week
3.00	1.0
2.40	1.5
1.80	2.0
1.20	2.5
.60	3.0

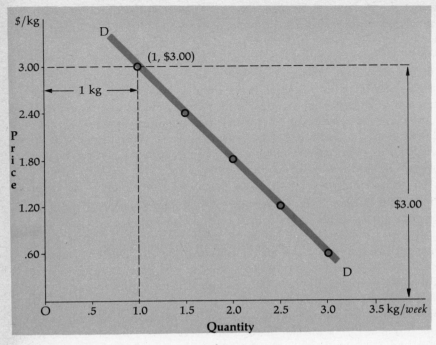

Figure 8-6

then we know that any point on that line measures $3.00 from the quantity (horizontal) axis. Along the horizontal axis we measure the distance from the origin that represents 1.0 kg of butter per week and extend a vertical line to mark it. The point at which the horizontal and vertical lines intersect (1,$3) gives us the information that at a price of $3.00 a kilogram, Mrs. Smith is willing to buy no more than 1 kg of butter in a week. This is one point on our demand curve. In precisely the same way we can plot the other points in the table. If we join these points together,[4] we derive the demand curve of the Smiths for butter—a schedule of the number of kilograms the family will buy at various possible prices in a period of a

---

[4] In joining the points and drawing a continuous curve, we are again making the assumption that all points on the line are meaningful—that butter will be sold in small fractions of a kilogram. We are assuming, for example, that it is possible to set a price of $1.275 per kilogram, and that at that price Mrs. Smith would be willing and able to buy 2.4375 kg of butter. We recognize that for an individual this degree of divisibility is not, in fact, possible, but any loss in accuracy is more than offset by the usefulness of a continuous curve as a tool of analysis.

week if such factors as the family's tastes, income, and the prices of related commodities like bread and margarine do not change.

Market Demand   The Smiths are only one family in the total market for butter, and for most purposes in economics the entire market demand for a good or service is more important than the demand of an individual or a household. To find the market demand we can sum the individual demands of the Smiths, the Browns, the Greens, and all the other families in the entire market. Again, to make things easier for us, let us simplify drastically and assume, as we have done in Table 8-5, that the market comprises only three families: the Smiths (whose demand for butter we have already discussed), the Browns, and the Greens.

Table 8-5
THE MARKET DEMAND FOR BUTTER

Price $/kg	Quantity Demanded by the Smiths kg/week	Quantity Demanded by the Browns kg/week	Quantity Demanded by the Greens kg/week	Market Demand kg/week
3.00	1.0	0.5	0	1.5
2.40	1.5	0.5	0	2.0
1.80	2.0	0.5	0	2.5
1.20	2.5	0.5	0.5	3.5
.60	3.0	0.5	1.0	4.5

The Browns are a wealthy couple of rather rigid habits. Butter comprises a very small part of their total food budget. They have no children, and Mrs. Brown is too busy with community work to do any baking, so regardless of what variations there are in the price of butter, the family buys only 0.5 kg a week. The Greens, we shall assume, are a low-income family. At the higher prices in Table 8-5, Mrs. Green feels that she cannot afford butter at all. However, her family likes butter, and if the price is as low as $1.20 a kilogram, she is prepared to buy 0.5 kg; and she would buy a maximum of 1.0 kg if the price happened to be 60 cents.

If these three families comprise the total market for butter, then it should be apparent that to calculate the market demand, we must sum the quantity demanded at each price by all three families. At a price of $3.00, then, the total quantity demanded is the 1.0 kg that would be bought by the Smiths and the 0.5 kg bought by the Browns—1.5 kg of butter in all. At a price of $2.40, the total quantity demanded would be 2.0 kg (1.5 + 0.5 + 0), and so on down the rest of the column labelled *Market Demand*.

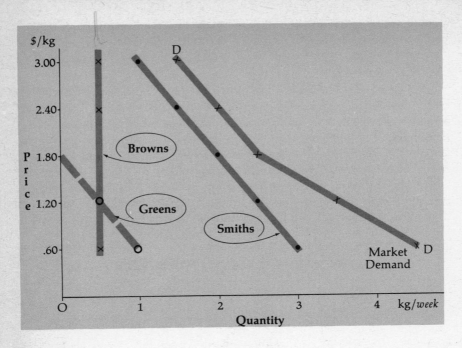

Figure 8-7

We can also arrive at the market demand from our *graph* by summing horizontally the individual demand curves for the Browns, the Greens, and the Smiths. At a price of $3.00, for example, we add the distance representing the Browns' 0.5 kg to the distance representing the Smiths' 1.0 kg, and we get a point on the market demand curve. At a price of $1.20, we add the distance representing the Browns' 0.5 kg to the same distance representing the Greens' 0.5 kg, and add both to the distance representing the Smiths' 2.5 kg. We can calculate the other points on the market demand curve in precisely the same way.

The Law of Demand Our market demand curve slopes down and to the right: the higher the price, the smaller the quantity demanded. This inverse relationship between price and quantity is sometimes referred to as "the law of demand" or the "law of downward sloping demand". The law states what we said earlier in our discussion of diminishing marginal utility—namely, that in a given period of time, *ceteris paribus*, the quantity demanded varies inversely with the price.

This is not an immutable law: the demand curves of some individuals may not, in fact, slope down and to the right. The Browns' curve in our simple example showed that in the price range we were considering, variations in price had no effect on the quantity demanded by that family. However, when the Browns' curve was combined with those of other consumers, the market demand curve did obey the law of demand and sloped downward to the right.

The inverse relationship between price and quantity for individuals is reinforced in the market by the fact that more and more people come into the market as consumers at progressively lower prices. The Greens, in our example, could not afford butter at a price higher than $1.20 a kilogram. Their entry into the market if price happened to be $1.20 or lower would reinforce the law of demand for the market curve.

There may even be exceptions to the law of demand in the case of the market schedule. However, such exceptions, while interesting, do not concern us here. For our purposes, we shall always assume a market demand curve that slopes down and to the right, illustrating the inverse relationship between price and quantity.

SUPPLY

Having studied consumers' demand for butter, we shall turn our attention to producers and the supply curve for butter. Supply may be defined as *a schedule of the quantities of a commodity that will be brought onto the market in a given period of time at various prices ceteris paribus.* When we derive the supply curve, it will become apparent that it is a *cost-output* relationship: for that reason we must understand the nature of producers' costs. Although we shall be discussing the costs of butter producers, the same kind of analysis will apply to producers of stereo sets or men's suits or any other product.

Costs, of course, are affected by a number of factors in addition to the volume of output: they are influenced by the prices of the inputs (factors of production). They are also affected by the size of the operation—the *scale* of the farm or manufacturing plant producing the product in question; a larger scale of operation, for example, may permit a farmer to use specialized machinery, or permit a businessman to take advantage of the techniques of specialization, which may reduce the cost per unit of output. The size of the production run is another factor that greatly influences costs; the short length of production runs in many manufacturing industries in Canada is one of the major explanations of our relatively high costs of production. Costs are also a function of technology: the invention of new and more efficient machines may enable a farmer to bring down his cost per unit of output; the development of higher-yield crop strains can do the same thing. These and other factors all influence costs. For now, however, we shall assume that all factors except the volume of output remain fixed. In other words, in the period that we are considering we shall assume that there is no change in factors like technology, or scale, or the size of the run; the only thing that we shall allow to change is the *volume of output*.

Fixed Costs Farmer Jones, like Mr. Black the theatre owner, incurs costs which do not vary with output during the particular period of time we are considering. Suppose he rents the farm on an annual contract (his lease could run for two or three years or more without in any way altering our analysis), then the rent will have to be paid that year whether he produces any butter or not: it is a fixed cost during that year. If he has bought the farm with borrowed money, then the interest he must pay is a fixed cost; if the farm is fully paid for, then in calculating his fixed cost he should include the interest forgone or what he could have earned by investing his money elsewhere, perhaps in Canada Savings Bonds. This is an example of what the economist calls the *opportunity cost* of his money, or its forgone alternative, and it is an important element in the economist's cost calculation, even though neither the accountants nor the income tax departments recognize it as a cost. There are other fixed costs, too: if he owns the farm, he must pay taxes. Then, there is a certain minimum level of upkeep on the barns, fences, and machinery that will have to be maintained whether he produces a lot of butter or none at all. The sum of all costs that *cannot* be altered during the time period we are discussing, as we said earlier, is called the total fixed cost (*TFC*).

If the only product that Farmer Jones produces is butter, then we can calculate his fixed cost per kilogram (his *average fixed cost*, or *AFC*) by dividing his total fixed cost by the quantity of butter he produces ($TFC/Q = AFC$). Since his total fixed cost by definition does not vary with output but remains constant at some sum—say \$120 a week (or \$520 a month or \$6 240 a year)—then as the quantity of butter produced increases, he can spread that cost over more and more kilograms of butter, and his fixed cost per unit will steadily decline over the entire range of output. There is an inverse relationship between fixed cost per kilogram and output—the greater the output, the smaller the average fixed cost.

Variable Costs On the other hand, Farmer Jones incurs costs that *do* vary with output. If he wants to increase butter production he may need more milk cows, and that will require more feed to carry them through the winter, more land for them to graze on, and more man-hours to look after them. The costs of these inputs are *variable* costs: within the time period we are discussing, they can be increased (or decreased) as the output of butter increases (or decreases). There is a direct relationship between total variable cost (*TVC*) and total quantity produced: the greater the output, the higher the total variable cost.

In the time period we are concerned with, then, there are both fixed and variable costs. There is enough time to vary some of the inputs, but not all of them. Such a time period in economics is referred to as the *short run*. If the time period is long enough that the entrepreneur can plan to vary all inputs (including the land, the barns, the rental contract, and the others which we have described in our example as fixed) so that we are dealing with a period of time in which *all costs* can be varied, then we are talking about the *long run*.

The next question is how those variable costs change as output increases. Do total variable costs increase steadily? Or do they rise at a relatively faster rate than output? Or do they increase less than proportionately, that is, at a decreasing rate? All may be possible for different kinds of firms and over different ranges of output. The assumption most commonly made in economic theory is that the TVC curve, while always showing a direct relationship with the quantity of output (the larger the output the higher the cost) increases at a decreasing rate to begin with, and then increases at an increasing rate, indicating that as output increases, costs at first increase less than proportionately but that as output continues to rise, costs rise more than proportionately. It is assumed, in other words, that the curve looks like the one in Figure 8-8.

As was the case in Figure 8-2 which showed the total fixed costs and total revenue of Mr. Black, we have measured total dollars per week on the vertical axis and output per week on the horizontal axis. From the diagram we can tell the total variable cost of producing any given quantity of butter: for example, when output is 300 kg a week, total variable costs is equal to $300.

Does the shape of the curve as we have drawn it seem logical? Consider what might be involved if the farmer decides to increase his output of butter. The additional inputs he would need would include more milk cows, additional feed, more man-hours and machine time. If he starts off with one milk cow on a farm that has a big barn and plenty of land and equipment, he obviously has excess capacity. By buying more cows, he can make more efficient use of the factors of production that are already there and thus increase productivity, which is the output per unit of input. While his costs will increase, they will increase relatively more slowly than output. As he continues to add cows, however, he may find that he needs more feed grain for the winter than he can grow on his fields as he is cultivating them at present, and that he must either bring more land under cultivation or cultivate his present land more intensively.

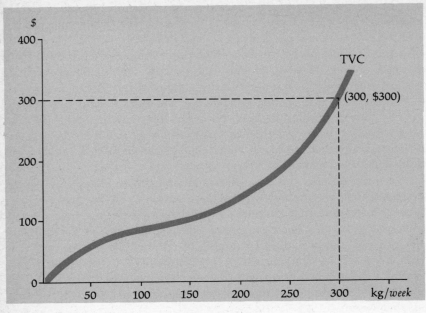

Figure 8-8

If he fertilizes his land, then the output of feed grain will likely rise, but a second and third application of fertilizer, while they may increase his output, will not likely yield as much as the first application. Wear and tear on his machinery increase with frequent use. He will need more help at milking time and more help in cleaning his barns, and the hired hands may not take as good care of his machinery and equipment as he does so that wear and tear accelerate. Costs in this situation will rise relatively more rapidly than output. What this discussion suggests is that the shape of the total variable cost curve drawn in Figure 8-8 seems logical.

With the aid of a table containing the hypothetical figures for the TVC curve in Figure 8-8, as well as the other costs, we can see fairly readily what happens to the *per-unit* curves, which are the curves most frequently used in an economic analysis of cost and pricing. Average variable cost (*TVC*/Output) when output is 50 kg a week is $1.20 a kilogram. By the time output has reached 200 kg a week, average variable cost per kilogram has dropped to 64 cents, but at an output of 250 kg a week, it has risen to 78 cents a kilogram and continues to rise as output increases. Given the shape that we have assumed for the total variable cost curve, we can see that the average variable cost curve must be "U"-shaped—a common assumption in the economic analysis of a firm.

Table 8-6

1	2	3	4	5	6	7	8
Output kg/week	TVC $/week	AVC $/kg	TFC $	AFC $/kg	TC $	ATC $/kg	ΔTC/ΔQ(MC) $/kg
0	0	0	120	—	120	—	
							60/50 = 1.20
50	60	1.20	120	2.40	180	3.60	
							20/50 = .40
100	80	.80	120	1.20	200	2.00	
							19/50 = .38
150	99	.66	120	.80	219	1.46	
							29/50 = .58
200	128	.64	120	.60	248	1.24	
							67/50 = 1.34
250	195	.78	120	.48	315	1.26	
							105/50 = 2.10
300	300	1.00	120	.40	420	1.40	

The total fixed cost which, we suggested earlier, might amount to $120 a week is also given in Table 8-6. As required by its definition it remains constant over the entire range of output. Total fixed cost divided by output yields the average fixed cost, which is set out in column 5 of Table 8-6.

Since the producer has both fixed and variable costs, it follows that if we want to arrive at his total cost (*TC*), we must sum total fixed cost and total variable cost (*TC = TVC + TFC*) to arrive at the figure in column 6 of Table 8-6. Similarly, if we want to get his *average* total cost we can either add *AFC* and *AVC* (column 3 + column 5) or divide total cost by the quantity of output (*TC/Q = ATC*). In either case we arrive at the figures in column 7.

Marginal Cost We are now in a position to calculate marginal cost, a tool that we need to determine the profit-maximizing output. Marginal cost is the additional cost of producing one more (or one less) unit of product, in this case one more kilogram of butter. Column 1 of Table 8-6 shows increases of 50 kg—rather large increments on which to calculate marginal cost; however, just as in the case of Mr. Black's advertising experiments when we used blocks of 100 tickets to get an approximation of his marginal selling cost, so in column 8 of Table 8-6 the same thing has been done for Farmer Jones' costs. The increase in total cost (ΔTC) has been divided by the increase in the quantity of output (ΔQ), and the figures shown give an approximation of marginal cost over that range of output. Once again the curve is U-shaped; but, as we shall see, the falling portion has no relevance for us at this time,[5] and we shall concern ourselves only with that part where there exists a direct relationship between marginal cost and the quantity of butter produced.

The Cost Curves We can use a diagram to illustrate the various relationships we have been describing. For convenience we shall draw smooth curves that have been constructed on the basis of much more information than that listed in Table 8-6. It is assumed, for example, that Farmer Jones can increase his output by infinitely small increments—an assumption which is unlikely to be fulfilled in the real world, but which makes it much easier to draw the graphs.

On the horizontal axis we plot kilograms of butter per week; on the vertical axis, unit costs are expressed in dollars per kilogram. The average fixed cost curve (AFC) falls steadily as output increases because the farmer is spreading his overhead (his total fixed cost) over a larger and larger number of kilograms of butter. As the quantity produced increases, the curve approaches, but does not touch, the horizontal axis; such a curve is called a *rectangular hyperbola*.

The average variable cost (AVC) is a U-shaped curve, as the information in Table 8-6 suggested it should be. Data for other shapes besides saucer-like curves have been calculated for other industries—curves that are horizontal over part or most of the relevant range of output, curves that look more like a "V" than a "U", and so on, but a U-shaped curve will serve our present purposes.

The average total cost curve (ATC) is the sum of AFC and AVC. For example, we know from Table 8-6 that at an output of 50 units, the average variable cost is $1.20 and the average fixed cost is $2.40 a kilogram, making an average total cost of $3.60 a kilogram, as illustrated in Figure 8-9. The average total cost curve is also U-shaped, although its minimum point will be reached at a larger output because, over a short range of output, steadily falling average fixed costs will tend to offset the first small increases in average variable costs, leaving ATC still falling as AVC rises.

---

[5] If we are talking about the long run, a period long enough for plant size to be varied, we can develop a *long-run marginal cost curve*. The long-run marginal cost of products like chemicals and petroleum may fall as plant size increases, and if so, the falling portion of the curve is relevant. In such cases, however, there will be a persistent tendency over time for large low-cost firms to develop and drive out smaller ones. This tendency is not found in agriculture: experiments with large farms have not been successful in the USSR or in North America. This suggests that the industry will remain atomistically competitive, rather than change into an imperfectly competitive one, as would happen if falling marginal costs were commonly found.

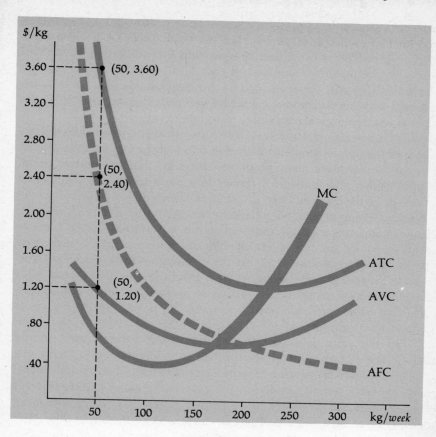

Figure 8-9

Marginal cost in this example is positively sloped over most of its range. It must intersect each of the U-shaped curves at the lowest point of the "U" for reasons which can be shown fairly readily, but which unnecessarily complicate our present analysis. In Figure 8-9 that part of the *MC* curve which lies above the *AVC* curve is shown as a heavy line: it is of particular significance to us because it is the schedule that shows how much butter Farmer Jones will bring to the market each week at various prices. It is his *supply curve*—one of the important tools to be derived from all the cost analysis we have been doing. Let us see why this should be the case.

Individual Supply Assume that, like Mr. Black the theatre owner, Farmer Jones' objective in producing butter is to make as large a profit as possible. As we already know, if he is a profit maximizer he will produce every unit of output that adds more to his revenue than it does to his cost, since each unit that does so adds to his total profit. If his aim is to maximize profit, he will not produce any unit that adds more to his cost than to his revenue since the loss on each such unit will reduce the size of his profit. The rule we developed for Mr. Black holds for Farmer Jones: he should continue to produce until he gets as close as possible to the output at which marginal cost equals marginal revenue.

What is his marginal revenue? We know that one of the key characteristics of the purely competitive market in which Farmer Jones is operating is that it comprises many producers, so many that no one by himself can affect price. The individual farmer is a price taker: it is the market that sets price for him and once it *is* set, the farmer is free to sell whatever quantity he wishes at the going market price. A fixed price for all units he sells means that his average revenue curve is a horizontal straight line at that price, as was the case when Mr. Black set his own price and decided to try to increase ticket sales at that price through advertising. The farmer's marginal revenue—the extra revenue from the sale of the extra kilogram of butter—is equal to the price, or average revenue, and as was pointed out earlier, this is always true when the average revenue curve is a horizontal straight line.

Given the price, what determines how much Farmer Jones should supply is the extra cost of producing the extra kilogram of butter. Consciously or unconsciously, he matches his extra cost (his marginal cost) against his extra revenue, which in this case is the going market price. If the price of butter increases, then Farmer Jones may argue that even though some of his cows are drying up it may pay him to go to the extra work and cost of milking them rather than slaughtering them or letting the calves run with them and thus converting the milk into veal. At the various prices that may be set by the market, it is the *marginal cost* that indicates how much of the product a profit-maximizing producer should bring to the market in a given period of time, other factors remaining constant. The marginal cost curve, then, is the individual producer's supply curve.

As shown in Figure 8-9, the supply curve does not comprise the entire marginal cost curve. Consider again the nature of the various costs. Since we are talking about the short run, Farmer Jones has both fixed and variable costs. If he decides not to produce any butter at all in the short run, he will eliminate the variable costs, but he will still have all his fixed costs such as the rent on the property if he is leasing the farm, or the taxes and the interest forgone on the money invested if he owns it, the minimum maintenance costs and depreciation, and the opportunity cost of his own labour (what he could earn working elsewhere). If the market sets a price so low that it does not cover even his variable cost per unit, that is, if it sets a price that lies below his *AVC* curve, then, since he has the choice of producing or not producing, he should choose *not* to produce, and hence not incur the variable costs. If he shuts down the butter-producing operation, his losses will be limited to the amount of his fixed costs, and he will not compound the problem and add to his losses by producing at a price (revenue) that is less than his variable costs. For this reason, the portion of the short-run marginal cost curve that lies below the *AVC* curve is not relevant for a profit-maximizing entrepreneur. Therefore, Farmer Jones' supply curve is that part of the *MC* curve which lies above the *AVC* curve. In Figure 8-9, the thickened section of the *MC* curve tells how much he will bring to the market per week over the range of prices indicated: it is his supply curve.

In the *long run*, as we have seen, all costs become variable. The farmer can build more barns, acquire more land; or alternatively, he can get out of the business. If the return from butter is not high enough to cover the rent on his land and the depreciation on his machinery and buildings, his own wages and those of his hired hands, then the farmer should get out of butter production and perhaps go into cheese production, or into cattle ranching, or grain farming, or perhaps he should give up farming completely. In the long run, if he is a profit maximizer, he will want to cover not merely the *extra* cost of producing a kilogram of butter, but also all other costs involved in butter production. If he cannot cover these costs, both fixed and variable, then he should give up butter production.

Market Supply A knowledge of what influences the quantity of butter Farmer Jones will bring to the market is an important stepping stone to understanding how the total market supply curve is derived. To calculate the market supply, we perform the same kind of operation we did in calculating the market demands of individuals: we sum the quantities supplied by individual farmers at various prices. From what we have said, it would be normal to expect that at a high price per kilogram ($3.60, for example) Farmer Jones and thousands of other butter producers like him would be prepared to bring to the market a large quantity of butter—say, 9.0 million kg a week. At a lower price of $3.00, the quantity supplied would be smaller—maybe 7.5 million kg. If the price happened to be as low as 60 cents a kilogram, most farmers would find this insufficient to cover the out-of-pocket costs of butter production, and they might switch into cheese production, or let the calves run with the cows. At that low price we shall assume that only 1.5 million kg a week would be brought to the market. These assumptions are set out in the supply schedule in Table 8-7.

Table 8-7

Price $/kg	Supply millions of kg/week
$3.60	9.0
3.00	7.5
2.40	6.0
1.80	4.5
1.20	3.0
.60	1.5

THE MARKET PRICE

We have described the individual farmer as a price taker and have said that Farmer Jones, by himself, is such a small part of the market that no matter what he does to his own volume of output, he cannot influence the market price. But how is that market price set? It is determined by market demand and market supply. When we have a price at which the quantity demanded is just equal to the quantity supplied—that is, a price that clears the market—then we have what is called an *equilibrium price*.

Equilibrium Price Equilibrium in economics, like equilibrium in physics, implies a balance among forces or variables. If a market system is in equilibrium, there is no tendency for it to change. On the other hand, if equilibrium does not exist, the market is not in balance and the equilibrium position is the one toward which price tends to move, provided, of course, that there are no government policies preventing such a move, and provided that the variables other than price that we have assumed to remain constant do, in fact, remain constant. In the economic system, because variables are changing constantly, equilibrium may never be reached. However, what is important for us is the tendency for the variable to move toward the equilibrium position and the direction of that move.

To illustrate the concept of the equilibrium price, we shall return to the example of butter. The hypothetical market supply schedule of Table 8-7 is reproduced in Table 8-8. It shows the usual direct relationship between price and quantity. Assume that there exists a market demand schedule like the one in Table 8-8, which was arrived at by summing the demands, not only of the Smiths, Browns, and Greens, but also of millions of other customers in the market. It shows the normal inverse relationship: the lower the price, the larger the quantity demanded.

In Table 8-8, the price at which the quantity demanded is just equal to the quantity supplied is $1.80 a kilogram. At that price (the equilibrium price) consumers are willing to buy 4.5 million kg a week, which is precisely the quantity that producers are willing to bring to the market. A price of $1.80 a kilogram clears the market: any buyer who is prepared to pay that price can get all the butter he wants, while any seller who will accept $1.80 a kilogram can sell all the butter he wants.

Suppose the price is less than the equilibrium level—$1.20 a kilogram, for example. Buyers are prepared to purchase 5.5 million kg, but sellers, according to our table, are willing to bring only 3.0 million kg a week to the market. Buyers, finding butter in short supply at that price, compete for the scarce commodity and in the process, bid the price up. A higher price discourages some buyers from buying any butter, and others from buying as much. At the same time, a higher revenue per kilogram encourages producers to increase output. The process of bidding the price up will end, if no other variables change, at that price at which the amount consumers want to buy is exactly matched by the amount producers are willing to bring to the market.

On the other hand, if the actual price happens to be above the equilibrium price—say, $2.40 a kilogram—buyers are prepared to buy only 3.5 million kilograms of butter a week, whereas producers are willing to bring 6.0 million kilograms to the market. In competing with each other for customers, some sellers will undoubtedly drop the price, thus encouraging consumers to buy more; and as we said before a lower price discourages sellers from producing as much butter and makes them switch over to the cheese or veal market. If all other variables remain constant, the process of price-cutting will continue until the quantity consumers are prepared to take off the market is matched by the quantity sellers are prepared to bring into it.

Table 8-8

Price $/kg	Demand millions of kg/week	Supply millions of kg/week
3.60	1.5	9.0
3.00	2.5	7.5
2.40	3.5	6.0
1.80	4.5	4.5
1.20	5.5	3.0
.60	6.5	1.5

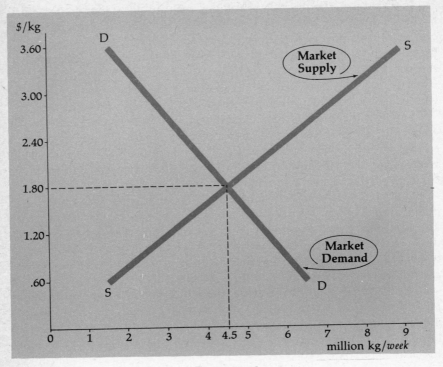

Figure 8-10

If we plot the supply and demand schedules from Table 8-8 and join the points with a smooth curve, then the equilibrium price (and quantity) is determined by the intersection of the market demand curve and the market supply, as shown in Figure 8-10. We can read the equilibrium price from the graph: a perpendicular drawn from the point of intersection to the vertical axis tells us that it is $1.80 a kilogram. By dropping a perpendicular from the point of intersection to the horizontal axis, we can see that the equilibrium quantity is 4.5 million kg.

Changes in the Equilibrium Price The equilibrium price will change with a *shift* in either the demand curve or the supply curve. Before such shift can take place, we have to relax some of our assumptions. So far in our analysis of demand we have assumed that the only variable affecting the quantity demanded is the price of a kilogram of butter; all other factors that might influence the demand schedule have been assumed to remain constant. What would happen if we relaxed that assumption and permitted a change in consumers' tastes, for example? Suppose consumers decide that margarine is better for the health than butter. What effect would that have on our demand schedule? At each price on the schedule, less butter would be demanded. At $1.80, for example, only 3.0 million kg might be demanded. In terms of Figure 8-11, the whole demand curve would *shift* to the left, from DD to D_1D_1. In economic jargon we would say there has been a *change in demand* or, more specifically, a *decrease in the demand* for butter.

On the other hand, if consumers' incomes were to increase, then it might very well happen that at each price in our schedule a greater quantity would be demanded. Instead of 4.5 million kg at $1.80, consumers might be prepared to buy 6.0 million kg. Instead of 5.5 million kg at $1.20, they might, with their higher incomes, be prepared to buy 7.0 million kg, and so on for all the other prices. Such a demand curve, D_2D_2 in Figure 8-11, would lie to the right of the one that we have drawn, illustrating an *increase in demand*.

Increases and decreases in supply are analogous. If, for example, there should occur a decrease in the number of farmers prepared to bring butter to the market at various prices, then, since the market supply is the summation of the outputs of all producers in the market, it follows logically that there would be a decrease in market supply. That

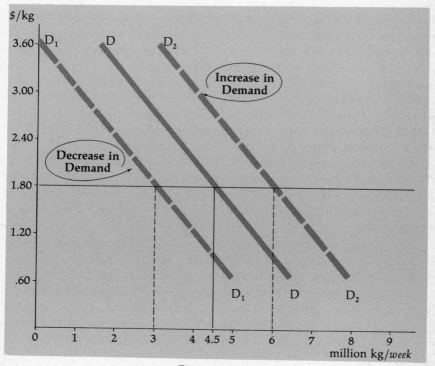

Figure 8-11

is, at each price in our schedule a smaller quantity would be supplied, and the entire market supply curve would shift up and to the left.

Alternatively, if there should occur an improvement in technology so that the cost of producing the extra kilogram of butter decreases—that is, if the entire marginal cost curve should shift down and to the right—then it would follow logically that the supply curve would also shift down and to the right, since the market supply is the summation of all of those marginal cost curves. The result of this is that at any price in the schedule, there would be an increase in the supply. An increase in supply also means that any given quantity will be brought to the market at a lower price than before.

THE INDIVIDUAL PROFIT-MAXIMIZING OUTPUT

The market price has now been set. This means that Farmer Jones can sell as much or as little as he wants at $1.80 a kilogram because the few hundred kilograms that he can produce are such an insignificant part of the millions that are brought to the market by all butter producers that they cannot affect the price. This means that his average revenue curve is a horizontal straight line at the price of $1.80 a kilogram; it also means that his *extra* revenue (his marginal revenue) for each kilogram sold is also $1.80, so that his MR curve coincides with the AR curve. At that price how much butter should he bring to the market? His MC curve will tell him, just as Mr. Black's MC curve told *him* how long to continue to advertise after he had set the price of his theatre tickets: he should get as close as possible to the output at which $MC = MR = \$1.80$. Figure 8-12 illustrates the solution. His AR (price) = MR curve is a horizontal straight line at the price of $1.80. The MC curve was derived in Figure 8-9. To maximize profit, Farmer Jones should operate at the output at which MC and MR intersect in the diagram —at about 260 kg. If the price had been less, say $1.20 a kilogram, then the intersection of marginal cost and marginal revenue would have occurred at a lower output, and his profit-maximizing output would have been closer to 225 kg a week.

The remaining question to be asked about Farmer Jones is, how is he faring? Is he making a profit? Or should the resources now allocated to butter production be reallocated elsewhere? To get the answer we need to use the cost curves derived earlier. ATC, AVC, and MC have all been taken from Figure 8-9. The AFC curve has been omitted: if need be, we can calculate the average fixed cost because, by construction, it is the vertical distance between AVC and ATC. If the market price is $1.80 a kilogram, then $AR_1 = MR_1$ is the relevant average revenue and mar-

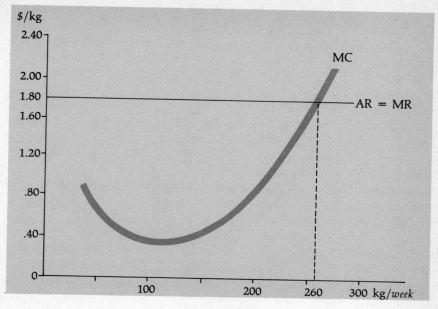

Figure 8-12

ginal revenue curve, and *OQ* is the profit-maximizing output. Profit per unit is the difference between average revenue and average total cost. His average total cost is measured by the vertical distance from the horizontal axis to the *ATC* curve—the distance *QC* in this case. His profit per unit is the distance *QR − QC* on the diagram, which equals *CR*—close to 60 cents a kilogram. If we multiply his profit per kilogram by the number of kilograms he produces (260) we can calculate a total weekly profit of about $150.[6] Farmer Jones is doing well.

Suppose, however, that this degree of profitability is typical of the entire butter-producing industry. It is a relatively easy industry to get

---

[6] A word of warning: owing to the economist's concern with achieving a proper allocation of resources, his definition of profit does not correspond to that of the accountant or the income tax department. If you look back at our various discussions of fixed cost, you will find that we have included as a cost the opportunity cost of capital (the interest that any money invested in the business could have earned if it had been put, for example, into Canada Savings Bonds). We also included the opportunity cost of the entrepreneur's labour (the revenue forgone by not working at some other job) if he happened to be running the operation as was the case with Farmer Jones. This means that we have already built into the cost schedules what the economist calls *normal profit*. The excess of revenue over cost that we are now calculating is usually described as "above-normal" profit.

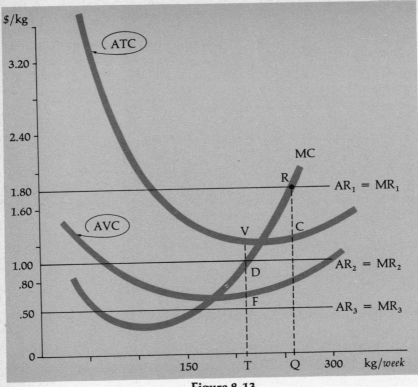

Figure 8-13

into[7] (a characteristic of the perfectly competitive market) and many farmers now producing cheese or beef or growing grain could shift to the profitable business of producing butter. As more and more farmers enter the industry, the market supply will increase, that is, the whole supply curve will *shift* to the right, to a position shown by the broken line S_1 in Figure 8-14, and the equilibrium price will drop.

Assume that the price drops from the $1.80 established in Figure 8-10 to $1.00 a kilogram. Farmer Jones now faces a very different situation. His average revenue curve in Figure 8-13 becomes $AR_2 = MR_2 = 1.00, and it intersects his MC curve between the AVC and the ATC. His average total cost at the output at which $MC = MR = 1.00 is now TV, and his average revenue, TD: average total cost exceeds average revenue and he is taking a loss (DV per unit). He is more than covering his variable cost, TF, but he is not fully covering his variable plus fixed costs. What should he do? In the short run when he has to meet his fixed costs anyway, he is better to keep

---

[7] Especially if you happen to be a cow or someone who knows about cows.

operating because he is not only covering his variable costs, but he is at least making a contribution to overhead. In the long run, however, he can vary all of his inputs: all costs become variable. Unless things are likely to improve, Farmer Jones should get his capital out of butter production. He should not replace his equipment as it wears out, and he should send his milk cows to the slaughterhouse or use them to raise veal, and thus either reallocate his resources to some more profitable kind of farming, or else get out of farming altogether.

Suppose, to compound Farmer Jones' problem, the bottom suddenly falls out of the butter market, perhaps because consumers become choles-terol-conscious overnight and switch to margarine; that means there is a *decrease in demand*, such as the shift from D to D_1 in Figure 8-14. With the decrease in demand superimposed on the increase in supply described above, suppose the price drops to 50 cents a kilogram ($AR_3 = MR_3$ in Figure 8-13); then what? At that price ($= MR$), the intersection of MR and MC occurs at an output of about 160 kg a week, but because Farmer Jones cannot cover even his variable costs, there is no point in producing butter at all. If he did, since his variable cost would exceed his revenue,

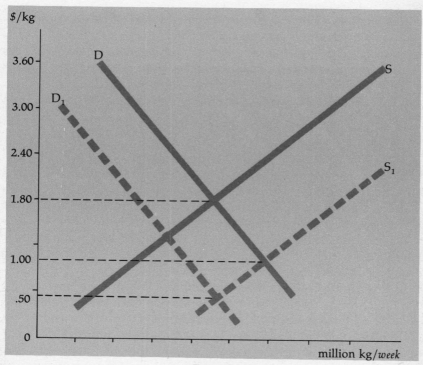

Figure 8-14

he would take a loss (an avoidable one) on variable costs as well as the unavoidable loss on his fixed costs. By not producing any butter, he would limit his total loss to his fixed costs.

The Spectrum of Markets

We have developed some tools of analysis by looking at two different kinds of businesses. Farmer Jones was producing a homogeneous product (graded butter) in a market in which there were many producers (so many that no individual farmer could affect the price) and where there were no barriers to entry. We described this market as purely competitive (and also as atomistically competitive) and indicated that if we had added the characteristics of perfect mobility of resources and perfect knowledge, we could have classified it as a *perfectly competitive* market. On the other hand, Mr. Black, the movie theatre owner, had a differentiated product and did not have so many close competitors. His market was different because his average revenue curve sloped down to the right. There were more ways available to Mr. Black to influence his sales, and he had a greater degree of control over price than Farmer Jones who could charge either the optimum price, or less than the optimum price if he did not care about maximizing his profit. Markets in which entrepreneurs have negatively sloped average revenue curves are sometimes described as *imperfectly competitive* markets, to distinguish them from the perfectly competitive market, which lies at one extreme of a wide spectrum of markets. It should be stressed that the use of the words "perfect" and "imperfect" does not involve a judgement about the two different classes of markets. "Perfect" markets are far from perfect.

IMPERFECT COMPETITION

At the other extreme of the market spectrum from perfect competition is *pure monopoly*, a market in which there is a single firm producing a product for which there is no close substitute. Barriers to entry are complete; if another competing firm gets into the market, then, by definition, there is no longer a pure monopoly. This is as rare in the real world as pure competition. A telephone system within a region might be as example; an urban transit system might be another.

In this kind of market, the firm and the industry are one and the same. The average revenue curve for the monopolist's product, therefore, is the *market demand* curve which, we assume, slopes down and to the right. This means that if all of the factors that might influence the quantity demanded (except price) are held constant, then the monopolist who wants to sell more of his product must lower his price. Raising price will result in a smaller sales volume. In the absence of government regulation, then, the monopolist can set the price of his product: he is a price *maker*, rather than a price taker. If he wishes to maximize profits, then the monopolist, like Mr. Black or Farmer Jones, should aim for the output at which $MC = MR$; the maximum price he can charge for that output is determined by his demand schedule. If we were to draw a diagram for this analysis, it would look very much like Figure 8-3, which we drew for Mr. Black.

Most industries in North America fall between the two extremes of pure competition and pure monopoly. Economics textbooks frequently distinguish two kinds of markets in this middle range: *monopolistic competition* and *oligopoly*. Monopolistic competition has some of the characteristics of pure competition: there is a large number of firms in the market and there are no serious barriers to entry and exit. Monopolistic competition differs from pure competition in that the product being produced is differentiated instead of homogeneous—that is, the units are not identical in the way that bushels of Number 1 Northern wheat are identical. In Canada, a good example would be factory-produced men's and women' s clothing. The businessman in monopolistic competition has a limited range within which he has some discretion over the price of his product: he has *some* power to administer his price. This is the monopolistic element in the competition, which gives the market its name. Since the product is differentiated, if the businessman operating in a monopolistically competitive industry raises the price of his product, he is likely to lose quite a large volume of sales to his rivals, who are producing close substitutes fot his product. However, he will not lose *all* sales, since his product is somewhat different from those of his rival (compare the loss to Farmer Jones if he tried to sell Number 1 Northern above the market price). In other words, there is an inverse relation between the quantity demanded and the price of the product of the *firm* in monopolistic competition. The quantity demanded is highly responsive to changes in price (in technical terms the demand is very elastic), but the curve does slope down and to the right. As in the other kinds of markets, the profit maximizing businessman will want to produce all of those units for which the marginal revenue exceeds the marginal cost.

The market that is perhaps most familiar to us in North America is *oligopoly*. In an oligopolistic market the significant factor is that there are relatively few firms—sufficiently few that the policies of one firm with respect to such factors as the price of the product, advertising campaigns, and packaging have a definite influence on the sales and on the policies of rival firms in the industry. Firms in an oligopolistic market soon recognize that their actions influence those of their competitors and that their rivals are likely to react to their various policies. In such situations, competition becomes something of a chess game. An intelligent competitor will begin to think several moves ahead. "If I put a dish towel premium in my package, I can probably take an extra 15 percent of the market. However, last time I tried a big premium, my main competitor retaliated with dishes in his package, and by the time he finished, I had lost about 80 percent of my gains. On balance he likely gained, though, and between the two of us we probably reduced the market shares of our three smaller competitors. If another couple of campaigns succeeded in persuading one of those smaller firms to give up business, a potential source of a price war would be removed. On the other hand, the Combines Branch may be eyeing us."

Since an oligopoly is a market in which there are only a few firms, it follows that there must be barriers to entry. They often take the form of a large amount of capital, as in the case of an oil refinery, or enough money to mount an advertising campaign that will permit a new variety of the product to break into a market where people are brand-conscious—a new brand of soap or toothpaste, for example.

Most of our best-known industries are oligopolistic in structure. In the case of oligopolies that supply products to the consumer market—automobiles, television sets, soap and cereals, to name only a few—the product is differentiated. They carry brand names, and their products vie for customers in many ways, advertising being the most obvious. In some oligopolies the product is undifferentiated, or homogeneous. The cement, sulphur, and asbestos industries are examples.

The term "monopoly" is sometimes given a much broader meaning than the narrow, theoretical definition of pure monopoly given above. Sometimes it simply implies the existence of a sloped demand curve and the power to set price. Since most businessmen face a sloped demand curve for their product, most have some degree of monopoly power. Even the farmer, in an atomistically competitive market, does not have to charge the optimum price: he is quite free (in the absence of government regulation) to charge less.

There is no sharp line of demarcation between the different kinds of markets. The spectrum is a continuum in which monopolistic competition and oligopoly blend. There is no obvious line that marks the desirable amount of monopoly power from the undesirable, or the inevitable monopoly from the avoidable.

In this digression into microeconomic theory we have acquired some important tools of analysis including the various cost and revenue concepts, supply and demand, the equilibrium price, and a set of characteristics that enable us to distinguish some different kinds of markets. These microeconomic tools will be used in later parts of the book to analyze a number of problems of the Canadian economy. Their value lies not only in their ability to further our understanding of these problems but also in helping us predict what will happen if underlying market forces change, either fortuitously or as a result of deliberate policy. Properly understood, they provide a valuable way of *thinking* about problems.

9

When discussing economic justice, we are concerned with equity in distributing income and in taxing. Although income distribution is largely determined in the market, governments have implemented programs to combat poverty. The poor comprise three groups: 1) those unavoidably outside the labour force, who cannot be expected to work, 2) the hard-core welfare cases, 3) the working poor, who are poor because of unemployment, low productivity, or discrimination.

Welfare policies in Canada include universal payments like family allowances, social insurance schemes like the Canada and Quebec Pension Plans, and social assistance measures like mothers' allowances and payments to the blind or disabled. Proposals for an income guarantee are gaining popularity; an income floor already exists for the elderly poor.

Topics like the equitable amount of redistribution, and the fairness of taxing according to the benefit principle (you pay for what you get) or the ability-to-pay principle constitute the subject matter of justice in taxation.

Income Distribution: Who Gets What?

The third in our list of Canadian economic goals is economic justice which, as we said earlier, is mainly concerned with the equitable distribution of income. "Distribution" is another of those difficult words in economics that has more than one meaning, and this can lead to confusion. First of all, there is the *process* of distribution, which deals with the progress of goods through the various levels of production, from manufacturer, to wholesaler, and to retailer. Then there is the *theory* of distribution, which explains how our national income is divided and distributed among the various factors of production. This theory explains how the earnings of the different factors of production, human and non-human, are determined.

The Distributive Shares

How is the national income pie divided? What is labour's share? How does it compare in size with the returns to the other factors? One answer to these questions can be found if we follow the *income* approach to national income[1], instead of the expenditure approach which we have been using so far. If we add up the earnings of the various factors of production, we arrive at one of the several important income measures: *net national income at factor cost*. Net national income at factor cost is composed of wages, salaries, and supplementary labour income, as well as military pay and allowances (returns to labour), rent (the return to land), interest (the return to capital), and profit (the return to the owners for taking risk and for their skill in combining other factors of production).

Figure 9-1 shows how the Canadian income pie is divided. The returns to labour (including Canada's armed forces) account for the giant's share—about 73 percent in 1975[2] (a percentage that changes little from year to year). And this figure does not tell the whole story, for labour

---

[1] See Ch. 4.

[2] Calculated from Statistics Canada, *National Income and Expenditure Accounts First Quarter 1976* (Ottawa: Information Canada, August 1976), Table 1, p. 3.

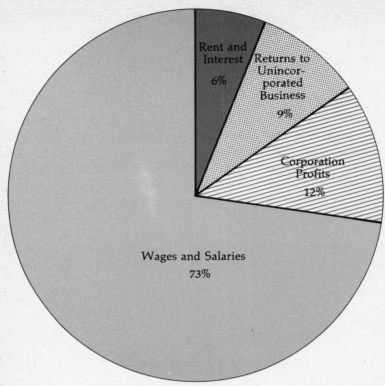

Figure 9-1

comprises an important part of the item called "returns to unincorporated business". Unincorporated business includes sole proprietorships and partnerships, both farm and non-farm. The doctor, the lawyer, the farmer, the man who runs the corner grocery store—they are all included here. Probably most of that item represents a return to labour, although some capital, rent, and perhaps a little entrepreneurial activity may be involved. Interest and other investment income account for about 6 percent, and corporate profits for about 12 percent of net national income at factor cost.[3] To call corporate profits a "distributive share" is somewhat misleading since corporate profits go not only to governments as taxes and to shareholders as dividends, but are also retained as earnings to be used to finance future investment by the firm.

---

[3] This 12 percent figure is calculated after profits paid to nonresidents have been taken out and after some account has been taken of the inventory valuation arising from inflation.

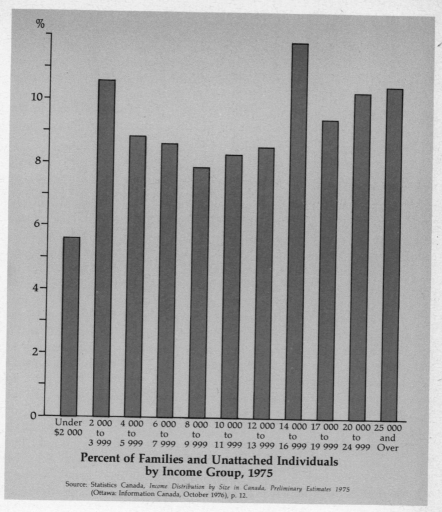

Percent of Families and Unattached Individuals
by Income Group, 1975

Source: Statistics Canada, *Income Distribution by Size in Canada, Preliminary Estimates 1975*
(Ottawa: Information Canada, October 1976), p. 12.

Figure 9-2

The way the income pie is divided among the factors of production gives one picture of the distribution of national output. We can get another picture if we look at the distribution of families and unattached individuals among the different income brackets.[4] As Figure 9-2 shows, 5.5 percent of Canadian families and unattached individuals surveyed by Statistics

---

[4] See Statistics Canada, *Income Distributions by Size in Canada, Preliminary Estimates 1975* (Ottawa: Information Canada, October 1976), p. 12.

Canada earned incomes under $2 000 in 1975. The percentage in the lower-income groups has been declining steadily. In the ten years from 1965 to 1975, for example, families and unattached individuals with incomes of less than $2 000 declined by almost 11 percentage points, from 16.3 percent to 5.5 percent. In the same period, those with incomes of $10 000 and over increased from 11.5 percent to 58.7 percent. At the upper end of the scale, 20.7 percent earned $20 000 or more in 1975. The median income in the same year was $12 106; that is, half the families and unattached individuals earned less than $12 106, and half earned more.

THE MARKET SYSTEM

What decides who will earn a high income and who will earn a low one, or what the distributive share of labour will be? In our mixed capitalistic system, for the most part we leave it to the market to determine the prices of the factors of production, just as we leave it to the market to determine the prices of most products. The greater the price a factor can earn for its productive services, or the more productive resources it owns, the greater the share of the total output of the economy's goods and services that factor can command. It is through these rewards to the factors that aggregate income is distributed. If a family earns an income of, say, $10 000 a year, it is because this figure is the sum of the returns to all members of that family in their role as factors of production. Their earned income will be the sum of the returns from their labour in the form of wages and salaries, plus what they earn as landowners, plus the interest they earn for the use of their money capital, plus any return in the form of profit for their activity as entrepreneurs—returns for their skills in combining other resources in order to produce goods and services, or for taking risk. The family's *total* income, as contrasted with its earned income, may be increased by gifts (in which case they are benefiting from someone else's participation in the productive process) or by transfer payments from the government in the form of such items as family allowance and unemployment insurance.

The market does not treat all comers equally. Figure 9-2 has shown that some who offer their services in the labour market get large returns, while others earn small ones. Why should this be? Consider the labour market, to begin with. It is a complex market because "labour" comprises the services of such different individuals as industrial psychologists, management consultants, architects, typists, waitresses, mailboys and janitors, to mention only a few. If we consider the market as a whole, we are ignoring important differences in the quality of labour—differences based on such factors as the education, training, skill, health, diligence, experience, and efficiency of the different members of the work force. It is more realistic to think of a large number of different markets for groups of workers with different abilities, skills, and educational levels.

In any labour market, as in any product market, the *demand* for the factor is an important determinant of its price, and this demand comes mainly from businesses that need the services of the various factors in order to produce the items that consumers want. It is because of the consumer demand for goods and services that businesses have a demand for labour and capital. In other words, the demand for these factor services is an indirect, or a *derived*, demand. If the demand for a product increases, businessmen wanting to produce more of that product will have to get more resources, and this will mean competing for these resources in the market by offering a higher price for the factors of production they need. The *productivity* of the factor is also important. The more a worker can produce in an hour or in a day, the more valuable he is to a producer, the greater is the demand for his services, and the higher is the price he can command.

The demand for labour is an important determinant of the return to that factor, but it is only part of the story: the supply also is important—the quantity of a given kind of labour that will be available at any particular time at the different wage rates that may be offered in the market. Supply and demand interact to determine the return to the factor, just as they interacted to determine the price of butter, as we saw in Chapter 8.

Institutional factors, which will be given closer attention in the next chapter, also influence the price that labour can command in the market. Returns to labour are affected by various laws as well as by the bargaining power of unions. Workers long ago discovered that if they banded together to bargain with their employers, they were usually more successful in getting what they wanted than if each tried to bargain individually. Thus, the existence of such bargaining groups, or unions, may affect the returns to particular groups of workers. It is an interesting and pervasive phenomenon, however, that labour's share of the national income pie has remained relatively stable: the ratio of profits to wages and salaries has changed little over time. This suggests that the actions of unions have resulted not so much in an increase in the returns to labour as a group, but rather in a redistribution from non-unionized workers, or workers in weak unions, to workers in powerful unions.

There are other conditions that influence the price labour can command in the market—for example, the region where the factors of production are located. There are large economic disparities between various parts of Canada, and incomes in the poorer areas, or in areas where unemployment is rife, will be generally lower than those in the more prosperous regions, even for people with the same training. If the economic disparities were removed, or if the labour force were fully mobile so that workers, obeying the dictates of the market, would move to those areas that offered higher wages, then the differentials in the returns to the factors of production would be reduced. Regional disparities and the immobility of labour, however, present Canada with major economic policy problems.

Poverty in Canada

The problem of the distribution of national income is solved primarily by the market. The market is an efficient institution, but that does not mean that we have to be purists and demand that the market be left free to make all decisions without interference. We are not compelled to accept what we consider to be an inequitable solution to the problem of the distribution of income. A coldly logical discussion about the use or misuse of a tonne of iron ore, or even the failure to use it, causes us no concern. Workers, however, are not just another tonne of iron ore: they are people, and the use of *human* resources raises quite a different problem. The market is an engine of progress: it rewards initiative, skill and personality, and it metes out punishment to the lazy, the badly trained, and the unfit. Unfortunately, it may also punish the unlucky, the victims of accidents, and the mentally retarded; and in these cases our sense of justice causes us to be dissastisfied with market decisions about income distribution. Left to itself, the market frequently does not provide enough jobs to keep everyone employed. Moreover, many of those who offer their services in the market can command such a small price for them that they cannot achieve a decent minimum standard of living. The problem of poverty is a serious one in Canada, as the Economic Council has pointed out:

> Poverty in Canada is real. Its numbers are not in the thousands, but the millions. There is more of it than our society can tolerate, more than our economy can afford, and far more than existing measures and efforts can cope with. Its persistence, at a time when the bulk of Canadians enjoy one of the highest standards of living in the world, is a disgrace.[5]

The Council made some estimates concerning the extent of poverty in Canada. If one accepts the definition that the poor are those families who spend 70 percent or more of their incomes on food, shelter, and clothing,

---

[5] Economic Council of Canada, *Fifth Annual Review* (Ottawa: Queen's Printer, 1968), p. 103. Reproduced with the permission of the Queen's Printer for Canada.

then the information collected in the 1961 census indicates that about 27 percent of the non-farm population in Canada—about 4.2 million people— were living in poverty at that time. If the farm population is included, the figure might be as high as 29 percent. If the definition of poverty is relaxed somewhat to assume that individuals and families who spend 60 percent, instead of 70 percent, on food, shelter, and clothing can be classified as poor, then the percentage of non-farm population so classified rises from 27 percent to 41 percent.[6]

WHO ARE THE POOR?

We can determine who the poor are if we say, for example, that they are those who fall below a certain income level. Poverty can be measured in either an absolute sense or in a relative sense. In the absolute sense it exists when people fall below a certain level of real income. One definition that Statistics Canada uses of low-income families is based on an income level below which low-income urban families normally spend 70 percent or more of their incomes on food, shelter, and clothing. Since 1961, when these income cut-offs were initially established, they have been updated by using the Consumer Price Index: in other words, changes in the price level have been taken into account, but the real incomes that define the poverty line have not been changed. For 1974 the updated low-income cut-offs were set at $2 518 for an unattached individual, and at $4 196, $5 034, and $5 872 for families of two, three, and four respectively. Defined in this way, poverty may decline over time as real incomes rise and if redistribution policies are successful. The data suggest that between 1971 and 1974, for example, the percentage of families below the updated low income cut-offs declined from 15.9 percent to 10.6 percent, and for unattached individuals, from 37.6 percent to 29.7 percent.[7]

On the other hand, poverty may be defined in relative terms. The Special Senate Committee on Poverty, for example, suggested that the poverty line should not be tied to fixed expenditures at a point in time, but rather should reflect changing patterns of expenditure; that they should reflect not only changes in the cost of living, but also changes in the standard of living.[8] Defined *relatively*, poverty is not a problem that the economy will grow out of.

---

[6] *Ibid.*, pp. 109-110.

[7] Statistics Canada, *Income Distributions by Size in Canada, 1971* (Ottawa: Information Canada, 1973), p. 72; and *Preliminary Estimates 1974* (Ottawa, October 1975), pp. 7 & 16. Comparable data are not available for 1975.

[8] Special Senate Committee on Poverty, *Poverty in Canada* (Ottawa: Information Canada, 1971), p. 7.

During the hearings of the Senate Committee on Poverty, the poor were frequently considered to fall into three categories[9]: those who are unavoidably outside the labour force, and they accounted for about a quarter of the poor; the "hard-core welfarites" who make up about another quarter; and the "working poor", who accounted for about half the poverty problem. Those in the first category cannot work, or should not be expected to work because they are disabled, blind, old, or are suffering from lengthy debilitating illness or the loss of the breadwinner of the family.

Those in the second category present a special problem for economic analysis. One of the basic assumptions of economics is that economic man is rational, and "rational" has a particular meaning. A rational *businessman* is one whose objective is to maximize profits, for profits are the motivating force that makes the market system work efficiently. This is not to say that economists assume that all businessmen maximize profits: a careful look at the business community would convince anyone that this is not always so. It simply means that our economic theory centres around the profit-maximizing businessman. A rational *individual*, on the other hand, is one who maximizes his satisfaction, who prefers more goods to fewer. It follows logically from this assumption that people will want to work in order to be able to get a larger basket of goods, and that if they are not working, it must be the fault of the economic system, which is not providing them with jobs. This idea was strongly reinforced by the experience of the 1930s, when about a fifth of the Canadian labour force desperately wanted work, but the economic system could not provide the jobs.

We have discovered, however, that not everyone wants to work. There is a group, sometimes referred to as the "unemployed unemployables" or "the hard-core unemployed", that has no desire to enter the labour force. For the most part they are people who have dropped out of school and have become used to life on the streets. Many of them are victims of poverty. They have developed major handicaps with respect to work habits, and frequently have police records and alcohol and drug problems. It is difficult to know how many of them there are because a considerable number of them in effect have dropped out of society: many have no fixed abode, and census takers have trouble in obtaining a record of them. No one wants to give such people jobs because they have no training. It is hard to persuade them to go to school because they have no motivation.

---

[9] T. Courchene, "Some Reflections on the Senate Hearings on Poverty" in *Economics Canada: Selected Readings*, eds. B. S. Keirstead, J. F. Earl, J. R. G. Brander, and C. M. Waddell (Toronto: Macmillan of Canada, 1974), pp. 205-206.

When they *are* persuaded to take jobs, they frequently give them up for no good reason.

Attempting to cope with the hardcore unemployed requires special kinds of policy, although, to the extent that they are successful in maintaining full employment, stabilization policies have an important role to play. If the economy is operating at its full potential output and if no production gap exists, then employers wanting to expand their work force frequently are compelled to hire workers whom formerly they would not have considered. Policies to maintain full employment are important for another reason: when there is slack in the economy, there accumulates a large number of *young* unemployables who may easily become a continuing problem. Such people tend to perpetuate the situation by passing on to their children their attitudes and their inability to adapt.

Full employment policies, though helpful, are not enough to solve the problem. Redistribution policies (merely giving unemployables more money) are not likely to be of much use if the objective is to rehabilitate this group and make them productive. Special policies are needed. There need to be policies for training, preferably on the job, so that training becomes work-related rather than merely classroom experience, where employers are vitally interested in the workers' progress, and where motivation may be supplied by fellow workers and by the wage earned at the end of the week. Social rehabilitation will be necessary, too, before any progress can be made in solving the intractable problem of the poverty of the hard-core unemployed.

The final group includes those who are in the labour force—employed or unemployed—whose incomes fall below the poverty line. The problem of this group, according to Harry G. Johnson[10], stems from three major causes: (1) unemployment, caused by the failure of the economy to maintain aggregate demand; (2) the low productivity of workers, caused by lack of skills, immobility, or cultural deficiencies; and (3) discrimination— against the aged poor who would like to work; against women; against the Indians, the Métis, and the Blacks; against the uneducated; and discrimination caused by limitations on the supply side, imposed by professional associations and unions on entry into different jobs.

The most important policy measure to fight poverty of this kind is to maintain full employment. Various kinds of discrimination must be eliminated; the skills of the work force must be upgraded; and the amount of capital must be increased so there will be a commensurate increase in

---

[10] Harry G. Johnson, "Poverty and Unemployment" in *The Economics of Poverty, An American Paradox*, Burton A. Weisbrod, ed. (Englewood Cliffs, N.J.: Prentice-Hall, Inc., 1965), pp. 166-168.

workers' productivity. It is important to adopt manpower policies that will improve mobility; but unless the demand for goods and services is sufficiently high that the derived demand for labour remains high, then these policies are unlikely to solve the problem of poverty.

SOCIAL SECURITY POLICIES

Over the years, provincial and federal governments have adopted a large variety of welfare policies. The Senate Committee on Poverty was very critical of them because these policies treat the symptoms of poverty rather than tackle the problem itself. There are four elements in the present welfare structure. The first is *universal payments* or demogrants, which include the Old Age Security Pension and family allowances. The pension was set at $100 per month in 1973, subject to escalation in step with increases in the cost of living. Family allowances were almost tripled in 1974 to bring them to an average of $20 per child under 18 years of age. These payments are universal, but because the federal regulations make them taxable income, low-income families and pensioners benefit more.

In addition to the universal payments there are *social insurance* schemes such as the Canada (and Quebec) Pension Plan, unemployment insurance, and Workmen's Compensation. The third element is *social assistance*. In Canada there is the Canada Assistance Plan. This comprehensive public assistance measure, which went into effect in 1966, provides the basis for coordinating the numerous public welfare programs in each province, including payments to the blind and disabled, as well as relief payments. The plan also covers assistance to needy mothers and dependent children, children being looked after by child-care agencies, youthful offenders, and needy persons in special care homes like homes for the aged and for unmarried mothers, and nursing homes. The agreement provides for the federal government to cover half the costs of assistance of agreeing provinces, provided the provinces satisfy the basic requirements of those who receive the aid. Basic requirements include food, shelter, clothing, fuel, utilities, household supplies, and personal requirements. All provinces in Canada except Quebec are members of this plan: Quebec opted out of the Canada Assistance Plan, as it had opted out of most shared-cost programs.

The most controversial part of any social security plan is the fourth element—*income guarantee*. The Senate Committee on Poverty recommended a guaranteed annual income for all Canadians with insufficient incomes and advocated that it take the form of a "negative income tax".[11] Under such a scheme, subsidies are paid to low-income households through the personal income tax machinery. If a given tax-reporting unit has an income below a certain level, it gets a subsidy; if its income is above that level, it pays a tax.

Canada started an income guarantee in 1967 with the Guaranteed Income Supplement, a scheme for old-age pensioners. In July 1976 about 55 percent of this group was receiving a supplement, the average amounting to over $69.[12] At the beginning of 1976 the basic pension amounted to almost $133; the guaranteed supplement, which is also adjusted upward with changes in the cost of living, amounted to an additional $93, so that pensioners were guaranteed a minimum of just over $226.

The idea of an income guarantee is gaining popular acceptance in Canada. It was an integral part of the *Working Paper on Social Security in Canada* (the "Orange Paper") presented by the Minister of National Health and Welfare as a set of proposals for reform which would be explored jointly by the federal and provincial governments. The paper proposes a full guarantee for those who are unable to work or who cannot find jobs, including the retired or disabled; single-parent families; and those who at present are not employable because of factors such as lack of skills, or age, or length of time out of the labour market. It also proposes income supplements, with built-in incentives to work, for those who are working but whose incomes are not adequate because of factors like family size, or too little work, or low-paying self employment.[13]

The form that any guaranteed income should take is highly controversial. The idea is not to create a system that appears to give people a free choice between leisure and work, or a system that would destroy the incentive to work. If eligibility is based on income alone, which is the assumption of negative income tax schemes, then there is concern on the part of many that it will be abused by all kinds of "free-loaders", although the experiments in the United States have suggested that in fact few people choose *not* to work when the guarantee is available.[14]

One of the worst features of the many diverse social welfare schemes in Canada is that there is little or no incentive to get off social assistance, no matter how much the welfare recipients may want to work. For one

---

[11] Special Senate Committee on Poverty, *op. cit.*, p. xv.

[12] Canadian Tax Foundation, *The National Finances 1975-76* (Toronto, 1976), p. 90.

[13] Marc Lalonde, Minister of National Health and Welfare, *Working Paper on Social Security in Canada* (Ottawa: Government of Canada, April 18, 1973), pp. 30-32.

[14] A. W. Johnson, "Canada's Social Security Review 1973-75: The Central Issue," *Canadian Public Policy*, 1:4, Autumn 1975, p. 467.

thing, social assistance for a larger family, which takes into account the number of children, may turn out to be higher in some provinces than employment at the minimum wage, which does not take size of family into account. Moreover, in most provinces, if anyone on social welfare takes a job, the loss in social welfare income has been dollar for dollar. A federal-provincial experiment is being conducted in a Manitoba community involving 2 500 families; its purpose is to see how income guarantees affect willingness to work. People under this scheme will have the guaranteed minimum, but will be permitted to raise their income level by working. Government support will be decreased gradually to zero as families earn more.[15]

Who Pays What?

Social security programs are expensive. They are paid for by taxes, and this raises a new issue of economic justice—equity in taxation. Taxes themselves can be a tool of redistribution: they have the effect of making incomes less unequal than they otherwise would be; therefore, we should not leave the goal of achieving economic justice without considering the question of taxes.

Benjamin Franklin once said, "The only human certainties are death and taxes", and in linking these two unpleasant prospects he fairly well summed up our attitude to taxes. The economist J. B. Say, writing about a century and a half ago, suggested that the best plan of finance was to spend little, and that the best of all taxes was that which was least in amount. Most people today would agree with him. Yet taxes provide the government with revenues, just as prices provide businesses (including some government businesses) with revenues. We do not object to providing industries with their revenues: we want the goods and services they produce, and we are willing to pay for them. We also want the goods and services the government provides—defence, education, roads, sidewalks, fire protection, social security, and so on—but we do not want to have to pay for them. We object to paying the taxes that are necessary to finance these goods and services.

It is a rather perverse attitude when you come to think of it. We can try to rationalize our position by saying that we want both the car and the road to drive it on, but while we can see, touch, and drive the car we pay for, none of us can point to a specific bit of road and say, "I paid for that." We do not see any *quid pro quo* for the taxes we pay. Pity the poor tax collector. It is no wonder that the cynical ones come up with the

---

[15] Canadian Tax Foundation, *op. cit.*, p. 95.

principle: the tax is best that gets the most feathers for the least squawking!

The private sector spends vast sums to persuade us to buy its output. Perhaps what we need is an advertising campaign by the government: admen might be able to come up with some slogans that would do for the government what TV commercials do for private business. In the future, we may be able to look forward to an interruption in the middle of hockey night in Canada to hear a message such as: "A tax a day keeps the recession away". Who knows, by offering an adequate reward (perhaps by agreeing not to collect income taxes for a year) the government might persuade a hero of the silver screen to let go of his cigarette long enough to intone sincerely, "I pay my federal taxes because I *enjoy* them."

EQUITY IN TAXATION

Economists and philosophers have always concerned themselves with developing guidelines or principles of taxation. The problem has been to find guidelines that would produce an equitable tax system. Everyone would agree that we must have a just system. There the agreement is likely to end, however, for as soon as specific proposals are discussed, some are bound to regard them as inequitable. Quite probably if someone were to ask you what constituted an equitable tax, the answer you gave would, in the last analysis, boil down to "The most equitable tax is one that somebody else pays." The argument about what constitutes equity in tax systems has been going on for centuries, and answers have changed from generation to generation. At one time the poll tax, a per person tax of fixed amount, was considered the most equitable tax. A tax on glass window panes in a house was another. Today we favour progressive incomes taxes, but it was not too long ago that proportional taxes were considered equitable.

One principle of taxation that has gained a certain amount of support is the principle of tax neutrality—the idea that an equitable tax system leaves people in the same relative position as it finds them. According to this concept of equity, taxes should not be a tool of redistribution. Obviously there is no right or wrong answer to the question of how much redistribution there should be, and it is not surprising to find suggestions at the other extreme that taxes and other redistributive tools should be used to make incomes *equal*: in a democratic society in which we believe in the equality of individuals (one man, one vote), they say, economic justice demands equality of income. Both the Bible and Karl Marx have suggested that the appropriate principle is "from each according to his ability, to each according to his need". Experience has shown that reliance on this principle has tended to cause production to falter and break down. Few argue for equality of income; but most support the idea that there should be *less inequality* than the free market system, if left to itself, produces. For the most part, however, the argument about equity has resolved itself into a discussion of two major principles of taxation: the benefit principle and the ability-to-pay principle.

The Benefit Principle According to the benefit principle, equity demands that those who receive equal benefits from the government should pay the same tax, and taxes on others should be adjusted according to the benefit each receives. This sounds fair enough: you pay for what you get. People who drive cars, for example, should pay for the roads, directly through tolls or indirectly through gasoline taxes. However, certain problems become evident when we try to apply the principle universally and attempt to make the orphans pay for the maintenance of the orphanage, or tax the unemployed and the disabled to pay for the relief that is being provided for them. If we adopt the benefit principle as the universal principle of taxation, then welfare services and transfer payments are ruled out.

An additional problem in using this principle is the very complex one of measuring benefits. One major reason for government spending is that it provides services that are collectively consumed—goods and services like education, defence, and police protection, for which it is almost impossible to determine the benefit derived by a single individual, and therefore almost impossible to decide how much each should pay to support that particular service.

The benefit principle is an equitable guideline for determining who should pay for certain goods and services. The consensus today, however, is that it is not acceptable as a universal principle of taxation.

Ability To Pay According to the ability-to-pay principle, equity demands that people with the same ability to pay should pay the same taxes, and that those with a greater ability to pay should pay more. Income is the customary measure of the ability to pay, though some argue that it would be more equitable to consider accumulated assets (wealth) either in addition to, or instead of, income. The principle of ability to pay, then, suggests that the more income (or wealth) people have, the more taxes they should pay. This still does not tell us whether the tax rates should be progressive, proportional, or regressive.

To make clear precisely what is meant by progressive, proportional, and regressive tax rates, consider Table 9-1, which deals with two individuals, Mr. Green who has an income of $5 000, and Mr. Brown, with an income of $10 000.

Table 9-1
TAX RATES

	Income	Progressive		Proportional		Regressive	
		Rate	*Tax*	*Rate*	*Tax*	*Rate*	*Tax*
Mr. Green	$5 000	10%	$500	10%	$500	10%	$500
Mr. Brown	10 000	20%	2 000	10%	1 000	5%	500

For the sake of simplicity, we shall assume that all income is taxable. If the tax rate on Mr. Green's income is 10 percent he will have a tax bill of $500. If the rate structure is to be progressive, Mr. Bown will have to pay a higher rate of taxes (not merely a greater absolute amount)—say 20 percent, so that his tax bill is $2 000. The system would also have been progressive if Mr. Brown had paid the same rate as Mr. Green (10 percent) on the first $5 000, and a higher rate, say 20 percent, on the second $5 000, giving him a total tax bill of $1 500.

Defining proportional and regressive tax rates may help to clarify the meaning of a progressive rate. If the tax rate is proportional, both tax payers will pay the same proportion or percentage of their income—say, 10 percent. As indicated in Table 9-1, Mr. Brown would pay more money than Mr. Green, $1 000, as compared with $500 in our example, but the tax *rates* are identical. Proportional taxes for a long time were considered to be most equitable. Even today there are some who advocate them on the grounds that progressive tax rates have an adverse influence on people's incentives to work and to invest, and thus tend to slow down the growth rate of the economy.

To complete the story, regressive taxes are those that bear more heavily on the poor. A poll tax is a good example. Suppose that every income earner is required to pay a tax of $500 a year. This represents 10 percent of Mr. Green's income, but only 5 percent of the income of the wealthier Mr. Brown. The higher the income, the lower the proportion of income represented by the poll tax. Regressive taxes are regarded as inequitable.

To return to the question of the kind of tax rate required by the ability-to-pay principle, the table shows clearly that both progressive and proportional rates ensure that more will be paid by those with higher incomes. Furthermore, the regressive rates could also meet the requirement: if we took $900 (9 percent) from Mr. Brown and $500 from Mr. Green, Mr. Brown would be paying more absolutely, but the 9 percent rate is still regressive since the $500 taken from Mr. Green represents 10 percent of his income.

The justification that economists sometimes give for progressive tax rates is the law of diminishing marginal utility, which we discussed in Chapter 8. This principle states that the extra satisfaction derived from each additional unit of a commodity (income, in this case) in any given time period is less than the extra satisfaction derived from the previous unit. The argument is that the 101st dollar of weekly income adds more satisfaction than the 201st dollar, and that the 201st adds considerably more than the 2 001st. This does not mean that $2 001 yield less *total* satisfaction than $201, which is obviously not true, and this is not what is meant by *marginal* utility. It is the extra satisfaction from the *last dollar* of income that we are discussing. If we agree that this principle has universal applicability, then when it comes to raising a dollar of government revenue through taxes, it follows that the total satisfaction of the community would be greater (the pain of taxation would be less) if we took that dollar from the person earning $2 001 a week rather than from the one earning only $201. This implies a heavier tax *rate* on higher incomes, which is what progressive taxation means.

We have confined our discussion to income taxes, but other taxes like sales taxes can be discussed in the same terms. If a sales tax of a fixed percentage is levied on all goods and services, then technically it could be considered a proportional tax because the rate is the same for everyone. Its *effect*, however, may be quite different, for if two people buy the same quantity of taxed goods out of different incomes, then the tax will bear more heavily on the person with the smaller income: it may be regressive in its effect, in other words. However, sales taxes may be made progressive: if food, children's clothing, and other necessities are exempted, while luxury items are taxed, then the sales tax can be made to bear more heavily on those with incomes high enough to buy luxury goods.

Equity in taxation is an important part of the broad goal of economic justice, and the way taxes are used as a tool of redistribution has an important effect on the objective of achieving an equitable distribution of income. There are other important factors that should be considered if we are to make a more complete study of redistribution. First of all there are the laws and institutions that affect the labour market and hence affect the distributive shares of members of the labour force. Then there is the problem of redistribution of income among the various provinces. There are great regional disparities in Canada, and one of the goals, ever since Confederation, has been to ensure that Canadians living in different parts of the country are equitably treated. We shall turn to these two problems in the next two chapters.

10

Governments try to improve the performance of the labour market by their manpower policies. Workers form unions and press for legislation to improve their position. The Canada Labour Code and similar provincial laws regulate employment practices, labour standards (including minimum wages, overtime, and holidays), safety practices, and industrial relations.

Three kinds of unions exist in Canada: local, national and international; many are affiliated with central labour congresses. An important union function is collective bargaining. If disputes arise while management and labour are negotiating an agreement, or during the life of a contract, a third party may conciliate or arbitrate. Only after the requirements of the contract or the industrial-disputes legislation have been met are unions legally free to strike, and management free to lock out workers.

Important contemporary issues include the role of unions in aggravating inflation, strikes in essential services, foreign domination, and unions' effect on the freedom of individuals.

Workers and the Distribution of Income

The role of workers in the economy has already been given some attention. The importance of the contribution of labour (its quantity, quality, and productivity) to growth was discussed in Chapter 7. In the previous chapter on distribution, it was pointed out that labour's share of Net National Income at Factor Cost (one of the important measures derived from the income approach to GNP) amounted to 73 percent, not counting the part included in returns to unincorporated business. The returns to labour depend on supply and demand in the labour market; and the demand derives from the demand for all of the goods and services produced in the economy.

There are imperfections in the labour market. One that has already been mentioned is the immobility of labour, which affects the returns to workers. In an industry where there is a strong demand for the product, wages may have to be raised to attract more workers, and the incomes of all workers in the industry are likely to be increased. At the same time, as some workers move out of an industry (or region) to a higher-paying one, the quantity supplied to the industry that is not expanding decreases, and our analysis of supply and demand suggests that as long as other conditions do not change, this will result in an upward pressure on the price (wages) of those who remain in the industry (or region). However, if workers are not aware of the existence of higher-paying jobs, or if they know but cannot afford to move, or are not properly trained, then this immobility can result in their earning a smaller share of the income pie.

Canada's manpower policies are administered by the Department of Manpower and Immigration. These policies were expanded greatly during the 1960s, giving Canada one of the most extensive programs in the world.[1] Through its large network of manpower centres, the Department works on both the demand and supply sides to try to improve the operation of the labour market. It offers job information and testing and counselling services; it helps students find summer jobs and refers people for full- and part-time courses under the Canada Manpower Training Program. The Canada Manpower Mobility Program helps workers move to areas where there are job opportunities. The Department also looks

---

[1] Sylvia Ostrey and Mahmood A. Zaidi, *Labour Economics in Canada*, 2nd ed. (Toronto: Macmillan of Canada, 1972), p. 180.

after the Local Initiatives Program and the Training-on-the-job Program—part of the government's plan to help alleviate the problem of seasonal unemployment.

To talk about *the* market for labour is to oversimplify greatly: as was pointed out in the last chapter, labour is by no means a homogeneous product. Members of the labour force include managers and professionals, barbers and baseball players, stockroom clerks and salesmen, farmers and fishermen, craftsmen and transport workers, as well as labourers, unskilled workers, and dog psychiatrists. There are great differences in the type of market that exists for the various kinds of labour. Some people operate as individuals in markets that might be described as competitive—that is, markets in which the forces of supply and demand operate relatively freely to determine the price of that labour. Non-unionized people fall into this category. More than two thirds of the total labour force in Canada do not belong to unions. There is no union of managers, for example, and many professions are not unionized. Agricultural workers, by and large, are not members of unions; nor are most of those who work in the service industries. Even in the industrial sector, where most unions are concentrated, there are many firms whose workers are not unionized. In such cases, it is the market that largely determines the returns to non-unionized workers, although its power is limited to some extent by certain provisions of protective labour legislation. Such returns can be very high, as we know from the incomes of doctors, hockey and baseball players, and managers. Workers in some non-unionized companies get returns higher than those in unionized companies, because management is sometimes willing to pay a premium to keep the unions out.

Sometimes unions have found that a single employer or group of employers is sufficiently large and powerful that it can influence the market and set the terms on which workers will be hired. One response to this power of employers has been for workers to organize into unions: this is the concept J. K. Galbraith called "countervailing power." When powerful unions bargain with powerful employers, the market cannot be described as competitive, for there are strong monopolistic elements on both sides. Neither side is a price taker: both can affect price. This situation in economic jargon is sometimes referred to as *bilateral monopoly*.

Legislation Affecting Workers

In addition to forming unions, workers have responded to the power of employers by pressing strongly for government legislation that would protect them and their share of income; and, like the farmers, they have been successful. The power to enact labour legislation in Canada rests with eleven legislative bodies—the federal government and the ten provincial governments. Section 92 of the British North America Act gives the provinces the right to make laws relating to property and civil rights. Through the process of judicial interpretation of the constitution, labour legislation has come to be regarded as a matter of civil rights, and hence primarily a matter of provincial jurisdiction. Though this has not always been the case, federal labour legislation today applies only to such industries as navigation, shipping, interprovincial railways, and radio broadcasting stations, which are specifically under federal jurisdiction, and to undertakings that Parliament has declared to be in the general interest of the country as a whole or of two or more provinces. As might be expected, similar legislation is to be found in all eleven jurisdictions covering a wide variety of subjects—minimum wages, hours of work, holidays, physical conditions of work, labour-management relations, workmen's compensation, and a great many others.

Under the federal jurisdiction the major pieces of labour legislation have been consolidated into one, the *Canada Labour Code*, which went into force in 1971. The Code, which is administered by the Department of Labour, is divided into various parts that relate to employment practices, labour standards, safety, and industrial relations. The fair employment section, for example, prohibits discrimination by employers and unions on the grounds of race, colour, religion, or national origin. Another section specifies equal pay for equal work for men and women. The section on standards covers matters like hours of work and overtime, minimum wages, annual vacations, and other holidays. The prime purpose of the section on safety is to ensure safe working conditions for employees in industries under federal jurisdiction. In the matter of industrial relations, the Code gives employees and employers in industries under federal jurisdiction the right to organize and bargain collectively, prohibits coercion and discrimination in union activity, and prevents employers from dominating or interfering with unions. The Department of Labour administers the provisions that relate to conciliation procedures, provides mediation services, and processes applications for certification and decertification.

Provincial governments have also enacted legislation relating to all of these matters for industries under their jurisdiction. There are minimum wage laws throughout the country, and the same wage rates are established for both sexes in the majority of provinces. Most provinces have anti-discrimination laws, general hours-of-work laws, annual vacation legislation, as well as factory or industrial safety acts. All provinces have workmen's compensation laws that provide for payments to employees for accidents suffered while on the job.

In addition, there is legislation in all provinces that is very similar to the industrial relations part of the *Canada Labour Code*. This legislation has the same general purposes as the Code: it ensures the right of labour to organize and bargain collectively; it provides for certification of unions as the exclusive bargaining agents of a group of employees; and it provides procedures to help settle disputes.

The effect of many of these laws is to increase the income level of workers and to increase employers' costs. The minimum wage laws, for example, make the lower range of the supply curve for workers irrelevant in some markets. Some workers who might be willing to work for less are prevented from doing so; employers are similarly constrained in their hiring. The result is that fewer people may be hired in some markets, but some of those who do work may earn more than would be the case if the law did not exist.

Unions

Unionism in Canada is at least a century and a half old. Union membership has grown by fits and starts. There was a forward spurt during and immediately after the First World War. It ebbed and flowed during the 1920s and fell back during the recession of the 1930s. The massive industrialization during the Second World War caused a tremendous growth; the number of union members doubled during the war years. Membership reached the million mark in 1949 and two million in 1968. At the beginning of 1975 a union membership of 2.9 million constituted almost 30 percent of the total civilian labour force and 37 percent of the non-agricultural labour force.[2]

Union objectives have also changed. In the early days, the major aim, often bitterly opposed by management, was to achieve union recognition. When this objective had been achieved by most unions, higher wage levels became the key issue at the bargaining table. Collective agreements in the early days tended to be short documents with relatively few clauses. In contrast, union contracts today are often spread over hundreds of pages, with clauses that cover not only the central issue of wages, but also everything from consultation procedures, medical plans, holidays with pay and hours of work, to the number of times a week eggs can be served in a bush camp. Union influence is becoming more and more pervasive in company affairs and, indeed, in the entire country.

---

[2] Canada Department of Labour, Economics and Research Branch, *Labour Organizations in Canada 1974-1975* (Ottawa: Queen's Printer, 1975), Table 1, pp. xviii-xix.

THE STRUCTURE OF UNIONS

There are three different kinds of unions in Canada: local unions, national unions, and international unions. *Local unions* are the smallest units. They are local organizations in which the local unit comprises the entire union; in 1975 there were 379 small local unions, accounting for less than 3 percent of total union membership. *National unions* are unions with many branches or locals that are chartered only in Canada. There were 98 such unions in 1975, and they accounted for 46 percent of total union membership. More than half (51 percent) of union members belonged to *international* unions — American unions with Canadian chapters.[3]

In 1975 there were four unions that had memberships in Canada greater than 100 000. These included the Canadian Union of Public Employees (198 900); the United Steelworkers of America (187 000); the Public Service Alliance of Canada (136 000); and the International Union, United Automobile, Aerospace and Agricultural Implement Workers of America (117 500).[4] An additional ten unions had memberships between 50 000 and 100 000.

In addition to the local, national, and international unions, there are central labour congresses that act as spokesmen for unions in policy matters. In Canada these central labour bodies include the Canadian Labour Congress (CLC); the largely Francophone Confederation of National Trade Unions (CNTU) or Confédération des Syndicats Nationaux (CNS); the Centrale des Syndicats Démocratiques (CSD) formed by a group who seceded from the CNTU in 1972; and the Confederation of Canadian Unions (CCU). The huge American organization — the merged American Federation of Labour and Congress of Industrial Organizations (AFL-CIO) — also operates in Canada.

Most of the international unions (78 of 94, representing about 43 percent of total union membership) are affiliated with both the CLC in Canada and the AFL-CIO in the United States. Four, however, are affiliated only with the AFL-CIO. The remainder are affiliated only with the CLC or do not have any affiliation with a central labour body. Beyond the 43 percent of union members who are jointly affiliated with the CLC and AFL-CIO, a further 28 percent are affiliated with the CLC alone. The other central bodies have a considerably smaller proportion of the affiliated membership: the CNTU (CSN) has just over 6 percent, the CSD just under 1.5 percent, and the CCU has less than one percent. The rest of the membership has no affiliation with a central congress.

---

[3] *Ibid.*, Table 3, p. xxiii.
[4] *Ibid.*, pp. xvi-xvii.

Aside from these national federations, there are also local and provincial federations. At all three levels federations have little in the way of economic power. They rely on the contributions of member unions for their funds; and the major functions that we associate with unions, like collective bargaining over wages and working conditions, and strikes, fall outside the jurisdiction of these federations. Most federations concern themselves with problems like research, education, and inter-union rivalry. Federations can try to discipline unions for corrupt or irresponsible actions; however, their tools of control are not very powerful. They can only rebuke the erring union or expel it, as happened to the Teamsters and the Seafarers' International Union.

The *political* power of federations is something else again. Federations represent a powerful lobby for labour in Canada; their greatest importance comes from their ability to speak for unions in many matters including social security, wages and hours of work, education, manpower uses, and so on. Union members are to be found on boards and commissions of all kinds—the Economic Council of Canada is one example. Labour is most effective when it can speak with a single voice, and throughout the history of unionism in Canada, continuing efforts have been made to unite unions into a single federation. It is apparent, however, that these efforts have not been successful. Labour does not speak with one voice on important policy matters; instead it speaks through several federations. Moreover, there are more than half a million union members in independent local, national, and international unions that have no affiliation with any federation, and these independent unions include some large ones like the Quebec Teachers' Corporation, which has close to 85 000 members, and the Teamsters' Union, with almost 76 000 members.[5] However, although union membership is at its highest in history, not much more than a third of the non-agricultural workers in the country are union members. One must hasten to add that the degree of unionization understates the influence of unions. The effect of their lobbying is evident in government legislation and affects both non-unionized as well as unionized workers. Furthermore, the wage increases, working conditions, and fringe benefits that unions get through collective bargaining have an important (if indirect) effect on working conditions in non-unionized establishments.

COLLECTIVE BARGAINING

Collective bargaining—bargaining by groups rather than by individuals—is a fundamental right of employees and employers in Canada. Unions may be recognized as the exclusive bargaining agents of employees or appropriate groups of employees. Such recognition may be accorded voluntarily

[5] *Ibid.*

by the employer, or it may be acquired through certification. In the latter case, a union that can show evidence of majority support, either by the number of members or by a supervised election, can be certified as the representative of the employees and thus accorded bargaining rights. These rights are made explicit for the industries under federal jurisdiction in Part V of the *Canada Labour Code*, whose provisions, in modified form, date from 1907. According to its terms, the Canada Labour Relations Board administers provisions dealing with the certification of unions. In the provinces, all of which have similar legislation, there are provincial labour relations boards that certify unions. Employers are required to bargain with the legally certified agents.

The objective of collective bargaining is to develop a collective agreement that defines the contractual relationship between the employer and the union. Wage rates, of course, are always a key item for negotiation, which explains why unions are an important part of any discussion of income distribution; but they are by no means the sole item. Hours, overtime, working conditions, health and welfare programs, the training and disciplining of workers, and policies with respect to layoffs and recall are equally important issues for the bargaining table. While the union must certainly concern itself with improving the status of the worker, it must also be concerned with preserving its own strength and security. Sometimes the issues under discussion may have an importance completely out of proportion to the economic effect, either on the company or on the workers, because they may involve a concession that would permit an encroachment on what management regards as its traditional prerogatives, or because they involve a concession on the part of the unions that might cause a loss of face that would damage its prestige. Collective bargaining is a difficult and complex procedure.

Collective bargaining aims to produce a mutually acceptable agreement that will set out the terms and conditions to be enforced during the life of the contract. The two bargaining parties, however, are not completely free to draw up any kind of agreement they want; for example, they cannot have an agreement that sets a wage lower than the legal minimum. Moreover, agreements must contain procedures for settling grievances. Throughout Canada, there is an almost universal requirement that the two parties must not engage in strike or lockout activities during the life of the agreement; instead disputes must be submitted to arbitration by an impartial third party. This gives rise to the controversial question of whether, if a conflict arises over matters not covered by the agreement, unions should have the right to strike even if an agreement is in force.[6]

---

[6] See H. D. Woods, *Labour Policy in Canada*, 2nd ed. (Toronto: Macmillan of Canada, 1973), pp. 348-354.

THIRD-PARTY INTERVENTION IN DISPUTE SETTLEMENT

When disputes that arise between labour and management cannot be settled by the two parties, then, whether the dispute is one that arises during negotiations over a new collective agreement, or one that arises during the life of an existing contract, an impartial third party is brought in to help the parties settle their dispute. The requirements for third-party participation, which differ in detail from province to province, are spelled out in the labour relations laws of the provincial and federal governments.

If disputes arise during the life of the contract concerning the meaning of a term in the agreement, or concerning an alleged violation of one or more of the clauses, in the absence of agreement between labour and management, they must be *arbitrated* by a third party who is authorized to impose a final and binding settlement on the two disputing parties: it is the function of an arbitrator to make an award. Arbitration may be carried out by a one-man board; or, as commonly happens in Canada, by a board made up of three people, one of them chosen by each of the disputants and the chairman chosen by the other two members of the board.

If the two parties negotiating a *new* contract fail to reach an agreement, then once again, there must be participation by one or more third parties before a strike can be called. In the past, there were two unvarying stages in this procedure, the first one involving a conciliator and the second involving a three-man conciliation board. However, a widespread feeling existed that this compulsory conciliation, which delayed the final pressure of the strike or lockout, weakened the earlier collective bargaining process. Various provinces began to make less use of conciliation boards, and the federal government amended the *Canada Labour Code* in 1972 to permit the Minister of Labour to use his discretion about whether, having received a request for conciliation, he would appoint a conciliation officer, a conciliation board, a conciliation commissioner (a Ministerial appointee with the powers of a board) or nothing at all, in which case any restraint on a strike or lockout would be lifted.[7] It was hoped that the air of uncertainty surrounding the Minister's response would cause the two parties to bargain more seriously at an earlier stage.

WORK STOPPAGES

When no agreement is possible, and when unions or management have complied with the legal restrictions imposed with respect to strikes and

---

[7] *Ibid.*, p. 367.

lockouts by various labour relations acts, then the union normally is free to call a strike, and management is permitted to lock out its workers. The cost of a strike acts as a deterrent to any extravagant demands or hasty action by either of the two parties because the losses and hardships it imposes on both sides encourage the two parties to come to an agreement through the collective bargaining process. However, when disagreements arise out of changing conditions that seemingly cannot be worked out by the two parties, with or without the help of a third party, then a work stoppage occurs.

In 1975, almost 10.9 million man-days were lost in Canada because of work stoppages; this amounted to just over half of one percent of the total man-days worked.[8] It was the worst strike record among the industrialized countries. Man-days lost for every 1 000 employed were five times as high in Britain, and they far exceeded the number in Italy and Australia, the second and third worst countries on the list.[9]

Problems of Industrial Relations

Many contentious issues in industrial relations create problems for the Canadian economy. There is the broad question of union power and public confidence as well as the more specific ones like the role of unions in causing inflation, the right to strike in essential services and in the public sector, foreign control, freedom of association and union security, and questions of automation and technological change, to name only a few.

UNIONS AND INFLATION

Powerful unions are one of a number of institutions that can exert an upward pressure on incomes, costs, and prices, almost independently, it would seem, of existing economic conditions. Even in the face of unacceptably high and rising unemployment some unions have been able to obtain remarkably large wage increases for their members. These, in turn, have set precedents and targets for other unions. Average settlements in recent years have been considerably higher in Canada than in the United States; but, as we are aware, the productivity of Canadian workers lags behind that of American workers by about 20 percent. If productivity

---

[8] *Labour Gazette*, Vol. 76 No. 8, August 1976, p. 455.
[9] *The Financial Times*, Toronto, 24 January 1977, p. 5.

were high, the inflationary pressure would be reduced, but Canada's dismal record in this respect aggravated the situation and created the additional danger that, at least in some areas, Canada might price itself out of the international market. Opinion polls indicate that the public believes that unions increase inflation, and this is a part of the crisis of public confidence that existed in the mid-1970s.[10]

In times of recession, or when industries are declining, unions have not been prepared to negotiate a commensurate decrease in wages. Given this downward rigidity in prices, employers in a declining industry, or during an economic recession, tend to respond by laying off workers, which produces a higher rate of unemployment rather than a lower level of prices. Thus, when prices begin to rise again, they are likely to start at the peak previously reached.

Clearly, then, unions, through the process of collective bargaining, can cause an upward pressure on prices in the economy. However, they are only one of many institutions that make the goal of full employment with reasonable price stability difficult to achieve.

STRIKES IN ESSENTIAL SERVICES

Labour's public image has deteriorated because of costly strikes, many of them in the public service and in essential services, where the effects of work stoppages are widely felt, creating in the public's mind the sense of being victimized. Work stoppages in these areas can cause great public hardship; but on the other hand, without the strike, unions have very little bargaining power and the collective-bargaining process is rendered almost meaningless. The right to strike has been extended to a number of sectors where heretofore workers have been subject to compulsory arbitration: in some jurisdictions the right has even been extended to policemen and firemen. But events like successive mail stoppages, and the disruption by longshoremen of grain shipments to Canada's international markets, not to mention strikes by policemen and firemen, raised in many people's minds the question of whether the right to strike should not be withdrawn from such services.

Disputes in areas of public interest are handled in different ways in different jurisdictions. In 1967, for example, the federal government, before the start of collective bargaining, gave almost all of its employees the right to choose either binding arbitration or a strike as the final method of settlement. For disputes in some public utilities the conciliation

---

[10] W. Donald Wood, *The Current Industrial Relations Scene in Canada 1974* (Kingston: Industrial Relations Centre, Queen's University, 1974), pp. S-U-5 ff.

board is still mandatory. In some places there is legislation that empowers the government to impose arbitration to end a strike and bring about a settlement in services relating to life and health or safety and order. Where strikes are permitted in essential services, there may be a prior agreement that a minimum level of service will be maintained. In all jurisdictions, of course, there exists the power of the legislature to order striking workers back to work—a device that has been used increasingly in recent years. In 1975, for example, Quebec ordered maintenance workers back to work to put an end to the Montreal transit strike. British Columbia legislated all of its striking workers in various industries back to work. The federal Parliament legislated the West Coast longshoremen back to work to get Canadian grain moving again, and shortly afterward ordered Quebec longshoremen back; the response of the latter groups, ominously, was to defy the back-to-work legislation for a short time.

Many groups are trying to find alternatives to the strike for settling disputes. One possible method is the use of *voluntary* arbitration, perhaps not on all issues involved, but only on those that remain unresolved. Another device that has been tried is the "final offer solution"; in this case the parties submit their final offers to an arbitrator who chooses one or the other, and whose choice is binding. A public referendum to settle issues in dispute has also been tried.[11] The need for some kind of alternative is clear because the public's tolerance for strikes and lockouts seems to be declining sharply.

FOREIGN DOMINATION

At a time when national identity is an issue in Canada, it is almost inevitable that the question of the independence of Canadian unions *vis-à-vis* their international affiliates should be raised. A number of fears have been expressed, among them that the international unions, backed by great power and large sums of money from the United States, may drive wages and fringe benefits to a level that the Canadian economy cannot support; that Canadian workers may be pulled out on strike for American purposes; that the protectionist stand of the AFL-CIO may prove harmful to the cause of Canadian unionism; and that large sums of money in the form of dues may flow into the United States out of the pockets of Canadian workers. With respect to the last concern, the *Corporations and Labour Unions Returns Act* (CALURA) requires fairly detailed reports from foreign-based unions and foreign-based companies. Its annual reports (which have

---

[11] *Ibid.*, p. S-CB-11.

been criticized by representatives of international unions in Canada for failing to give the full picture) suggest that American parent unions on balance receive more from dues and other payments from their Canadian branches than they have been paying out in Canada.[12]

The degree of autonomy in Canadian branches of international unions varies widely. Very few of them, however, can be described as completely autonomous. Some of the bigger ones in Canada have made progress toward acquiring the power to take care of the needs of their Canadian members. The Canadian membership of some can elect the top Canadian officers; other unions have a central Canadian office authorized to speak for the union, and a competent staff to serve the particular needs of Canadians. In a few cases there is a regular Canadian policy conference to deal with the union's affairs in Canada.[13] The CLC in 1970 made a recommendation that Canadian branches of American unions should achieve certain minimum levels of autonomy.[14] A great deal remains to be done, however.

DEMOCRACY IN UNIONS

Concern is frequently expressed about the right of individual union members to freedom of association. Unions have powers that they use on behalf of the group, but there always exists the possibility that such powers may be abused. Many unions have the power to control the entry of individuals into the union as well as to control the right to continue as a member. Once a union is certified and becomes the sole bargaining agent for the group, it can then proceed to bargain for whatever type of union security it chooses. It can bargain for anything from a closed shop (workers must be members of the union before they can work) at one extreme, to an open shop (workers are under no obligation to join the union or pay dues to it) at the other extreme, or any variation in between. One variation is the union shop, which means workers must join the union after a certain waiting period. Another derives from a formula, developed by the late Chief Justice Ivan C. Rand, which requires that workers pay union dues, but they are not required to join the union. Some of these forms of security give the union a great deal of power over the individual members, and little has been done to establish policies to prevent abuse of this power, except when the abuse has been flagrant.

---

[12] R. W. Cox and Stuart Jamieson, "Canadian Labor in the Continental Perspective," *International Organization*, Vol. 28 No. 4, Autumn 1974, pp. 814-815.

[13] For a detailed treatment of this issue, see John H. G. Crispo, *International Unionism* (Toronto: McGraw-Hill, 1967), Ch. 3.

[14] Cox and Jamieson, *op. cit.*, p. 814.

The Task Force on Industrial Relations pointed out a number of areas where individual freedom might be in jeopardy. For example, there is the problem of the right to union membership, particularly when employment is not available to anyone who is not a union member. There is also the question of fair treatment in distributing the work that is available, or, if jobs depend on a minimum level of competence, of ensuring that there is easy access to the necessary training. It is imperative that members have the democratic right to freedom of speech and freedom to seek office in the union without danger of reprisal. In the United States, abuses of these rights of individual members led to the passage of a wide-ranging federal law guaranteeing freedom of speech and assembly and other basic democratic rights to union members. The Task Force did not see any need for such a comprehensive act in Canada, though there appeared to be a need for some safeguards.[15]

The basic democratic rights of union members need to be safeguarded; but, on the other hand, there is also a need to guarantee the security of the union and its leaders, so that collective bargaining is possible. If union leadership is not strong and secure, then it becomes impossible to make difficult decisions and to take part in genuine collective bargaining. Union membership appears to have been restive in the past few years, and has been expressing its dissatisfaction with the process of collective bargaining and with its officers by wildcat strikes (strikes not sanctioned by union officials) and by refusals to ratify agreements. Thus, any legal step to protect the rights of individual members must be large enough to protect the individual against abuses, but at the same time, not so large as to render union leadership powerless to take responsible but unpopular positions in bargaining.

OTHER ISSUES

Several important issues in industrial relations deserve at least a brief mention. The problem of technological change, for example, has been a contentious issue in the post office. Technological change is inherent in growth, but it involves a cost: by altering or eliminating jobs, it renders some workers unnecessary. The government can help lessen the ill effects of technological change by creating policies geared to maintaining a high level of employment and providing labour mobility as well as retraining, relocation, and income-maintenance programs. Unions have attempted in various ways to cope with the problem. Occasionally they have tried to

---

[15] *Canadian Industrial Relations, The Report of the Task Force on Labour Relations* (Ottawa: Queen's Printer, 1969), pp. 103-104.

obstruct change, but for the most part they have accepted it as inevitable and have attempted to get clauses in their agreements that would minimize the ill effects of technological change on their members. Such clauses set out procedures for consulting and informing workers in advance, and for providing retraining or relocation, severance pay, early retirement, and other matters. The *Canada Labour Code* was amended in 1972 to require employers under federal jurisdiction to give the bargaining agent notice of technological change if it was likely to affect the job security or terms and conditions of work of a significant number of employees. This had been recommended by the Task Force on Industrial Relations. The Task Force also proposed that the existing laws requiring all disputes arising during the life of an agreement to be settled without recourse to a strike be changed in order to give unions the right to strike when the dispute involve the permanent displacement of workers because of technological change.[16]

One reason commonly cited to explain the increasing public demands for more curbs on work stoppages is union violence and corruption. The shocking stories of intimidation, blackmail, extortion, black-listing, kickbacks, and political payoffs that were revealed in the report in 1975 of the Cliche Commission (which investigated Quebec's construction industry) provide perhaps the worst example. The investigation was launched after a construction site of the James Bay project was deliberately destroyed by unionists, at a cost to the Quebec taxpayer of some $35 million. In response to the recommendations of the Cliche Commission, the Quebec government put several unions affiliated with the Quebec Federation of Labour (QFL) under trusteeship. The QFL countered by calling for strikes at all construction sites (including the site of the 1976 Olympic Games, which raised fears that the games might be cancelled) and by holding protest rallies. After one such rally, protesting strikers turned violent and caused between one and two million dollars' worth of damage to plant property.

As mentioned earlier, strikes in certain sectors of the public service have been causing some concern. Firemen, policemen, nurses, doctors, and teachers have been involved in work stoppages. Strikes had not occurred before in these occupations, and now there is strong public opinion that they should not be allowed. Many people would favour *compulsory* arbitration in cases of dispute. The Task Force, however, expressed its opposition to compulsory arbitration and suggested that although a strike or lockout is costly, it may in the long run prove to be less costly and better able to clear the air than compulsory arbitration. If

---

[16] *Ibid.*, p. 195.

disputes are settled rather than merely contained, it is possible in many instances to take steps to make up for time lost in strikes. Furthermore, removal of the right to strike does not ensure that there will be no resort to other kinds of economic weapons like working to rule (which is a powerful weapon), slowdowns, rotating study sessions, absenteeism (the Anglophone teachers of Quebec blamed their absences on "Garneau grippe", named after the Minister of Education who did not make them a contract offer they considered acceptable), or industrial sabotage.[17]

Since by far the largest distributive share of national income is earned by labour, it is important if we are to understand the distribution of income to have discussed some of the laws and institutions, like unions, that affect labour. But there is another way of looking at the problem of income distribution—the way a Newfoundlander, for example, might look at the higher average income of his counterpart in Ontario or British Columbia. We shall give some attention to the matter of regional distribution of income in the next chapter.

---

[17] *Ibid.*, p. 119.

11

Average income varies from region to region. For example, it is higher than the national average in British Columbia and considerably lower in the Atlantic Provinces. Reasons for the income lag in the Atlantic Provinces include the smaller percentage of the population employed, lower educational levels, and Canada's tariff policy.

Many efforts have been made to reduce income disparities. The federal Department of Regional Economic Expansion administers special rural development projects, offers development incentives to encourage investment and job creation in designated regions, and has signed general development agreements with the various provinces to foster cooperative efforts to promote development in areas of slow growth. All of the provinces have established their own development agencies to stimulate economic development and employment within their boundaries. Transportation subsidies have been used to help some regions. In addition there are the federal-provincial fiscal arrangements that provide for equalization payments, stabilization payments and aid to some kinds of education.

Regional Distribution: What Region Gets What?

In the previous two chapters we discussed the goal of equity in the distribution of income as it related to individuals and groups in the Canadian economy. Here we touch on another equally important aspect of the problem: the equitable distribution of income among the various regions of Canada. Regional equity is a subject whose importance goes beyond the national level: it is a major international problem. The difference in wealth, industrial development, and standard of living between the "have" and the "have not" nations are an important source of world tension, and the advanced economies are shouldering increased responsibility for trying to improve the position of the poorer nations. In Canada there is a long-standing and persistent problem that is similar in kind, though not in degree, to the problem of the have and the have-not nations of the world. It is not so much a question of having or not having: rather, it is a problem of regions that have more and regions that have less. In Canada, just as on the international scene, these gaps in income are a source of tension and discontent; many policies have been tried, and many new ones are being developed to encourage the growth of lagging areas and to reduce regional disparities.

At the international level there are examples of lagging countries that have caught up with the more developed ones. Not long ago the level of income in Sweden lagged far behind that of Canada, which could claim to rank second only to the United States in average income and living standards. Today Sweden and several other countries appear to have surpassed the Canadian performance.[1] Japan's performance has been remarkable: in the postwar period it has shown the highest rate of growth of any of the OECD countries and is rapidly closing the income gap.

There have been similar cases in Canada itself. The Prairie Provinces used to be one of the most economically depressed regions; now their

---

[1] The Hudson Institute estimated that in 1970 Canada ranked eighth among seventeen countries in income per person, and forecast that it would slip to eleventh place by 1985. Cited in Economic Council of Canada, *Looking Outward: A New Strategy for Canada* (Ottawa: Information Canada, 1975), p. 28.

income level is not much below the national average. The great change was brought about largely by the discovery of oil in Alberta, the development of potash deposits in Saskatchewan, and the mechanization of agriculture. Incomes in Alberta have increased sufficiently that the province no longer qualifies for equalization payments under the federal-provincial fiscal arrangements (payments designed to bring provincial revenues per person up to the national average). On the other hand, in spite of the amount of attention devoted to the problem, incomes in the Atlantic Provinces continue to lag and policy makers are constantly faced with the dilemma of whether people should be moved to jobs or jobs moved to people in order to solve the problem of equity.

Regional Disparities

National income data dating from the mid-1920s show that for twenty-five or thirty years, average incomes per person in Ontario and British Columbia were equal to about 125 percent of the national average.[2] Since then their average has dropped: it is now closer to 115 percent. During the depression incomes in the Prairies were well below the national average; but since the war, with the improved markets for agricultural products, the rationalization of agriculture, and the development of new resources in Alberta and Saskatchewan, personal income per person has increased to a level that is only somewhat lower than the national average. Quebec incomes have been, and still remain, slightly below average. In the Yukon and Northwest Territories incomes are also a little below average. Except for a brief time at the end of World War II, the level of personal income in the Maritime Provinces has been 75 percent or less of the national average.

The data on regional incomes suggest that any study of the contentious contemporary problem of regional disparities should concern itself with questions of why the incomes of certain areas—the Atlantic Provinces particularly and Quebec to a lesser extent—lag behind the national average; what, historically, has been done to try to close the gap; and what current efforts are being made. We shall deal very briefly with Quebec, then turn to the problems of the Atlantic Provinces before considering past and present policies.

---

[2] See Economic Council of Canada, *Performance and Potential mid-1950's to mid-1970's* (Ottawa: Information Canada, 1970), Chart 13, p. 37.

QUEBEC

As mentioned earlier, incomes in Quebec are somewhat below average. The province is richer than the Maritimes but not as wealthy as Ontario. The problem is compounded by ethnic differences, tempting some Quebec nationalists to blame ethnic discrimination for their lower level of income. The Royal Commission on Bilingualism and Biculturalism has made a detailed study of this. Some of the research that has been done suggests that there is very little truth to these charges of discrimination.[3] If one may argue by analogy, one could claim that since those working in the Maritimes have lower incomes on average than Quebec workers, there must be even greater discrimination against the Anglo-Saxons living in the Atlantic provinces. Moreover, if it were true that Quebec workers were as productive as Ontario workers and that they were paid less, then if the market system works it would pay businessmen to locate factories in Quebec rather than in Ontario. The result of this would be that the demand for workers in Quebec would increase, and this would drive up the wages of Quebec workers. Statistics dating from the 1920s indicate the existence of a gap that shows no marked tendency to close; it is like the persistent gap in income between the United States and Canada. This lends force to the argument that it is not a question of discrimination but rather of productivity: the productivity of Quebec workers on average is not as high as that of Ontario workers. This reinforces the contention, more and more frequently expressed, that the level and kind of education in Quebec, as well as the differences in attitudes among the various ethnic groups, have been important factors in explaining the lower productivity. Hopefully, the "quiet revolution", which has greatly altered the educational system in Quebec, will in time effect a narrowing of the income spread that exists between Quebec and Ontario.

THE ATLANTIC PROVINCES

Since Confederation, the Maritimes have presented the most intractable regional problems. Many attempts have been made to determine their causes and to find solutions to them. The region and its resource endowments have been intensively studied. Products peculiar to specific areas (lobsters, shrimps, forests, and coal, to name only a few) have been

---

[3] Donald E. Armstrong, *Education and Economic Achievement*, Number 7 of Documents of the Royal Commission on Bilingualism and Biculturalism (Ottawa: Information Canada, 1970), Chs. 3 & 4.

thoroughly investigated. It emerged in Parliament early in 1969 that since Confederation about eighty-five economic studies had been undertaken by the federal government in the Maritimes, together with another forty-four conducted in cooperation with the governments of that region.[4] There have been others since then.

In the years just prior to Confederation, the Atlantic region reached the peak of its prosperity: The "golden age" of the Maritimes was based on the wooden ship-building industry and the export of lumber and fish. With the advance of technology came the steamship; wooden sailing ships became obsolete, and the whole foundation of the Maritime economy was undermined. Shortly after Confederation there began a twenty-year depression that seriously affected the market for Maritime fish and lumber. Coal for many years was an important Maritime resource, but when oil replaced coal for heating and railway transportation, it too became a dying industry in spite of the efforts of both the federal and provincial governments to keep it alive. Forest resources in the Atlantic Region, though valuable, are not as good as in other places in North America. The Atlantic forest industry has been threatened by the cheap southern pine of the United States. Moreover, the forest products industry in the Maritimes is not a multi-product operation like that in British Columbia where the trees are bigger and the scrap wood from large and profitable lumbering operations can be used for the pulp and paper industry. Tourism has been fairly successful; but it is only a summer operation in the Maritimes, and the season is short as compared with the Laurentians in Quebec, or the Banff region of the Rocky Mountains where there are both summer and winter tourist seasons.

In addition to the resource endowment of the area, there are other problems that must be considered if we are to explain the income gap. The percentage of the population employed in the Atlantic region is smaller than elsewhere in Canada. Educational levels, an important factor in explaining economic growth and development, have been lower than those in the rest of Canada. Lastly, the Canadian tariff structure has reinforced the regional disparity.

The Employment Base   Whenever a region has a smaller-than-average percentage of its population employed, the level of income per person is reduced. A number of factors can affect the size of the employment base; for example, if there is a relatively high proportion of old people or of

---

[4] *The Gazette*, Montreal, 17 March 1969.

children, the employment base will be smaller. In the Atlantic Provinces the proportion of population of working ages is lower than in any other region. This can be attributed in part to the high rate of out-migration, as people of working age move to other provinces—British Columbia, Ontario, or Alberta, for example—where the employment opportunities are better. Other factors that affect the employment base are the participation rate (the proportion of people of working age in the labour force, whether they are employed or unemployed) and the unemployment rate.

The participation rate in the Atlantic Provinces is the lowest of any region in the country, and it lags as much as ten percentage points behind Ontario, for example. Until very recently the rate of increase in the region's labour force was slow, and as we saw in Chapter 7, an increase in the quantity of labour is a potential source of growth in income. It is too early to tell whether the above-average increase in the labour force in 1972-74 marks the beginning of a trend. The Atlantic region has also had a poor record of creating new jobs—a factor that has helped to give it the highest unemployment rate in Canada. All of these factors relating to the employment base help to explain the relatively low average level of income per person that exists in Atlantic Region.

Educational Levels Another factor that helps to explain the persistent gap in income per person has been the lower educational level in the Maritimes. Historically, a smaller percentage of the labour force in the region has had high school and post-secondary education than elsewhere. This has had an adverse effect on industry, for a region with a relatively low educational level does not support or attract industries that rely on a highly skilled or well-educated labour force. A vicious circle develops: a poor region cannot afford the high costs of good education and thus has to make do with an inferior school system; an inferior school system, for its part, results in fewer productive workers who, with their lower incomes, can support fewer social services. Roads and municipal services are poorer; industry, which needs these services, is not attracted into the area, with the result that fewer taxes are paid; poorer services result; and the vicious circle continues. Nothing fails like failure. Good social services, such as a good educational system, reduce the costs of doing business and help to attract more industries. More industries mean higher incomes for individuals and higher tax revenues for a region; and higher revenues make it easier to support good services. In the last decade expenditures on education have increased rapidly in the Atlantic Provinces, and in the long run this should contribute to closing the income gap.

Tariffs   Tariffs have been a contentious issue ever since Sir John A. Macdonald's National Policy was enunciated in 1879. The purpose of that policy was to create and maintain national unity in the new federation by ensuring an east-west flow of trade, rather than the more natural north-south movement between various parts of Canada and the adjacent regions of the United States. To ensure that such a flow of goods would take place, an east-west transportation system was built; to make sure that there would be goods to move on that transportation system, tariffs were used to restrict the flow of American goods. In order to minimize costs of transportation, manufacturing industries tended to locate in central Canada rather than in the Maritimes or in the West.

The National Policy dealt a blow to the Maritime economy. Prior to the erection of the tariff barriers, this region had been able to buy manufactured commodities on the world market at the going world prices, and to import manufactured goods very cheaply from the industrialized American north-east. After the imposition of the tariffs, however, many of these manufactured goods were excluded. The Maritimes, like the West, were forced to purchase from central Canada at a cost that was increased not merely by the higher costs of production, but also by the higher transportation costs. This was not all. Because of the low cost of transportation by water, the world market was the natural market for the resource-based products of the Maritime region. The effect of the tariff barriers was to reduce the volume of trade; as a result the demand for Maritime products declined and these regions were forced to look for markets in central Canada. To be competitive with suppliers in central Canada, Maritime producers sometimes had to bear the costs of transportation, and their returns were reduced correspondingly. It is understandable, therefore, that complaints against Canadian tariff policy and the cry that the high cost of transportation has frozen the Maritimers and the Westerners out of the large markets of central Canada should have reverberated through all the decades since the late nineteenth century. These are some of the reasons cited as justification for the various investigations, special projects, and redistributional devices that have been designed to reduce regional disparities.

Projects to Reduce Regional Disparities

Since Confederation many efforts have been made to reduce regional disparities and to move toward the objective of achieving an acceptable level of services in poorer areas without forcing them to bear a heavier tax burden than that in other regions of the country. These efforts have taken many forms, such as subsidies to reduce transportation costs so that goods from one region could compete in other areas. Incentive programs have been designed by all levels of government to attract industry to slow-growth areas. There have been special projects aimed at special areas, such as the Maritime Marshland Rehabilitation Project which was designed to convert 80 000 acres that had reverted to salt-water marshes into agricultural land. Comprehensive development projects are being undertaken to reorganize the economies of certain poorer areas, including the massive program involving the entire economy of Prince Edward Island. These special projects are now being administered by the Department of Regional Economic Expansion (DREE). In addition to projects of this kind, there are federal-provincial fiscal arrangements, including subsidies to education, which are supposed to reduce regional income disparities. These various programs deserve further attention in view of the importance attached by various governments to the achievement of a more equitable regional distribution of income. Since most of the special projects aimed at reducing regional economic disparities are housed in the Department of Regional Economic Expansion, that is a good place to start.

REGIONAL ECONOMIC EXPANSION

The projects being supported by DREE fall into three groups. First there are the special projects begun before DREE was established in 1969, including ARDA (Agricultural Rehabilitation and Development), FRED (the Fund for Rural Economic Development), and the PFRA (Prairie Farm Rehabilitation). These are essentially rural economic development projects. The second group includes development incentives. Finally, there are the General Development Agreements, which provide for cooperation between the federal government and the provinces to encourage projects for economic and social development in areas of slow growth.

Rural Economic Development Projects The most important of the special projects aimed at rural development in the 1960s were undertaken under the terms of the *Agricultural and Rural Development Act*, which was passed by Parliament in 1961 and revised in 1965. The Act authorized the federal government to enter into agreements on a shared-cost basis with the ten provinces to undertake projects aimed at rehabilitating rural lands and developing rural economies. ARDA provided that projects could be undertaken that would find alternative uses for marginal lands, develop income and employment opportunities in rural regions, carry out land and water conservation projects, and conduct research related to any of these programs. The 1971 agreement signed with all provinces except Prince Edward Island emphasized the development of certain industries, such as fishing in Newfoundland, tourism in New Brunswick and Nova Scotia, agriculture in Quebec, and projects like livestock production, farm consolidation, and recreation development in the Prairie Provinces. Such development programs are likely to be merged into the General Development Agreements as soon as the present arrangements expire.

The Fund for Rural Economic Development provided special federal assistance, not necessarily on a shared-cost basis, to designated low-income areas. The largest project, agreed to in 1969, is now under way in Prince Edward Island. It is a 15-year, $725-million plan designed to aid the Island's agriculture and the tourist and fishing industries, to upgrade roads and the water supply, overhaul the educational system, and improve the government's health and welfare programs.

When drought hit the southern plains of the Prairie Provinces during the Great Depression, it caused even further damage to an area already hard hit by the disastrous decline in farm prices. As a result, the federal government passed the *Prairie Farm Rehabilitation Act* in 1935 to aid in the reclamation and conservation of land and water resources in the area. Since then, the Act has been expanded to include the entire settled area of the Prairies. The project was successful in ending the major problem of soil drift and in bringing thousands of acres back into crop and pasture land. Its water conservation program has also been successful, particularly on individual farms where assistance is given to build inexpensive farm dug-outs—excavations designed to catch surface runoff. Tree belts have been planted and numerous community water projects have been undertaken to support cattle farming; the PFRA also provides for large-scale irrigation and reclamation projects such as the South Saskatchewan River development project.

Development Incentives Development incentives are available under the terms of the *Regional Development Incentives Act* to encourage investment and job creation in designated regions. These regions change from time to time, but until the end of 1976 they comprise the Atlantic Provinces, Quebec excluding the Montreal-Hull corridor, northern Ontario and all of Manitoba and Saskatchewan. The incentives may take the form of nonrepayable grants, development loans, or incentive grants that may become repayable if the enterprise reaches a certain level of profitability. The amount of money given depends on the size of the capital cost involved and the number of jobs created. The subsidies are intended to persuade firms to build new plants in designated areas, to enlarge existing ones, to encourage firms to build now rather than later, or to make viable a project which, without a subsidy, might be only marginal.

The *Regional Incentives Development Act* has come under attack for a number of reasons. Concern has been expressed that the subsidies are biased in favour of capital and that this is inconsistent with the objective of creating jobs.[5] It has also been suggested that although the incentives are supposed to be paid only for investments that would not likely have been undertaken otherwise, a significant amount of funding has gone to plants that probably would have been set up anyway. There is also concern that subsidized firms may reduce or supplant investment by firms already in place, and that the investment and employment creation claimed may be overstated.[6]

The Cape Breton Development Corporation (DEVCO) provides a different kind of development incentive. Through this organization the governments of Nova Scotia and Canada are cooperating in an effort to reorganize and, given the change in the world energy situation, to reestablish the coal mining industry in Cape Breton Island, and to encourage the development of other industries in the area.

All provincial governments have development agencies that attempt to stimulate economic development and employment within their boundaries. The New Brunswick Development Corporation, for example, can lend money or guarantee loans, or buy shares in firms if it will encourage them to come to New Brunswick. The Quebec Industrial Development Corporation provides loans at or below prevailing rates, or grants subsidies, while the General Investment Corporation can enter into joint ventures with the private sector in the chemical, metallurgical, forest-products, or petroleum-based industries. Ontario has three development corporations operating in different regions: the Ontario Development Corporation, Northern Ontario Development Corporation, and Eastern Ontario Development Corporation. They provide advisory services and loans at favourable rates to encourage industrial and economic development. Loans may be made for purposes such as expanding manufacturing businesses and tourist facilities, purchasing pollution control equipment, and supporting exports.[7]

---

[5] R. S. Woodward, "The Effectiveness of DREE's New Location Subsidies," *Canadian Public Policy*, 1:2, Spring 1975, pp. 216 ff.

[6] Dan Usher, "Some Questions About the Regional Development Incentives Act," *Canadian Economic Policy*, 1:4, Autumn 1975, pp. 563 ff.

[7] For more details on provincial development corporations see, for example, Canadian Tax Foundation, *Provincial and Municipal Finances 1975* (Toronto: 1975), pp. 233-238.

General Development Agreements The General Development Agreements are the most recent vehicles for regional development. Ten-year agreements have been signed with all provinces (except Prince Edward Island, which already has a comprehensive development scheme which is being carried out under the terms of the Fund for Rural Economic Development). The Agreements provide that DREE, in cooperation with provincial and local governments, the federal Department of Transport, the Department of Industry, Trade and Commerce, as well as the private sector, will try to identify obstacles to growth and development and to find means of promoting economic and social development projects in areas of slow growth. There will be subsidiary agreements to cover specific projects, which are very diverse in nature. Some examples include the development of forest resources and building infrastructure including roads in Newfoundland; mineral exploration and building highways in Nova Scotia; fisheries, agriculture, and tourism in New Brunswick; steel production in Manitoba; and the development of the northlands of Saskatchewan, to name only a few.

TRANSPORTATION SUBSIDIES

In 1927, in an effort to make central Canadian markets more accessible to Maritime products, the federal government passed the *Maritime Freight Rates Act*. Implementing the suggestions of the Duncan Royal Commission, the Act reduced railway rates by 20 percent on traffic moving within, or moving west across, the territory east of Lévis, Quebec. In 1957 the rate reduction was increased to 30 percent on rail shipments moving out of the region to other parts of Canada, and in 1974 the subsidy went up to 50 percent on certain goods with a high manufacturing content. In 1969 subsidies were extended to commercial trucking and railway express companies, instead of being restricted to the railways.

In view of the importance of the coal industry to the Maritimes, special transportation subsidies existed for more than forty years to enable Maritime coal to be competitive with imported coal in the iron and steel industries of central Canada. These subsidies were phased out in the early 1970s.

FEDERAL-PROVINCIAL FISCAL ARRANGEMENTS

Under the *Federal-Provincial Fiscal Arrangements Act*, which is renegotiated every five years, there are financial arrangements designed to help reduce regional income disparities. Of particular importance in this regard are the *equalization payments* which attempt to raise provincial revenues to a national average. By means of a rather complex formula, a national average yield from twenty-three provincial revenue sources is calculated and divided by population to arrive at an average per person. If provincial revenues per person from these sources fall short of the national average, there is a payment equal to the shortfall per person multiplied by population. The returns to Alberta, British Columbia, and Ontario are above the national average and, therefore, these provinces receive no equalization payments. In 1975-76 Quebec was entitled to just over half of the total amount paid for equalization purposes because of its large population. Prince Edward Island's entitlement was the smallest, amounting to less than 3 percent of the total.

The entire equalization payments scheme was threatened by the sharp jump in world oil prices which greatly increased provincial royalty payments. If the additional revenue to Alberta and Saskatchewan had all been counted for equalization purposes, then even Ontario and British Columbia would have been entitled to equalization payments. To prevent this from happening, the federal government in 1975 redefined oil and gas revenues from various sources to limit the amount that would be subject to equalization.[8]

The federal government also makes *stabilization payments* which are designed to put a floor under provincial incomes. In the 1972-77 agreement, the stabilization payment is the amount of money needed to bring a province's current income up to the revenue of the previous year, provided there have been no changes in provincial taxes.[9]

Disparities in educational levels have been regarded as a cause of regional disparities in income. Although education is a provincial responsibility in the *British North America Act*, the federal government helps finance some of the costs, particularly at the post-secondary level. Thus, it helps fund universities, community colleges, Quebec's CEGEPs (Collèges d'enseignement général et professionnel), teachers' colleges, classical colleges, and senior matriculation high schools. The federal government originally paid subsidies; but now, under the *Federal-Provincial Fiscal Arrangements Act*, it has withdrawn further from the personal and corporate income tax field to leave provinces with more room to collect their own revenues. It has specifically tied an abatement of four percentage

[8] See Canadian Tax Foundation, *The National Finances 1975-76* (Toronto: 1976), p. 124.
[9] *Ibid.*, p. 159.

points of personal income tax and one percentage point of corporate income tax to expenditures on post-secondary education. If the revenues collected by the provinces do not amount to half of the operating costs of post-secondary educational institutions, or in the case of the provinces that have opted to be paid on the basis of population (an amount equal to $15 per person, escalated by the rate of growth of operating costs), the federal government pays a subsidy to make up the difference. The total federal assistance in the agreement that expires March 31, 1977 cannot increase by more than 15 percent annually.

A study by the Economic Council of Canada of the effects of these post-secondary education agreements[10] suggests that they resulted in a considerable amount of redistribution: fiscal transfers were made mainly by Ontario and British Columbia to other provinces. In absolute terms, Quebec got the most. In relative terms, Prince Edward Island and Newfoundland received the largest share. Since British Columbia and Ontario are the provinces to which workers tend to move, one must remember that their fiscal transfers to other provinces for post-secondary education are offset, in part at least, by transfers in the opposite direction of human capital.

What we have just said makes it clear that there is a transfer from provinces with incomes that are above average to the poorer provinces. The exception in this study was Alberta which was a recipient province because of its large expenditures on education, notwithstanding the fact that it had a relatively high average income.

Under the terms of the *Adult Occupational Training Act*, the federal government has taken over full responsibility for the occupational training of adult workers who have been out of school for at least a year and who are at least a year beyond school-leaving age. Included are the costs of the course, compensation for buildings and equipment used, as well as training allowances for those adults who have been in the labour force for three years or who have dependants. The Government also pays part of the wages of workers who are retrained on the job.

Federal-provincial fiscal arrangements, together with such shared-cost programs as federal health grants, hospital and diagnostic service payments, and the Canada Assistance Plan, have helped to shift some of the tax burden to the federal government and thus bring about a redistribution of income. In any program for which the federal government picks up the bill in whole or in part, there is likely to be some redistribution,

---

[10] Economic Council of Canada, *Eighth Annual Review: Design for Decision Making* (Ottawa: Information Canada, 1971), pp. 215 ff.

since more of the government's revenues are collected from the wealthier provinces.

12

Foreign trade is beneficial because it enables countries to improve the international allocation of resources and raise standards of living. Yet many trade barriers exist. Arguments favouring barriers include defence needs, protecting infant industries, dislocative effects of removing tariffs on certain industries and regions, protection against low wages elsewhere, and national identity. These arguments are opposed by the Economic Council of Canada, which advocates free trade.

The balance of international payments is a summary of monies received from and paid to foreigners. It has two parts: the current account (merchandise and nonmerchandise) and the capital account.

The foreign exchange rate is the price of one currency expressed in terms of another. Flexible (floating) rates respond freely to changes in supply and demand; fixed (pegged) rates do not.

Foreign aid enters into the international accounts. Canada's development assistance programme, therefore, affects the achievement of a viable balance of payments.

Trade and a Viable Balance of Payments

International trade is vital to Canada, as it is to many other nations of the world. Trade affects the level of our national income and our standard of living. Trade between nations is carried on for precisely the same reason as trade between individuals, or trade between provinces in this country; the greatest difference is that international trade is more complex because it is carried on in the currencies of different countries.

Each individual could grow his own food, make his own clothes, build his own house, and cut his own hair. Robinson Crusoe did it, but his standard of living was not very high. Man discovered long ago that it was better to unite in families, tribes, and nations so that the members of the group could specialize in producing those things for which they had particular skills, or so that they could acquire skills by learning to perform a specific operation well. International trade is one form of the division of labour: it is an example of geographic specialization. History shows that the greatest advances in the world have been made when specialization was carried to its limit—when large free-trade areas developed. The great development in the British Empire was an example. The United States, which grew from a small colony into the most productive country in the world, is itself one massive free-trade area. Europe has seen the advantages to be gained from specialization and has formed itself into a free-trade area. Similar moves are being made in Africa and Latin America. These countries have recognized that, individually, they cannot exploit fully the advantages of specialization, and that all will be better off if each concentrates on producing the goods and services for which it has a natural or acquired bent, if it exports its surpluses, and if, with the earnings from those exports, it buys goods and services that it is relatively less efficient in producing. In this way real national income will rise.

Canada is a large country with regions that differ from each other in many respects. Unlike the United States, however, it lies wholly in the frigid and temperate zones, which means that many products cannot be grown. The population is small, and lacking a large domestic market, the country is unable to take full advantage of specialization. Thus, unlike the United States, trade is vital for Canada, and the objective of achieving a viable balance of payments has far greater importance as a goal.

Canada has a natural advantage in producing goods for which the climate is particularly suited—high quality wheat and forest products such

251

as lumber and newsprint. The country has rich mineral resources: nickel, copper, iron ore, and uranium, all of which are exported in both primary and semi-fabricated forms. Canada also exports some manufactured goods: hydro generators, chemicals, pleasure boats, small aircraft, and farm implements. On the other hand, because the limited size of the market makes it difficult to achieve low costs of production, many manufactured goods are imported. This process of exporting goods that the country has in abundance and can extract or produce efficiently, and of importing goods that can be produced at a relatively higher cost in terms of the resources used, makes possible a higher standard of living for Canadians; it is an illustration of the gains that are made from trade through a more efficient international allocation of resources.

The Gains from Trade

To illustrate the gains to be made from international specialization, we shall look at two highly simplified arithmetic examples. Assume that we have two countries, Canada, and the hypothetical country, Alpha. Assume that in each country there are 200 units of labour available for the production of two products, fish and bananas.

Table 12-1
THE GAINS FROM TRADE

BEFORE TRADE:		Fish		Bananas
Canada	100 men	450 000 kg	100 men	25 000 kg
Alpha	100 men	300 000 kg	100 men	300 000 kg
		750 000 kg		325 000 kg
AFTER TRADE:				
Canada	200 men	900 000 kg	—	0
Alpha	—	0	200 men	600 000 kg
		900 000 kg		600 000 kg

In Table 12-1, we have assumed that 100 men in Canada can produce 450 000 kg of fish in a year. If it were necessary, Canada could produce bananas, too, given enough glass and heat, but the productivity of the workers would not be high. Alpha, too, can produce both products. Its labour force is less productive than Canada's in fishing: 100 men produce only 300 000 kg of fish. On the other hand, the cost to Alpha of producing bananas is less than the cost to Canada: 100 men produce 300 000 kg of bananas. Total output at a *real cost* of 200 men in each country is 750 000 kg of fish and 325 000 kg of bananas.

ABSOLUTE ADVANTAGE

In our example, Canada has an *absolute advantage* over Alpha in producing fish. Alpha, on the other hand, has an absolute advantage in producing bananas: with 100 men it can produce 300 000 kg, whereas with the same expenditure of labour—at the same real cost—Canada can produce only 25 000 kg. If both countries specialize completely in the products they produce best—if Canada, for example, employs 200 men to produce wheat, and Alpha devotes its total labour force to produce bananas—then as can be seen from Table 12-1, Canada can produce 900 000 kg of fish and Alpha can produce 600 000 kg of bananas. Total production has increased considerably. If the countries exchange their surpluses with each other, each will have more bananas and more fish—a higher real income—because of the specialization permitted by trade.

COMPARATIVE ADVANTAGE

There is no question about the gains to be made from trade in a situation like this in which each country has an absolute advantage in producing one product. It is obvious that both countries benefit. But assume now that one country is better in the production of all goods—a not inaccurate description of the United States. Can it gain anything from trading? An excellent analysis done more than 150 years ago by David Ricardo shows that even in such circumstances trade is advantageous.[1] A highly productive country, in other words, can gain from importing a commodity that it produces less efficiently—at a lower real cost—than the country from which it procures it. As long as a country is *relatively* better than others in producing certain goods—as long as it has a *comparative advantage* in producing those goods—it will gain by specializing in those areas of production and exporting its surpluses in order to pay for the import of goods that it is relatively less efficient in producing.

We can illustrate this with another simplified arithmetic example of trade between Canada and Alpha. Assume this time that the two commodities that can be produced by the 200 men in each country are fish and wheat. If each country devotes 100 men to the production of each commodity, then, according to Table 12-2, Canada can produce 450 000

---

[1] David Ricardo, *The Principles of Political Economy and Taxation*, Everyman's Library Edition (London: J. M. Dent & Sons Ltd., 1911), pp. 81 ff.

Table 12-2

BEFORE TRADE:		*Fish*		*Wheat*
Canada	100 men	450 000 kg	100 men	3 million kg
Alpha	100 men	300 000 kg	100 men	1 million kg
		750 000 kg		4 million kg
AFTER TRADE:				
Canada	50 men	225 000 kg	150 men	4.5 million kg
Alpha	200 men	600 000 kg		0
		825 000 kg		4.5 million kg

kg of fish and 3 million kg of wheat. As before, 100 men in Alpha can produce 300 000 kg of fish and, we have assumed, 1 million kg of wheat. Canada can produce both wheat and fish at a lower real cost per unit and thus has an absolute advantage in the production of both.

Would Canada gain from trade? The law of comparative advantage says yes, provided the country has a comparative advantage in producing one of the commodities. In the example in Table 12-2, Canada has a 1.5:1 (450 000/300 000) advantage over Alpha in producing fish, and a 3:1 (3 million/1 million) advantage in producing wheat; the country has a comparative advantage in wheat production, and it would pay to shift some of the factors of production from fish into wheat. Alpha, on the other hand, is relatively better at producing fish, and it would pay that country to shift its men from wheat production into producing fish. We shall assume, for the sake of illustration, that Canada shifts half of the men formerly in fish production into wheat, so that with 150 men producing wheat, production rises to 4.5 million kg. Fish production from the remaining fifty men drops to 225 000 kg. Assume that in Alpha all resources are devoted to the fishing industry so that 600 000 kg of fish are produced by 200 units of labour. Total output of the two commodities for the same expenditure of labour as before has risen to 825 000 kg of fish and 4.5 million kg of wheat. Both countries can be made better off by trade even though Canada, according to our assumptions, is more efficient in producing both.

Arguments Against Trade

International trade is one of the greatest forces for good in the world. Without it resources would be allocated less efficiently, the standard of living in almost all countries would decline sharply, and in many densely populated areas, famine would take the lives of thousands. Yet every country in the world puts up trade barriers, and there are powerful lobbies that spend a large amount of time and money trying to persuade governments to apply more and higher tariffs. Only the economists seem to favour free trade. Why? There are several arguments that one commonly hears against free trade and in defence of trade barriers; we shall consider five of the most common.

DEFENCE

First of all, there is the defence argument. Some industries are protected by tariffs on the grounds that they are strategic—essential to national security. Exporting certain products to potential enemies is forbidden for the same reason. The defence argument is a political argument, and one that is probably much overused.

INFANT INDUSTRY ARGUMENT

An argument that has a sound economic foundation is known as the infant industry argument. According to this argument, if certain new industries are given protection in their formative stages when they are vulnerable to competition,they will then expand and develop, and having achieved the low costs that go with economies of scale—with growing up—they will be able to stand on their own feet and compete in the world market without any further need for protection. The argument is a valid one. The trouble is that the infants seem to have a habit of never growing up. Tariffs, once imposed, often are still there twenty or thirty years later, and the economy is left protecting industries that cannot face world competition. These are industries in which productivity is relatively low and in which the country has no advantage. From the point of view of the standard of living in Canada as a whole, the country would be better off without them; for if the factors of production could be shifted over into the relatively more productive areas in which there exists an advantage, then real national income would rise.

DISLOCATIVE EFFECTS

This brings us to one of the most telling arguments against free trade and in favour of retaining Canada's present barriers. Many Canadian industries have grown up behind tariff walls. Tariffs have been there for historical reasons, and people have gone into the industry in good faith, assuming that the tariffs would remain. It is true that the productivity of factors may be low relative to that of factors in export industries; and it is true that from the aggregate point of view it could be better if the tariffs were removed and if those firms that would not compete in world markets were to close down and the factors were to move into industries in which Canada has an advantage. But the dislocation caused by such a policy, while soon remedied from the aggregate point of view, may be drastic as far as many individuals, or even entire towns and regions, are concerned. What would happen to many of the textile towns in Quebec, for example, if the tariffs on textiles were removed? Clearly, if Canada introduces policies to reduce the protection of domestic industries, there will need to be generous adjustment assistance programs to mitigate the dislocative effects.

PAUPER LABOUR ARGUMENT

One of the most frequent arguments for protection is one that long ago was shown to be false, and yet has persisted, because unfortunately, it sounds so plausible. It is commonly called the pauper labour argument. According to this argument, we must protect our workers and our standard of living against the cheap labour of other countries. Japan, it is often said, is flooding the Canadian market with goods produced by a work force that is paid a mere pittance, and if Canadian workers are to keep their jobs, we must keep Japanese goods out. And there seems to be a certain logic to the argument: if a Canadian worker and a Japanese worker are producing the same good, and if the Canadian is paid $7.50 an hour and the Japanese only $2.50, then ought not one to expect that everyone would want the Japanese good because it would be cheaper, and that the Canadian worker, therefore, would be put out of a job?

The only meaningful interpretation of the statement that "cheap Japanese goods are flooding the Canadian market" is that the Japanese are selling to Canada far more goods than they are buying, which is causing a deficit in Canada's trade with Japan. However, this is not true, and statistics for merchandise trade tell the reverse story. In 1975, for example, for every dollar Canadians spent on Japanese goods, the Japanese spent about $1.75 on Canadian-produced goods.

The pauper labour argument is wrong for two reasons. It is wrong, first of all, because it ignores workers' productivity: a high wage does not necessarily mean a high-priced good. If the Canadian worker earning three times as much as the Japanese worker produces more than three times as many goods, then the cost of the Canadian product will be lower. American workers, as we know, are more productive than Canadian workers and produce many goods at a much lower cost, and this was true all through the years when hourly wage rates in the United States far exceeded those in Canada. The problem in Canada at present is the low rate of increase in productivity combined with an increase in wages so rapid that in 1974 average hourly earnings in Canadian manufacturing actually overtook comparable American rates.

The pauper labour argument is wrong, too, because it fails to take account of the fact that Japanese wages are only one of two important factors that determine the price of Japanese goods in Canada. Equally important is the exchange rate—the price of one currency in terms of another. If by chance Japanese goods did begin to flood the Canadian market, there would be an increased demand for Japanese yen to pay for them; the price of the yen would rise, and this would have the effect of making Japanese goods more expensive in Canadian dollars, so that Canadian consumers would buy fewer of them.

PROTECTING THE NATIONAL IDENTITY

The question of national identity—the freedom to remain Canadian—is a political issue with strong emotional content which, depending on the kind of response to that emotional content, can have major economic implications, as we shall see when we discuss the issue in more detail in the next chapter. The argument favouring protection in the name of preserving national identity runs roughly as follows: in the first place, to be a nation Canada needs to have more secondary industries, and the only way to get them is to let them grow up behind tariff walls. In the second place, tariffs are necessary to limit the purchase of goods from foreigners, particularly the United States, for without tariffs there would be even larger deficits that would have to be financed with an even greater inflow of American capital, which would mean a further increase in foreign ownership and control, and hence a further loss of national identity.

These arguments are rejected by the Economic Council of Canada, which advocates a policy of free trade for Canada. The Council argues that Canadian protection policies have not resulted in a great increase in secondary industry. On the contrary, the pattern is much the same as it has traditionally been: Canada remains to a large extent a buyer of highly manufactured products and a seller of natural resources in spite of being a high-tariff country.[2] Moreover, high tariff walls have encouraged American firms to establish subsidiaries in Canada, and the limited possibility for achieving economies of scale and specialization that we discussed in Chapter 7 has also meant that when nonresidents have taken over Canadian companies, they have found it more profitable to run them as branch plants and to take advantage of the economies of scale available

---

[2] Economic Council of Canada, *Looking Outward, A New Trade Strategy for Canada* (Ottawa: Information Canada, 1975), Ch. 1.

from the parent company in marketing, advertising, research, and other head-office services.[3] As we shall see in the next chapter, strong objections to the effects on national identity of a branch-plant economy have been raised by opponents of foreign investment.

Tariffs impose a high cost on the Canadian economy. In the first place there is a large out-of-pocket cost for Canadian consumers. Moreover, the tariff structure has grown up in a haphazard manner that creates an unevenness in the treatment of different industries, and this can have only an adverse effect on the allocation of resources. Then there is the inefficiency in industries that have grown up behind tariff walls; the resulting failure to achieve economies of scale and specialization has had deleterious effects on the Canadian economy. Because of the high costs to the economy of tariffs, the Economic Council has strongly recommended that Canada move to establish multilateral free-trade, arguing that to do so would be to take the single most important step possible to improve the economic well-being of Canadians. The Council calculated that such a move could result in a jump in GNP of at least 5 percent.[4]

The Balance of International Payments

An understanding of a country's international accounts is important if we are to understand the problems of achieving the goal of a viable balance of payments. When countries trade with one another, payments are made across international boundaries. All such payments by a country are set out in the *balance of international payments*, which is a summary of all the monies received from foreigners and paid to them. It includes payments for and receipts from goods and services, private gifts, government gifts, international purchases and sales of securities and other assets, as well as borrowing and lending. This total statement must always balance: total payments and total receipts must be equal.

The balance of payments has two parts: the *balance on current account* and the *balance on capital account*. The current account balance, for its part, is subdivided into two accounts: the *merchandise account*, which includes the payments for imports of goods and receipts for exports; and the *nonmerchandise account*, in which are included such items as interest and dividend payments to foreigners who own Canadian securities, and receipts by Canadians from foreign assets they own. Travel is another big item in the nonmerchandise account: Canadians who visit the United States purchase American-produced meals, gasoline, and motel and hotel

---

[3] *Ibid.*, p. 36.
[4] *Ibid.*, pp. 81-82.

services, and these constitute payments to the United States. On the other hand, American tourists in Canada by their expenditures provide Canada with receipts on current account, just as a merchandise export like newsprint does. Canadians flying on an American airline (or a British or Dutch airline) purchase a foreign service for which there must be a payment on current account, just as there is for the import of merchandise like Florida oranges.

Merchandise and nonmerchandise payments and receipts taken together give us the current account balance. Payments on current account are not necessarily equal to receipts on current account: if receipts are greater than payments, there is a surplus on current account. Or, a situation Canadians are more accustomed to, payments may exceed receipts, in which case the balance on current account is unfavourable: there is a deficit on current account.

The balance on current account may be favourable or unfavourable, but total payments must be equal to total receipts. The balancing item is to be found in the capital account. Items that enter into the capital account can be subdivided into three parts: long-term capital flows (items like investment by foreigners in Canadian companies or by Canadians in foreign companies, and Government of Canada loans), short-term flows (involving items like bank deposits, holdings of currency and treasury bills), and official monetary movements (exchanges of monetary reserves). As this classification indicates, a large number of capital transactions take place across international boundaries. A Canadian corporation, for example, may float a stock issue in the New York market: Americans buy the issue and this receipt of American dollars constitutes a capital inflow. On the other hand, a provincial government may retire an issue of bonds that previously had been floated in the American market and was held in American investment portfolios. There will have to be a capital outflow—a payment on capital account by Canadians.

Assume now that there is a deficit on current account: payments for goods and services have exceeded receipts. Where does the extra foreign currency come from to settle the bill? It must come from a capital inflow— from investments by foreigners in Canadian industries, from borrowing by Canadian corporations or governments on American security markets, or from loans made to Canada by foreign countries or by an international body like the International Monetary Fund. Canada also has official international reserves, its stocks of foreign exchange, gold, and special drawing rights. If the Bank of Canada, as agent for the Exchange Fund Account, draws on the country's official reserves, this transaction, too, appears as part of the capital account. Any deficit on current account must be matched by net receipts on capital account.

On the other hand, if receipts from the sale of Canadian goods and services exceed payments, then foreigners will not have enough Canadian dollars to settle their bills. There will have to be a capital outflow sufficient to balance the surplus on current account, through Canadian purchases of foreign securities, direct investment abroad, or a build-up of official international reserves.

The Foreign Exchange Rate

The foreign exchange rate is a price ratio. It is just like any other price ratio, but it seems more complicated because the ratio involves *two* currencies.

When we used a graph to discuss the price of butter,[5] we measured kilograms per week along the horizontal axis: in other words we measured what we were talking about (the product for which there was a demand and supply in a given period of time) along the horizontal axis. When we discussed theatre tickets, we labelled the x-axis "tickets per week." Price was measured along the vertical axis. That price was expressed as a ratio (as it always should be, but frequently is not in common usage), as dollars per kilogram of butter or dollars per theatre ticket. Notice that we put what we were talking about (kilograms of butter, or theatre tickets) in the *denominator* of that price ratio.

The commodity we are interested in now is a foreign currency: it could be any currency—the Japanese yen, the British pound, the French franc, or the American dollar. Let us discuss the American dollar and its price. Just as we have done before, we shall put what we are talking about (American dollars per period of time, in this example) on the horizontal axis, and the price of the commodity expressed as a ratio, on the vertical axis. The American dollars appear as the denominator of the price ratio, and the ratio is expressed as Canadian dollar per American dollar. If we draw a demand curve and a supply curve for American dollars as in Figure 12-1, then we can determine the equilibrium price (the exchange rate) of the American dollar in terms of the Canadian dollar. What *is* the price of the American dollar? Between 1962 and 1970, the banks sold it at a fixed price of close to $1.08 Canadian. Since 1970 it has varied considerably: in 1973, for example, it did not get too far from par, but by the spring of 1974 the price of an American dollar had dropped close to $0.96 Canadian; a year later it was back to over $1.03, and at the end of 1976 it was $1.01.

---

[5] *Supra*, Figure 8-10.

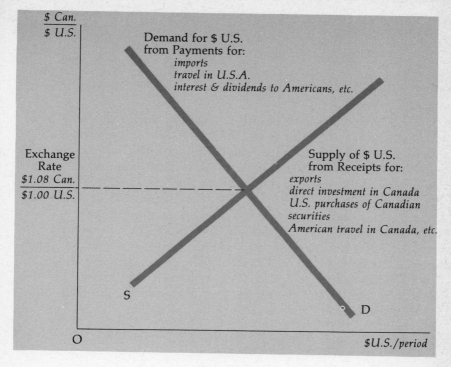

Figure 12-1

INVERTING THE RATIO

Price ratios, or exchange ratios, can be inverted. We normally talk about the price of bread in terms of of dollars: we say that it costs 50 cents a loaf, or half a dollar a loaf. But we could also talk about the price of a dollar in terms of bread, if we had any reason to. We could ask, how much bread would it cost to buy a dollar, and the answer would be just the reciprocal of (one over) the price of bread in terms of dollars. Instead of half a dollar per loaf, the price ratio would be two loaves per dollar.

In the same way, we can look at the exchange ratio between two currencies from the point of view of a foreigner. Thus we can ask, what is the price of a Canadian dollar in terms of the foreign currency? How many American dollars does it take to buy a Canadian dollar? The reciprocal of $1.08 Canadian/$1.00 U.S. is $1.00 American/$1.08 Canadian— the famous "92.5-cent dollar". In other words, in the period when the rate was fixed, it took only 92.5 American cents to buy one Canadian dollar.

THE DEMAND FOR AMERICAN DOLLARS

The exchange rate is the price of a foreign currency, and like the price of butter, it is determined by the interaction of demand and supply—this time the interaction of the demand for American dollars and the supply of them. The question now is, what gives rise to the demand for, and supply of, a foreign currency?

Anything in the balance of international payments that causes a *payment* to Americans will give rise to a *demand* for American dollars. Canadians like to eat California oranges and California fruit growers want to be paid in American dollars; therefore, the Canadian importers of oranges have a demand for American dollars to pay the California fruit growers. If you plan to visit New York, you go to the bank and demand (buy) American dollars to pay for the tickets to all of those Broadway shows you want to see, or to finance visits to discotheques or purchases on Fifth Avenue. Interest and dividends on Canadian securities owned by Americans cause a demand for American dollars because Americans do not want Canadian dollars to spend: they want their own currency. These transactions, summarized in Figure 12-1 alongside the demand curve, indicate the sources of the demand for American dollars.

THE SUPPLY OF AMERICAN DOLLARS

The *supply* of foreign currency comes from the *receipts* from foreign transactions. Paper companies, for example, export newsprint to the United States; they take the American dollars they get from the sale to the bank and sell (supply) them to get the Canadian dollars they need to pay the Canadian workers who produce the newsprint. Direct investment in Canada gives rise to a capital inflow—a receipt of foreign funds. American purchases of Canadian securities and American travel in Canada bring a supply of American dollars into the foreign exchange market. These transactions are summarized in Figure 12-1.

The equilibrium price, the exchange rate, is established by the intersection of the demand curve and the supply curve of American dollars.

CHANGES IN THE EXCHANGE RATE

What might make the price of the American dollar rise? We know from our previous use of demand and supply curves that an *increase in demand*, other factors remaining constant, will increase the equilibrium price. In Figure 12-2 when demand increases from DD to $D'D'$, the exchange rate increases from ER to ER_1. An increase in demand might be caused by an

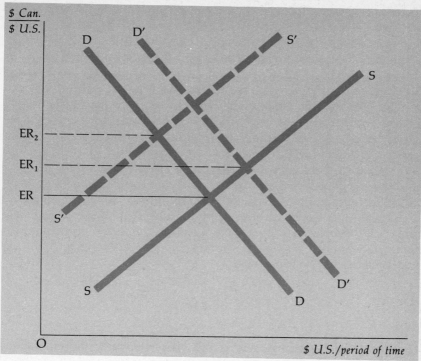

Figure 12-2

increase in imports that must be paid for in American dollars, or by more travelling in the United States by Canadians.

The exchange rate might also increase if there occurred a *decrease in supply*—if the supply curve shifted to the left. In Figure 12-2, if supply decreases to $S'S'$, the new equilibrium price, determined by the intersection of DD and $S'S'$ increases to ER_2. This might occur if, for example, fewer Canadian goods were sold to Americans, or if Americans invested less in Canada, or if bombing incidents prevented as many tourists from travelling in Canada.

A decrease in the price of the American dollar would come about in the opposite way. The exchange rate would fall if there occurred a decrease in demand (a shift to the left in the demand curve) or an increase in supply (a rightward shift in the supply curve).

FLEXIBLE EXCHANGE RATES

If the exchange rate is left free to respond to changes in demand and supply and to move toward the equilibrium price, then it is described as a free-floating, or flexible, exchange rate. For more than a decade (October

1950 to May 1962), Canada was unique among nations because of its flexible exchange rate. The price of foreign currencies in terms of Canadian dollars shifted in response to changes in demand and supply. The International Monetary Fund frowned on Canada's floating rate: it favoured the fixed, or pegged, rate that all its other members had. Many economists, however, prefer to see the market left free to find its own level. This does not mean that the monetary authorities ignore the operation of the market; the exchange rate can be a volatile price, and to iron out large, day-to-day fluctuations, the Bank of Canada used to step in regularly to buy and sell foreign exchange.

The Canadian dollar, which had been pegged since 1962, was so seriously undervalued by the middle of 1970 that the government decided to let it float once again. This second decision to switch to a floating rate was greeted with a good deal less opposition because in the intervening period many people had been persuaded of the logic of letting the exchange rate adjust over time to market forces. By 1974 most countries had adopted flexible exchange rates.

PEGGED EXCHANGE RATES

A fixed or pegged exchange rate is one that is *not* free to respond to changes in demand and supply except within narrow limits. In 1962 Canada became involved in such a severe exchange crisis that it had to turn to the International Monetary Fund for help, and in return for giving this help, the IMF required that the Canadian rate be pegged. It was fixed at a price of just over $1.08 Canadian for an American dollar.

In accordance with the articles of agreement of the IMF the Canadian government had to maintain the dollar within a margin of one percent on either side of any established par. As long as changes in the supply of, and demand for, American dollars were small, the price stayed within the allowable range. However, if anything happened to push the price above or below these limits then the Bank of Canada, as agent for the Exchange Fund Account, had to act to bring the exchange rate back within the allowable range.

Assume that in Figure 12-3, *DD* and *SS* represent the demand for and supply of American dollars. Assume that the equilibrium price of American dollars is at the old pegged rate of $1.08. The allowable range within which the price is free to move is bounded by the two horizontal lines, one at slightly over $1.09, and the other one at slightly less than $1.07.

Assume now that the demand for American dollars increases to $D'D'$, perhaps because Canadians buy more imports from the United States. The intersection of $D'D'$ and SS establishes a price (ER_1) higher than the

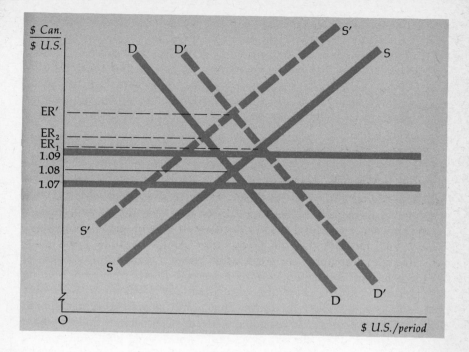

Figure 12-3

allowed $1.09. The price might also be driven up above the allowable range to ER_2, for example, if there occurred a decrease in supply to $S'S'$, because of, say, decreased American investment in Canada. A decrease in supply and an increase in demand could also combine to drive up the price, to a position like ER' on our diagram.

Now the Bank of Canada must act. It can attempt to decrease the demand for American dollars and thus move the equilibrium price below $1.09, by restricting imports through quotas or higher tariffs. This is what happened in 1962 when Canada was in an exchange crisis, but trading partners, except in emergencies, are not prepared to see such action taken against them; moreover, such actions normally contravene the terms of the General Agreement on Tariffs and Trade (GATT), which Canada supports as a matter of policy. The objectives of GATT are to bring about mutual *reductions* in tariffs (such as those of the Kennedy round) and to forestall unilateral increases. The other way of lowering the price of the American dollar is to increase its supply in the market: the Bank of Canada can do this by selling its official reserves of American dollars and gold in the exchange market. This causes the supply curve to shift to the right (back toward SS) and brings down the price of the American dollar.

The problem is that stocks of American dollars are limited, and Canada does not have the right to print them. If Canada cannot earn enough by exporting, or by selling assets to Americans, and if reserves run short, the only way to get more is by borrowing. Alternatively, Canada may have to accept the fact that the American dollar is pegged at an unrealistically low level, and that its price in Canadian dollars will have to be increased to $1.09 or $1.10 or higher—that is, that the Canadian dollar will have to be *devalued*.

We might also face the reverse problem: the price of the American dollar might be forced below the allowable limit of $1.07. This could occur because of an increased supply of American dollars, caused perhaps by a large capital inflow. If Canadians lost their taste for American goods or for travel in the United States, then the demand curve would shift to the left, and this, too, could cause a decrease in price. If changes in supply and demand are such that the price of the American dollar falls below the allowable minimum, then the appropriate policy for the Bank of Canada is to increase the demand for American dollars by buying them in the open market. This procedure created serious problems between July 1963 and December 1968, for during that time Canada had an agreement with the United States that Canadian reserves of American dollars would not be permitted to rise above a given limit.[6] In 1970 the government, once again, found itself in the position of having to buy such large quantities of American dollars that it decided to free the Canadian dollar and permit it to float to a more realistic price.

It was clear that with the established pegged rates many of the world currencies were improperly valued. In December 1971, the so-called Smithsonian Agreement was worked out whereby the United States undertook to devalue the American dollar relative to gold and to special drawing rights,[7] while Japan and European countries agreed to revalue their currencies. The bands within which currencies could fluctuate were to be widened from one percent to 2.25 percent. Given the world economic situation, the fixed rates could not hold, and most countries ultimately followed Canada's example and abandoned the pegged rates.

THE CONFLICT WITH MONETARY POLICY

At times there have occurred basic conflicts between the objectives of

---

[6] The ceiling, originally set at $2.7 billion, and later decreased to $2.6 billion and then to $2.55 billion, was agreed on in exchange for exempting Canada from the American Interest Equalization Tax.

[7] Special drawing rights (SDRs), sometimes referred to as "paper gold", are international reserve assets that were created by international monetary authorities in the late 1960s as a means of settling accounts. They represent a composite of the currencies of 16 nations weighted according to their importance in international trade.

monetary policy on one side, and the attempt to maintain a viable balance of payments on the other. How this conflict is resolved is greatly influenced by whether the economy is operating with fixed or floating exchange rates. It is widely though not universally conceded that flexible exchange rates give the country greater power and autonomy to deal with domestic issues.

Let us consider the problem of inflation which has been a major problem of the Canadian economy on a number of occasions since the Second World War. It was a serious problem in the immediate postwar period and after the Korean War, present though not so serious after the 1956 investment boom, a serious problem again at the end of the 1960s; and it became acute in the 1970s. The appropriate anti-inflationary policy is a tight money policy. However, if in attempting to achieve a tight money policy the Canadian rate of interest is set higher than the American rate, this would encourage Americans to purchase Canadian securities, and Canadian firms and governments in search of low interest rates to float issues in the American security markets. The supply of American dollars would increase; the supply curve would shift to the right; and the price of American dollar would fall. If the exchange rate is fixed, the Bank of Canada must keep purchasing foreign exchange in order to prevent the price from dropping below the allowable limit. In the years when not only was the exchange rate fixed but there was an agreed ceiling on reserves (July 1963 to December 1968), the monetary authorities had very little room for maneuvering: they could not buy for long without reaching the ceiling; once they could no longer buy foreign exchange, they faced the necessity of abandoning the tight money policy necessary for the health of the domestic economy. The problem is less acute without such a ceiling, but obviously there will be a conflict of interest with the United States if the reserves of American dollars get too high and cause balance-of-payments problems for the United States. The Canadian authorities again would face the possibility of having to abandon the monetary policy that they regarded as appropriate.

In the years prior to the 1962 exchange crisis, there occurred a clear example of a conflict between the efforts to pursue a domestically-oriented monetary policy and the achievement of a viable international payments position. Through poor monetary policy, the interest rate in Canada rose higher than that in the United States. Large issues of securities (the Toronto subway issue, for example) were floated in the United States, and the inflow of capital caused a rightward shift in the supply curve, with the result that at one time the price of the American dollar was less than 95 Canadian cents. This made American imports most attractive to Canadian purchasers because, as we have noted before, the price of imports is made up of two components: the domestic price in the producing country and the price of the foreign currency. The cheap American dollar meant low prices for American imports, and this encouraged Canadian purchasers to buy American goods. At the same time, the high price of the Canadian dollar in terms of other currencies discouraged foreigners from buying Canadian goods, and Canadian exporters were being penalized. When newsprint was sold in the world market for American dollars, for example, the newsprint manufacturers could get less than 95 cents Canadian for every American dollar they earned; as a result their profits fell, and they were discouraged from exporting. It is no wonder that Canada ran into such large deficits on current account. The government then began to discuss actions to raise the price of the American dollar from 95 cents up to a maximum of $1.05. However, for a number of reasons—speculation being important among them—the supply of American dollars dropped rapidly; the price rose, and in spite of large sales of exchange from the stabilization fund by the Bank of Canada, the price rise got out of hand. Canada lost exchange reserves so fast that the monetary authorities had to turn for help to the International Monetary Fund.

There can occur a conflict of objectives during a recession. The appropriate policy in a time of high unemployment is to have easy money in order to encourage investment and consumption and thus to put people back to work. Assume that the easy money policy is successful and that consumption increases. There will be increased consumption not only of domestically produced goods but of American-produced goods as well. More American dollars will be needed to pay for these imports; the demand for American dollars will shift to the right and the price will increase. If there is a fixed exchange rate the government, trying to hold down the price, may then have to sell its supplies of foreign currency, just as it had to do during the speculative assaults of 1962 and 1968. If it begins to run short, it may be forced to abandon its easy money policy and to dampen domestic economic conditions by using a restrictive monetary policy. If there is a floating exchange rate, the effect may be quite different. The government would not have to sell its reserves of foreign exchange to keep the exhange rate within the allowable limit. Instead, as the price of the American dollar rose, American imports would become more expensive compared with Canadian-produced products; Canadians would be encouraged to substitute import-competing Canadian goods for the more expensive American goods, and this ultimately could have the effect of increasing employment in Canadian industries and of reinforcing the original easy money policy.

Foreign Aid

Foreign aid transactions—international transfers of resources on concessionary terms—enter into a country's international accounts and thus are related to the goal of achieving a viable balance of payments. Foreign aid is undertaken for a number of reasons—political, economic, and humanitarian. There are contradictory views about development assistance: at one extreme there are those who believe that the developed countries have a major responsibility to assist the poor nations of the world, and they argue that in view of Canada's wealth, the country's contributions are disgracefully low. On the other hand, there are those who say that there are poverty and development problems within Canada, and domestic under-development problems should take precedence over foreign ones. The common sentiment appears to be that the rich nations do have a major responsiblity to help the poor nations.

The needs of the underdeveloped countries are immense. These countries are impatient to achieve the higher standards of living they know to exist in other parts of the world, and their demand for capital for this purpose, as well as for capital to keep pace with their rapidly increasing populations is great. The situation of some of the poorest nations is particularly distressing: these are the countries with annual incomes of about $100 per person, literacy levels of less than 10 percent, and life expectancies of less than fifty years. They have suffered acutely in the recent world inflation in items like food, oil, and fertilizers. It is to these countries (which include much of Africa and several Asian countries) that the United Nations and the OECD are trying to direct more aid.

The United Nations Conference on Trade and Development (UNCTAD) some years ago suggested that government and private sources in the developed countries should give aid equal to one percent of their annual national income. This target has been reached by relatively few countries. According to the Development Assistance Committee of the Organisation for Economic Co-operation and Development, only Belgium, Canada, France, the Netherlands, Sweden and the United Kingdom achieved that level of aid in 1974. The United States, with a total contribution (private and official) of $9.9 billion, gave 0.71 percent of its gross national product. Canada's contribution (private and official) of about $1.7 billion amounted to 1.18 percent. Russia and China are listed as having disbursed 0.16 and 0.24 percent, respectively, of their estimated national incomes.[8]

---

[8] Development Assistance Committee, *1975 Review: Development Co-operation* (Paris: Organisation for European Co-operation and Development, November 1975), Chs. vii & ix. In the fall of 1975 the United Nations General Assembly adopted a target for *official* development assistance of 0.7 percent of GNP by the end of the century. Canada's official aid reached 0.5 percent of GNP in 1974, according to the *1975 Review* (p. 131).

Canadian Development Assistance

Canada has been giving aid to underdeveloped countries for more than twenty-five years. Most of the funds have gone into the Colombo Plan countries in South and Southeast Asia, the first and largest of Canada's regional programs. Assistance to the Carribean began in the late 1950s. A special aid program was started in 1961 for new Commonwealth African countries, and an educational assistance program was launched for Francophone African countries. The newest region of interest is Latin America, where a technical assistance program concentrating on agriculture, forestry, fisheries, education, and community development was begun in 1971.

The Canadian International Development Agency (CIDA) administers Canada's development assistance program. It expected to dispense close to a billion dollars in 1975. Most of the aid is bilateral (given directly by Canada to a region), although CIDA does put considerable emphasis on multilateral aid which is given to organizations like the United Nations and its agencies and the World Bank group, to be distributed to underdeveloped countries. Some multilateral aid is funneled through four regional development banks: the Inter-American, African, Asian, and Carribean Development Banks. A good deal of private aid is channeled through organizations like the Red Cross, Oxfam, Care, and the Save-the-Children fund.

Bilateral aid, in the form of grants or loans, is of three general types: technical assistance, economic assistance, and commodity aid (mainly food aid, though commodities such as fertilizers, aluminum, nickel, copper and newsprint have also been given away). Canada in 1975 greatly increased its food aid in line with the pledges it made at the 1974 World Food Conference in Rome. Food aid was expected to account for about 30 percent of CIDA's total aid budget, and a sizable portion of it was to be administered multilaterally through the World Food Program of the United Nations.

Technical and educational assistance is another important part of development assistance. Large numbers of students and trainees from developing countries come to Canada to study, and many Canadian teachers and technical advisors serve in underdeveloped countries. Capital is also made available to build and support schools and other institutions.

Much of the bilateral aid has been in the form of grants for specific projects, many of them in the energy, transportation, and communications field. Such aid is tied to procurement in Canada of things like equipment, materials, and engineering services. In principle, about 20 percent is not tied and therefore is available to meet the local on-site costs of labour and local materials used.[9] This minimizes the balance-of-payments problems that might be caused by giving foreign aid. In the balance-of-payments statements, grants and other unilateral transfers by the government or by private agencies to foreign countries comprise part of the payments to foreigners in the nonmerchandise account. If aid is tied to purchases in Canada, then the money used to purchase domestic goods and services show up as exports, and the receipts then partially offset the payments and improve the current account balance. Furthermore, there is a good chance that these contacts with foreign countries will result in the establishment of long-term markets for domestically-produced goods and services. Unlike the bilateral aid, almost all of the multilateral development assistance is untied.[10]

Loans comprise a substantial portion of development assistance, and the terms on which they are made are crucial to the developing country. If they have to be serviced and repaid in foreign currency, the interest charges can take up a large part of the foreign exchange being generated by the aid program. The International Development Association, an affiliate of the World Bank, was established in 1960 to provide "soft loans"—that is, loans with little or no interest and with long maturity dates. Most Canadian loans are very soft—interest-free, maturing in fifty years, with no repayment for the first ten years.

Foreign trade is an area where many goals of the economy meet, if not collide (sometimes in a cloud of theory). Greater opportunities for specialization exist if there is trade, and this affects growth. World-wide developments affect prices of imports and exports and have a direct influence on inflation and employment. The ability to implement stabilization policies is constrained by the need to maintain a viable balance of payments. One current collision path involves foreign investment, an important component of the balance of payments and national identity. We shall turn to the subject of foreign investment in the next chapter.

---

[9] Development Assistance Committee, *1974 Review*, p. 127.

[10] *Ibid.*

13

Throughout most of its history Canada has welcomed foreign investment. Benefits include new industries, new techniques of production, technical "know-how", and access to new markets. More growth has meant a higher standard of living, more jobs, and increased revenues for Canadian governments. Costs include payments for interest, dividends and head-office services, less research and fewer exports than there might otherwise have been, and the spillover into Canada of foreign laws.

Some subsidiaries are owned by multinational enterprises— organizations that invest in several countries. Their power derives from their size, financial strength, flexibility, and mobility.

Canadian governments have responded to opposition to foreign direct investment by limiting access to key sectors, enacting guidelines to influence the behaviour of foreign-owned firms and passing the Foreign Investment Review Act to ensure that foreign investment is of significant benefit. They have also encouraged Canadian ownership through tax concessions, business incentives, and the Canada Development Corporation.

Foreign Investment: Who Controls What?

Now that we have looked at Canada's trade and the balance of payments we are in a better position to understand some of the issues relating to foreign investment that are currently being discussed all over Canada. We saw in the previous chapter that flows of capital are the offsetting item to imbalances in the trade of goods and services in the balance-of-payments accounts. It follows, then, that the flows of capital associated with foreign investment have a role to play in the objective of achieving a viable balance of payments. Moreover, various payments associated with foreign investment, such as interest payments and dividends, enter into the current account; and to the extent that foreign investment results in the production of goods and services that are exported or that take the place of goods and services that might otherwise be imported, there is also an effect on the current-account balance. Foreign investment, then, is involved in the objective of achieving a viable balance of payments.

Foreign investment is also involved in achieving other economic goals. It has made an important contribution to growth, with the result that Canadians enjoy a higher standard of living then they otherwise would have. The most sensitive issue, however, is the question of economic nationalism: if, as was suggested in Chapter 3, we define economic freedom as encompassing the right to pay the costs of being Canadian, then the entire question of foreign investment becomes a component of the goal of economic freedom. Historically the Canadian economy has always been freely accessible to foreign investment, and notwithstanding a noticeable change in attitude, particularly in the last ten or fifteen years, and the imposition of some restrictions (the most recent being the *Foreign Investment Review Act*) Canada's economy still remains one of the least restrictive towards foreign investment.

According to Harry G. Johnson,[1] the tangible benefits of economic nationalism are likely to accrue to only a limited number of nationals; nevertheless, its emotional appeal in Canada has been growing, reinforced by the efforts of a small but influential group in the country. Evidence of

---

[1] H. G. Johnson, "A Theoretical Model of Nationalism in New and Developing States," in H. G. Johnson, ed., *Economic Nationalism in Old and New States* (Chicago: University of Chicago Press, 1967), pp. 8 ff.

the change in attitude is to be found in the explosion of literature on the problem and in the unfavourable opinions being publicly expressed in news commentaries and after-dinner speeches. Opposition to the free flow of foreign investment was the rationale for the formation of the Committee for an Independent Canada in 1970. It is a basic component of the platform of the Waffle Group, a left-wing offshoot of the NDP which advocates nationalizing foreign-owned subsidiaries. The change of attitude also shows up in the opinion polls.[2]

Governments, both federal and provincial, have become so concerned about the issue that they have undertaken a number of studies, which include the federal government's *Report of the Task Force on the Structure of Canadian Industry* (the Watkins Report) in 1968, the *Report of the Commons Standing Committee on External Affairs and National Defence* (the Wahn Report) in 1970 and *Foreign Direct Investment in Canada* (The Gray Report) in 1972; and the Government of Ontario's *Report of the Interdepartmental Task Force on Foreign Investment* in 1971.

The concern is focused on foreign *direct* investment, as opposed to foreign *portfolio* investment. Foreign portfolio investment occurs when nonresidents buy long-term bonds issued by corporations or by any of the various governments of Canada, or when they buy shares in companies in which nonresidents have a minority interest—that is, not enough equity to give them control. Foreign *direct* investment carries with it the concept of control over physical assets. It involves investment by nonresidents in Canadian companies that are controlled in the country of residence of the investor. Direct investment can take place even if no capital moves across the border: as frequently happens in Canada, foreign subsidiaries may increase their asset holdings by reinvesting some of their retained earnings.

The federal government has responded to public pressure by restricting foreign direct investment in certain key sectors like finance and communications. Parliament passed the *Foreign Investment Review Act* in 1973, which created a screening agency to look into all takeovers beyond a certain size and to permit only those investments considered "of significant benefit" to Canada. In addition, there have been measures to encourage Canadian ownership, such as favourable tax laws and the establishment of the Canada Development Corporation. There have been several sets of government guidelines designed to improve the performance of foreign-owned firms in Canada, the most recent being the 1975 *New Princi-*

---

[2] See John Fayerweather, *Foreign Investment in Canada* (Toronto: Oxford University Press, 1974), pp. 13-28; and J. Alex Murray and Lawrence LeDuc, *A Cross-Sectional Analysis of Canadian Public Attitudes Towards U.S. Equity Investment in Canada* (Toronto: Ontario Economic Council, Working Paper No. 2, June 1975), pp. 10 ff.

ples of International Business Conduct enunciated by the Minister of Trade and Commerce. Finally, some measures have been taken by both the federal and provincial governments to try to limit the application of foreign laws to Canadian companies.

What the advocates of policies to limit foreign investment are essentially saying is that Canada would be better served if a company like Coca Cola were owned by Canadians rather than by shareholders in the United States; and, by inference, that the outsiders who do own Coca Cola could influence the country in a negative way. On the other side there are those who argue that it makes no difference who owns or controls the company; what matters is the performance of the foreign firms and the efficiency with which they allocate economic resources; that as long as there are some Canadians in the executive suite, as long as some research is being done, as long as the company is aggressively trying to sell its products at home and abroad, what difference does it make *who* controls it?

Where people stand on such an emotional issue depends on a number of factors, three of which might be mentioned. The first factor is whether or not people accept nationalism as an ideology. Those who are internationalist in outlook are less concerned with who owns or controls a company, arguing that the free flow of resources on a worldwide scale increases the efficiency with which they are allocated and improves the welfare of all. The important question for such people is performance: economic, political, and social. Obviously, these are not the people who get so upset when they see an American license plate in a Canadian city that they rush out to paste a "Yankee go home!" sticker on the car.

The second factor is whether people believe that the advantages of foreign investment outweigh the disadvantages. Those who argue that the benefits are greater than the cost suggest that foreign-owned firms have contributed much to economic growth, citing their contribution to Canadian "know-how" and the reciprocal access to foreign markets which the presence of these firms facilitates. On the other hand, those opposed to foreign control suggest that the costs of a "branch plant economy" in research and development, in the extraterritorial application of foreign laws, and in the loss of jobs for top management are costs that are not matched by the benefits that have accrued to the Canadian economy.

A final factor that might be mentioned is the concept people have of the power of business. Those who feel that the business community is not very powerful will be less concerned with whether the decision-makers in the business are American, British, French, Japanese or Canadian. On the other hand, for those who believe that "big business" controls the economy or the government (or both), the nationality of businessmen then becomes of major importance.

The Growth of Foreign Investment in Canada

Canada has had a long history of foreign investment. Before World War I foreign investment formed a relatively greater proportion of total investment than it does at present.[3] Large amounts of capital poured into the building of canals and railways, and into the mining and pulpwood industries; the government borrowed heavily in foreign markets to finance its own operations. There was some foreign investment in manufacturing industries, but Canada relied mainly on imports because the local market was too small to support much secondary industry. Much of the investment was portfolio rather than direct. Just before the war almost three quarters of total foreign investment was provided by the United Kingdom.[4]

After World War I, the major supplier of investment funds became the United States instead of the United Kingdom. The change in source was accompanied by a shift from portfolio to direct investment. By the time of the Great Depression, direct investment accounted for over two fifths of the total; it was concentrated in industries like pulp and paper, electrical equipment and cars, and in the extractive and processing industries.

During the 1930s when all economic activity was at a low ebb, foreign investment in Canada declined. There was some divestment of securities by nonresident owners, and some foreign-held Canadian securities were repatriated by the issuers.

After World War II the flow of foreign investment increased rapidly. The size of the domestic market for manufactured goods was also growing. The continuation of Sir John A. Macdonald's National Policy—a policy that encouraged the development of secondary manufacturing industries in Canada—meant that the market was heavily protected by tariffs. Investment was made even more attractive since firms located in Canada could get access on favourable terms to markets in the British Commonwealth because of the British Preferential Tariff. In the resource domain, the discovery of oil in Alberta's Leduc field in 1947 attracted huge amounts of foreign capital to finance exploration and development of Canada's oil fields. With large markets for iron ore assured in the United States there was a surge of capital investment to develop the iron ore industry in Labrador. Similarly, captive markets for newsprint in the United States encouraged investment in the newsprint industry.

---

[3] Government of Canada, *Foreign Direct Investment in Canada* (Ottawa: Information Canada, 1972), commonly known as the *Gray Report*, p. 13.

[4] *Ibid.*, Table 1, p. 15.

SOME FACTS AND FIGURES

We have used the phrase "huge amounts of foreign capital": some data[5] may convey a more accurate idea of the magnitudes of the variables we are discussing. At the end of 1974 foreign long-term investment in Canada amounted to $60.2 billion—more than an eightfold increase since 1946. Of this total, almost 60 percent was foreign direct investment. Most of the foreign long-term investment came from the United States: in 1974 it contributed just about 77 percent of the total. Britain, the next largest source, supplied about 9 percent. The largest amount of foreign long-term investment at the end of 1974 was to be found in manufacturing, which accounted for 28 percent of the $60.2 billion. The next largest amount of investment (about 19 percent) was in government securities of various kinds. Long-term investment in petroleum and natural gas accounted for another 17 percent.

Attitudes toward foreign investment are affected not only by the level of ownership and control but also by the trend of ownership patterns. There tends to be less concern if the relative share of foreign ownership is declining than if it is increasing. The very rapid increase in the postwar proportion of direct foreign investment in the manufacturing and resource industries provided a good deal of the content of the speeches of various members of the Committee for an Independent Canada. Data on Canada's international investment position indicate that in the postwar period foreign investment outpaced domestic investment until about 1960, but that during the 1960s the *rate* relative to domestic investment declined in some sectors—manufacturing, for example—although the absolute amount of foreign investment continued to increase. In the petroleum and natural gas industry during the latter period the rate seemed to have levelled off.[6]

Data that measure foreign participation by control of assets, equity, sales and profits are collected under the *Corporations and Labour Unions Returns Act* (CALURA).[7] If foreign participation in the various industrial divisions is measured by assets and equity, then it is greatest in mining and in manufacturing (it is over 55 percent in both). It is lowest in construction (about 15 percent) and utilities (over 10 percent); it amounts to over 25 percent in the wholesale and retail trades and to somewhat less than that in the service industries.

Within the manufacturing sector there are some industries where foreign control (measured by assets, equity, sales and profits) is very high.

[5] From *Statistics Canada Daily*, Ottawa, 8 October 1976.
[6] See Fayerweather, *op. cit.*, pp. 6-8.
[7] Statistics Canada, *Corporations and Labour Unions Returns Act, Report for 1973, Part 1— Corporations* (Ottawa, 1976), pp. 39-74.

It is amost complete in the petroleum and coal products manufacturing industry, for example, and it amounts to more than 75 percent in the transport equipment and machinery industries.

CANADIAN DIRECT INVESTMENT ABROAD

When discussing the impact of foreign direct investment on Canada we must not lose sight of the fact that at the same time as foreigners are investing in Canada, Canadians are taking over foreign companies and building plants in foreign countries. Direct investment abroad by Canadian residents has been growing rapidly. At the end of the war (1946) it started off at $772 million, doubled by about 1953-54, doubled again by 1963, and again by 1970; by 1974, the most recent year for which figures are available, it amounted to $9 307 million.[8]

Foreigners have poured almost four times as much money into direct investment in Canada as Canadians have invested abroad, but then Canada has a much smaller population than have all of the countries that invest in Canada. If we compare direct investment on a *per person* basis with, say, the United States, the major investor in Canada, we find that the average Canadian owns more of the United States than the average American owns of Canada. In 1974, for example, the average American had an investment in Canada of $137. The direct investment per Canadian in the United States amounted to $219—more than one and a half times as much.

One must recognize, of course, that Canadian direct investment abroad includes investment by some Canadian companies which, themselves, are foreign-owned. Some companies have found it to their advantage to have third-country subsidiaries held by a Canadian company—in Commonwealth countries, for example. Foreign companies have occasionally taken over Canadian corporations with foreign operations, and this has resulted in Canadian direct foreign investment by nonresidents.[9]

The Benefits of Foreign Direct Investment

Throughout its history, the Canadian economy has offered virtually free entry to foreign investment because of a widespread belief in its benefits to

---

[8] Foreign Investment Division, Office of Economics, Department of Industry, Trade and Commerce, *Direct Investment Abroad by Canada, 1946-1967* (Ottawa, 1971), p. A-2, and *Statistics Canada Daily*, Ottawa, 14 September 1976.

[9] A. J. Cordell, The Multinational Firm, *Foreign Direct Investment and Canadian Science Policy*, Background Study for the Science Council of Canada, Special Study No. 22 (Ottawa: Information Canada, 1971), p. 68.

Canada. Only relatively recently have concerns been expressed about some of the costs; still more recently the Canadian government has begun to develop stronger policies which, it is hoped, will retain most of the benefits while reducing some of the costs.

The benefits most commonly cited include the inflow of foreign capital that has made possible the development of many industries for which adequate Canadian financing was not available. Foreign direct investment has been instrumental in introducing new production techniques and technical "know-how" into the Canadian economy and has provided managerial skills in many industries. It has increased trade: a large export business has been generated, particularly in resource industries. Investment in manufacturing industries has increased the output of import-competing goods. Other benefits deriving from foreign investment include access to markets that would otherwise not have been available, and the increased efficiency of some established firms resulting from the competition generated when foreign firms came in.

The favourable impact of foreign investment on growth has been the contribution that Canadians have most universally appreciated. The higher rate of growth has given Canadian consumers a higher standard of living, has provided Canadian workers with more jobs and Canadian governments with more tax revenues than would have been possible if the country had not had access to foreign capital. Resource development in particular has required vast amounts of capital for exploration and for development. Large and secure markets are essential before companies find it worthwhile to push developments into remote regions where resources are to be found. At the time when many resources were being developed—the Quebec-Labrador iron ore deposits, for example—the necessary pools of capital, much of it high-risk, were not available in Canada; nor was the Canadian market large enough to absorb the output of these huge developments.

The transfer of capital that occurs when foreign investment takes place makes a major contribution to growth, but of great importance also is the transfer of techniques and skills including research and development, management, marketing, production skills, and so on. These, too, have increased productivity and have helped raise real wages and salaries in Canada.

Canada has always been dependent on foreign technology: most product innovation and process development have resulted from scientific and technological developments elsewhere. Canada is a small nation, which means that the absolute level of resources is more limited than in other developed countries. Moreover, the proportion of gross national product devoted to research and development lags far behind that of the United

States, the United Kingdom, France, or Holland, for example.[10] In contrast to industry in the United States, the United Kingdom, or Japan, Canadian industry undertakes relatively little research and development: most of it is carried out in government laboratories and universities in Canada, where there is no close link with the demands of the marketplace.[11] Because of this, access by Canadian subsidiaries to the research and development of the parent company has been a major factor in making possible the innovations in Canadian industry which permit it to turn out the many products that Canadians want.

Nor is it only access to research and development, as we understand it, that is important: there is also the "know-how" of investing, producing, selling the product, and administering the subsidiaries in Canada. Efficient management is crucial for the successful practical utilization of inventions and in the organization of production and sales. Studies of educational achievement suggest that Canadian entrepreneurial skills have been in short supply, and there is evidence to suggest that much of the needed entrepreneurship in Canada has been provided by foreign parent companies.[12]

Some Canadian subsidiaries have had access to markets in the home country of the parent; some have been able to use the marketing skills and distribution channels of the parent company to sell abroad, thus increasing exports and helping to create a more favourable balance-of-payments position. Many manufacturing firms that have been established primarily to sell in the domestic market, rather than abroad, have helped the balance-of-payments position by producing import-competing products, which have the effect of slowing down the flow of imports.

The Costs of Foreign Direct Investment

Foreign capital flows into Canada because its owners foresee returns on their investments. These returns may either be distributed as interest and dividend payments, or they may be retained by the company in order to make further investments and thus increase the capital value for the owners. Interest and dividends show up in the nonmerchandise account of the balance of international payments as payments to foreigners. There are

---

10 Economic Council of Canada, *Fifth Annual Review: The Challenge of Growth and Change* (Ottawa: Queen's Printer, 1968), p. 40.
11 G. Bruce Doern, "The Allocation of Research-and-Development Resources" in *Issues in Canadian Economics*, L. H. Officer and L. B. Smith, ed. (Toronto: McGraw-Hill Ryerson Limited, 1974), p. 344.
12 Gray Report, *op. cit.*, p. 37.

other financial outflows that enter into the nonmerchandise account—the payments for various head office services such as management and other professional services, royalties, payments for franchises, for research, for advertising and for insurance.

The use of these various head office services has given rise to a great deal of controversy in Canada. On the one hand, there are the benefits, already mentioned, such as access to the skills and techniques developed by the parent company. On the other hand, this dependence on the parent company is an important element in the emotion-packed charge that all of this direct foreign investment is making the Canadian economy little more than "branch-plant economy", or that foreign-owned subsidiaries are "truncated", to use the language of the *Gray Report*. "Truncation" is described as a tendency to limit the managerial, developmental and planning activities of subsidiaries and concentrate them in the parent company, whether to achieve economies of scale, to limit risk, to effect savings, or for any other reason.[13]

Other costs associated with foreign direct investment are the costs of extraterritoriality (the spillover of foreign laws into Canada) and the cultural domination that may accompany foreign direct investment. The issue of cultural domination has less economic content than others, and for this reason, we shall not deal with it directly, although we shall note some of the policies that have been implemented to try to maintain the Canadian cultural identity.

THE PERFORMANCE OF FOREIGN-OWNED SUBSIDIARIES

We shall consider a few of the costs of foreign direct investment in more detail. Our immediate task is to look at the performance of foreign-owned subsidiaries with respect to exports and imports, research and development, and management. Then we shall turn to the issue of extraterritoriality.

External Trade   Concern over Canada's balance of payments has led to a closer study of the export performance of foreign-owned subsidiaries, particularly in the manufacturing sector. Canada has a major disadvantage in being about the only fully industrialized country that does not have free access to a market of at least one hundred million people. To achieve potential economies of scale and become competitive, it is essential for many industries to expand sales beyond the domestic market into foreign ones. Recognizing this, many Canadians have begun to ask whether sub-

---

[13] *Ibid.*, p. 42.

sidiaries of foreign companies may be neglecting to export to the degree that they might, and hence failing to become as efficient as they should be. Some parent companies impose restrictions on subsidiaries: for example some are licensed to supply only the domestic market. The parent company, in limiting the subsidiaries' exports, may be obeying laws that exist in its home country, or may be responding to policies or pressures of its home government. Alternatively, the parent company may be trying to minimize its own risk, or to allocate markets in the most efficient way possible among all of its subsidiaries in order to maximize the profits of the entire operation. According to the Gray Report there is evidence that such restrictions exist in a "significant number" of cases, and the fear is being expressed that they may remain there through inertia even though the performance of subsidiaries, and hence their potential to export, may improve.[14] A study by A. E. Safarian suggests that restrictions (on patent rights, for example) exist in a minority of firms, but in many cases they are potential rather than actual, since the high costs of production in these subsidiaries would prevent them from competing in international markets. His findings also indicated that as far as export performance was concerned there was no significant difference between resident-owned and nonresident-owned firms.[15]

A large and growing portion of exports by foreign-owned subsidiaries is sent to affiliated companies, and since most parents of Canadian subsidiaries are in the United States, this means increased trade with affiliates in that country.[16] In many quarters in Canada there is a desire to diversify trade and limit, as far as possible, dependence on a single trading partner. Proponents of diversified trade feel that this objective is being thwarted by foreign-owned subsidiaries which deal to such a large extent with their American affiliates.

Limitation of exports by parent companies and decisions to divide the export market on grounds that may be rational from the point of view of the parent companies may reinforce certain attributes of a branch-plant operation that are considered undesirable: they may constrain Canadian managers from becoming aggressive entrepreneurs who seek out export opportunities. It has also been suggested that, given the significant correlation between the export performance of American firms and the level of research and development, which lead to product innovations and hence to the development of unique products, export limitations that prevent access to large markets may also aggravate the research and development

[14] *Ibid.*, p. 154.

[15] A. E. Safarian, *The Performance of Foreign-Owned Firms in Canada* (Montreal: Canadian-American Committee, Private Planning Association of Canada, 1969), pp. 36 & 38.

[16] Gray Report, *op. cit.*, pp. 171 ff.

problem[17] and perpetuate the role of subsidiaries as means merely of providing a distinctive product of the parent company for the Canadian market.

In all of this, it must be said again that there is little difference between the performance of foreign-owned subsidiaries and Canadian companies in the matter of export.[18] Much more important than ownership in determining the export performance of these subsidiaries are such matters as the Canadian tariff structure and trade arrangements with different countries, the general level of efficiency of industry in Canada, and the general economic environment. The data indicate, moreover, that foreign-controlled firms, in both manufacturing and in resource industries, account for a large and growing proportion of total Canadian exports.[19]

When discussing the possible effects of direct foreign investment on Canada's balance-of-payments position, we should look at *imports* by foreign-owned susbidiaries as well as exports.[20] As in so many matters relating to direct foreign investment, the data available are very limited. Foreign-controlled firms appear to be more oriented to imports than resident-controlled firms; moreover, American-controlled subsidiaries in Canada seem to import more than American subsidiaries in other countries. Imports tend to come mainly from the country where the parent is located, which, for Canada, means mainly from the United States. Subsidiaries may import for a number of reasons: the products they need may not be produced in Canada, or if they are they cost more; it may be possible for the parent to get discounts from bulk buying if it buys for itself and its subsidiaries simultaneously. The close link between parent and subsidiary may prevent a Canadian supplier of a product, or of some service like advertising or management consulting, from getting the business, however efficient he may be. The purchase of large quantities of goods and services from parent companies abroad may slow down the development of competing Canadian manufacturing and service industries, and it is feared that it may introduce some undesirable rigidities into the balance of payments. Furthermore, when there is trade between affiliates, the products exchanged do not go through the market, so that a market price is not set; this raises the question of what price is charged. *Transfer prices*, as they are called, can be raised or lowered in such a way as to influence the profits of the subsidiary, and hence its taxable income, which is of concern to governments in Canada.

---

[17] *Ibid.*, p. 170.

[18] Safarian, *op. cit.*, p. 5.

[19] Gray Report, *op. cit.*, p. 170.

[20] *Ibid.*, pp. 195-208.

Research and Development Research and development are important contributors to productivity and hence to growth, and Canada has had extensive access to foreign technological developments through the links that exist between subsidiaries and their parents, through the ability to purchase the rights to use foreign technology, and through licensing arrangements. There appears to be no significant correlation between *indigenous* research and development and growth: it is access to the outcome and the readiness of Canadian manufacturers to adopt new technology that count. The *Gray Report* points to the cases of Japan and the United Kingdom, the former with a relatively low technological output of its own but a very high rate of growth, and the latter in the opposite position.[21] Concern, however, is being expressed about the possible costs that may accompany Canada's heavy dependence on foreign technology. One indicator of this dependence comes from a report of the Patent and Copyright Office showing that of the patents issued in Canada, 95 percent were taken out by foreigners, mainly Americans. According to a study made for the Economic Council of Canada, Canada had the highest percentage of foreign-owned patents and the lowest percentage owned by nationals.[22]

The dependence on foreign technology may be partly attributed to the relatively small size of the economy. Firms are encouraged to spend on research and development if there is a prospect of a return from the process, and that usually means that there must be a large market against which the costs can be written off. Technological dependency may also exist because there is a large degree of foreign control in high-technology industries where one would expect research and development to be undertaken. The *Gray Report* points to a series of industries like transport equipment, electrical products, machinery and chemicals, where research and development expenditures in the United States are very high but where, in the foreign subsidiaries in Canada, there is relatively less research and development.[23]

Why should Canadians care about having indigenous research and development as long as there is access to innovations that result from it? First of all, there is the matter of the out-of-pocket costs that must be paid for foreign patents not yet in the public domain, as well as for licenses and for technical "know-how". There is also some concern that because there are fewer research and development facilities than might be the case if there were fewer foreign subsidiaries, employment in this area is lim-

---

[21] *Ibid.*, p. 120.
[22] *Ibid.*, p. 118.
[23] *Ibid.*, p. 122.

ited, and trained researchers may have to go outside Canada to find jobs. Products developed in foreign countries may not be as well adapted to the Canadian market; furthermore, the fact that we do not develop products with a distinctive Canadian flavour may mean that our ability to export is diminished. Moreover, there is concern because it is the parent company that has the right to say *what* research and development is done, and whether and where new developments will be turned into salable products.

What has been said so far about research and development should not be taken as an implication that foreign-owned subsidiaries do little research. Although the data are almost a decade old and refer to a period before there was much of a government incentive program, it seems clear that much of the research done in Canada is concentrated in those industries where foreign direct investment is high.[24]

Management   Another cost often attributed to foreign direct investment is that it has adverse effects on the supply and performance of managers in Canada. A parent company can limit the autonomy of its foreign subsidiaries by making a range of decisions itself. It is argued that this form of truncation limits the scope for Canadian managers. Parent companies sometimes appoint senior executives or members of boards of directors from the home country, and this may not only limit the range of employment possibilities for good managers (who may then feel obliged to emigrate) but it may also mean that managerial decisions are being made by people with outside cultural and political inclinations, who, it has been suggested, may not be as responsive to Canadian priorities.[25]

EXTRATERRITORIAL APPLICATION OF FOREIGN LAWS

The issue of extraterritoriality—the application of foreign laws to Canadian residents and Canadian companies—is different in kind and different in emotional impact from the issues of truncation that have just been discussed. In this case, we are not interested so much in its effects on economic variables like efficiency, employment, or growth. Such effects appear to have been rather insignificant; the efficiency of some Canadian firms may even have been improved because of the spillover of American laws. But the issue is not one of benefit or harm; instead it is a matter of national sovereignty, which is a sensitive political issue. It is the kind of issue that people do not readily forget: perhaps you remember having

---

[24] A. E. Safarian, *op. cit.*, pp. 45 ff.
[25] Gray Report, *op. cit.*, p. 145.

heard the story about Ford of Canada which, in the late fifties, was apparently not permitted to fill an order for trucks for Communist China even though it would have been quite legal under Canadian law to do so. The spillover of American antitrust laws in the Radio Patents Pool case is almost as well known: Canadian subsidiaries of American firms joined in an agreement designed to increase the manufacture of radio and television sets in Canada. An American company, not party to the agreement, filed a complaint that this was impeding its exports to Canada, and the American parent companies were forced to deny their Canadian subsidiaries the right to take part in the patent pool.

Late in 1974 the Canadian Minister of Industry, Trade and Commerce berated Washington strongly for intolerable interference in Canadian affairs because it looked as if the *Trading With the Enemy Act* was preventing the sale of office furniture to Cuba by the Cole Division of the California-based Litton Industries. In fact, the parent company had failed to file a formal application for exemption from the Act, and when it did, the exemption was granted by the American State Department, but the headlines crowed "U.S. Bows to Canada."[26]

The three best-known vehicles for extraterritoriality are the laws that affect our exports (of which the most important example is the *Trading With the Enemy Act*), the antitrust laws, and the balance-of-payments guidelines and regulations which have been published from time to time in the United States. There have been instances when the regulations of the Securities and Exchange Commission have also had some extraterritorial application, but they appear to have been somewhat less of an issue in Canada.

The Trading With the Enemy Act   The regulations under the *Trading With the Enemy Act* in the United States virtually prohibit trade with Cuba, China, Vietnam, and North Korea, and they extend to exports made by foreign subsidiaries or affiliates of Americans or American firms. The rules try to prevent the export not only of goods that have some American content but also of goods, even if they are entirely Canadian in origin, produced by a company that has United States citizens in any way involved in its management. As is evident from the Cole-Canada example mentioned earlier, it is possible in individual cases to obtain an exemption from the provisions of the Act.

It is not difficult to see why the United States would want to have such laws. Countries, including Canada, do not renounce all jurisdiction over their nationals just because they are in foreign countries; if they did,

---

[26] *The Gazette*, Montreal, 15 February 1975.

imagine the tourist traffic into a country that permitted the consumption of bothersome mothers-in-law. The laws are in place not because of a desire to control Canada, but rather to prevent American nationals from setting up and operating firms in Canada simply to circumvent American laws. However, Canadian sovereignty clearly becomes an issue when the rules spill over to control the export of goods that are Canadian in origin.

Antitrust Legislation   American antitrust legislation is stricter than Canadian, and it is because of this difference that extraterritoriality has occurred. The United States government, unwilling to see American citizens establish foreign subsidiaries in order to circumvent American antitrust policy, has made it clear that the regulations applicable to American firms are also to be applied to foreign-owned firms, just as in the case of the *Trading With the Enemy Act*. The spillover of U.S. antitrust laws has occurred in a number of ways: individuals in Canada have been named as defendants by the courts in the United States; the courts have tried to get evidence from the files of a Canadian company, and they have issued directives to Canadian companies that certain actions are to be undertaken or are to cease. There have not been many cases where these orders have affected the actions of Canadian firms, and where they have, they may even have had the effect of increasing the efficiency of Canadian industry.[27] But the problem is there. Suppose the Canadian government should decide to make Canadian industry more efficient, perhaps by providing market cooperation in order to overcome the disadvantages of a fragmented market, then those Canadian firms that are subsidiaries of an American parent could well find themselves in difficulties with American antitrust legislation. It is quite likely that American parent companies, when planning for their subsidiaries, will take into account the more stringent rules of the United States' antitrust legislation rather than the more permissive Canadian Combines Act, and this may prove disadvantageous to Canada.

Host governments like Canada have indicated their preference for joint ventures with foreign partners instead of wholly-owned subsidiaries. The argument is that when stocks are held at least in part by Canadian nationals, and when Canadians sit on boards of directors, the foreign-owned companies will be constrained to respond to domestic government policies. Canadian participation will also help maintain national control over Canada's industry. However, the concern about antitrust action in the United States is one reason why American parent companies find it easier

---

[27] Gray Report, *op. cit.*, p. 272.

simply to own the subsidiary outright: the law cannot accuse a company of conspiring with itself.[28]

Balance-of-Payments Problems During the greater part of the post-Second World War period the United States ran a balance-of-payments deficit. This deficit, caused mainly by private investment outside the United States and government aid and military programs, provided the rest of the world with the dollars needed to settle international accounts, because for a couple of decades the American dollar was universally acceptable as a key currency. As the deficit continued, however, it became an increasing cause for concern, and the United States took a series of actions designed to improve its payments position. The first move was the *Interest Equalization Tax* of 1963, which imposed a tax on foreign borrowers using American markets in order to discourage foreigners from raising funds in the United States. Then came the voluntary restraint program of 1965, part of which became mandatory in 1968, and the "new economic policy" of 1971, when President Nixon suspended the convertibility of gold, put a 10 percent surcharge on imports, and a temporary freeze on prices and wages. There were also the devaluations of the American dollar in December 1971 and February 1973.

The effects of these actions immediately spilled over into Canada, and Canada worked hard to negotiate exemptions from the earlier ones. On the specific matter of extraterritoriality, however, the voluntary controls of 1965 caused the greatest problem. The American guidelines were issued by the Federal Reserve Bank for banks and other financial institutions and by the Department of Commerce for business firms. The U.S. Department of Commerce guidelines, which became mandatory in 1968, and which initially included Canadian subsidiaries, requested companies not only to expand exports, to limit direct investment in developed countries and to increase the proportion of foreign investment financed abroad, but also to increase the rate of repatriation of foreign earnings and short-term assets. The use of American law to influence the behaviour of American-owned subsidiaries resulted in heavy pressure on the Canadian dollar as capital flowed back to the United States; and Canada was pushed into an exchange crisis.[29] Canada negotiated exemptions from the American balance-of-payments measures that affected capital flows on the grounds that Canada's current account deficits with the United States were larger than its capital imports; therefore, Canada was helping the United States to

---

[28] J. N. Behrman, *An Essay on Some Critical Aspects of the International Corporation, Background Study to the Interim Report on Competition Policy* (Ottawa: Economic Council of Canada, January 1970), p. 13.

[29] *Supra*, Ch. 12.

finance its balance-of-payments deficit. If the American government restricted Canadian borrowing in the United States, or ordered foreign subsidiaries to repatriate capital, then the only response that Canada could make would be to adjust some other parts of its transactions with the United States—to decrease the size of the trade deficit—which would have an adverse effect on the American balance of payments. Examples of extraterritoriality like these have led some Canadians to argue that it is one of the greatest costs of foreign direct investment.

The Multinational Enterprise

So far, in discussing foreign investment in Canada, we have paid no attention to the nature of the parent company. For the most part the implications for Canada are the same whether we are discussing bilateral foreign direct investment, or whether the parent has direct investment in several different countries. In the last decade or two, however, more and more attention has been focused on multinational enterprises. Multinational enterprises (MNEs) have been variously called multinational corporations, international corporations, supranational corporations and transnational corporations. To qualify as a multinational enterprise, an organization should have direct foreign investment in several different national economies. The characteristic that brings MNEs most into conflict with individual national interests is their attempt to integrate operations in order to maximize profit globally.

Some indications of the size and rate of growth of these powerful international corporations are to be found in the *Gray Report*.[30] There are about 300 major MNEs, of which some 200 are American-controlled; the remaining 100 are largely European- and Japanese-based. The American-based MNEs are estimated to account for 80 percent of all foreign direct investment of the United States. The estimated value of output of subsidiaries of American firms surpasses by six or seven times the value of American exports. There was almost a tenfold increase in the book value of MNEs between 1929 and 1969, and there is reason to believe that they will continue to grow. In his background study for the Economic Council of Canada, J. N. Behrman suggested that we might expect to see a five or sixfold increase in the annual value of output of MNEs in the two decades to 1990, making their output as large as the gross national product of the United States, or equal to about half of what he forecast the free world's gross national product would be. Such a huge growth is to be expected, he suggests, because the MNEs are to be found in dynamic sectors of the world's economies; they have the capacity to generate capital funds easily;

---

[30] Gray Report, *op. cit.*, pp. 52-53.

they emphasize research and development; and they can and do attract a core of young, able and aggressive managers.[31]

CHARACTERISTICS OF MULTINATIONAL ENTERPRISES

Multinational enterprises are powerful. Their power derives from their size, their financial strength, and their flexibility and mobility. Based on data collected under the *Corporations and Labour Unions Returns Act* (CALURA), the *Gray Report* concluded that the average size in terms of assets of foreign-owned firms in 1965 was more than four times the size of Canadian-owned firms—$7.8 million as compared with $1.7 million.[32] Not all foreign-owned firms can be classed as MNEs, but the differential is still significant.

Because MNEs are large they can raise funds relatively easily. They have easy access to capital markets in different countries; moreover, they tend to have large sums available from their own retained earnings.

An important source of strength of the MNEs is their mobility and flexibility. With operations in several countries, they can readily shift purchases or production from one subsidiary to another in response to economic need or political pressure: they might shift resources to circumvent local monetary policies, for example. When MNEs buy and sell among their affiliates, they do not deal at arm's length; that is, they do not transact business in the market, and by altering the prices of sales between their various affiliates (by altering their *transfer prices*), they can alter their costs and profit levels in different countries if it is to their advantage to do so. The efficiency of these enterprises is maintained by the core of able and mobile managers whom the MNEs with their financial strength and the excitement of multinational activities have the ability to attract.

With all of these characteristics, MNEs are a major force for any government to contend with. They have the same impact as a domestic firm on things like competition, employment, the capital market, or on the economy as a whole. But they may have more bargaining power than domestic companies owing to their mobility. This is particularly true when the MNE is negotiating to set up a new operation in a foreign country: it can bargain in many places for assistance or for absence of interference, and it can go where the best terms become available. Once an investment has been made, the local government's authority increases, and the MNE becomes more like a domestic company; but even then it

---

[31] J. N. Behrman, *op. cit.*, p. 7.
[32] Gray Report, *op. cit.*, p. 55.

has the possibility of altering transfer prices, or shifting market areas, or simply disinvesting in that country by writing off its capital.

Government Policies Relating to Foreign Direct Investment

The openness of the Canadian economy to foreign direct investment has already been commented on. Canadians, wanting to enjoy the same standard of living as Americans but lacking the necessary capital, skills, and technology, have traditionally been happy to import them. Foreign direct investment has been encouraged by special tax treatment; Canada's high tariff wall has lured many firms into the manufacturing sector.

It was not until the late 1950s that opposition to Canada's policy of keeping the doors wide open for foreign direct investment began to grow so strong that government policies to limit it started to appear. The *Gray Report* identifies three kinds of policies that have emerged in response to this opposition.[33] First of all, there have been policies to limit direct foreign investment in "key sectors" of the economy. Next, certain measures have been taken whose objectives are to increase the benefits from foreign direct investment and to reduce its costs—measures to "optimize" foreign direct investment, one might say. Finally, there have been policies that have been designed to increase Canadian ownership of the Canadian economy.

RESTRICTIONS ON FOREIGN DIRECT INVESTMENT

Legislation has been passed limiting foreign investment in sectors of the economy like finance, broadcasting and publishing, which are considered to be politically or culturally essential to Canada. For example, the revision of the *Canadian and British Insurance Companies Act* in the mid-1960s limited to 25 percent the proportion of shares that could be transferred to nonresidents; no one nonresident is permitted to acquire more shares if the transfer would take his holdings to a level over 10 percent. Similar provisions were introduced for existing federally-incorporated trust and loan companies; the Bank Act revision of 1967 put the same limitations with respect to the transfer of shares of chartered banks to nonresidents. Regulations were introduced governing the minimum proportion of Canadian directors for various financial institutions. In 1971, legislation was passed to prevent the acquisition by foreigners of more federally-incorporated sales finance firms.

---

[33] *Ibid.*, Ch. 20.

As for Canadian control over the means of disseminating culture, first of all there exists the publicly-owned network of the Canadian Broadcasting Corporation, which has been in existence since the 1930s. The *Broadcasting Act* of 1968, which brought broadcasting and cable television under the supervision of the Canadian Radio-Television Commission, required that the entire broadcasting system be owned and controlled by Canadians; a limit of 20 percent was set on nonresident holdings. Regulations with respect to Canadian content in programs have been greatly strengthened.

Magazines and periodicals have constituted one of the most contentious and most publicized areas of discussion over foreign control, mainly because of the controversy over the Canadian editions of *Time* and *Reader's Digest*. In 1956 a tax was levied on the advertising revenues of magazines that contained a sizeable portion of the material that appeared in the parent edition, as well as ads aimed at the Canadian market which had not appeared in the home edition; it was removed in 1957 when the Conservatives took office. In the mid-1960s the *Income Tax Act* and *Customs Act* were amended to prevent newspapers and periodicals that are not at least 75 percent Canadian-owned from deducting for income tax purposes the costs of ads aimed primarily at the Canadian market; exemptions were made for *Time* and *Reader's Digest* because they were foreign-controlled publications already being produced in Canada. In the spring of 1975 the federal government moved to eliminate the tax privileges of *Time* and *Reader's Digest* and to take steps to increase their Canadian content. *Time*, in response, discontinued its Canadian edition.

Book publishing has been another problem. In a debate in the House of Commons a few years ago, it was suggested that the English-language book publishing industry was about 95 percent foreign owned, and that only about 20 percent of Canadian textbooks were being supplied to Canadian schools by Canadian publishers.[34] Concerned about possible foreign impact on Canadian education, governments began to support what was left of the Canadian publishing industry. The Ontario government lent money to five Canadian firms to help them publish Canadian books, and the federal government allocated money for the purchase of Canadian books for libraries at home and abroad and for opening distribution centres in the United States. The Canada Council increased its grant for books by Canadian authors.[35]

The move to prevent the sale of Denison Mines to American interests in 1971 suggests that the uranium industry was regarded as a key sector.

---

[34] House of Commons, *Debates*, 9 December 1971, p. 10335.
[35] John Fayerweather, *op. cit.*, p. 157.

The attempted takeover by an American company of Home Oil Limited in 1972 was forestalled because the industry already had such a high degree of foreign ownership. Such takeovers do not now require special legislation: they are screened by the Foreign Investment Review Agency, which will be described in the next section.

MEASURES TO IMPROVE COST-BENEFIT RATIO

Several sets of guidelines have been issued in Canada to encourage better performance of foreign-owned subsidiaries. In 1966, for example, the Honourable Robert Winters, then Minister of Trade and Commerce, issued a set of a dozen guidelines to good corporate practices to about 3 500 foreign subsidiaries. They constituted a form of moral suasion designed to make firms aware of what the Canadian government considered to be desirable patterns of behaviour in such controversial areas as exports, growth, transfer prices, procurement, research and development, management, financial disclosure and so on. The government also began to collect data from these firms, and this has given the Department of Industry, Trade and Commerce a basis for assessing their performance; the government had previously (in 1962) passed the *Corporations and Labour Unions Returns Act*, which required yearly reports from foreign-owned companies.

The Winters guidelines were updated and expanded in 1975 by the Ministry of Industry, Trade and Commerce. The *New Principles of International Business Conduct* take account of Canada's concern over matters such as the need for more autonomy for subsidiaries in many areas, including technological innovation and participation in the social and cultural life of Canada.[36] Provinces, too—Ontario, in particular—have taken measures to reduce what they have regarded as the costs of foreign investment. Ontario, Manitoba, and Alberta have legislation limiting foreign control of provincially-incorporated trust and loan companies. Limits are set on some kinds of land sales in British Columbia, the Prairie Provinces and Prince Edward Island—and in the last case, the "foreigners" to whom land sales in excess of ten acres may not be made include anyone, Canadian or otherwise, who does not live in that Province. Ontario imposes a 20 percent tax on the sale of all land to nonresidents. Several provinces have legislation that limits foreign ownership of certain financial institutions, and Quebec's law is similar to Prince Edward Island's land sale law in that it requires 25 percent *Quebec* ownership of securities firms in that Province. Ontario also limits foreign control of businesses engaged in book

---

[36] *The Globe and Mail Report on Business*, Toronto, 19 July 1975.

publishing and in the distribution of periodicals and paperbacks. Quebec requires all of the institutions that it supports by grants, such as libraries, universities and school boards, to buy books from booksellers who have headquarters in Quebec and are at least 50 percent controlled by Canadians who live in Quebec.

Foreign Investment Review Act   In the *Gray Report* there was a great deal of discussion of the benefits of having some sort of reviewing agency to screen proposals for foreign takeovers and for establishing new foreign-owned businesses.[37] In December, 1973, Parliament passed the *Foreign Investment Review Act* which provides for a screening agency to look at prospective foreign takeovers as well as potential foreign investment in Canada. The Act is supposed to ensure that future foreign direct investment will be of "significant benefit to Canada."

The first part of the bill, which requires Cabinet approval of foreign takeovers of Canadian businesses with assets of more than $250 000 or sales of more than three million dollars, has been in force since April 1974. In the first eleven months of its operation, it was not at all clear what constituted the criteria for being of "significant benefit to Canada." During that time eighty cases came before the Review Agency; ten applications were turned down. The reasons for approval or refusal of the applications were not made public; the government released only the name of the purchasing companies and the companies purchased, and the early refusals left the firms quite bewildered about the respects in which they did not meet the criterion of being of "significant benefit to Canada."

Early in 1975, ten criteria used to assess applications were made public.[38] They required things like compatibility with Canadian industrial and economic policies; improved productivity and efficiency; increased employment; new investment; participation by Canadians as managers, directors and shareholders; increased resource processing or use of parts and services made in Canada; technological development; improvement of the competitive environment and increased exports. This action went some of the way towards meeting the objection raised by critics of the bill who argued that a screening agency would discourage many desirable investments, in large part because of the uncertainty that prevailed about the rules the Agency was working under and also in part because of the need to prepare a detailed dossier in order to submit the case to the Review Agency. The Act does not suggest embarking on a "buy back Canada" campaign; as a result, it does not meet the objections of critics at the other end of the scale.

---

[37] See, for example, the *Gray Report*, Ch. 25.
[38] *Financial Times of Canada*, Montreal, 10 March 1975, p. 23.

It was originally expected that Part II of the Act, the part dealing with the registration and screening of new investment, would be put into operation after the Review Agency had had a few months to assemble the personnel needed for administration and to get some experience with the problem of screening foreign investment. The implementation of Part II was delayed until late in 1975, partly because of the united opposition from the provinces, which were concerned that the Act might slow down development by discouraging foreign investment, and partly because of the concern that such discouragement would increase the already high level of unemployment that existed in 1975.

MEASURES TO ENCOURAGE CANADIAN OWNERSHIP

One way to help reduce the proportion of foreign direct investment in Canada is to encourage Canadians to increase the amount of the economy they own. Taxes and business incentives have been used for this purpose: dividend tax credits on income tax are available to stockholders; lower withholding taxes on dividends to nonresidents are paid by corporations that are partly Canadian-owned; there are incentives to small businesses to generate the pool of capital needed to finance growth and development that are available only if they are Canadian-controlled. Pension funds must pay a special tax unless they hold at least 90 percent of their assets in Canada. Canadian firms that buy shares in other corporations can deduct the interest charges for financing them. It is hoped that such devices will persuade Canadians to invest in their own economy and help to generate the pool of capital needed to finance growth and development.

Another device designed to encourage Canadian investment in the Canadian economy is the Canada Development Corporation (CDC) which was set up in 1971. Like Panarctic Oils and Telesat Canada, CDC is not an agency of the Crown, but is an independent company that does not report to Parliament. Initially all of its funds were provided by the federal government although, ever since its inception, it has been the stated intention that it should be a joint government-public operation. Early in 1974 it placed an issue of preferred shares with Canadian financial institutions, and in 1975 it offered convertible preferred shares to the general public, thereby furthering one of its major aims: to give Canadians a greater opportunity to participate in the economic development of Canada.

Another objective of the Canada Development Corporation is to help develop and maintain strong Canadian-controlled and managed firms in the private sector: in view of this objective there was widespread criticism of CDC's initial purchase of Polymer (now Polysar Inc.), a Crown corporation in the petrochemical industry. Since then, CDC has invested heavily in the health care and medical equipment field, with its purchase of

Connaught Medical Research Laboratories in Toronto, and a holding company, Omnimedic Inc., in Quebec, which has acquired three Quebec-based companies in the pharmaceutical and medical supplies field, and a biochemical research firm in Edmonton. Such investments have strengthened the Canadian presence in an industry where American investment has been heavy. The CDC's most publicized investment occurred in 1973 when it moved to become an international corporation by making a $290 million bid to buy about ten million shares of Texas Gulf. These shares, together with what it already owned, would give it effective control. Texas Gulf, a company with extensive mining operations and a large profit base in Canada, managed to stall the matter in a Texas court on a number of charges including conflict of interest on the ground that the sole shareholder of CDC was the Canadian government. CDC won the case both in Texas and in the Appeal Court, which gave it the right to buy all of the shares that had been tendered to it.

According to an annual report, the Canada Development Corporation had assets of almost $1 300 million by the end of 1975, about half of which were invested in the petrochemical field (Polysar and Petrostar) and over 30 percent in Texas Gulf. Its gas and oil assets amounted to $135 million, and $90 million were invested in the health care field. The Corporation, which is supposed to be a profit-making institution, had a return of almost 4 percent on its equity.[39]

Looking Ahead

As we have seen, Canada has relatively more foreign ownership and control of its economy than any other industrialized country. Direct foreign investment has brought substantial benefits in the form of additional output of goods and services, higher income levels, more employment and greater tax revenues than would have been possible without it; there have also been costs on which an increasing amount of attention has been focused in the last fifteen to twenty years—costs deriving from a less than desirable level of exports and research and development, and costs that have accompanied the centralization of certain functions and powers in the parent company. The spillover of foreign (especially American) laws and regulations into Canada has aroused strong opposition to this infringement on national identity. There have been suggestions that subsidiaries are inefficient. However, studies imply that while the perform-

---

[39] The Financial Post Corporation Service, *Canada Development Corporation*, 12 October 1976.

ance of foreign subsidiaries lags behind the performance of their parents in matters like research and development, exports, and effecting economies of scale, in fact, they are not much different from Canadian-owned firms in similar situations. This raises the questions of how much of the problem is foreign, and how much is simply a matter of Canada's domestic tax, tariff and competition policies. Canadian governments, both federal and provincial, have tried to eliminate some of the costs of foreign investment by establishing guidelines, regulations and incentives of various kinds, the most recent of these being the *Foreign Investment Review Act.*

The size, power and flexibility of some multinational enterprises create problems that go beyond those normally associated with such foreign direct investment. These are problems that are difficult for any single government to tackle and cooperation among governments will be necessary if they are to be coped with satisfactorily.

What policies are likely to emerge in the future? The country could move in one of three directions: Canada could do away with some of its present restrictions and open its doors wide to foreign direct investment; it could maintain the *status quo* with its present legislation and guidelines; finally it could put on more restrictions and, in the extreme, it could follow the preferences of the most nationalistic groups and embark on "buy back Canada" or "take back Canada" campaigns. Both extremes, given the attitudes that exist in Canada, seem unlikely: public opinion is unlikely to tolerate opening up the country even more to foreign capital, which would entail backtracking on the steps that have already been taken to control foreign investment. At the other extreme, there seems to be relatively little support for a policy to prevent any further foreign investment, or to go even further to establish a policy of buying back what is now owned and controlled by nonresidents.

Maintaining the *status quo* is a possible policy. Legislation of various kinds now regulates foreign control in key sectors. There are some incentives to Canadians to invest in their own economy, and a screening agency is now trying to ensure that takeovers and new investment will be for the benefit of Canada. The country is growing wealthier, and as wealth increases, reliance on foreign capital will decrease. Much of the funding even of foreign direct investment is now financed domestically. Once such massive capital intensive projects as James Bay and the Mackenzie Valley pipeline have been completed, Canada may even become a net exporter of capital. As a result, the relative share of foreign direct investment will decline. Some countervailing power may develop in the form of more Canadian multinationals. As long as there are serious unemployment problems, there is unlikely to be much pressure from public opinion to make restrictions on foreign direct investment more stringent.

Many other kinds of regulations exist in other countries,[40] and advocates for a number of them are to be found in Canada. The key sectors, for example, could be expanded: in Sweden and Norway, foreign control of forest resources, water falls and minerals, as well as real property and shipping are restricted; in Mexico and Japan where relatively little foreign investment of any kind has been permitted, one might argue that the entire economy is regarded as a key sector. Regulations could be implemented to ensure that residents of the host country have shares in subsidiaries: in Mexico at least half of the shares must be held by residents. Or there could be a requirement, such as exists in Norway, Denmark and Sweden, that a majority of the board of directors should be nationals. France and the United Kingdom require that nonresident takeovers be financed entirely from abroad; France also requires that at least half of the financing for new enterprises should come from abroad. The list could go on.

It must be recognized, however, that further restrictions will make Canada look less desirable as a place to invest, and that some of our big projects cannot be financed internally. Moreover, there has not been much evidence of any lessening desire on the part of Canadians for the jobs, the technology, and the improved standard of living that have been the immediate benefits of direct foreign investment.

Multinational enterprises present some particular problems of their own. Their bigness compared with the size of the economies of many of the host countries causes concern over their economic and even their political strength. Companies which can be classed as multinationals, which means that they must have affiliates in several countries, will almost inevitably be large. To the extent that they can bargain about investing or not investing in a particular country or province they may have political strength, at least in the short run. But it is in the area of economic power that there may be the greatest cause for concern, particularly if the multinational happens to be a conglomerate—a company that produces many diversified products. In the case of multinationals that have essentially one product—computers and related products in the case of IBM, for example—one may expect to achieve all of the economies that go with scale, specialization and improved technology. Such a company is able to compete in the market because it has a better product, or a cheaper one. If it becomes so large that it grows inefficient and the smaller companies can equal its performance, or even outperform it, then as has happened in the computer field, small companies will spring up.

Many multinationals, however, are conglomerates. International Telephone and Telegraph Company (ITT), one of the first of this species to

---

[40] See the Gray Report, *op. cit.*, pp. 329-337.

develop, produces thousands of products across much of the world: it produces everything from telephones to television sets, cosmetics to lamps, automotive products to frozen foods and ham; it is involved in insurance, business schools, publishing, rent-a-car and the Sheraton Hotels. Whether one is dealing with a Canadian conglomerate or a multinational conglomerate, the issue is the same: market decisions may be made without any relation to efficiency, and this is undesirable. If a company with a food outlet and a newsprint plant can go to a newspaper and say, "If you do not buy our newsprint, you cannot have the ads from our food store," then that newsprint producer has an economic clout that has nothing to do with the price or quality of its merchandise.

With companies like multinationals, policies may need to be developed cooperatively by governments, instead of unilaterally. There is also need for intergovernmental cooperation to solve the issues related to the spillover of foreign legislation. Regulations relating to such matters as these would probably get public support in Canada now, but it appears unlikely that there will be moves to implement new stringent regulations on foreign direct investment in the near future. The benefits of foreign investment together with Canada's growing ability to finance more of its own capital needs, as well as the prospect of becoming a net exporter of capital in the not-too-distant future, all give reason to expect that the matter will become somewhat less of an issue, and that Canadians will regard additional restrictive legislation on foreign direct investment as unnecessary.

14

A strong wave of consumerism has emerged in the last two decades. Contributing factors include inflation, discontent concerning the information available about a growing range of increasingly complex products, and decreased public confidence in business. The rights consumers are working for include 1) the right to safe products, 2) the right to be informed, 3) the right to choose, and 4) the right to be heard.

The object of regulating business is to maintain a reasonable degree of competition and hence improve the allocation of resources. One way to measure competition is to look at the level of concentration in an industry. Another is to look at industry performance. The government's methods of regulating business include nationalizing, establishing regulatory boards, reducing tariffs to expose business to international competition, and enacting laws like the Combines Investigation Act, which outlaws agreements, monopolies and mergers that lessen competition to the detriment of the public, as well as certain unfair trade practices.

Consumerism and the Regulation of Business

The protection of consumers' rights and the regulation of business by the government are both important issues in Canada today. The two issues are closely related because out of its desire to protect the consumer the government has enacted a body of legislation to regulate business practices (an example of this is the legislation against misleading advertising). Both issues affect more than one goal. They play an important role in maintaining competition, which was described in Chapter 3 as part of the objective of achieving a proper allocation of resources. They also affect freedom of choice, and growth. Although the protection of some consumers' rights results in legislation to regulate business and may therefore be considered simply as a part of the regulation of business, the issue of consumerism is a broader one, and it seems more useful, therefore, to consider it separately.

Consumerism

Consumers —are they sovereigns or pawns? Are they free to choose what to buy and to determine what it is that corporations will produce? Or are they so conditioned by Madison Avenue (and whatever its Canadian counterpart is) and skilled behavioral scientists hired by big, remote, impersonal corporations, which can be conversed with only through the frustrating link of computers, that they are mere pawns in a chess game in which they have no real power? So far in our discussion of consumer sovereignty, we have accepted the notion of consumer as sovereign—not an absolute monarch because the government frequently interferes with the market solution, and monopoly, in the strict sense of a single firm producing a unique product, may interfere with consumers' choice and limit consumer sovereignty.

Some consumer activists are vocal in their support of the view of consumers as pawns and are working to rouse consumers and governments to increase the amount of regulation of business to ensure that more weight is given to consumers' demands. Many consumers have felt that they have not had a fair deal and that inadequate attention has been given to their rights. Politicians and journalists have frequently agreed with them. In the late 1960s and the 1970s there occurred a strong surge of action on the part of consumers to assert what they considered to be their rights. *Consumerism* became a popular term in the 1960s to describe this movement; consumers' rights, as listed in a directive to the Consumer Advisory Council by John F. Kennedy when he was President of the United States were: the right to safety, the right to be informed, the right to choose, and the right to be heard.[1]

Consumer organizations and consumer activists obviously are not the only ones who are involved in consumerism. Businesses, too, have an important role. Many corporations have established their own high standards of safety, of honesty in advertising, and of consumer relations, which they enforce themselves, thus obviating any need for government regulations. As we are only too well aware, however, some businesses set no standards at all and so we find that to an ever increasing extent, governments are becoming involved and are promulgating more and more regulations in an effort to ensure that the rights of consumers are respected.

The strong surge of consumerism in the 1960s and the 1970s has had politicians, economists, political scientists, and marketing men asking why the movement started, why it started at the time it did, and for how long it is going to last. Is consumerism going to be a permanent force in the marketplace, or will interest in it soon decline and the movement fade into oblivion? Numerous explanations have been given for the strength of the current wave of consumerism.[2] The movement seems to get its strongest support from those in the middle and upper-middle income brackets, so that rising educational levels and income have been a factor. People have had more leisure time to devote to such causes, and the communications revolution has meant that the issues have received greater publicity. Rising standards of business conduct and social responsibility have also contributed. Inflation has been an important factor. In one analysis of the American consumer movement, it was pointed out that the current period of consumer unrest is not unique. There have been two other periods, one in the early 1900s and the other in the 1930s, when consumers resorted to boycotts in response to rising food prices, when they joined together to form new organizations, and when journalists were active in writing exposés of the dangers inherent in some widely used products. In each case, inflation was a contemporary economic problem.[3] Not all inflation-

---

[1] Quoted in Richard H. Buskirk and James T. Rothe, "Consumerism—an Interpretation", in *Consumerism the Eternal Triangle*, Barbara B. Murray, ed. (Pacific Palisades, Calif.: Goodyear Publishing Company Inc., 1973), p. 34.

[2] *Ibid.*, p. 33.

[3] Robert O. Herrmann, "Consumerism: Its Goals, Organization, and Future", in Consumerism the Eternal Triangle, *op. cit.*, p. 21.

ary periods, however, achieved the same result. The inflationary periods that accompanied the First and Second World Wars and the Korean War did not give rise to such consumer unrest, perhaps because the consumers' main problems were shortages of goods which, in the name of patriotism, they were prepared to put up with.

Consumer discontent over information available has been another important factor in keeping the consumer movement strong. Products have proliferated and have become technologically more complex. Comparative shopping has become difficult. As products have become more complex, servicing them has become more of a problem, and as consumers' frustration has increased, so have demands for performance indicators, standards, unit pricing, and intelligible and honest warranties and guarantees.

Consumers have reacted against the size and remoteness of businesses. They complain about "buck passing" and getting the "run around"; they believe that products are getting more and more shoddy, and that they are not as safe as they should be.[4]

Consumer scepticism has mounted, too, and consumers are less willing to trust business. This decline in confidence is reinforced by such cases as the businesses in Quebec that for over a decade sold meat from diseased cattle for human consumption. The decline in the confidence level of consumers has shown up in studies by the Better Business Bureau, which found that the level had dropped to almost half in a period of six years.[5] The decrease in confidence has been further reinforced by the revelations of the consumer activist Ralph Nader in his much-publicized David-Goliath fight with General Motors over the issue of auto safety. This was the first of a long series of battles by Nader and his "raiders" that have earned a great deal of publicity and have done much to create suspicion about big business and to enlist support for consumerism.

Since all of us are consumers, it might seem logical to expect strong consumers' organizations. Such is not the case, however. The consumers' voice traditionally has been a whisper rather than a shout, which explains why observers of consumerism frequently raise the question of whether consumerism as a force in the economy will last for long. Consumers are harder to organize and keep organized than, say, unions. Consumers'

---

[4] *Notes for an Address by the Honourable André Ouellet, Minister of Consumer and Corporate Affairs to the Annual Meeting of the Canadian Advertising Advisory Board, Toronto, Tuesday, November 26, 1974* (mimeographed), Department of Consumer and Corporate Affairs, p. 11.

[5] Referred to in *Notes for an Address by the Honourable André Ouellet, Minister of Consumer and Corporate Affairs to the Better Business Bureau of Canada, Toronto, Ontario, May 13, 1975* (mimeographed), Department of Consumer and Corporate Affairs, p. 7.

interests are so disparate that until an issue arises such as the use of a dangerous drug like thalidomide or the failure of the provincial meat inspection legislation in Quebec to prevent the sale of carrion and tainted meat for human consumption, it is difficult to find unifying objectives that will make consumers pull together in one direction. The importance of peoples' roles as factors of production seems in their own minds to outweigh the importance of their roles as consumers. Consumer protection is very much like other collectively-consumed goods and services which promote the welfare of all but whose benefits cannot be accurately attributed to specific individuals. Individuals who devote their attention to attempting to decrease the number of package sizes in order to increase consumers' ability to "comparison shop" will get very little personal gain: most of the benefit of their efforts spills over on the thousands of consumers who try to buy rationally. The *social* benefit of having a regulation passed preventing meat packers from packaging bacon in red-striped paper, which tends to mislead the buyer about how lean the bacon is, far outweighs the private benefit to the individuals who worked to get the legislation on the books: there are *externalities*, to use the technical economic jargon. Unions that bargain for four weeks of holidays, on the other hand, benefit themselves almost exclusively; there is little spillover effect unless the union happens to be a trendsetter and other unions can benefit from the precedent it sets. Basically, however, unions work for their own members, and as long as the leaders can keep winning benefits they can keep a loyal and active following. The existence of externalities tends to work against the continuation of consumerism as an active force. It may also be that many consumers feel that they can look after themselves: how many consumers have *you* talked to who have admitted to being misled by advertising? On the other hand, support for consumerism tends to come from the better educated in the middle and upper-middle income brackets and since levels of education and income are likely to continue to increase, this constitutes a positive force that suggests that consumerism will continue.

Consumerists have been concerned about the plight of low-income consumers. The problem of high prices in the ghetto market and the ease with which low-income consumers become victims of fraud and exploitation have been highlighted in studies like David Caplovitz's *The Poor Pay More*[6] which was written under the auspices of the Consumers Union in the United States. The broadening scope of consumerism suggests that it might expand to encompass problems of the economic environment—like poverty and the distribution of income in general, and the problem of a deteriorating physical environment—problems which impinge, at least

---

[6] David Caplovitz, *The Poor Pay More* (New York: The Free Press of Glencoe, 1963).

indirectly, on consumers' rights.[7] Issues of this kind will be with us tomorrow, and if consumerism broadens to encompass them, it is likely to continue to be a force in the economy for some time. Consumerism in Canada has an even better chance of continuing as a strong force because of the existence of ministries at the provincial level and also because of the creation in 1967 of the Department of Consumer and Corporate Affairs whose Minister has been named the "consumer advocate" of the government. The Department was the first government department in the world to be given the explicit mandate of promoting consumers' interests.[8]

THE RIGHT TO SAFETY

The list of consumers' rights mentioned earlier—the right to safety, to be informed, to choose, and to be heard—provides a convenient framework within which to look at some of the laws and regulations imposed on business that have resulted from the wave of consumerism. The protection of consumers against safety hazards is an issue that has had a long history. When the seeds of consumerism in North America were sown around the turn of the century in the United States, the issue that resulted in the first consumer regulation was protection against adulterated and unsafe products in the food and drug industries.[9] The *Canadian Food and Drugs Act*, which is enforced by two government agencies—the Department of Consumer and Corporate Affairs and the Department of National Health and Welfare—controls the safety, purity, and quality of foods and drugs throughout Canada. The Department of National Health and Welfare develops safety standards in drugs and purity standards in food. These standards are maintained through regular inspection. The Act also has provisions to prevent misrepresentation in labelling and advertising. The *Hazardous Products Act* of 1969 is a more recent piece of consumer protection legislation; it provides the basis for regulations covering thousands of individual products in some fifty categories. This Act, for example, ensures that manufacturers put symbols on labels to warn consumers about the kind of hazard (poisonous, flammable, explosive or corrosive), and the degree of hazard of a wide variety of products used in the home.

---

[7] See David A. Aaker and George S. Day, "Introduction: A Guide to Consumerism" in *Consumerism: Search for the Consumer Interest*, David A. Aaker and George S. Day, eds. (New York: The Free Press, 1971), pp. 5-6.

[8] Notes for an Address by the Honourable André Ouellet to the Better Business Bureau of Canada, *op. cit.*, p. 2.

[9] Barbara B. Murray, "Introduction" in Consumerism, op. cit., p. xi.

It establishes safety hazards for toys—the kind of regulations that prevent the use of straight pins to attach bows and decorations to dolls and ensure that electrically operated toys meet the safety standards set by the Canadian Standards Association.

THE RIGHT TO BE INFORMED

Consumer frustration over the absence of information or the presence of false or misleading information has been an important catalyst in generating consumerism. It is not possible for consumers to become experts in the purchase of all consumers' goods. They can develop some expertise with commodities they buy frequently because they can build on their own experience; but on goods that are bought infrequently, perhaps only once or twice in a lifetime, they do not have their own experience to rely on. Such goods are often technologically advanced or are of a kind that keeps changing with changing technology so that consumers cannot assess their potential performance before purchasing. If independent appraisals such as those of the Consumers' Association of Canada or the Consumers Union in the United States are not available, then consumers must rely on the marketing departments of the seller. Consumers have complained that they are not given enough information; businessmen tend to argue that consumers do not make use of the information they have. Moreover, they suggest, the consumer's greatest protection lies in the brand name of the product or in the reliability of the store from which it is purchased. "Satisfaction or your money refunded", which is the self-imposed policy of reliable department stores, for example, has done much for consumer protection. Store buyers for The Bay or Eatons have expertise and know the products they offer for sale; if customers' dissatisfaction over a particular kind of stove can take the form of returning it to the store and getting a refund, then the consumer's need for information is lessened.

Not all goods, however, are bought on the basis of "satisfaction guaranteed or your money cheerfully refunded". And while there are many manufacturers who do care, there are some who do not, causing consumers to demand more reliable information, to press for universal standards, honesty in warranties and guarantees, ticketing that gives comparable performance information for different models of the same product, unit pricing, more uniform package sizes, and so on. Consumers' organizations like the Consumers' Association of Canada and the Consumers Union in the United States have contributed substantially to increasing the information available to consumers. They test and rank various products and publish the results in their respective journals, *Consumer Canada* and *Consumers Report*.

The federal government has been active in its programs and its legislation aimed at making sure that consumers are informed. Legislation against misleading advertising in the *Combines Investigation Act* antedated the formation of the Department of Consumer and Corporate Affairs. Stage I of the revision of this Act provides for the extension of the provisions relating to misleading advertising and other kinds of misleading information that can be disseminated through door-to-door selling, direct mail, flyer advertising, and telephone sales.

Several other pieces of legislation have been passed by the Department of Consumer and Corporate Affairs to improve consumers' information. The *Textile Labelling Act* and its regulations, which have been in effect since 1972, were designed to minimize consumers' confusion over the rapidly proliferating man-made fibres and the host of new technical terms and trade names. Supplementing the Act are two voluntary programs, the Canada Standard Sizing System for children's clothing and the Canadian Care Labelling System—those variously-shaped symbols in traffic-light colors that most of us are beginning to look for (or should be looking for) when we shop for clothes. The *Packaging and Labelling Act*, whose basic regulations went into effect early in 1974, and the *Weights and Measures Act* are designed to increase consumers' ability to buy wisely by ensuring that labels will list the ingredients of a package and prevent the consumer from being defrauded by short weight or faulty weighing machines.

Apart from its regulations to ensure that businesses inform the consumer and that the information is accurate, so that in making his dollar vote the consumer in fact has the information necessary to be the rational individual that the economic model assumes, the Department has an extensive consumer education program. *Consumer Contact*, an informative newsletter for consumers, is published eleven times a year; it is available free of charge from the Department and had a circulation of over 175 000 in 1975.[10] The Department's television game show "It's Up To You" ("C'est pas sorcier" on the French network) proved so popular (it was estimated to have been seen by 5 million Canadians in 1973, its first year) that further series were planned. Binkly and Doinkle, the puppets from outer space, who each summer since 1973 have instructed 75 000 to 100 000 children in parks and playgrounds across the country on a variety of safety hazards

---

[10] Department of Consumer and Corporate Affairs, *Annual Report for the Year Ending March 31, 1976* (Ottawa, 1976), p. 39.

(the series are also available to schools on video cassettes and film) are educational tools of the Department of Consumer and Corporate Affairs. Post Office Box 99, the Department's consumer complaint and enquiry service together with the Department's regional offices processed close to 40 000 requests for information in the year 1975-76." [11]

Another method of providing information (as well as other services) to such consumers as low-income groups, the elderly, and recent immigrants who might not otherwise make use of the services of the Department of Consumer and Corporate Affairs is through neighborhood Consumer Help Offices, which are operated on a contract basis by local organizations that are active in the community, rather than out of government offices. Several, for example, are affiliated with the National Anti-Poverty Organization. Early in 1976 seventeen of these offices were in operation across Canada, and the objective of the Minister was to have forty eventually. [12] It is apparent that the government has been active in its efforts to ensure that consumers are informed.

THE RIGHT TO CHOOSE

Consumers' right to choose is a subject that we have met before. In discussing economic freedom as a goal, we saw that in the market economy the right to choose meant not only the freedom to buy any of the goods that are brought to the market, which is a freedom open to consumers in a command economy, but also the freedom to determine what goods and services will be produced. This is what is meant by consumer sovereignty. In Chapter 8 it was suggested that pure monopoly was undesirable because it limited the right of consumers to choose, and hence limited consumer sovereignty. This is one of the important reasons for wanting a reasonable amount of competition in the marketplace. As we shall see later in this chapter, the government uses the *Combines Investigation Act* to maintain competition. It has been regarded by successive Ministers of Consumers and Corporate Affairs as an important piece of consumer legislation on the grounds that the consumer's interest is best served by an equitably and effectively functioning marketplace and that the key to such a marketplace is competition.

---

[11] *Ibid.*, p. 13.
[12] *Notes for an Address by the Honourable André Ouellet, Minister of Consumer and Corporate Affairs to the National Anti-Poverty Organization March 18, 1975* (mimeographed) Department of Consumer and Corporate Affairs, p. 3.

THE RIGHT TO BE HEARD

In order to develop what J. K. Galbraith termed "countervailing power" (in other words to achieve a better balance of power in a market where corporations are large and growing larger), consumers must find means of making their voices heard. They have made great strides in this direction in recent years through various consumers' organizations. The Consumers' Association of Canada, the largest such organization in the country, traces its history back to 1941 when the federal government sought the aid of women's organizations throughout the country to help maintain the wartime price ceilings. The organization not only tests products and provides information and counsel to consumers, but also lobbies in their interest. The Minister has suggested that the existence of the Department of Consumer and Corporate Affairs to a large extent is due to the lobbying of consumers' groups.[13]

Consumers' organizations have emerged at all levels—local, provincial, and national. The Department of Consumer and Corporate Affairs gives grants to support the work of more than twenty such groups, including the Consumers' Association of Canada, the Consumer Action League, the Automobile Protection Association, as well as some local organization. Provincial governments have also begun to give grants to local consumers' organizations.

The Canadian Consumer Council, a body of representative citizens who serve as an advisory board to the Minister, has been concerned about the ineffectiveness of, or absence of, representation of consumers' interests before various federal and provincial regulatory boards, tribunals, and commissions. Preparing and presenting briefs to such bodies is costly and frequently requires legal and economic expertise. The Council considered various proposals for creating new types of consumer representation including consumer appointees as members of regulatory boards, a consumer ombudsman, and (the one it found most promising) a consumer advocate—an official subsidized by the federal government who would present the consumers' case before various regulatory bodies. To ensure that the independence of such an individual would be maintained, the Council, in a report to the Minister, recommended that the office be financed by a separate federal grant but established within the Consumers' Association of Canada. The Department of Consumer and Corporate Affairs had previously given substantial additional grants to the Consumers' Association of Canada to enable it to carry out an experimental

---

[13] Notes for an Address by the Honourable André Ouellet to the Better Business Bureau of Canada, *op. cit.*, p. 2.

program to determine whether such a voluntary agency could represent consumers' interests effectively.[14] Representation has been made at such hearings as those held by the Canada Transport Commission on the proposed increases in telephone rates by Bell Canada, and the proposed increases in air fares by Canadian airlines.

Militant consumer activists have also been effective in making the consumers' voice heard. Canada has not produced its own Ralph Nader—yet. However, Canadian housewives have become activist enough on a few occasions to use the weapon of the boycott in an effort to force prices down; in 1973, for example, they used it to try to stop the climb in meat prices.[15] A boycott is a very difficult weapon to use because, in order to be effective, it requires widespread support, and for consumers it is very difficult to achieve the necessary singleness of purpose.

P.O. Box 99 and the regional offices of Consumer and Corporate Affairs, mentioned earlier as sources of consumer information, also give individual consumers an opportunity to be heard by receiving their complaints. In the year 1975-76 nearly 50 000 complaints were processed[16] (as compared with about 3 000 in the first year of operation). About half of them related to food, real estate and housing, motor vehicles and appliances. Complaints in such numbers are an indicator of what is causing consumer discontent and can have an effect on the shaping of government policy.

There can be little doubt that the existence of a government department that focuses on consumer interests has been a major factor in developing in Canada a large body of laws and regulations of business that have been designed to ensure that the rights of consumers are being guarded. Various services provided by the Department have had the same effect: government support for the different consumers' organizations has contributed substantially to their continued existence. Certainly there is no evidence that the Department of Consumer and Corporate Affairs sees its work as coming to an end: the Minister has been discussing a switch of focus from putting out bushfires to preventive actions such as developing, in advance, the regulations that will protect the consumer as society

---

[14] Department of Consumer and Corporate Affairs, *News Release*, NR-74-22, (Ottawa: April 11, 1974), p. 4.

[15] Even companies have promoted buyer restraint in an effort to hold down prices. In a recent period of world shortages and runaway prices of sugar, for example, Redpath Sugar took out advertisements urging consumers to buy less sugar.

[16] Annual Report 1976, *op. cit.*, p. 13.

moves into a cashless and chequeless economy.[17] The countervailing power of consumers seems more likely to grow than to decline.

The Regulation of Business

Consumerism, the movement to protect consumers' rights, has precipitated a considerable amount of government regulation of business. Much of what remains to be studied under the heading of government regulation of business might be looked on as an extension of the discussion of consumerism to include the creation of a competitive environment. It is assumed that if businessmen operate in a competitive environment, they will be forced to keep in mind their consumers' interests. Maintaining a competitive environment creates some difficult problems because there is no consensus on the meaning of the word "competition" or on precisely how much competition is appropriate in Canada.

CONCENTRATION IN INDUSTRY

One of the measures that economists use to describe the amount of competition, or potential competition, in an industry is the level of concentration, which indicates the degree to which output (or employment, or assets, or income) is concentrated in the largest firms in an industry. An index of concentration commonly found in American literature is that part of total output produced by the four companies with the largest outputs; if the four largest companies produce 5 percent of total output, then the degree of concentration (5 percent) is not as large as if the four produce 50 percent. In other words, the larger the index, the greater the degree of concentration. In one well-known Canadian study, Gideon Rosenbluth[18] used as his index of concentration in the manufacturing industry the number of the largest firms required to account for 80 percent of *employment*. The greater the number of firms required to account for 80 percent of employment, the smaller was the degree of concentration.

In a study for the Economic Council of Canada, M. D. Stewart substituted *shipments* for employment. The results of his study, which was based on 1964 data, indicated that in more than one third of 181 Canadian manufacturing industries examined, eight or fewer firms accounted for 80

---

[17] *Notes for an Address by the Honourable André Ouellet, Minister of Consumer and Corporate Affairs to The Retail Council of Canada March 5, 1975* (mimeographed), Department of Consumer and Corporate Affairs, pp. 5-6.

[18] Gideon Rosenbluth, *Concentration in Canadian Manufacturing Industries*, National Bureau of Economic Research (Princeton: Princeton University Press, 1957).

percent of shipments. This is a high degree of concentration. On the other hand, there were also many industries in which the concentration was relatively low; in more than one third of the industries studied, it took twenty or more firms to account for 80 percent of shipments.[19] As for changes in the level of concentration since the time of Rosenbluth's study, of 61 industries for which the data were roughly comparable, more than half had a higher degree of concentration in 1964 than in 1948; more than a quarter had a lower degree of concentration.[20] There is no clear trend.

In 1971 the Department of Consumer and Corporate Affairs published a study on concentration in 159 of Canada's manufacturing industries. The manufacturing industries that were included accounted for about 94 percent of the total value added by manufacturing.[21] Concentration in the study was measured for manufacturing *establishments* (which means essentially for individual plants) and for manufacturing enterprises (companies with one or more plants in an industry). Various measures of concentration were used. For example, industries were looked at in terms of the number required to account for 80 percent of *shipments* (as in Stewart's work). The study described 60 manufacturing industries (which accounted for 37 percent of total manufacturing shipments) as "highly concentrated" because eight or fewer enterprises accounted for 80 percent of shipments. At the other end of the scale there were 57 industries (which accounted for 42 percent of shipments) in which it took more than 20 enterprises to account for 80 percent of shipments. When information on employment (Rosenbluth's measure) instead of shipments was used, the level of concentration turned out to be lower.[22]

The evidence on the historical trend once again was mixed. In the case of forty of the industries used in the Rosenbluth study the Department of Consumer and Corporate Affairs felt that its data were comparable. At the level of the *enterprise*, concentration increased between 1948 and 1965, but if the *establishment* is the basis of comparison, increases in concentration were offset by decreases. If one looks at all nonfinancial corporations, there appears to have been a decline in concentration between 1958 and 1965.[23]

[19] See the pre-publication summary of M. D. Stewart's report in Economic Council of Canada, *Interim Report on Competition Policy* (Ottawa: Queen's Printer, 1969), Table A-1, p. 209.

[20] *Ibid.*, p. 210.

[21] Department of Consumer and Corporate Affairs, *Concentration in the Manufacturing Industries of Canada* (Ottawa: 1971), p. 3.

[22] *Ibid.*, pp. 3-4.

[23] *Ibid.*, pp. 42-43.

One of the findings of both the Rosenbluth and the Consumer and Corporate Affairs studies was that comparable industries in Canada are more highly concentrated than in the United States.[24] Firm sizes tended to be much the same in the two countries, and given the relatively small size of the Canadian market as compared with that of the United States, it is logical to expect fewer firms in an industry—that is, a higher degree of concentration.

WHY MAINTAIN COMPETITION?

Why should we care what form of market structure exists, or what degree of concentration there is? Numerous arguments are given for supporting competition and hence, by implication, for supporting government intervention to ensure that competition exists.

One argument is that competition provides a better allocation of resources: one branch of economic theory, welfare economics, gives support to pure or perfect competition as the kind of market that gives the best possible allocation of resources. It is argued that monopolies and oligopolies make large profits by charging high prices and restricting output. This means that they hire fewer factors of production: fewer resources, then, are being allocated to these goods than consumers would like and would buy if prices were lower.

In our economy it seems scarcely practical to advocate setting up a market in which a vast number of small producers produce a homogeneous product. What would happen to the economies that go with large-scale production? In many industries, large capital-intensive plants have made possible dramatic cuts in production costs. The techniques of mass production have enabled us to achieve the highest standard of living in history. It would seem rather unwise to break such firms up into small inefficient units. Homogeneity of the product—everyone in identical suits of nondescript grey—is another characteristic of the purely competitive market that consumers are unlikely to accept. Obviously, they are prepared to sacrifice some of the allocative superiority of pure competition for variety in the products they buy.

Pure monopoly, on the other hand, is undesirable. It, too, limits consumers' choice and interferes with consumer sovereignty. Early in the discussion of our mixed capitalistic system we said that the Canadian

---

[24] Gideon Rosenbluth, *op. cit.*, p. 20, and Department of Consumer and Corporate Affairs, *op. cit.*, pp. 5-6.

economy relied mainly on the market to make the basic decisions about the production of goods and the distribution of income. Consumers by their dollar votes decide, in large measure, what is to be produced by voting for the goods they like with a large number of dollars; as a result, firms producing those goods earn large profits, which are a clear indication that consumers want more resources to be allocated to those goods. If above-normal profits are being made, other entrepreneurs will want to get into that industry and produce the profitable good too. However, with the barriers to entry characteristic of pure monopoly (and oligopoly) new firms may not be able to get in, and the firms already there may simply respond to an increased demand by raising the price of the product, rather than by expanding output.

The one-brand product of a pure monopoly can be a source of dissatisfaction to consumers. Assume that there is only one model of a refrigerator available on the market, and that it has a very small freezer. The customer who would prefer a larger freezing capacity has no way of indicating his preference: either he buys the model that does not give him the feature he wants, or he does not buy a refrigerator at all; with a single brand, it is a matter of take it or leave it. If two models are available, one with a large freezer and one with a small one, then consumers who prefer the former can encourage the production of that model by buying it. If four models are available, the consumer may be able to express his preference for round, revolving shelves as compared with pull-out rectangular ones, as well as different freezing capacities. This is not to say, however, that if an infinite number of varieties is available, the consumer will achieve the greatest satisfaction. It is quite possible that when the number of models gets to some level, perhaps six or eight, the consumer's satisfaction is increased very little by the addition of yet one more model; and if he is a conscientious comparative shopper, that extra model, involving the extra time required to investigate its price and various features, may even *reduce* his total satisfaction. Having only one (fresh) milkman delivering milk could cause housewives (or their husbands) considerable unhappiness. The existence of two or three alternatives provides choice and the right of effect protest. However, ten deliveries a morning, with all of the attendant noise and traffic, might start residents complaining and taking steps to reduce the number of deliveries in their neighbourhood.

Competition is supported on the ground that it increases other freedoms of choice, as well as the freedom of consumers to choose the products they want. If competition exists, producers are not barred from getting into an industry: they have greater freedom in their choice of entrepreneurial activity. Furthermore, if the response to above-normal profits is the competitive one of having more entrepreneurs go into the industry, rather than the monopolistic one of raising price without increasing output, then more resources will be allocated to the production of these goods, which opens up a greater freedom of choice to workers looking for jobs.

Competition, as we suggested in Chapter 7, may act as a spur to growth because it encourages rapid implementation of inventions. If one producer in a competitive industry innovates and produces a better product, or produces the same product more cheaply, then others are forced to follow suit if they want to survive. Large and powerful monopolies, on the other hand, could impede growth by, for example, finding, patenting, and then shelving new products or techniques. It is a common characteristic of industries into which entry is restricted that they use large amounts of capital, and they are frequently accused of resisting innovations that would render their present equipment obsolete, and of delaying the retirement of capital until it has been fully depreciated.

On the other hand, we must remember that research and development are essential to growth. Entrepreneurs in pure competition, who are price takers and who can sell all they produce at the going price, do not have either the incentive or the pool of profits necessary to carry out research; but in industries in which monopoly profits are being made, entrepreneurs, who can see the possibility of profiting from their own inventive efforts, will have the funds necessary and will be encouraged to do research and thus contribute to growth. It is apparent that if manufacturers were not permitted to brand their products (that is, to differentiate them from those of their competitors) and thereby introduce an element of monopoly into the market, they would have no incentive to improve their products, to innovate, or to offer their customers something new. It is often argued, therefore, that a degree of monopoly is a powerful engine of progress and growth. Indeed, it is sometimes suggested that it may be too powerful an engine of progress. Some progressive firms with a large share of the market have been accused of innovating too rapidly, thereby making it more difficult for their smaller rivals to catch up.

Another argument in favour of competition is that a high degree of concentration implies "bigness" and bigness is regarded by many—particularly in the United States—as inherently bad, whether it is found in large powerful corporations or in large powerful unions. Bigness has become a political as well as an economic question in the United States, and a number of economists argue strongly that the government should step in and break up giant corporations into smaller units. They argue that many of these corporations have achieved their mammoth size not because of economies of scale, but through mergers—buying up competitors—and these economists want strong legislation to prevent this from happening.

PERFORMANCE AS A CRITERION OF COMPETITION

On the other hand, there are economists who argue that in order to have competition it is not necessary to have a large number of firms, or to have price competition. They suggest that "trust busting" is unnecessary; for if competition is not forthcoming from within the industry, then it will come from outside. The power of steel companies to raise price, for example, is kept in check by the existence of industries producing potential substitutes like aluminum, copper, lumber, and plastics. Even if there is no competition from other domestic products, there can be competition from imports, provided tariffs are not prohibitive. Competition exists among all products for the incomes of consumers: diamonds compete with second cars or mink coats, and golf clubs compete with camping equipment. In addition to this competition from existing products there can also be competition from newly-developed products and processes.

Firms also have to face competition in the resource or factor market. It may seem at times that huge corporations like General Motors or Dupont have almost unlimited power, but, in fact, they have to compete for raw materials and labour. Automobile companies compete for their steel and aluminum, not merely with each other, but with the manufacturers of farm implements, boats, domestic appliances, and a host of others who use the products. Workers are mobile enough that if the productivity of the industry lags and their wages fall below those of other companies, then they will move. This suggests that we might look, not so much for a definition of competition that might emerge from the theory of the structure of markets, as for a *performance* definition. One might say that an industry, regardless of its structure, is competitive if certain desirable kinds of behaviour are present. It is desirable to have freedom of entry: there should not be legal barriers, nor should we allow the predatory competitive tactics of firms already in the industry to prevent the entry of other firms that might be attracted by the profits to be made. Products and processes of production in an industry should improve; production should be efficient, and prices should decline when costs decline. If an industry performs well on the basis of such criteria, then, the argument runs, it should be regarded as *workably* competitive, even though it might conceivably be composed of a few giants.

There is a large and growing volume of literature on this subject. The "trust busters" argue for the breakup of large firms and for strong anti-trust legislation to prevent mergers. Others argue that such legislation is unnecessary because workable competition already exists in industry in North America. Factual evidence is offered to support both sides; the verdict remains "not proven".

GOVERNMENT REGULATION OF BUSINESS

Without consensus in the community on how much competition should be maintained, there can be no agreement on how much government regulation of business there should be. The government has a number of policies that it can, and does, use. We shall consider briefly four: nationalization, establishing regulatory boards, lowering tariffs, and using legal restraints such as the *Combines Investigation Act*. The government might also use its tax (and subsidy) powers as a regulatory device to influence profits and the quantity purchased.

Nationalization One way the government can regulate a business is to take over and run it. This has been done with a number of utilities. Such takeovers are sometimes rationalized on the ground that utilities are natural monopolies—that is, they are industries in which one firm (or a very few firms) achieves its lowest production cost at an output large enough to supply the entire market. And since a single firm is most efficient, the government should operate that firm for the benefit of all consumers.

Nationalization has its strong opponents in the community: one objection frequently expressed is that government ownership paves the way for political interference. Governments, moreover, are not always as efficient, as innovative, or as responsive as they should be to consumers' wishes. Government post offices and liquor stores do not always convey the impression that the customer is always right or even that he is always welcome.

Regulatory Boards The government may not go so far as to take over an industry. If it is inefficient to have more than one producer, or more than a few, the government may simply issue an exclusive licence or franchise, and then prevent the company from exploiting its monopoly position by putting it under the aegis of a regulatory board. Since two telephone systems in a single area would just increase consumers' costs, Bell Canada is allowed to have a monopoly on telephone communications in a number of regions; but it is regulated by the Canada Transportation Commission, which attempts to keep the price of the service down and to prevent the firm from making profits that are too high. The Canada Transportation Commission also regulates railways, inland waterways, and airlines.

Regulating industries to ensure that they get a fair rate of return is a difficult task. Costs and demand are hard to calculate, and there is no consensus on what a fair rate means. It is generally assumed that regulation results in a lower price and a higher output than would be forthcoming in the absence of the regulatory board. About all we can say for certain, however, is that regulation holds down profit; whether this is accomplished by lowering price and increasing output, or by increasing costs because of the removal of the incentive to be efficient, is a good question. It is not always clear, in other words, whether or not the effect of regulation is really to protect the consumer.

Reducing Tariffs Another control over businesses whose profits appear to be unreasonably high or which do not appear to be performing competitively is to lower the tariffs that protect their products. Such a policy, increasingly popular with economists, has been scarcely used in Canada. Some years ago it was used against the newsprint industry. If firms are not performing competitively (if, for example, prices and profits are too high, and output is being restricted), then lowering protective tariffs provides an excellent way of introducing competition. Not many protected industries in Canada are so efficient that they could retain high profit rates in the face of international competition.

A policy of reducing tariffs would not only increase the amount of competition; it would also mean that a wider range of products would become available to consumers because there would be fewer tariff barriers to keep products out. Moreover, as was pointed out in Chapter 12, tariff reductions are supported by economists as a means of bringing about increasing specialization and higher productivity.

Legal Restraints There are many devices that companies can use to lessen competition, and the government may simply pass laws to restrict the use of them. The most common of such devices are agreements to limit competition—combinations in restraint of trade, as they are called in Canadian law. The most obvious kind of departure from competition is for firms to agree to fix prices. Such an agreement requires a great deal of cooperation among the agreeing parties, and, if it is to have the desired effect, must be strictly adhered to by all of them. It is usually necessary to form a cartel with some kind of central authority that can set a price that will maximize the joint profits of all members. However, there is a strong temptation for any member of the cartel to cheat, because there are large short-run gains to be made if the firm can get away with it. The agreement is in constant danger of breaking down because of problems like deciding who will get what share of the market, and what share of the profits. Since such agreements are against the law in North America (in the domestic market at least) they are not enforceable in the courts. They are not illegal on the international level, and probably the best known cartel today is OPEC (the Organization of Petroleum Exporting Countries), the cartel made up of the governments of the oil-producing countries.

Sometimes indirect methods of getting agreement can be used, since overt agreements are not legal. There are several common practices which are normally quite innocuous, and sometimes desirable from the industry's point of view, but which can sometimes be used to limit competition.[25] The publication of statistics can act as the signal for concerted action in the industry; standardization of products, normally a desirable practice, can be used as a barrier to entry to keep out unwanted rivals; uniform accounting schemes can be used as a device for controlling prices.

In addition to price agreements, there can also be agreements about shares of the market. Firms can agree not to produce more than a certain amount, or can agree not to sell in one another's territory. Such agreements have the same effect on competition as agreements to fix price.

Agreements need not be overt in order to limit competition: they can be tacit. Without any formal agreement firms may adopt policies that have the same effect as an overt agreement. Such behaviour is sometimes described by lawyers as "conscious parallelism". It is quite common to find in mature industries a general live-and-let-live attitude with respect to the share of the market, for example: firms do not agressively compete for markets; their objective is merely to hold their share.

There can be conscious parallelism in pricing as well as in market-sharing policies. Perhaps the commonest form is price leadership, in which one firm changes price, and others follow suit. If the price leader is the most efficient firm in an industry, then it can set a price that maximizes its own profit; and other firms, if they wish to remain competitive, or perhaps avoid a price war and remain in business, will follow. Sometimes the largest firm in the industry is the price leader. Sometimes no single firm acts as leader: the firm that first recognizes changes in demand and supply conditions may adapt its price to these changes, and other firms may follow its pricing policy. This is sometimes referred to as barometric price leadership.

Unfair business practices are another departure from competition. These can include practices like improper branding, misleading advertising, misrepresenting the geographic origin of products, rigging bids, stealing trade secrets from other businessmen, and predatory pricing—that is, setting prices low in order to force a competitor out of business.

---

[25] Corwin D. Edwards, *Maintaining Competition: Requisites of a Governmental Policy* (New York: McGraw-Hill Book Company, Paperback Edition, 1964), pp. 25 ff.

THE COMBINES INVESTIGATION ACT

The *Combines Investigation Act* contains regulations prohibiting the use of a number of these devices that may limit competition. Provisions against combinations in restraint of trade have existed in Canada since 1889, but the history of legal regulation since that time shows little consistency in efforts to enforce or strengthen the law. This should not be surprising in view of the absence of any consensus on how much competition we want, or even what competition is.

L. A. Skeoch has pointed out[26] that in the early parliamentary debates, there was no broad support for policies to maintain competition; there appeared simply to be opposition to monopolistic practices that were detrimental to the public interest. Moreover, repeated attempts have been made through the subsequent history of the Act to weaken the constraints that were there. As a result, the Act is limited in its range of activity. It renders unlawful three main kinds of offences: first, price and other collusive agreements; second, monopolies and mergers that lessen competition to the detriment of the public; and finally, unfair trade practices including price discrimination, predatory pricing, resale price maintenance (to be explained later), misrepresentation of the regular price, and misleading advertising. However, it exempts government practices that tend to restrict competition—for example, licensing and operating marketing boards such as the Canadian Wheat Board. Until 1975 the Act applied only to goods, and in the service field, to insurance; the first stage of the new competition bill, passed late in 1975, extended its coverage to service industries. Unions are exempt from the Act.

Agreements Section 32 of the Act outlaws combines (by which is meant price and other agreements). The most commonly used provision is paragraph (c), which makes it unlawful to combine to prevent or lessen, unduly, competition in the production, manufacture, purchase, barter, sale, storage, rental, transportation, or supply of an article, or in the price of insurance. The courts have interpreted "unduly" to mean that the agreement must affect a sizable part of the market: in most prosecutions, the market share affected by the agreement has been 80 to 90 percent, though it has gone as low as 56 percent.[27] Most cases considered under the Act have involved price fixing, but combinations can also take the form of agreements to rig bids when making tenders, to share markets or profits, and to limit output.

---

[26] L. A. Skeoch (ed.), *Restrictive Trade Practices in Canada* (Toronto: McClelland & Stewart Limited, 1966), p. 3.

[27] D. H. W. Henry, *Notes for an Address to Business Press Editors' Association* (mimeographed), January 18, 1968, p. 14.

The courts are not concerned with the performance definition of competition. Economic factors such as the question of whether, by getting together, firms make the industry more stable, or more efficient, or whether consumers are getting an adequate quantity of the product, or whether the price of the product can be regarded as reasonable and the profits moderate, have been ruled out as irrelevant to the meaning of lessening competition unduly.

Not all forms of "cooperation" are ruled out by the *Combines Investigation Act*. For example, it is quite acceptable for people in the same industry to exchange statistics or credit information, or to cooperate in research and development. This last results from a typical Canadian problem: because many companies are too small to accumulate the funds necessary for large-scale research and development, the Act makes it possible to combine for this purpose. An example of such a combination is the Pulp and Paper Research Institute, a research body supported by a number of Canadian newsprint companies.

Another common problem of Canadian industries is developing enough efficiency to compete in world markets. Sometimes a market-sharing arrangement, for example, may enable firms to specialize and thus achieve the economies of large-scale operation that would permit them to compete. The law against combines does not apply if the arrangement relates only to the export of articles from Canada. Other forms of collusive action that are exempt from the Act include defining product standards, exchanging credit information, and restricting advertising.

Mergers and Monopolies It is illegal under the *Combines Investigation Act* (section 33) to take part in the formation of a monopoly or merger that will lessen competition to the detriment, or against the interest, of the public. A merger involves acquiring control over a competitor or supplier; a monopoly exists when there is complete or substantial control of a class of business. There has been very little legal action under this section of the Act. In two important merger cases, *Western Sugar* and *Canadian Breweries*,[28] the Crown was unsuccessful in its prosecution. As a result of the verdicts in these cases, the Restrictive Trade Practices Commission, a three-man body which forms part of the enforcement machinery of the *Combines Investigation Act*, came to the conclusion that before detriment to the public could ever be proved, the Crown would have to show that the effect of the action of merging was virtually to eliminate competition.

The Crown was more successful in some of its later cases. In 1970, for example, the Supreme Court of Canada fined Electrical Reduction Com-

---

[28] *Regina v. Canadian Breweries Ltd.* (1960) O.R. 601 and *Regina v. British Columbia Sugar Refining Company Limited et al.* (1960) 32 W.W.R. (N.S.) 577.

pany of Canada for its merger with Dominion Fertilizer; the merger gave the company a virtual monopoly over industrial phosphates. The Crown was also successful in getting the Supreme Court of Alberta to issue orders of prohibition against Canada Safeway Limited and therefore did not pursue in the courts the charge of monopoly offences in Calgary and Edmonton. Among other things, the orders of prohibition prevented the grocery chain from expanding its retailing space and from buying up the desirable retail sites, for a specified period of time, as well as from buying shares in rivals' operations. The intent was to encourage the growth of competition in the retail and grocery trade in the two cities.

The situation is very different in the United States where the courts have stepped hard on mergers, and even on corporations that are thought to have grown too large. If a firm shows a tendency to dominate the American market—nothing so extreme as virtually eliminating competition—then it is in danger of action under the antitrust laws.

In Canadian industry, the number of mergers has been increasing rapidly, as it has in the United States. All are kept under surveillance by the Combines Branch; most, however, are of no significance under the Act. There has been a growing practice on the part of businesses of referring proposed mergers to the Combines Branch so that companies can ascertain whether or not such an action is likely to attract an inquiry under the Act.[29]

Unfair Trade Practices   The *Combines Investigation Act* makes illegal a number of trade practices such as price discrimination (giving preferred treatment to one purchaser but not to another buying similar quality and quantity) and predatory price cutting (the practice of selling at lower prices in some localities than others, or at unreasonably low prices anywhere, in order to drive competitors out of business). Promotional allowances, if they are made available at all, must be offered on proportionate terms to all purchasers. Misleading advertising is not allowed; nor is resale price maintenance. This means that a manufacturer cannot dictate the price at which a good will be sold; all he can do is *suggest* a retail price. He cannot withdraw a franchise from a dealer who sells below that suggested price unless the dealer fails to provide an adequate level of servicing or makes a practice of using it as a loss leader—that is, selling below cost as an advertising gimmick or to get people into the store in order to sell them other goods.

Stage I of the revised bill makes a number of changes in the sections

---

[29] *Report of the Director of Investigation and Research Combines Investigation Act for the Year Ended March 31, 1974* (Ottawa: Information Canada, 1974), pp. 10-11.

relating to unfair trade practices, such as strengthening the part dealing with misleading advertising practices and adding new protection for the consumer in the area of warranties and guarantees and certain undesirable selling practices. It gives the Restrictive Trade Practices Commission a new power under *civil* law (which is a major innovation) to review certain practices like tied sales, market restriction, refusal to deal and the implementation of foreign judgements, laws, or directives in Canada; and to issue corrective orders if they are considered contrary to the public interest.

The Machinery of Enforcement The *Combines Investigation Act* provides for two bodies to investigate the actions of companies that may limit competition to the detriment of the public. First of all, there is the Director of Investigation and Research and his staff in the Combines Branch of the Department of Consumer and Corporate Affairs. The second body is the three-man Restrictive Trade Practices Commission. Beyond these groups the enforcement machinery consists of the courts.

The first investigation is carried out by the Director of Investigation and Research, usually on his own initiative. Any six Canadian citizens may file a request for investigation, however, or the Minister of Consumer and Corporate Affairs may ask him to investigate an industry. If the preliminary investigation suggests that some action may be warranted, the Director can instigate a formal inquiry, and has the right to search business premises, seize documents, and call witnesses. If there seems to have been no contravention of the law, he can discontinue the inquiry. If further action seems advisable, he may present a statement of evidence to the Restrictive Trade Practices Commission and to the party involved in preparation for a hearing; or, if the case is not breaking new ground, or if it must be dealt with quickly (as in the case of misleading advertising), then he can refer it directly to the Attorney General of Canada who will decide whether or not to initiate legal procedings.

The Restrictive Trade Practices Commission receives evidence from the Director, conducts a hearing, and writes a report about the case and the appropriate action to be taken. That report must be published. Publication, it is hoped, will have a beneficial influence on firms' behaviour.

If, on the advice of counsel, the Attorney General of Canada deems it advisable, the case will go forward to the courts, and the offending parties will be prosecuted for breach of a statute. If the parties are found guilty, they are fined or given prison terms, or the court may issue a writ of prohibition to ensure that no further actions will be taken to diminish competition. There are also little-used provisions for lowering tariffs or revoking the patents of offending parties.

Current Issues in the Regulation of Business Economists as a group favour competition, usually because it is a means by which our goals can be better achieved: resources will be better allocated; consumers, producers and workers will have greater freedom of choice; incomes will be better distributed; and; hopefully, growth will be promoted: The objective of the *Combines Act* is to keep industries competitive. The problem is that what is wanted in the law appears to be competition for competition's sake, rather than competition for what competition can do. The courts have not taken into consideration the economic performance of the industry: monopoly control has been purely a legal matter in Canada, and contravention of the law is a criminal offence. There has been no room for making economic tests to find out whether the industry is investing and expanding output in accordance with consumers' wants.

There are cases when the law can put businessmen into a difficult situation. If firms are producing a homogeneous product for a market in which the buyers are experts, then our common sense as well as our theoretical analysis tell us that there can be only one price. If an entrepreneur tries to sell above that price, he will lose all of his customers: in a free market who would buy Farmer Brown's Number 1 Northern at $4.00 a bushel if they can get it next door at $3.80? The businessman who does not eliminate the hazards of guesswork by deliberately setting out to discover what his competitors are charging and who does not consciously charge the same price is not a very good entrepreneur. Yet the law makes no provision for this: if there is an open attempt to achieve the same price then it is an offence, and a criminal one at that.

Why should it be a criminal offence? Fear has been expressed that if it were to become a civil matter, the old problem of the division of powers between the federal and provincial governments might arise. Judicial interpretation of the cases has confirmed that as long as it is a criminal matter, regulation of business clearly lies within the purview of the federal government. As a result, there has been reluctance to change. However, one of the recommendations of the Economic Council's report on competition policy[30] was that some parts of the Combines Investigation Act should be shifted into civil law to permit an increased use of economic analysis in what are essentially economic problems.

Provisions to exempt certain actions from criminal procedures and to provide for looking at the effects of some moves to restrict competition to see whether they are beneficial or detrimental are expected to be included in Stage II of the revision of the *Combines Investigation Act*. The issues have

---

[30] Economic Council of Canada, *Interim Report on Competition Policy* (Ottawa: Queen's Printer, 1969), pp. 107 ff.

been under intensive discussion since mid-1971 when a revised competition bill was first introduced. It is anticipated that mergers and monopolies, export agreements, and agreements to rationalize industries in order to encourage specialization and achieve economies of scale (agreements that could have beneficial effects even though they may limit competition) will be treated as exemptions to the general criminal provisions of the law. Stage II may appear in 1977 although there is speculation on whether or not passage of the bill might be slowed down by the work of the Royal Commission on Corporate Concentration (the Bryce Commission).

15

Sharp increases in world oil prices by the Organization of Petroleum Exporting Countries (OPEC) have reinforced inflation throughout the world, making it more difficult to achieve economic stability. Energy industries raise special problems of resource allocation; oil and gas, for example, are exhaustible resources, and conservation and the quantity to be exported are controversial issues. Environment problems are created by the development and transportation of energy resources. Pricing policies are important for resource allocation: artificially low prices in the past have encouraged consumption and discouraged the development of alternative sources of energy.

Agriculture is another resource-based industry whose problems affect the achievement of several economic goals. Increases in food prices in the 1970s contributed to inflation. Canadian governments have enacted a number of measures to improve farmers' share of income, including price supports and marketing boards. These policies frequently interfere with efficiency and hence with the proper allocation of resources.

Issues in Energy
and Agriculture

Energy and agriculture are two resource-based industries that attracted a great deal of attention in the mid-1970s. Both affected the achievement of several goals of the Canadian economy, but the most widely-expressed concern related to the unwelcome contribution they made to destabilizing the economy by causing the rate of inflation to accelerate.

Energy

If Canadian or American companies had banded together into a cartel, had almost quadrupled the price of oil in the short space of three months, and had imposed an embargo on sales to countries that they considered to be friends of Israel, as did the Organization of Petroleum Exporting Countries (OPEC) in the period from October 1973 to January 1974, their executives would have landed in jail. However, OPEC is a foreign government cartel. It includes the governments of Ecuador, Iran, Iraq, Indonesia, Kuwait, Libya, Saudi Arabia, and half a dozen more. The staggering price increases consisted almost exclusively of returns to these various governments: they did not reflect any additional real costs in terms of extra resources needed to get the oil out of the ground, or extra returns to the companies.[1] However, there are no antitrust laws protecting sovereign states from economic exploitation by other sovereign states. The embargo was removed early in 1974, but the price of oil delivered to Eastern North America did not drop; indeed, the additional increases in the fall of 1975 and 1977 suggest that the price is more likely to rise in step with world inflation than to fall, although, as with all cartels, this depends on whether or not the members maintain discipline in their ranks and play by the cartel rules. There are strong pressures on the cartel because of the existence of large, low-cost reserves, and because there would be some benefit to any individual member who could cheat and get away with it. So far, there have been few cracks in the structure of the cartel. The response to the excess capacity created as sales dropped has been well disciplined: the operators of the facilities in the various countries have done as they were directed and

---

[1] M. A. Adelman, "Policy and the Cartel," in *Energy: Update and Outlook—November 1974*, ed. L. Lund (New York: The Conference Board, 1975), p. 9.

have cut back on production, and the price has risen. It has been suggested that to break the discipline maintained by the multinationals that have become instruments of the cartel, the American government should exploit the vulnerable aspect of excess capacity of auctioning import rights using sealed competitive bids in such a way as to prevent policing of the various members of the cartel by the OPEC administration.[2]

The impact of the huge price jump on developed and underdeveloped countries all over the world was very sharp—almost catastrophic in some cases. The vast flow of revenues to the exporting countries[3] and their resulting huge surpluses on current account[4] had to be matched by equal payments on the part of importing countries, with the result that many of them faced serious balance-of-payment problems. If the oil-producing countries could import enough from their customers to offset their huge deficits on current account, or if they were prepared to invest in the countries with deficits (and if those countries were prepared to accept the investment) or to give large amounts of foreign aid, then the petro-dollars, as they are called, could be "recycled". Imports by the oil-producing countries of machinery and other durable goods, as well as food, have increased sharply; however, the imports these countries seem to be most interested in are military goods, and this creates its own problems. Many oil-consuming countries are being forced to borrow, and there is concern over the possibility of default in payment by some that are particularly hard-pressed. The need to recycle the petro-dollars is putting pressures on the international banking community and the precariously balanced system of international payments.[5]

The effect on world liquidity of recycling petro-dollars is a problem for Canada, of course; but the country was well-cushioned from the *direct* impact of the price increases because, from 1971 to 1974, it was in a unique position, vis-à-vis other western industrialized nations, of exporting more oil than it imported. The problems created by the energy crisis in that period, then, did not include concern over the immediate effect of expensive OPEC oil on Canada's balance of payments, although this could become a serious issue by the end of the 1970s.

---

[2] *Ibid.*, "The World Oil Market," in *The Energy Question: An International Failure of Policy*, Vol. 1, *The World*, eds. E. W. Erickson and L. Waverman (Toronto: University of Toronto Press, 1974), p. 14.

[3] It has been estimated at about $100 billion for 1974 as compared with $15 billion in 1972. *The Gazette*, Montreal, 9 September 1975.

[4] The United States Treasury Department has estimated that OPEC may accumulate *excess* reserves of $195 billion (over and above imports) by 1980. *The Gazette*, 11 September 1975.

[5] See, for example, R. L. Heilbroner, *The Economic Problem Newsletter*, Vol. VI, No. 2 (Englewood Cliffs, N.J.: Prentice-Hall, Inc., 1975).

The impact of higher oil prices on an already unacceptably high rate of inflation in Canada *was* a matter of concern. On January 1, 1977 the Canadian government raised the price throughout the country to $9.75[6] for a barrel of oil—considerably above the price of $4.00 that existed prior to the embargo or the 1972 price of $3.00. An export tax brought the foreign price of Canadian oil up to the world level, and the revenue from it was employed to subsidize consumers east of the Ottawa Valley who used imported oil. It has been estimated[7] that the direct effect on consumers of higher oil prices plus the indirect effects from the increasing prices of competing fuels, and of domestic and foreign goods whose prices rose because energy costs involved in their manufacture rose, caused the GNP implicit price deflator to rise by more than 3 percent in 1974, and that prices would be more than 5 percent higher in 1975 than they would have been without the energy crisis. Since these estimates did not take into account the additional excise tax imposed on gasoline in the federal budget of June 1975 or the increase in the price of a barrel of oil to $8.00, the inflationary effect for 1975 would have been even greater than the model forecast.

The adverse effect on prices and employment is a vital issue, particularly in the midst of the current vicious wage-price spiral in Canada and the attempts to achieve the goal of stability. There are other major economic issues, however, and they are related to the objective of achieving a proper allocation of resources. Energy in Canada, as in the United States, derives primarily from fossil fuels. Hydro power, with a slight boost from nuclear power, accounts for about 35 percent of the electrical power generated in Canada, but this amounts to less than 10 percent of total primary consumption. More than 90 percent (the remaining 65 percent of electrical power generation plus transportation, commercial, residential, and industrial consumption) derives from fossil fuels.[8] Oil and gas, therefore, are the resources under scrutiny in the present energy shortage, and they are nonrenewable resources. The knowledge that fossil fuel deposits are finite and that there is an energy shortage has given rise to scare stories about the possibility of having to turn out the lights permanently and live in cold houses.

Because oil and gas are nonrenwable resources, several important economic issues arise. They include the problem of how much of each is available, the responsiveness of supply to increases in price (the *price*

---

[6] *The Financial Times of Canada*, Toronto, 3 January 1977, p. 5.

[7] G. V. Jump and T. A. Wilson, "Macroeconomic Effects of the Energy Crisis in 1974-75," *Canadian Public Policy*, Vol. 1, No. 1 (Winter 1975), p. 35.

[8] E. M. Erickson and Leonard Waverman, "Introduction," in *The Energy Question: An International Failure of Policy*, Vol. 2, *North America*, ed. E. W. Erickson and L. Waverman (Toronto: University of Toronto Press, 1974), p. vii.

elasticity, in other words), the role of research and development in finding new sources of energy, the problem of conservation (including the question of exports), and the environmental impact of exploiting known reserves. Related to these issues is the whole problem of pricing policy including the role of governments in setting price, the jurisdictional conflict between the federal and provincial governments of Canada, and the effects of pricing policies on the distribution of income. An issue that we shall not discuss again, except in passing, is the heavy foreign ownership in the oil industry. Foreign control of assets in the petroleum industry amounts to over 91 percent as compared, for example, with only one percent in the electrical industry.[9] Those who strongly oppose foreign ownership consider energy even more of a problem because of its foreign ownership aspects. To many, leaving profits in the hands of foreign-controlled companies so that they can invest and explore seems like giving money away to foreigners; it is causing widespread concern over whether Canadians are receiving the benefits they should from their own oil and gas reserves. Some of the issues relating to oil and gas deserve further attention.

FOSSIL FUELS: A NONRENEWABLE RESOURCE

Back in the eighteenth century, the Reverend Thomas Malthus, a contemporary of David Ricardo, was concerned about the niggardliness of nature, particularly as evidenced by the limited capacity of the soil to produce food. He saw food production increasing only in an arithmetic progression (1, 2, 3, 4, ...) while population increased in a geometric progression (2, 4, 8, ...) with a resulting pressure on food supplies that could be coped with either by late marriages and sexual abstinence, or by war, pestilence, and famine. Malthus seemed to consider the latter more likely. One wonders what he would have said about the depletion of wood and coal stocks in the 1900s, when 95 percent of Canada's energy derived from these sources.[10] Surely this was niggardliness of nature more extreme than the limited food-producing capacity of the soil. However, Canadians stopped relying on wood and coal long before sources were depleted. Technology gave us oil and natural gas and efficient hydro transmission lines which offered energy that was more convenient and less costly than wood or coal.

---

[9] Department of Energy, Mines and Resources, *An Energy Policy for Canada Phase 1, Volume I Analysis* (Ottawa: Information Canada, 1973), pp. 239-240.

[10] Leonard Waverman, "Energy in Canada: A Question of Rents," in *Issues in Canadian Economics*, eds. L. H. Officer and L. B. Smith (Toronto: McGraw-Hill Ryerson Limited, 1974), p. 136.

Numerous sources of energy are available today. Geologists tell us that there are extensive reserves of oil and gas in the Arctic and in offshore areas. With improved recovery-technology techniques more oil can be extracted from existing wells; the reserves in the Athabasca Tar Sands and the shale oil of Western United States are huge. Gas can be generated from coal, garbage dumps, crop residue and farm animal wastes as well as industrial wastes, which are all renewable resources. Hydrogen gas can be used. A report from the Science Council of Canada suggests that even with present technology solar energy could supply 40 percent of residential cooling and heating needs, or about 8 percent of the total energy used in Canada, and that tidal power from all sources in the Maritimes could produce about six times the present output of the Maritime Power Pool.[11] These sources of energy are expensive, but if cash flows and profits to oil companies had been higher it seems probable that many of the alternative sources of energy would have looked like a worthwhile investment and would now have been closer to coming onstream.

As things stand, proven reserves are decreasing annually as conventional sources in the Western Provinces are consumed, and new sources are not being discovered and developed. Canada could encounter short-run problems of supply in the early 1980s unless there are increases in proven reserves or producible capacity. Low proven reserves, or producible capacity, do not mean that we are running out of oil and gas; they refer to sources that can be recovered *economically*, given present prices and present technology. Their existence has been demonstrated by drilling, and they are within economic range of a pipeline. Proven reserves have been compared to a grocer's shelf inventory: to acquire and hold such an inventory costs money, and the oil and gas industry has no incentive to invest prematurely in proving reserves. This is why the ratio of proven reserves to annual production always seems to indicate that our proven reserves will be depleted within a relatively short time period. Increased oil and gas consumption in the world has been more than matched by discoveries of new reserves.[12] Geologists believe that huge amounts of gas and oil lie below the earth's surface; the problem is that there is a time lag of perhaps a decade or more between finding new reserves and getting them to the consumer. What is clear is that the supply of gas and oil is responsive to changes in price; that is why the pricing policy for energy is so important.

Conservation is an important part of the allocation problem for an exhaustible resource. Do we use the resources ourselves or save them for

[11] Science Council of Canada, Report No. 23 *Canada's Energy Opportunities* (Ottawa: Information Canada, 1975), pp. 69 & 75.

[12] Erickson and Waverman, "Introduction to the Energy Question," pp. vii-viii.

our children? Do we share our supplies with foreigners, or do we keep all of them for ourselves and our children? If we keep our own gas and oil do we risk loss of their export value as Americans adapt to new forms of energy supplies and become self-sufficient again, perhaps within twenty-five years?[13]

The question of whether or not to export energy or energy-producing products is a major contemporary problem of the Canadian economy because of the short-run energy shortage now foreseen and the relative unreliability of foreign sources, and because any decision is bound to affect Canada's relations with the United States, which has long favoured a continental energy policy. For more than two decades after the discoveries of huge oil deposits in Alberta, energy policy in Canada was aimed at persuading the United States to import more Canadian oil. Much of the development in the industry has been export-related. The major pipeline systems would not have been economically feasible in the late 1940s and 1950s without the prospect of exporting to American markets. The Interprovincial Pipeline became economically feasible because oil could be carried not only to Sarnia, but also to the American Midwest. Trans-Mountain Pipeline could be built because it carried oil from Edmonton to the Puget Sound area as well as to Vancouver. When Canadian exports to the United States fell in the mid-1950s, partly because of a recession and partly because of a voluntary American import reduction program, producers in Canada began to look for increased domestic markets, and began to demand either that Interprovincial extend its pipeline to Montreal or that a new all-Canadian pipeline be built to that market. This was strongly opposed by the international oil companies and the American government, which agreed to exempt Canada from import restrictions if the Alberta-Montreal pipeline was abandoned and if oil to Montreal could be freely imported.[14] The agreement formed the basis of Canada's National Oil Policy, according to which consumers west of the Ottawa Valley, as well as customers in the American Midwest, are supplied by domestic oil, while the markets east of the Ottawa Valley, including Montreal, are supplied by imported oil. In 1959 the National Energy Board was created to maintain this policy.[15]

Exports were also an integral part of the proposal by Canadian Arctic Gas Pipeline, a consortium of twenty-seven Canadian and American companies to build a 4 000-kilometre pipeline from the Arctic at an estimated

---

[13] Anthony Scott and Peter H. Pearse, "The Political Economy of Energy Development in Canada," in *The Mackenzie Pipeline*, ed. Peter H. Pearse (Toronto: McClelland and Steward Limited, 1974), p. 9.

[14] Eric J. Hansen, "Economics of Oil and Gas," in *Canadian Perspectives in Economics*, eds. John Chant *et al* (Toronto: Collier-Macmillan Canada, 1972), n.p.

cost of $7 billion. There are major economies of scale in building a large pipeline, and to make it feasible to build one four feet in diameter, the company proposed to transport gas from Prudho Bay in Alaska to American markets, as well as from the Mackenzie Delta; a substantial quantity of the Canadian gas was to be exported in the early years of operation. Many Canadians have expressed concern about the prospect of exporting Mackenzie Delta gas when it may soon be required to meet domestic needs. No decisions on the building of a Mackenzie Valley Pipeline are expected until the report of Mr. Justice Thomas Berger has been studied: he was appointed as a one-man commission to enquire into the effects of such a development, and the social and environmental conditions that should be imposed on any builder of a natural gas pipeline from the Western Arctic. He must also consider the proposal for the shorter, smaller-diameter (42 inches as compared with 48 inches), less costly ($4.5 billion as compared with $7 billion) Maple Leaf Pipeline, an all-Canadian pipeline designed to carry gas from only the Mackenzie Delta, and not from Prudho Bay.

Clearly the question of whether or not to export is controversial. If Canada does not export, there will be a high cost in terms of incomes both to the government and to the private sector. There will be major implications for the balance of payments. On the other hand, as a result of its 1974 study, the National Energy Board indicated that if Canadian demand west of the Ottawa Valley was to be met from domestic crude, exports would have to be cut off by 1984; if 250 000 barrels a day were to be provided to Montreal through the approved Sarnia-Montreal pipeline, then exports would have to cease a year or two earlier. The response of the government was to cut allowable exports progressively. From a high in 1973 of over 1.1 million barrels a day, allowable exports were expected to drop to 305 000 barrels a day by the beginning of 1977, and to be eliminated by 1981. In the 1980s the possibility of domestic self-sufficiency will depend on whether or not enough new sources of energy are exploited to offset the predicted decline in the output from the existing ones. If exploration and development are to be encouraged, the critical problem will be the price of the product and the revenues to the oil companies, and hence their incentive to do the necessary exploration, research and development. Another important factor is the impact on the environment of any proposed development.

---

[15] The National Energy Board is a five-man body with wide powers to exercise federal jurisdiction in energy matters. It has two key functions: to regulate and advise. It regulates matters like the export and import of energy, and the construction of interprovincial pipelines; in its advisory capacity it does a great deal of research, and makes forecasts of such things as energy demand and supply.

IMPACT ON THE ENVIRONMENT

The impact on the environment of the demand for and supply of gas and oil imposes costs on society which, until recently, have not been a consideration in the price to consumers and producers of the fossil fuels. Such costs are normally discussed by economists under the heading of *externalities*: they are costs which are external to the industry and which are borne by society in general. An example is the air pollution that results from the consumption of fossil fuels: it causes or aggravates respiratory ailments; this health problem in turn increases medical costs and may pressure people into spending money on the installation of costly air cleaners on their furnaces; it makes clothes dirtier, which necessitates the use of more laundry detergents which may cause increased pollution of the water systems; it makes buildings dirtier, thus, environmentalists argue, decreasing the beauty of our cities and adversely affecting the quality of life, as well as necessitating considerable expenditures for periodical building cleaning. Laws regulating emission standards have been passed so that pollution has been reduced, but the decreased efficiency of automobile engines that meet the standards for emission control has been a factor in causing the increased demand for gasoline. Similarly, emission standards for stationary engines and furnace stacks in the United States have resulted in large shifts from coal to oil and gas for industrial use.

There are environmental problems on the production and transportation side of energy: they relate to tanker spills, the ecological effects of building pipelines and of pipeline spills in the Arctic, refinery wastes, strip mining, offshore drilling, valley flooding, and so on. Coal is a key energy source, but the environmental effect of strip mining on the eastern slopes of the Alberta foothills or of the air pollution from burning it are serious deterrents to its use. The delay in starting the construction of the Trans-Alaska Pipeline from Prudho Bay to the port of Valdez is another example of how environmental considerations conflict with the desire to get energy: the *National Environmental Protection Act* in the United States makes environmental objectives a national policy and requires that in federal decisions environmental values be taken into account, and that federal agencies compile and publish reports on the potential environmental impacts of their decisions. Both the Trans-Alaska Pipeline Company and the American Department of the Interior spent a couple of years compiling a report on the effects of the pipeline on the tundra, pipeline spills in the Arctic, and tanker spills along the coast of British Columbia which was challenged in the courts by both Canadian and American environmental groups who were concerned about such matters. The effect of this was to delay the commencement of the pipeline for several years.

In the long run, acceptable environmental standards can be set and prices can rise to cover the costs of the additional economic resources that will have to be allocated for these standards to be met. Meanwhile, more research is needed in the Arctic on how to transport gas and oil over vast distances without jeopardizing the biological environment or damaging the permafrost. Damage to the permafrost is a particular problem in the Mackenzie Delta where the soil has a very high ice content; it is less acute for the gas pipeline which is now proposed because gas can be cooled to below-freezing temperatures. However, if oil pipelines are built, there will be problems because the oil is hot when it comes out of the ground; and if large-scale damage to the environment is to be avoided, engineers must find a method of transporting it without causing the permafrost to melt.[16] The number of biological species that exist in the Arctic is limited and there is concern that the balance of the food chain may be upset. Alternative pipeline routes cross through the calving grounds of the caribou, the den sites of grizzly bears and the prime trapping grounds of the native peoples. Furthermore, Canada has international responsibilities relating to migratory wild fowl that collect in large numbers in the area. The impact on the social environment of native peoples together with their land claims create problems of immense complexity. Other resource developments, it is argued, have had an adverse social impact on the native peoples, and fear is being expressed that the long-run costs, social and economic, of destroying the native culture that has developed in that hostile environment may outweigh any benefits brought to them by the pipeline.[17]

Tens of millions of dollars have been spent in the 1970s by industry and the government on research into Arctic wildlife and how the ecosystem works. Guidelines have been issued by the Department of Indian Affairs and Northern Development which are designed to reduce the cost in terms of disruptions of the social environment of the natives as well as damage to the physical and biological environment. All of these issues as they relate to the Mackenzie Valley Pipeline have been studied by Mr. Justice Thomas Berger in his capacity as a one-man commission of inquiry.

To those who see the heavy reliance on cheap energy that exists in Canada, who foresee an imminent shortage of domestic fossil fuels and who fear the political instability of the oil-producing countries and their use of oil as a political weapon, these delays in building the pipeline appear as a very serious threat to the Canadian economy. There are others who argue in favour of a postponement for perhaps another decade, when

---

[16] See Judith Maxwell, *Energy From the Arctic: Facts and Issues* (Montreal: Canadian American Committee, Howe Research Institute, 1974), Ch. 3.

[17] Stuart Jamieson, "Impact of an Arctic Pipeline on Northern Natives," in *The Mackenzie Pipleine*, ed. Peter H. Pearse, pp. 107-111.

the project might be economically more advantageous, and additional time would be available for further ecological research, for settling the land claims of the native people more equitably and for putting adjustment programs into motion. They also argue that more time is needed to permit the Canadian GNP to grow to a level where the country could more easily absorb the impact of financing this multi-billion-dollar project.[18] There are also those who urge the abandonment of the whole idea of pipelines in the Arctic because of the threats to the physical and social environment.

PRICING POLICIES

For nonrenewable resources like fossil fuels it seems logical to permit the market to perform its task of rationing scarce resources by allowing their prices to rise relative to the prices of other goods. In view of the inverse relation that exists between price and quantity demanded, such increases in price would encourage people to cut back on consumption, to substitute other energy sources and thus conserve the exhaustible resources for their most important uses. Prior to the establishment of OPEC, energy prices did not rise in real terms; on the contrary, the fell.[19] As a result North America adapted to an era of cheap energy. Low gasoline prices have meant that North Americans could afford to drive big heavy cars, whereas Europeans (who have always paid two or three times the North American price for gasoline) have had to compensate by buying considerably smaller cars. A few years ago many new buildings were not equipped with room controls to turn off the lights: electricity was so cheap that it did not pay to put in the extra wiring and switches necessary to enable light fixtures to be individually controlled. People have been casual about insulating their homes and have not felt any economic pressure to leave their cars at home and use the public transit system. Industry substituted cheap natural gas and oil for other energy sources: not only did the quantity demanded increase as we rode down the long-run demand curve, but the whole curve shifted to the right.[20]

Government policy was responsible for the low prices of natural gas

---

18 John Helliwell, Peter H. Pearse, Chris Sanderson, and Anthony Scott, "Where Does Canada's National Interest Lie?—A Quantitative Appraisal" in *The Mackenzie Pipeline*, pp. 213-217.

19 It has been estimated that in the period from 1951 to 1973 the real price of gasoline fell more than 25 percent and that the same was true of fuel oils. Erickson and Waverman, "Introduction to the Energy Question," pp. xv-xvi.

20 Erickson and Waverman, "Introduction to the Energy Question", p. xvi. If you have forgotten what is meant by a shift in the demand curve, see Ch. 8.

and oil. For many years the wellhead price of natural gas in the United States was regulated and kept at a level that was too low to cover the cost of exploration and development of new reserves. The return to companies on the sale of the natural gas that was a by-product of the oil was so low that it did not pay to transport it to users, and much of it was simply flared. Natural gas is a premium fuel and the fact that its price was low put a downward pressure on the price of oil and other competing energy sources.

Other government policies have affected price: the Alberta Energy Resources Conservation Board controlled the quantity of oil coming onto the market by setting a maximum permissible rate of extraction on all producing wells. Maximum quotas also exist in Saskatchewan and British Columbia. Governments levy taxes on gasoline, and those taxes, while large, have not been nearly as high as in Europe, where they raised the price much closer to the real cost of replacement of supplies in North America. Artificially low prices attributable to the policies of various governments had the effect of shifting the demand toward the fossil fuels while at the same time failing to provide companies with sufficient revenue to cover the long-run marginal costs of finding and bringing into production new sources of fossil fuels or of doing the research, and developing the technology necessary to make practicable the use of non-conventional fuels. There is widespread agreement that the failure to remove the government control from the wellhead price of gas was a key reason for the world energy crisis late in 1973; the crisis was not the result of some abrupt fundamental change in the *real* costs of fossil fuels, that is, in the quantity of resources or factor inputs required to get the fossil fuel out of the ground and delivered to consumers. Other failures in government policy blamed for creating the crisis were the American price controls and the uncertainty and delays caused by American policy.[21] These policies, it is argued, created a fundamental imbalance between demand and supply in the United States, the world's largest producer and consumer of energy, and made it and the rest of the world susceptible to the embargo and price increases of the OPEC cartel.

If self-sufficiency in energy was indeed an objective in North America, then it should have been apparent to the governments concerned that they could not keep the price of oil at $3.00 and $4.00 a barrel and expect companies to go out and develop $10.00-a-barrel oil reserves or develop equally costly non-conventional sources. Geological surveys indicate that there is no world shortage of fossil fuels in an absolute sense: there is only a shortage at present prices and with the present tax structure. Experience has shown that if the oil industry sees the possibility of

---

[21] Erickson and Waverman "Introduction to the Energy Question," *loc. cit.*, Vol. 1, p. xix.

profits, it will take all of the risks and make the huge expenditures necessary to locate the fossil fuel deposits that geologists believe exist and bring them into production. Supplies of fuel, in other words, are *responsive* to changes in price. In economics, the responsiveness of one variable to changes in another is called *elasticity*: the responsiveness, in this case, of the quantity supplied to changes in price (revenue to the company) is called the *price elasticity of supply*.

Price Elasticity of Supply   If we wish to be technical, we can calculate a number—a coefficient—that tells us the price elasticity of supply by *dividing the percentage change in quantity by the percentage change in price*. If the percentage change in quantity is *less* than the percentage change in price, then the coefficient will have a value of less than one, and we say that the supply curve is inelastic with respect to price. One limit to the size of this coefficient is shown in supply curve S_1S_1 in Figure 15-1. In this case there is no change at all in quantity regardless of the percentage change in price, so that the resulting coefficient is zero, and we say that the supply curve is *perfectly inelastic*.

On the other hand, if the percentage change in quantity is *greater* than the percentage change in price, then the resulting numerical coefficient will be greater than one, and we say that supply is *elastic* with respect to price. At the limit we have a case where for an extremely small percentage change in price there is an infinitely large increase in quantity: the value of the coefficient then approaches infinity, and the curve, which we describe as *perfectly elastic*, is horizontal and looks like S_2S_2 in Figure 15-1.

If the percentage change in quantity just equals the percentage change in price, then the value of the coefficient of elasticity is one. Unit elasticity marks the boundary between elastic and inelastic.

It has been suggested that the elasticity of supply of crude oil discoveries in North America is about unity;[22] if this is true, then it means that at least in the price range where the studies of elasticity were made, an increase of one percent in the price that companies receive will lead to an increase of one percent in the quantity of oil discovered and ultimately brought onto the market.[23] The long run supply curve, therefore, looks something like S_3S_3 in Figure 15-1. In the short run, however, it may look a good deal more like S_1S_1.

---

[22] *Ibid.*, Vol. 2, p. viii.

[23] The important fact that should be emphasized here is that if higher prices are to encourage exploration and development they must benefit the producer. Most of the increased revenue from the sale of oil and gas in the last few years has gone to governments.

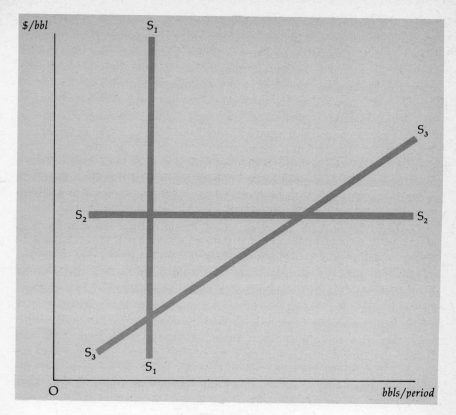

Figure 15-1

The Demand for Oil   Until the 1970s the United States was able to meet its objective of being self-sufficient in oil, but as the demand for fossil fuels at the then-prevailing prices increased sharply—more sharply than predicted[24]—the United States, too, became dependent on oil from the Middle East and vulnerable to the pressures of the OPEC cartel. Canada joined the roster of oil-deficient nations in 1976. How long the country will remain in that position depends partly on what policies are developed to bring supply and demand into balance. On the demand side, the most obvious policy is to raise price; the government might also introduce energy-saving legislation as happened in the United States, or in an emergency, resort to rationing.

The responsiveness of quantity demanded to increases in price

---

[24] Erickson and Waverman, "Introduction to the Energy Question," *loc. cit.*, Vol. 2, pp. xiii-xvi.

depends on the *price elasticity of demand*, which is a concept analagous to price elasticity of supply. In the case of demand, as we are well aware, a positive change (increase) in price will bring about a negative change (decrease) in quantity demanded, and the coefficient therefore normally carries a negative sign. However, when we discuss the size of the coefficient, we are interested in its absolute value—its value without regard to sign. Thus, demand is described as *elastic* if the percentage change in quantity is greater (without regard to sign) than the percentage change in price, and the coefficient, therefore, is numerically greater than one. Demand is said to be *inelastic* if the percentage change in quantity divided by the percentage change in price yields a coefficient that is numerically less than one; it is said to have unit elasticity if the percentage in quantity equals the percentage change in price.

Elasticity of demand for fossil fuels has usually been described as being low, as low perhaps as -0.1,[25] which means that it would take a 10 percent increase in price to bring about a one percent cutback in the quantity demanded. Long-run elasticities tend to be greater than short-run; that is, the quantity demanded is more responsive to price changes when more time is allowed for consumers to adapt to that particular price change. Economists are beginning to wonder whether the long-run coefficients may not be higher than previous studies had suggested, and whether the time for adjustments may not be shorter than believed, as indicated by things like the decline in sales of large cars and the decreased consumption of gasoline and oil for heating. It has been reported that whereas in previous years American demand for petroleum and petroleum products had increased at the rate of about 5 percent annually, consumption actually declined by about 4 percent in the first nine months of 1974.[26] Of course, other factors such as the mildness of the winter and the economic recession also had an effect. As prices continue to increase, consumers will be encouraged to switch to smaller cars and to use public transportation; they will insulate their homes; industrial users will adapt to substitutes like coal; and the quantity of oil demanded will either not increase as much as it otherwise would, or it may decline. Oil prices in Canada rose, but not as much as in the United States. From a 1972 price of about $3.00 a barrel, domestic oil had reached a price of $9.05 in 1976, still considerably below the world price of over $13.00 a barrel. Obviously there was less pressure on Canadian consumers to cut back on their demand for oil because they were being shielded

---

[25] *Ibid.*, p. xvi.
[26] Quoted from a study for the Chase-Manhattan Bank by John M. Hennessy, "The Year Reviewed," in *Energy: Update and Outlook*, op. cit., p. 7.

from the full impact of the world price by price ceilings on domestic oil and subsidies on foreign imports. Canada was the only country in the western world in which consumption rose substantially in 1974.[27]

Economic Rent in the Oil Industry If the government is unwilling to let the domestic oil price rise to the world price in order to limit the quantity demanded, then, from what we know about supply and demand, we might expect an economic policy that would result in an increase in supply. It would seem logical to expect that unless the government itself plans to pour vast amounts of money into exploring for new sources and into research and development on non-conventional fuels, it should be encouraging the private sector to do so. Since, as we have seen in the discussion of the elasticity of supply, companies do respond to increases in the price they earn, and since new oil sources in North America are very expensive to locate and develop, we should expect to see government policies which would permit large increases in the revenues to oil companies.

The sudden price increases by the OPEC governments created the possibility of similar increases by Canadian oil companies, which would then get unexpectedly large profits on the oil they themselves were producing—large "windfall profits" or "economic rent". Economic rent may be defined as returns in excess of opportunity cost: it is the revenue that can be taxed away without making it rational for the supplier to get out of production altogether.[28] The question was, who was to benefit from these economic rents? Should it be the companies, so that they would be encouraged to explore and develop more sources of energy? Should it be consumers? Should it be the government, and if so *which government*? Should it be the federal government so that the benefits could be spread around? Or should it be the governments that own the resources—British Columbia, Saskatchewan, and, above all, Alberta? In that case there would be a geographical redistribution of income away from Ontario to the Western Provinces, to which Ontario would object. Alberta has argued that if the rest of the country wants to talk about "a reasonable price for oil" then it would like to discuss "a reasonable price for transportation" or "a reasonable level of tariffs" to stop the geographical redistribution of income which, that Province claims, has been going on for decades in the East's favour. The ten-

---

[27] The Bank of Nova Scotia, *Monthly Review*, July-August 1975.

[28] For a discussion of economic rent, see Economic Council of Canada, *Eleventh Annual Review: Economic Targets and Social Indicators* (Ottawa: Information Canada, 1974) pp. 139-141.

sions between governments over the division of the spoils echoes the tensions on the world scene where the Arabs have been criticized for trying to use oil as a political weapon. Ill feeling ran so high over the apparent inequity created by the Arabs' getting so much at the expense of others when they merely owned the oil and did nothing about finding it or developing it, that there was talk about the possibility of military intervention if the OPEC cartel pushed the price up too far.

In the midst of the jurisdictional dispute in Canada, both levels of government have laid claim to so much of the economic rent that the oil industry has found itself with little incentive to find and develop new sources of oil. The governments cannot help but be aware of this fact but neither level is prepared to compromise very much. The federal government in its budget in 1974 discontinued the practice of allowing royalties paid to the provincial governments as a deduction from federal income tax. *The Financial Times of Canada* estimated that the budget cut one billion dollars a year from the industry's cash flow and suggested that the cash payback in the United States to companies that shifted their operations from Canada to that country would be about three times as high.[29] Premier Lougheed of Alberta argued that federal tax policies would be such a deterrent to oil and gas exploration that the energy shortage would arrive even sooner than within the seven years forecast by the National Energy Board. When the price increase was announced in the middle of 1975, Alberta cut its royalty rate in order to give some encouragement to companies.

The oil and gas industry is rather unique. Before a single barrel of oil can be sold, the industry must develop the field and prove the existence of many years' supply—enough to warrant the heavy cost of building transportation facilities, which usually means building a pipeline. Virtually all of the production costs must be incurred before the industry can earn a penny of revenue from a particular field. Once production begins, the ongoing cost for that field drops virtually to zero. All the company needs for an oil field already in production is a few men to check the lines and to check the valves. The marginal cost, therefore, of getting oil from a developed field is almost zero.

Marginal costs of zero are what we assumed in the example of Mr. Black's movie theatre[30], but the situation here is different; in the case of the cinema we assumed that there were no additional costs incurred by Mr. Black whether he accommodated one customer or three hundred; however we also assumed that if Mr. Black decided not to open his door

---

[29] *The Financial Times of Canada*, Montreal, 3 December 1974.
[30] See Ch. 8.

to *any* customers, he could in time escape a number of costs by getting rid of his ushers, projectionists and ticket sellers when their contracts were up; he might even level up the floor of his theatre, convert it into a warehouse and recoup a little of his capital costs. But in a producing oil field there are virtually no escapable costs: the industry cannot pull up a well, cut it in lengths and sell it for post holes. If a price war should break out, the price could drop close to zero until the existing supply is used up: preventing such price wars is one reason why there has almost always been a government presence in the industry.

By the same token, governments can tax the revenue down to zero, for the return to the company is almost entirely economic rent, which the government could continue to extract until the supply in that particular field ran out. The effect of such a policy on future supply from the private sector would likely be rather drastic. To finance the heavy cost and huge risk of exploration, companies must foresee a commensurable return. They have shown themselves willing to take such risks when there has been promise of profits. But they have been discouraged by recent government policies: as a result of taxes at a rate of 100 percent on increases in export prices, and drastically increased royalty rates, producers in Canada have found little increase in their own net revenues.[31] Instead of being encouraged to explore by being allowed to retain some of the economic rent, their cash flows have been depleted; as a result drilling rigs have been leaving Canada in great numbers for the more favorable revenue climate of the United States.

There are those who argue that the government should take over the oil industry, which is dominated by foreign-owned corporations. This was evident in 1973 when the minority Liberal government first introduced the bill to establish Petro-Canada, a national petroleum corporation: it was under pressure from the New Democratic Party to move massively into the oil industry. The bill, reintroduced in 1974 and passed in 1975, gives the government sweeping powers, including the power to nationalize the industry, although the stated intent of the government is to concentrate on research and exploration. Before the establishment of Petro-Canada the federal government had a limited involvement in exploring for oil and gas through its participation in Panarctic Oils, a consortium comprising oil and gas companies, individuals and governments. When the costs of development of synthetic oil from the Athabasca Tar Sands escalated so rapidly, and when the withdrawal of one large member of the Syncrude

---

[31] R. S. Ritchie, "Public Policies Affecting Petroleum Development in Canada," *Canadian Public Policy*, Vol. 1, No. 1 (Winter 1975), p. 73.

consortium threatened to cause the collapse of the enterprise early in 1975, the federal government stepped in with some financial help.

Many who advocate government operation of the industry instead of supporting the traditional pattern of leaving it to the private sector with its expertise, appear to believe that profits are so high that we should depart from our normal reliance on the private sector. However, when one considers the firms that have gone into the exploration business and made only marginal profits or none at all, and when one looks at the profit performance over time of the leading companies[32] one is left with the feeling that governments can do better for themselves by letting private companies take the risks and participating through leases, royalties, and taxes. Alberta, for example, has a rather ingenious method of capturing some of the economic rent through its leasing policy: the Province leases land to companies for drilling "wildcat" wells, stipulating that they must progressively give up part of their leases in a pattern that ensures that what is given up includes some of the best land. The Crown then puts these lands up for auction and other oil companies bid on it, the price they offer depending on their estimates of the amount of oil and the costs of bringing it into production. On a good field the price is likely to be very high, and the Alberta Government in this way lets the market forces siphon a sizeable portion of the economic rents into government coffers without creating major disincentives to further exploration.

Had the oil companies been permitted to keep a larger share of the revenues generated because of the actions of the OPEC cartel, there is no doubt that, encouraged by increased profits, they would have spent vast sums on exploration in the Arctic and offshore in Eastern Canada. On the other hand, by establishing a two-price system on Canadian oil and preventing the domestic price from rising to the world price and by taking a large share of the economic rent to subsidize eastern consumers, the government mitigated the inflationary impact on the economy, and greatly reduced the geographical income redistribution from the oil-consuming to the oil-producing provinces. However, the jurisdictional problem generated by the fact that the *British North America Act* gives the provinces control over natural resources, and the resulting confrontation between the federal and provincial governments, has resulted in so much uncertainty in the industry and so little encouragement from increasing profit that exploration research and development are being cut back. The outcome of this could well be an acute shortage of energy by the early 1980s, which will necessitate either heavy dependence on oil from Venezuela and the Middle East, or else very severe restrictions on the demand side.

---

[32] See Erickson and Waverman, "Introduction to the Energy Question," pp. xvi-xviii.

Agriculture

Agriculture is another resource-based industry where attempts to deal with current problems affect the achievement of a number of Canada's economic goals. The most pressing problem related to agriculture in the mid-1970s was the sudden jump in prices of agricultural products, which dated back to changes in world market conditions in 1972, and the pressure that continuing increases in food prices, like increases in the price of energy, put on the Consumer Price Index. The key issues in agriculture have traditionally centred on income maintenance and income stabilization in an economically and politically important sector. Most policies in agriculture—price-support policies, the payment of subsidies, and the creation of marketing boards, for example—have been aimed at achieving the goal of an equitable distribution of income, and they have often been in conflict with the objective of achieving efficiency in the agricultural sector and thereby obtaining a proper allocation of resources. Now there is the added problem of a conflict between the goal of *stability* and the goal of equity: notwithstanding the problem of inflation, unless agricultural prices remain high enough to assure farmers of an adequate income, output of agricultural commodities is likely to decline and thus reinforce future inflationary pressures.

Agricultural products—grains in particular—are important components of Canada's trade, and hence are a matter of some concern when we consider the objective of achieving a viable balance of payments. Historically, of course, agriculture was one of the dynamic forces of Canadian growth: the move west to open up new fertile farmlands provided a great spur to Canada's early development. This is no longer the case: *encroachment* on the most fertile land is one of today's problems.

INFLATIONARY PRESSURES

The sudden jump in agricultural prices that further complicated the problem of achieving stability can be traced back to the worldwide problem of poor harvests in 1972. The Soviet Union was particularly hard hit, and before the rest of the world was aware of the seriousness of the shortage, Russia moved quietly in and bought up most of the world's grain surplus —an action that has been described as "the great grain robbery". High quality wheat which sold for $1.50 a bushel in August 1972 had risen to over $5.50 a year later; Durum wheat in the same period rose from $1.69 to $9.00 a bushel. Feed grain prices spiralled, and since feed grains represent an important part of the costs of meat, poultry and eggs the effect was a sharp rise in the Consumer Price Index.

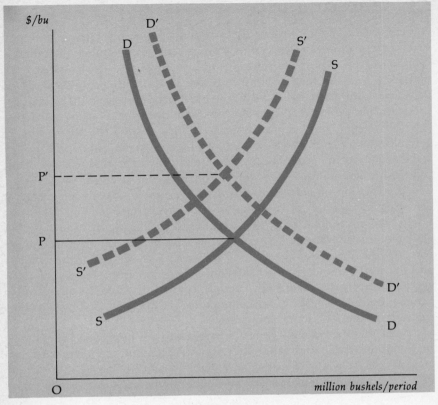

Figure 15-2

Figure 15-2 illustrates what happened. *DD* and *SS* represent the original demand and supply curves,[33] and *P*, the equilibrium price. Assume that adverse weather conditions in North America cause a poor harvest, then there is a *decrease* in supply: the entire supply curve shifts to the left, say, to *S'S'*. If, at the same time, serious crop failures in other parts of the world bring Russia, and other countries, into the market as large customers, then the entire demand curve shifts up and to the right (to *D'D'*, for example). The result is a jump in prices to a level like *P'*. The size of such price changes is affected by the elasticity of demand and supply for agricultural products. The more *inelastic* these curves (that is, the more

---

[33] The careful reader will note that the supply and demand curves in Figure 15-2 are curved, whereas in most of our diagrams they are straight lines. Supply and demand functions *may* be straight lines (which makes them much easier to draw and explains why they predominate in diagrams) but, in fact, curvilinear functions are more likely.

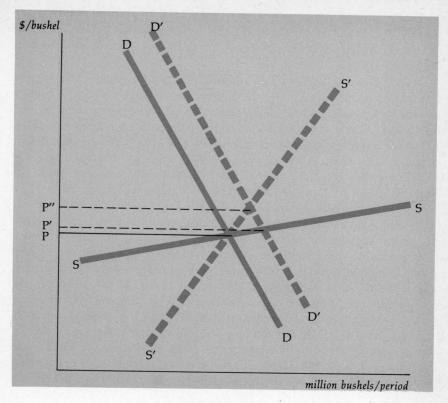

Figure 15-2A

unresponsive quantity is to price changes), the larger the effect on price.[34] The evidence suggests that in the case of agricultural products both demand and supply tend to be inelastic. Moreover, in the case of the supply of certain products like beef, the increase in supply comes only after a considerable lag since the farmer needs time to breed his stock and

---

[34] This statement can be most easily demonstrated on a diagram. Let us compare the difference in the effect on price of a change in the demand for Canadian wheat caused, say, by a failure of the Russian wheat crop, when the Canadian supply curve is elastic and when it is inelastic. In Figure 15-2A, *SS* is an elastic supply curve (it resembles S_2 in Figure 15-1). *S'S'* is an inelastic curve through the same point of intersection with *DD*, the initial demand curve. Because of an increase in demand for wheat by the Russians, the demand curve shifts to *D'D'*. If the relevant supply curve is *SS*, the *elastic* curve, then the price increases to *P'*; if however, the curve is *inelastic*, like *S'S'*, then the price jumps much more, to *P'*. The reader might like to test his knowledge of the subject by showing that the price change resulting from a change in supply (for example, a decrease in Canadian supply caused by severe crop damage from widespread drought on the Prairies) is greater, the more inelastic the demand curve.

let them grow to a marketable size. As a result even relatively small changes in demand or supply tend to cause wide swings in price, and this helps to explain some of the price instability in agricultural products during the 1970s.

While the crop yields in North America and in many other regions returned to about average in 1973, they were not large enough to build a reserve back up, particularly in the face of strong world demand for agricultural products of all kinds and continuing crop failures in a few countries. Hopes for bumper crops did not materialize until 1976, and the size of Russian purchases through the summer of 1975 suggested that the drought in that country had created problems as serious as they had been in 1972. The situation meant high incomes for North American grain farmers, but created serious problems for cattle and hog producers, dairy farmers and egg and poultry producers, for whom feed grains constitute a large part of costs. In beef production, for example, herds were expanding in response to sustained demand, and prices were beginning to ease, but with the cost of feed grains outstripping the return on cattle, beef producers were threatening to kill off their herds, which could only result in higher prices in the long run. Similar conditions existed in the hog, poultry, and egg markets. Even with the two-price system for wheat (which keeps the price of wheat for domestic milling below the world price and compensates the farmer by paying him a subsidy) price increases in wheat products have spilled over into the retail market. Moreover, there have been inflationary pressures at every stage along the line—increases in the cost of transporting, processing, packaging and selling the products. Bumper crops in 1976 may help to cut costs and help relieve the inflationary pressures on food.

THE TECHNOLOGICAL REVOLUTION

Bad harvests and inflationary pressures in the mid-1970s tended to obscure what had been happening in agriculture in the quarter-century after the Second World War. There had occurred what can only be described as a revolution in agricultural techniques: the development of new and improved high-yield crops, better methods of cultivation and more efficient machinery resulted in a great increase in output. Output per man (productivity) increased tremendously—so much so that in spite of the fact that over half of the work force left the agricultural industry, total output increased. There was a large increase in the supply of agricultural products: in terms of Figure 15-3, the entire supply curve shifted markedly to the right, from SS to $S'S'$ with the result that at any price—the old equilibrium price, P, for example—producers were prepared to bring a greater quantity (OQ' as compared with OQ) onto the market.

If this had been the only change, there would have been a new

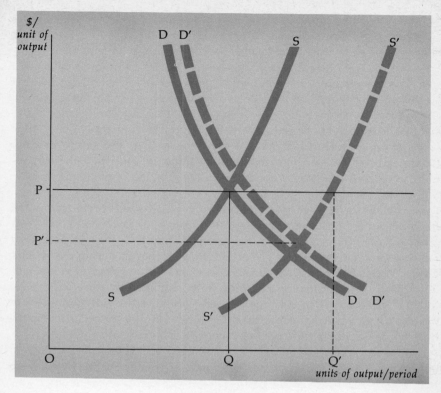

Figure 15-3

equilibrium price far below the original, at the level indicated by the intersection of the new supply curve *S'S'* and the original demand curve *DD*. As it happens, the factors influencing demand changed, too: population increased and incomes rose. These are the items that we normally hold constant when we draw the price-quantity relationship that we call the demand curve. As incomes rise, people tend to increase their consumption of all goods; and because some who were not able to afford the product before now have the money to buy it, a greater quantity is demanded at all prices. Demand increases with an increase in income: the whole curve shifts to the right. Unfortunately for the farmers, the rightward shift has been small because the demand for agricultural products tend to be *unresponsive* to increases in income: it is *income inelastic*, in technical economic terms. While there was some increase in demand to a position like *D'D'*, for example, it was not as sharp as the increase in supply. As a result, the prices of many agricultural products tended to fall, and the agricultural price level failed to keep pace with increases in other prices in the economy. In Figure 15-3, the intersection of *D'D'* and

$S'S'$ indicates a new and lower equilibrium price, P'.[35]

Low prices for farm products meant low incomes for the labour employed in agriculture; low incomes encouraged a great exodus of workers from the agricultural sector into sectors where incomes were higher. The increasing output per employed person left in the industry made a significant contribution to the increase in real output per person employed in the economy as a whole.

Not surprisingly, farmers asked for special consideration. In a time when incomes were rising rapidly, they argued that agriculture had not fared nearly as well as the manufacturing industry, and since the agricultural sector still constituted a sizeable portion of the population, its buying power (not to mention its voting power) merited some attention. Farmers pointed out that the manufacturing industry had protection in the form of tariffs; this had the effect of raising the prices of goods that farmers had to purchase, and in the face of falling agricultural prices, they felt that they deserved some protection, too. Moreover, during the Second World War when Canadian farmers were in a position to earn tremendous profits through high prices, they were restrained by price ceilings set by the government; if the free market solution was not permitted to operate then, was it equitable that the rather ruthless forces of competition should be permitted to operate when prices were relatively low?

Different kinds of policies can be used to raise real incomes in agriculture. One is to encourage economic efficiency in the industry so that returns to the resources employed in it will increase. In theory, if this route is followed, workers will be encouraged to leave agriculture and inefficient marginal farms will be abandoned. Appropriate policies would include training and manpower policies to reeducate and relocate redundant farm workers, and income supports for those who are unable to change occupations. As we shall see, this route of economic efficiency was the one supported by Canada's Task Force on Agriculture when it reported in 1970.

Other types of policies include a variety of actions to support and stabilize farm prices. These, rather than policies to promote economic efficiency, are the kinds of policy that have predominated in Canada, although as was noted above, they were not used extensively enough to halt the mass exodus from farming.

---

[35] As consumers who keep an eye on the consumer price index, we may find it difficult to believe that farm prices either declined or failed to keep pace with other prices in that period. However, what we must bear in mind is that in this generation an entire industry has grown up between the farmer and the food retailer (and purchasers): the processing and packaging industry. At the supermarket we now buy everything, from instant breakfast and instant mashed potatoes to TV dinners. Processing and packaging costs are relatively high so that rising prices of food to consumers are not inconsistent with falling prices to farmers.

INCOME DISTRIBUTION AND STABILIZATION POLICIES

In Canada, as in the United States, farmers have been granted special assistance of many kinds, including price supports (prices that are higher than the equilibrium price when the supports are effective), subsidies, crop insurance, relatively easy access to credit, and assistance in research. Some of these policies can most easily be understood with the aid of our tools of supply and demand.

Price Supports As a result of government policy, not all agricultural prices are determined by the free interaction of market demand and supply. In some cases the government sets minimum prices. If these support prices (or *floor prices*, as they are frequently called) are to be effective, they must be higher than the equilibrium prices. If not, the free market will operate to give the farmer a higher price than the support price. Price support programs for agriculture in Canada derive mainly from the Agricultural Stabilization Act of 1958. The Canadian Dairy Commission has the authority to support the price of major dairy products, and the prices paid for various grains by the Canadian Wheat Board may, in certain circumstances, turn out to be support prices. The marketing policies of provincial marketing boards may also result in price supports for agricultural products. Under the terms of the Agricultural Stabilization Act, support of nine specified commodities is mandatory, and support of other agricultural products may be given if the need arises. Before this Act was passed in 1958, price supports had all been optional at the discretion of the Prices Support Board. On the nine mandatory commodities (cattle, hogs, sheep, industrial milk and cream, corn, soy beans, and eastern oats and barley) the support price must not be less than 90 percent of the price of the product averaged over the preceding five years. There is no maximum, and from time to time support prices have been so high that they have acted as incentive prices—that is, they have encouraged farmers to increase output greatly. Three methods of supporting prices may be used: subsidies, offers to purchase commodities at fixed prices, and deficiency payments.

OFFERS TO PURCHASE

Originally, the government used what is called the "offer-to-purchase" method of supporting farm prices, that is to say, the government set the support price, consumers purchased whatever they wanted at that price, and the government then offered to purchase the output that consumers would not buy. The tools of supply and demand can clarify greatly the operation of this support program.

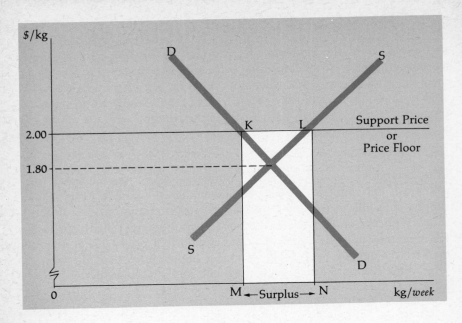

Figure 15-4

Assume, for example, that the equilibrium price of butter is $1.80 a kilogram. In Figure 15-4, this is the price that is indicated by dropping a perpendicular from the intersection of the supply and demand curves to the vertical axis. Assume further that the government decides to support butter at $2.00 a kilogram. The demand curve, which is a schedule of the quantities that consumers want at various prices, indicates that at $2.00 a kilogram, the quantity that consumers are prepared to buy amounts to *OM*. The supply curve, being a schedule of the quantity producers are prepared to bring onto the market in that time period, suggests that at $2.00, *ON* will be supplied—far more than consumers want to buy at that price. A surplus equal to *MN* develops and, unless the government takes some action, suppliers wanting to get rid of their stock of butter will cut price in order to attract customers; thus the price will be driven down below the support price. What the government must do under the offer-to-purchase method is buy the surplus (the quantity *MN*) at the support price. The cost to the government—or to the Canadian taxpayers, to be precise—of supporting butter would be $2.00 (the distance *MK*) times the number of kilograms of surplus butter (the distance *MN* in Figure 15-4). It would be equal to the rectangle *MKLN*.

Having purchased the surplus, the government faces the problem of what to do with it. It can store it for a time, as has been done with many commodities including butter, and in that case the government must absorb the costs of storage and deterioration; sooner or later, however, it must dispose of the surplus. There is no alternative but to sell the surplus abroad and take the loss, or to give it away and take an even greater loss. It cannot sell it on the domestic market; for, unless the commodity has been stored long enough for market conditions to have changed, such an action would simply drive the price below the floor price and thus would defeat the purpose of the support price. Presumably the world price is less than the domestic price, otherwise farmers could have sold the product on the world market in the first place, and would not have needed price supports. It is possible that the government might be lucky enough to store the commodity and find that the world price had improved sufficiently for it to recoup its losses.

DEFICIENCY PAYMENTS

Because of the price-support policies of the late 1950s, huge surpluses developed in Canada, particularly of eggs and hogs, and this led the government to attempt to improve its support policies. In 1959 it altered the form of its price supports on some products: it began to use deficiency payments. With this kind of support program, the government, as in the case of its offer to purchase the surplus, sets the minimum level below which the price to farmers will not be permitted to fall. It then leaves the market free to find its own level: buyers pay the price necessary to clear the market; the government then pays producers the difference between the market price and the support price. In terms of Figure 15-5, the government sets the support price for butter, as before, at $2.00 a kilogram. At that price, the supply curve tells us, producers will produce ON kilograms of butter. The demand curve is not only a schedule of the quantities that will be taken off the market at various prices at a given time; it is also a schedule of the maximum prices that can be charged if various quantities are to be sold, provided that the various other factors which influence demand remain constant. The demand curve, then, tells us that if consumers are to be persuaded to buy ON kilograms of butter, the maximum price that can be charged in the market is P_m—say $1.60. The support price (P_s) is $2.00; the price that clears the market is $1.60. In our hypothetical example, if the government pays the support on all butter produced, it will have to pay 40 cents a kilogram for all ON kilograms—a total outlay indicated by the area $P_m P_s FG$.

In Canada, the government does not make deficiency payments on the total output. When deficiency payments were established for eggs and hogs, for example, a limited output per producer was set as an eligibility standard for the subsidy. The effect of this policy was to assure the smaller farmer of a higher income. It kept the cost to the taxpayer down;

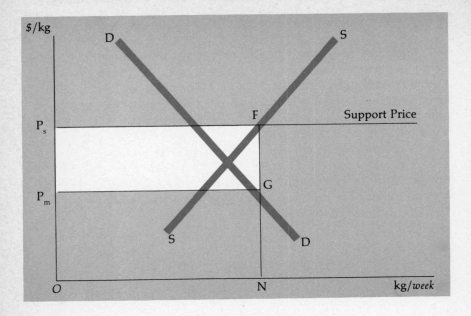

Figure 15-5

but it also discriminated against the large, efficient farms in favour of the smaller ones.

CROP RESTRICTION

A method of supporting price that has been used fairly extensively in the United States, but not in Canada, is one that involves bringing supply and demand into equilibrium at the support price by decreasing supply—in other words, by shifting the supply curve to the left. Assume that demand and supply are as illustrated in Figure 15-6 and that P_s represents the support price. The problem for the government is to find a means of persuading producers to cut output through some form of crop restriction or marketing arrangement, so that the supply curve shifts left to $S'S'$. In the United States devices like marketing quotas and acreage allotments are traditionally coupled with price-support programs. Acreage allotments do not always constitute a successful method of restricting crops, because when the acreage is cut back, farmers often utilize good land more intensively, applying fertilizers and pest control methods, so that output may *increase* above previous levels.

One successful Canadian attempt to divert acreage from a particular product was begun in 1970: Operation LIFT (Lower Inventories for Tomorrow) was introduced in order to cut back on huge carry-overs of wheat stocks. Under this plan there was an acreage payment of $6.00 for summer-

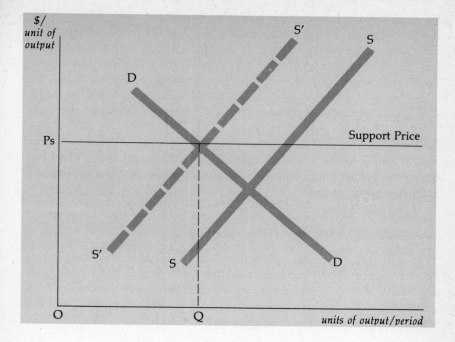

Figure 15-6

fallow or forage, to be followed by a further $4.00/acre for acreage still in forage in 1971.

The Canadian Wheat Board is another body that, in certain circumstances, can provide price supports for grain. The Board is a marketing agency that purchases wheat, oats and barley from farmers in Western Canada for interprovincial and export trade. Every year, on the basis of its estimates of the future selling price of wheat, and of farmers' needs, Parliament sets an initial price which (minus the cost of handling the grain in the country elevator and railway freight from the delivery point to an export point) is paid to farmers when they deliver their grain to a country elevator. If the Board sells the grain at the price higher than this initial payment, as it normally does, it pays the farmer the difference. If by chance it gets less, then the government absorbs the loss and the initial payment becomes, in effect, a support price.

The postwar technological revolution created major problems for wheat producers and the Wheat Board. Bumper crops throughout the late

1960s, even in years of rather poor weather conditions, resulted in surplus stocks that filled storage elevators and piled up on the farms. In the 1970-71 crop year there was a carry-over of more than a billion bushels of wheat—an all-time high. With domestic consumption of about 175 million bushels, and exports of 300 to 350 million bushels considered likely, by the time the 1971 wheat crop came in, the Wheat Board faced the prospect of having almost enough wheat to fill all foreseen demands, domestic and foreign, for the next three years. The Task Force on Agriculture advocated a sharp cutback in wheat production over a period of three years[36] to help cope with such surpluses. By 1973 the position had been reversed: the Wheat Board had to cope with shortages and the problem of rationing a scarce resource.

MARKETING BOARDS

Marketing boards, which are mainly a provincial responsibility, have grown up in all provinces. There are more than 100 of them in Canada. Milk marketing boards, for example, are to be found right across the country. An important objective of these bodies is to raise producers' income, and the economic theory is the same as that illustrated in Figure 15-6. If farmers can band together to market a product, and if the arrangement can be made binding on all of the producers in an area, then a marketing board can raise the price to buyers by restricting output (by decreasing supply to $S'S'$, for example). Boards may do this by setting quotas, if they have the power. They may also stabilize farmers' incomes by pooling crops at the beginning of the crop year and storing them to prevent farmers from dumping their entire output on the market as soon as it is harvested and thus driving the price down. The chief problem of marketing boards has been to get the participation of all farmers in an area. This is essential, otherwise those who participate will have to accept quotas, or finance storage facilities for the crop, while those outside the arrangement may ignore quotas, or may take advantage of the higher price achieved by withholding the crops of others and selling their own newly harvested crop, thus reaping all the benefit of the marketing arrangement while paying none of the cost. That is why the legislation in all provinces now provides that when support is forthcoming from a majority of producers in an area, the marketing arrangements become binding on all.

Provincial boards are limited to controlling marketing arrangements within a given province unless the federal government chooses to delegate

---

[36] Federal Task Force on Agriculture, *Canadian Agriculture in the Seventies* (Ottawa: Information Canada, 1970), p. 131.

some of its power over interprovincial trade. During the Great Depression the federal government attempted to establish national marketing boards to ensure the orderly marketing of produce, but the courts declared that such authority was outside federal jurisdiction. The Canadian Wheat Board was established by the federal government in 1935; the next national marketing board to be set up was the Canadian Dairy Commission, which went into operation in the mid-1960s. In addition to administering subsidies and price supports for major dairy products, this body has the power to purchase any such product and to store, process, package and dispose of it in any way it sees fit. With the cooperation of most of the provincial milk boards it operates a comprehensive market-sharing program.

The Task Force on Agriculture[37] advocated establishing more marketing boards of various kinds at the national level. The federal *Farm Products Marketing Agencies Act* passed in 1972 provides the authorization for such boards. If producers of a product as well as the provinces feel that marketing cannot be effectively handled by the individual provincial boards, national agencies may be set up. The Act established a National Farm Products Marketing Council to advise the Minister of Agriculture on all matters relating to the establishment, operation and performance of national agencies.

Because of all of the adverse publicity it received in the mid-1970s, the best-known of the new agencies is the Canadian Egg Marketing Agency, which was the first to be set up under the Act. Its purpose was to guarantee a fair return to egg producers who had suffered through several years of low prices and provincial egg-dumping wars. At the price the Agency established to purchase eggs, most provinces exceeded their quotas, surpluses developed, eggs rotted, and the Chairman of the Food Prices Review Board launched a stinging attack on the agency because of the detrimental effect of the rising egg prices on consumers' food budgets. The Consumers' Association of Canada labeled it "a mismanaged monopoly".

Marketing boards, though frequently the centre of bitter controversy among producers who are bound by the arrangement but who would like to be free to compete independently, seem to have had some success in levelling out fluctuations in income and in raising the prices of agricultural products. To the extent that the boards succeed in raising farm incomes by raising the prices of farm products, they do so largely at the expense of urban consumers, with the result that the rural-urban income gap is somewhat narrowed.

---

[37] *Ibid.*, pp. 328-329.

ALLOCATION OF RESOURCES

The objective of most agricultural policies has been to improve the incomes of farmers. These policies are frequently criticized because too little attention has been paid to their effect on the allocation of resources. The Federal Task Force on Agriculture came down very firmly on the side of economic efficiency. Having made the assumption that some form of guaranteed income would be available for low-income farmers, it argued that agriculture should be operated the way other industries operate. Policies should be designed to encourage efficient producers; inefficient producers should be encouraged to change jobs. Its key recommendations included extensive rationalization of both private and government organizations in agriculture, the improvement of farm management and the introduction of modern management techniques. It viewed overproduction as a major long-run problem. A widespread series of crop failures in the early to the middle 1970s saw excess supplies replaced by shortages and sharply rising prices; however, the longer-term trend reasserted itself in 1976 as the weather improved, and technological changes continued to bring about higher productivity. Concerned about surpluses, the Task Force advocated strong policies to control supply, expand demand, particularly in the international scene, and to phase out price supports and subsidies such as those for wheat and milk which, it felt, had insulated farmers from the realities of world markets and had encouraged them to produce more than the market could absorb.[38]

Price supports, as is evident from Figures 15-4 and 15-5, encourage farmers to produce more. In each case, farmers, instead of producing the quantity indicated by the intersection of the supply and demand curves, produce the larger quantity, *ON*. The more responsive is the supply schedule to price increases (the more *elastic* the supply curve), the greater will be the increase in the quantity supplied as a result of the support price. Moreover, farming is becoming increasingly capital intensive,[39] and efficient production is possible only on large commercial units; by using price supports, and by setting quotas on the amount of output on which deficiency payments will be made, the government is encouraging marginal farms to remain in the industry, and it is discriminating against the large producers. This has probably slowed down the rate of orderly economic adjustment in the industry.

Research in agriculture is one of the pillars of Canadian agricultural

---

[38] Federal Task Force on Agriculture, *op. cit.*, Ch. 1.

[39] A capital-intensive industry is one in which capital costs constitute a large portion of the price of the product. A labour-intensive industry, by contrast, uses relatively more labour. A business that washes cars by hand is labour intensive; a business that uses an automated jet spray and dryer is capital intensive.

policy. The output of an individual farm, no matter how large, is minuscule relative to the total size of the market; this is a characteristic of atomistic (or pure) competition. As a result, individual farmers have nothing to gain from undertaking research themselves. Fishermen are in the same position. The federal government, therefore, has stepped in and does most of the research for the agricultural and fisheries industries, with universities and some private companies doing the rest. The result of the research in agriculture has been a remarkable improvement in technology, and a greatly increased supply of agricultural products. While this increased supply has been one of the roots of the problems of the agriculture sector, this is not to argue that research is a bad thing. Research has enabled Canadian farmers to produce at a lower cost and to compete in world markets where they do not have any great influence on price. If they are to survive economically, Canadian farmers must be able to keep up with farmers in other parts of the world.

Another important policy of the federal government is to make credit readily available to farmers through such acts as the Farm Credit Act and the Farm Improvement Loans Act. These acts enable farmers to obtain money on favourable terms. In theory, this should enable them to become more capital intensive and to take advantage of new techniques and thus improve their operations and earn a satisfactory living. However, loans are normally tied to the assets farmers already have—their land, buildings, machinery, and livestock. From the point of view of a proper allocation of resources, the danger is that marginal farmers (of whom there are far too many in Canada, living at the poverty level and slowing down the increase in productivity) will be able to borrow only enough to keep them in farming (thus adding to the total supply), but will not be able to borrow enough to convert their marginal operations into efficient commercial farms.

The question of achieving a proper allocation of resources in the agricultural sector and of giving that objective priority over the maintenance of farm incomes is likely to become more of an issue. The work of the Task Force, together with the shock to the economy of rising food prices (they were rising at a rate of about 15 percent in the years 1973 to 1975) in a time of inflation, and an active Food Prices Review Board, have drawn public attention to the issue of efficiency in agriculture. Moreover, the political power of the farm sector is declining. In 1939 the farm population accounted for almost 32 percent of the total; by the time of the 1971 census it had dropped to 6.6 percent and the Task Force forecast that it might be as little as 3 or 4 percent by 1980. In an increasingly urban economy, it is being argued, what is needed is a food policy whose objective is to supply the urban population with food at the lowest possible stable prices, not the maintenance of high stable prices to support farmers, whether they are efficient or inefficient.

16

Conflicts occur because the goals of the Canadian economy cannot all be achieved simultaneously. The market economy is unsurpassed for giving freedom of choice, but that freedom is limited by policies to redistribute income, maintain competition, and promote growth. Income-redistribution policies may adversely affect the allocation of resources. The growth rate may be reduced by anti-inflation policies and by efforts to maintain competition. A conflict may occur between policies to achieve domestic stability and a viable balance of payments.

Stagflation (the simultaneous existence of inflation and unemployment) was the major problem of the mid-1970s. Controlling inflation tends to worsen unemployment, and vice versa, and there is disagreement about which is the lesser of the two ills. The federal government's stabilization policy of price and wage controls adversely affects several other goals.

Other problems in Canada need attention, including problems relating to urbanization, discrimination, and adapting to rapid changes in technology.

Conflict: A Problem in the Canadian Economy

Problems abound in the Canadian economy, and solutions are difficult to find. The man on the street argues that the fault lies with economists, who cannot agree among themselves on the facts and the theories, with the result that there are as many solutions proposed as there are economists. This is far from the case. Economists are in agreement on important theories; such disagreements as remain are mainly on marginal issues. Moreover, disagreements about economic theory are relatively unimportant. Much more crucial is the problem of determining the objectives or goals of the economy, and this is a realm that lies beyond economics.

A nation can be defined as a group of individuals with common goals or objectives. Goals—whether political, cultural, or economic—are not the substance of theory; they are a matter of values, or the moral sentiments. Selecting goals that are appropriate for a country, therefore, may give rise to honest differences of opinion—to conflict—among reasonable men. It is not necessary, or even possible, for all conflicts in a country to be resolved. A person or a family, or a country, at any one time, will find all kinds of unresolved internal conflicts. But if consensus about key goals cannot be achieved, then the nation will disintegrate into smaller units in which there *is* consensus.

There are threats to the Canadian nation because of conflicts that have arisen over finding goals that are mutually acceptable. For political and cultural reasons, some individuals in Quebec are discussing separatism, and so are some in the West. In both parts of the country it is argued that objectives are not being met within the Canadian federation, and that they might be better achieved if these regions were independent of the rest of Canada. If such conflicts over the national goals cannot be resolved, and if consensus cannot be reached about national objectives, then we can expect to see the disintegration of the Canadian federation.

Conflicts among Goals

Throughout this book, we have assumed that there exists consensus in Canada about the desirability of a set of half a dozen economic goals, including stability (by which we mean full employment without inflation), growth, an equitable distribution of income, a viable balance-of-payments position, economic freedom, and—a catch-all for a heterogeneous set of contemporary problems—the proper allocation of resources. These broad goals have achieved wide acceptance in Canada. As soon as we consider implementing them, however, major areas of conflict open up. We have already encountered some conflicts that have arisen because all goals cannot be simultaneously achieved and because disagreements arise over the relative importance to be attached to the various goals, but the subject deserves further elaboration.

ECONOMIC FREEDOM

We value economic freedom, and the free market is a vehicle that is unsurpassed for giving us freedom of choice. Every time there is interference with the working of the market, someone's freedom of choice is circumscribed. Many of the economic policies designed to achieve other goals involve interference with the working of the market, and there is the danger of a steady loss of freedom. Boards have been established to regulate monopolies; the *Combines Investigation Act* is supposed to maintain competition and thus protect consumers' sovereignty and improve the allocation of resources. We may agree that competition is a good thing and well worth the cost to firms in terms of reduced economic freedom, but we must recognize that the economic freedom of some groups *is* being limited.

We favour an equitable distribution of income, whether for individuals or for regions. As a result, minimum wages are imposed by both federal and provincial governments, but this conflicts with the freedom of groups to make contracts: there are circumstances in which workers might be quite prepared to sign a contract that they would regard as advantageous even though the wage rate was below the legal minimum.

It is commonly accepted that an equitable distribution of income means a more equal one, so that what is required is the redistribution of income from wealthy individuals, corporations, and wealthy regions to the poorer ones. By taking away relatively larger sums from those with higher incomes, we are circumscribing the freedom of those individuals, corporations and regions to use their incomes as they see fit.

A similar conflict may occur between the goals of economic freedom and growth. We have seen that the education of the labour force is an essential element in the growth of the economy. Education is expensive, and in establishing a policy of taxing heavily in order to provide it, we are imposing limits on the freedom of bachelors, for example, who are forced to contribute to the education of the offspring of others.

One aspect of the goal of economic freedom is the freedom to pay the cost of remaining Canadian. This is essentially a political goal, with strong economic implications. Tax revenues are used to support institutions like the Canadian Broadcasting Corporation, for example, in an attempt to maintain a Canadian culture and identity. Canadian content rules in broadcasting result in a growing demand for Canadian performers and encourage the development of a Canadian culture; but they also raise the costs of local television stations, limit their freedom to import television shows, and, many viewers argue, limit *their* freedom to see the programs they want to see.

The idea that tariffs are essential to national identity was discussed in Chapter 12. Tariffs raise prices to consumers, and like any other tax, they limit the freedom of the person paying them to use his dollars as he sees fit. Protection of inefficient secondary Canadian industries means that productivity is less than it would be if these resources were transferred to more efficient uses, and therefore, that national income is lower. Thus, the objective of maintaining national identity is achieved at the cost of a poorer allocation of resources.

EQUITY IN INCOME DISTRIBUTION

We have already noted the conflict between the objective of achieving an equitable distribution of income and economic freedom. Equity in income distribution can also conflict with the proper allocation of resources,[1] particularly in the case of *regional* equity in distribution. Capital and labour, if controlled only by the market, tend to move out of the underdeveloped regions of Canada into the more developed ones. Policies that attempt to reverse this flow—incentives to attract industries, for example— can lead to a misallocation of resources.

Since the term "equitable" has been taken to mean "more equal than the income distribution determined by the operation of the free market", policies to achieve equity will end up taking money from those with higher incomes and giving it to those in the lower-income brackets. This, too, can have an adverse effect on the allocation of resources. Income is better thought of as a flow to be divided rather than a pie to be shared, and the way it is divided will have a good deal to do with the size of the

---

[1] For an extended discussion of the conflict between equity in income distribution and efficiency in resource allocation, see Arthur M. Okun, *Equality and Efficiency: The Big Tradeoff* (Washington, D.C.: The Brookings Institute, 1975), especially Ch. 2.

flow. When people do extra work and produce and sell more output, then they are likely to feel that the additional earnings should belong to them. If people know that the government, in order to achieve greater equality, is likely to take away all or most of the extra income, then the flow may diminish in size.

A common argument against redistribution by means of progressive income taxes is that such a policy has an adverse effect on the incentives of people to work. The heavier the tax on work, the more attractive leisure becomes as a consumer's good, the more total output may fall short of what it might otherwise be, and the lower may be the rate of growth. Moreover, the heavy taxes on high incomes have been effective in preventing large pools of risk capital from accumulating in Canada. There is a commonly expressed opinion that Canadians are not risk takers, and that this is why American risk capital has moved into many industries in Canada, helping increase the Canadian rate of growth but creating national-identity problems for the country. One possible explanation for the apparent unwillingness of Canadians to take risk is the efficiency with which the government has taxed high incomes in the interest, in part, of achieving an equitable distribution of income.

Old age is one of the causes of poverty. An equitable distribution, then, will involve redistributing income from young to old, so that there is a conflict of interest between the generations. Rural incomes lag behind urban: is the appropriate policy, therefore, to support farm prices? The majority of consumers are taxpayers who live in urban areas, so that price supports create a conflict between urban taxpayers and consumers on the one side, and agricultural workers on the other.

Areas of Eastern Quebec and the Maritimes lag in income, and any policies that will decrease the gap will also cause a conflict of interest between these regions and the relatively wealthy regions of Ontario, British Columbia, and Alberta, which must bear much of the burden of financing improvements in income in the other regions of Canada. The equitable distribution of income seems like a simple goal on which we can expect to get widespread agreement; yet we can see that any policy to implement it involves conflicts.

GROWTH

Anti-inflation policy can conflict with the achievement of a high rate of growth. One of the objectives of a tight money policy is to discourage investment. To the extent that the monetary authorities are successful, they may stand in the way of maintaining or increasing the rate of growth. If the anti-inflationary policy takes the form of cutting back government expenditures on education, or on social capital essential to growth (like roads and harbours), it may have an adverse effect on the growth rate. On the other hand, efforts to counter a recession by encouraging private investment and by increasing spending on social capital may have the effect of increasing the rate of growth.

Research and development are important to growth. However, the firms that can contribute most to research and development are large firms whose profits provide them with money for this purpose. A conflict then arises between our desire to have a high rate of growth, which may mean allowing the existence of large corporations that have the resources and facilities necessary to carry out research and development and hence to further the growth rate, and our desire to control big business in the interests of maintaining competition.

There is a conflict between the goals of growth and what some consider to be a proper allocation of resources, namely allocation in a way that would preserve the environment and improve the quality of life. This conflict has been most evident in the controversy over the energy question. The pressing problem of the simultaneous existence of an unacceptable rate of inflation and an unacceptable unemployment rate has upstaged concerns over the environment, and, indeed, over most other concerns—but only temporarily, in all likelihood.

STABILIZATION AND STAGFLATION

A potential conflict between achieving domestic stability and a viable balance of payments was pointed out in Chapter 12. Monetary policy may influence the interest rate and affect the movement of capital across international boundaries in such a way as to cause balance-of-payments problems; or fiscal policy, through its effect on expenditures by consumers and business, may adversely affect the merchandise account. The dominant problem of the mid-1970s relating to the goal of achieving stablility in the Canadian economy, however, was undoubtedly the simultaneous existence of double-digit inflation and an unacceptably high level of unemployment. A new vocabulary developed to describe this new disease, including terms coined from the words inflation and stagnation or slump, such as "stagflation," "slump-flation" and the even less euphonious "inflump". Devising policies to solve this intractable problem was complicated by the large number of causes that contributed to its existence, by the internal conflict within the goal of stability, and by the conflict between anti-stagflation policies and policies designed to achieve other goals like growth, an equitable distribution of personal and regional incomes, and a viable balance of payments.

The existence of the internal conflict was pointed out in Chapter 6 in the discussion of the trade-off between unemployment and inflation. There we used a trade-off curve to help explain the nature of this problem. Normally we think of using the tools of monetary and fiscal policies to move the economy toward the middle range of the curve: precisely *where* we aim, whether for more unemployment and less inflation or the reverse, is not a question of economic theories or facts, but rather a question of our values. Not all groups in the economy have the same values, and this gives rise to another conflict. The values of the dwindling number of members of the labour force who experienced the hunger and degradation of the dole and the bread lines of the 1930s tend to be different from those of a generation that has known little but the inflation of the period after the Second World War. The older members of the labour force are prepared to sacrifice a little more price stability for a higher level of employment. Those who have retired and who see their savings eaten up by rapid price increases tend to support policies that keep inflation under control. The existence of stagflation compounds the problem of where we aim on the trade-off curve; it does not eliminate it. It would be quite possible to use a tight money policy to curb aggregate demand, to limit growth, and control inflation, but the result would be an even higher level of unemployment.

Why Stagflation?   Numerous explanations for the existence of stagflation have been given. Monetarists point to an excessive growth in the money supply as the chief culprit. The balance-of-payments deficits of the United States in the 1960s, which resulted in the buildup of huge liquid reserves and strong inflationary pressures in the OECD (Organisation for Economic Co-operation and Development) countries have been blamed. Some economists point to the increased power of unions and the widespread wage explosion as *the* cause. Still others have singled out the shocks of increased oil and food prices, which were discussed in Chapter 15, as the main source of the problem. The rapid increase in government expenditures is another explanation that has been put forward. It seems more reasonable to use an eclectic approach and agree that all of these are important contributing factors and that no one of itself can be pinpointed as the single cause of stagflation.

Inflation became a serious problem in Canada in the early 1970s when it reached a rate of 5 percent and higher—considerably above the maximum of 2 percent in the implicit GNE price deflator which the Economic Council of Canada had defined as constituting reasonable price stability. To a considerable degree, it had been externally generated. Because of the openness of the Canadian economy, the inflationary pressures in the

OECD countries had a major influence. The large volume of trade with the United States and the close economic links via international unions and American subsidiaries made Canadian prices particularly sensitive to inflationary pressures from the United States. The sharp impact of price increases in oil and food reinforced the external pressures already in existence.

External forces were not wholly to blame, however; domestic policies also played a part. The "92.5-cent-dollar" policy discussed in Chapter 12 encouraged exports and discouraged imports during the 1960s and thus helped to achieve a viable balance of payments. But as the economy began to run out of excess productive capacity, the continued existence of this low price of the Canadian dollar, though it helped the trade position, also meant that fewer goods were available and that inflationary pressures were increased for Canadian consumers.[2] In the late 1960s and early 1970s the rate of increase in the money supply was considerably in excess of the rate of increase in real output or potential output.[3] The abundant supply of money helped to keep the interest rate down and prevent the price of the Canadian dollar from developing a premium that could have had serious implications for the balance of payments, but it did not help curb inflation. An easy-money policy was politically easier to pursue because the unemployment that would have accompanied tight money could have generated more unrest in the country and could have given the opposition parties a major advantage in fighting the election battles of the period.

Wage and salary earners responded strongly to the rapid rise in the cost of living. Having become accustomed to increases in real income every year, they grew militant in their efforts not only to protect themselves against any erosion of income caused by rising prices, but also to achieve the annual increases in real income that they had come to expect. Strikes and threats of strikes increased, and in many industries where strikes did not occur there were settlements that were excessive and inflationary. Since wages constitute a large part of the cost of doing business, employers tried to pass these costs on to buyers in the form of higher prices, and the inflation rate was reinforced by a wage push.

---

[2] See Grant L. Reuber and Ronald G. Bodkin, "Stagflation: The Canadian Experience" in *Issues in Canadian Economics*, eds. L. H. Officer and L. B. Smith (Toronto: McGraw-Hall Ryerson, 1974), p. 29.

[3] *Ibid.* See also Judith Maxwell, "The Vicious Circle of Inflation" in *Policy Review and Outlook, 1975: Restructuring The Incentive System* (Montreal: C. D. Howe Research Institute, 1974), p. 11.

[4] Government of Canada, *Attack on Inflation, a Programme of National Action*, Policy Statement tabled in the House of Commons by the Honourable Donald S. Macdonald, Minister of Finance, 14 October 1975, p. 5.

The increase in government spending at a rate in excess of the rate of growth of real output[4] is another factor that has been widely blamed for feeding the fires of inflation. The impetus for such increases has come in large part from attempts to achieve a more equitable distribution of income. The government had launched a series of new services including medicare, more generous unemployment insurance schemes, larger family allowances and pensions, and regional development incentives. Desirable as an equitable distribution of income may be, such policies conflict with the objective of controlling inflation. There is concern that some of them may adversely affect the allocation of resources through a negative influence on peoples' incentive to work. Critics argue that the level of payments for welfare and unemployment insurance are becoming so generous that a significant number of people have opted to avoid the costs and inconvenience of work and prefer, instead, to stay home and collect welfare payments.

Another cause of stagflation that might be added to our list is the tremendous growth in the labour force. As was suggested in Chapter 7, Canada has achieved remarkable success in creating new jobs; nevertheless, job creation did not keep pace with the growth of the labour force, and unemployment increased.

Anti-Stagflation Policies In view of the number of factors that contributed to the existence of stagflation (and our list is by no means exhaustive) it follows that there are several policy options. To control inflation the government could rely on its traditional tools of monetary and fiscal policies and embark on a strong deflationary path using tight money, a cut in its own expenditures, and increased taxes. The likely outcome of such policies would be a more severe constraint on the growth rate and a rise in the unemployment rate. However, there was no evidence in the mid-1970s that the country was prepared to accept the discipline of massive doses of unemployment. The government rejected this option.[5]

Some devices, such as more use of subsidies and indexing, have been suggested as means of cooling wage demands and lessening the militancy of workers. The two-price system for oil and wheat, for example, has been used to keep prices below what they would otherwise be. Indexing has been applied to Old Age Security payments, family allowances, the Canada Pension Plan, unemployment insurance, and the federal personal income tax. Cost-of-living adjustments (COLA clauses) are becoming more and more common in labour contracts in the private sector. It is

[5] *Ibid.*, p. 4.

hoped that such adjustments will make wage demands more reasonable. At the same time, it is apparent that these adjustments, if made frequently enough to be effective in restraining wage demands, will speed up the rate of transmission of price increases to all parts of the economy.

Some economists support the idea of *growing* out of stagflation by finding methods of increasing productive capacity and the productivity of Canadian workers. The target of the Economic Council of Canada for 1972-76 was a real growth rate of 6 percent.[6] It was a cause of concern, then, when the growth rate in 1974 dropped to 2 percent from a realized rate in 1973 of 6.8 percent (in constant 1971 dollars), and to one fifth of one percent in 1975. The low productivity of Canadian workers and its effect on growth is another matter of serious concern. It was suggested in Chapters 7 and 12 that productivity in Canada could increase if the country moved toward free trade. Unless there occurs a major improvement in productivity, the prospects of growing out of inflation do not look very bright.

The state of the stock market in the mid-1970s made it very clear that potential investors were cautious about helping finance productive capacity. They had discovered that the rate of return to shareholders was not keeping pace with inflation, and rather than make their savings available for investment purposes, Canadians were putting their money into land, pictures, stamps, and antiques as a hedge against inflation. Another possible anti-stagflation policy would be to attract investment by offering positive incentives in the form of reduced corporation taxes or faster write-offs.

Several kinds of policies dealing with specific problems related to stagflation have been suggested. Manpower policies, for example, might increase the mobility of labour. More extensive training programs could be made available; moving costs could be subsidized; and the flow of information could be improved. Policies should be enunciated to limit the control of unions and professional associations over the supply of labour.

WAGE AND PRICE CONTROLS
In October 1975 the government adopted the controversial policy of imposing income and price controls. These controls were described as voluntary, but there were legislative powers available to back them up. Canada first tried voluntary restraints in 1969 when the government established the Prices and Incomes Commission. This body, while it achieved a degree of success in persuading companies and governments to go along with its pro-

---

[6] Economic Council of Canada, *Eleventh Annual Review: Economic Targets and Social Indicators* (Ottawa: Information Canada, 1974), p. 24.

posals for restraint, failed completely to get the support of labour and was disbanded in 1972. In the spring of 1975 the Minister of Finance tried verbally, but without success, to persuade business and labour to restrain price and wage increases voluntarily. Increasingly, demands began to be heard for mandatory controls—the kind tried out in the United States for ninety days, from August to November 1971. Such controls are controversial because they create conflicts with the goal of a proper allocation of resources by removing the rationing and allocating power of the pricing mechanism. Past experience has indicated that controls can create dislocations in the economy which, many have argued, make the cure worse than the disease. Opponents argue that they will not work except in times of major crises like wars, when patriotic citizens are prepared to put up with policies that normally they would regard as an unacceptable infringement on their economic freedom. The very openness of the Canadian economy means that external influences can upset guidelines set on price increases. Moreover, there is the whole constitutional problem in Canada of how to impose such controls successfully because they are wide areas in which the provinces control prices owing to the way the powers are divided in the *British North America Act*.

The 1975 controls established guidelines for price and income increases which, the government hoped, would be adhered to voluntarily by everyone for a statutory period of three years. For large organizations— those employing 500 or more people—the rules are mandatory, and if they are not obeyed, legislation is available for enforcement. The idea of the guildelines is to permit wages and salaries to rise enough not only to cover the effects of inflation but also to share in the improvement in overall productivity that is expected to take place at the national level. The productivity factor incorporated in the guidelines is 2 percent, which equals the average increase in productivity in the period 1954-1974. Exemptions from the guidelines are allowed if the result would distort historical wage relationships among groups of workers or if there is a need to permit workers to do some catching up because they had experienced below-average increases in the previous two years, or if adhering to the guidelines would prevent adjustments to tight labour markets in certain industries. A maximum of $2 400 and a minimum of $600 were set as limits to the amount to be paid, regardless of the size of the increases in the previous two years. An Anti-Inflation Board was established to investigate performance and, if necessary, to enforce rollbacks in prices and incomes. Before announcing the new controls, the Prime Minister conferred with provincial premiers in an effort to secure their cooperation. If the voluntary system failed to work, and if the strong opposition from unions increased the possibility of failure, the government said that it intended to legislate comprehensive mandatory controls.

Changing Problems

The dislocative effects of stagflation attracted considerable attention through much of the 1970s and tended to push other issues of the Canadian economy offstage. But these problems remain, and some of them are growing to such proportions that they can no longer remain in the background, and solutions must be found.

Perhaps one of the biggest and most costly problems to be solved is the vast, sprawling, unplanned cities that are growing in Canada. The trend to urbanization, already strong, is likely to continue, and with it, the problems that go hand-in-hand with population concentration in urban areas. The air above the cities, and the water and land around them, are becoming polluted. City centres are decaying; people who can are moving to the suburbs; many of those who stay behind are culturally deprived; recreation facilities are inadequate; crime rates are increasing. Problems of municipal finance, urban transportation, housing, pollution, congestion, and poverty are growing to such proportions that they cannot be ignored.

Canada must also face problems of discrimination. The Indians, the Métis, and the Eskimos may not pose as acute a problem as the Blacks in the United States, but these groups have incomes that are well below the average. They are getting restive, and there have been some ugly confrontations. There is growing evidence of discrimination against women in the labour force, and corrective policies are needed.

In some cultures, tasks in the economy have been performed in the identical manner for centuries; one of the most remarkable developments of our time is the incredible pace of technological change in the developed countries. As a result of technological change, physical capital rapidly becomes obsolete, and as more sophisticated techniques evolve, they either remove old jobs or change their nature, so that *human* capital, too, rapidly grows obsolete. Along with the rapid pace of technological change has gone a managerial revolution. Entrepreneurs face the same problem of rapid obsolesence as workers. It will be a major problem of the Canadian economy to find policies that will assist the labour force to adapt to rapid changes. Such policies have immense implications for many of our goals: for growth, for an equitable distribution of income, for the balance of payments, and for resource allocation. If the economy is to keep up with changing technology and continue to grow, to increase productivity, and to compete with other industrialized nations, there must be heavy investment in human capital. Demands for resources for this purpose, already large, are likely to increase in the next generation. Our entire concept of education may have to change. We may have to develop a system in which, for example, people must be reconciled to going back to school every few years for retraining so that they may remain productive members of the labour force.

These are new frontiers for the Canadian economy. They will create new problems and new conflicts. The Canadian economy is one of the wealthiest and best-endowed in the world. Whether or not it can survive as an entity will depend on whether or not Canadians have the ability to find mutually acceptable goals, and to resolve the host of conflicts that stand in the way of implementing policies appropriate to the solution of the problems of the Canadian economy. These problems are complex. Anyone who thinks that the solutions are easy to find simply does not understand the problems.

Index